CONSCIENCE AND CONFLICT

A Biography of Sir Dominic Corrigan
1802-1880

Conscience and Conflict

A BIOGRAPHY OF SIR DOMINIC CORRIGAN
1802-1880

Eoin O'Brien

THE GLENDALE PRESS
DUBLIN

First published in Ireland by
THE GLENDALE PRESS
18 Sharavogue
Glenageary Road Upper
Dun Laoghaire
Co. Dublin, Ireland

ISBN 0 907606 16 4

Typeset by Print Prep (Ireland) Ltd., Dublin
Printed by Mount Salus Press, Dublin

For Aran, Aphria
and Emmet
whose today will
all too soon be history

Contents

List of Illustrations

Acknowledgements

To my father I owe my interest in the history of medicine, and to his admiration of Corrigan's success against all the odds I attribute my interest in the subject of this biography.

Dr. Peter Froggatt, whose obligations as Vice-Chancellor of the Queen's University in Belfast make extraordinary demands on his time, was painstaking in reading the manuscript. His advice and encouragement influenced the final shape of the biography, and whatever merit there may be in *Conscience and Conflict* I share willingly with Peter.

An especial tribute is due to the late Francis Cyril Martin who cared for the Corrigan papers and memorabilia placed in his charge. Had he not given these to the Royal College of Physicians this biography would not have been written. To his son Clive Martin, and to Sister Constantia Martin, sister of the late Mother Mary Martin, I am indebted for information on the Martin family, and to Sister Mairead Butterly of the Medical Missionaries of Mary who also assisted me in my enquiries.

Robert Mills, Librarian to the College of Physicians of Ireland has helped me over many years in my researches of the medical literature, and to him also has fallen the important task of cataloguing the Corrigan papers and memorabilia.

I have received help and advice from a large number of people who deserve greater acknowledgement than that which space permits. Without their assistance the book would have been much the poorer, and I would have been denied a lively acquaintance with many people who have since become friends.

Professor P.D. Holland, President of the Royal College of Physicians of Ireland, gave enthusiastic support to this study of his predecessor, and the College generously provided me with a grant to travel to Arcachon in Bordeaux. David Davison of Pieterse Davison International, Dublin gave generously of his expertise in providing me with much of the photography, and it is a tribute to his talents that the early Victorian photographs are reproduced with such remarkable clarity. I am grateful to John Hall and Philip Curtis of the Audiovisual Department in the Royal College of Surgeons in Ireland, who provided much of the photography for the book, and very much more from which the final selection of illustrations was made. The staff of the National Library of Ireland never lost patience with me, and I am particularly indebted to Mr. Richard Mooney who directed me to appropriate sources for answers to many apparently insoluble problems. Mr. J. Kenny, Secretary Manager of The Charitable Infirmary, and St. Laurence's Hospital, provided assistance in many ways, and Miss Noreen Casey of the Charitable Infirmary assisted me in consulting the minute books of the hospital. In Edinburgh, Rosemary Gibson, Archivist to the University, Joan Ferguson, Librarian to the Royal College of Physicians, Lesley De Jean, Archivist to the Royal College of Surgeons, Mr. M.

11

Matthew, Regius Keeper to the Royal Botanic Garden, and Dr. Andrew Doig and Professor M.F. Oliver of the Royal Infirmary all provided me with valuable material and information. At St. Patrick's College in Maynooth, the President, Monsignor Michael Olden, and the Reverend Donal Kerr, revealed to me many features of this historic and beautiful institute, and I regret that I did not have more time to peruse the archives that were so generously placed at my disposal. Ms. Honor Quinlan and Ms. A. Meagher of the National Gallery of Ireland gave me valuable last minute assistance in tracing some of the illustrations. Dr. Terry Murphy, the Director of the Dublin Zoological Gardens was enthusiastic as always in providing material from his archives. Mr. Patrick Healy of the Royal College of Surgeons in Ireland directed me to sources in the college archives and elsewhere, and Mr. Niall Sheridan kindly advised me in planning the biography. Ms. Alison M. Deveson translated Corrigan's thesis and final examination papers from the Latin, and Dr. J.B. Finn of Navan, kindly presented me with a 'Corrigan's Button' that had been in his father's possession. Mr. Peter Folan of the Dublin Diocesan Library, Father Michael O'Donoghue, and Father M. O'Halloran of the Pro-Cathedral in Dublin, Mr. F. Shalvey and Mr. G. Gleeson of the Board of Works, Ms. Tessa Sidey and Ms. Jean Coxsey of the City Museums and Art Gallery, Birmigham, Sir Gordon Wolstensholme, Harveian Librarian to the Royal College of Physicians in London, Professor J.H.M. Pinkerton of the Queens' University of Belfast, Mme. D. Fernandez of the Bliotheque Municipale in Arcachon, Fr. Kevin Condon of All Hallows College, Sister Marie Peter of St. Mary's Orthopaedic Hospital, Cappagh, Dr. Patricia Horne and Ms. Margaret Horne, Professor J.B. Lyons, Professor J. Fleming, and Dr. F.O.C. Meenan, all responded to many queries the answering of which often called for much time and effort.

For secretarial assistance I am indebted to Ms. Ina Doran and Ms. Mary Corcoran who dealt with a large correspondence and provided the many photocopies of the manuscript. *Conscience and Conflict* owes its existence in the printed form to Mrs. Rosemary Byrne who not only typed and retyped the manuscript patiently through its many drafts but also compiled the index.

Mr. Thomas Turley of Glendale Press possesses a characteristic not common among publishers in always being ready to acquiesce to the author's suggestions for improving the quality of the work.

I would like to thank Mr. Leo Vella, Professor John Fielding and Mr. Patrick Crowley for assisting me in ways that cannot, at least for the moment, be acknowledged fully, and to the Minister for Health, Mr. Barry Desmond, I owe a debt of personal gratitude for the honour he has conferred on me and the College of Physicians by officiating at the publication of *Conscience and Conflict* in the Royal College of Physicians in Ireland, on October 13th, 1983.

Finally, to Tona whose advice, criticism and encouragement was essential, and to our children an expression of gratitude, not devoid of apology, for permitting Corrigan to lay claim to time that was of right theirs.

Introduction

The bond that develops between a biographer and his subject is, like all relationships, susceptible to human emotion. The biographer may come to love or hate, admire or despise, be attracted to or repelled by the subject of his researches. He cannot, and indeed must not, fail to become involved, but he must avoid the extremes of sentiment which can only force him to paint in his picture that which is in the eye of the beholder. The consequence of such emotional indiscretion will be to either flatter or discredit the subject; in either event a great disservice is done to his readers and to history.

Anxious to present an accurate portrayal of Dominic Corrigan I feel it would not be amiss, therefore, to describe how my relationship with him began and developed. It is important also for another reason. Not being a professional historian, the reader has a right to be acquainted with my approach to the task, so that he may decide on the veracity or otherwise of my conclusions.

As a doctor specialising in cardiology in a teaching hospital in central Dublin I have much in common with my subject, also a doctor, whose interest in the days before medicine fragmented into specialities was cardiology; and moreover, Corrigan was physician, as I am, to The Charitable Infirmary in Jervis Street. Striking though the similarities may be, they would not suffice to account for this biography.

I first heard the name Dominic Corrigan as a second year medical student in the Royal College of Surgeons in Dublin. The professor of physiology at that time, the late Frank Kane, would describe how the volume of the pulse might vary in disease, and how in extremes it could have a collapsing

quality, often called "Corrigan's pulse" after a nineteenth
century Dublin physician. Progressing through the wards of
the Richmond Hospital I came to recognise this pulse, and as
I learned to use the stethoscope I heard the heart murmur that
is diagnostic of "Corrigan's disease." From time to time my
late father, (then a chest physician in the Richmond Hospital), would enliven a bedside clinic with an anecdote
about the man who had been one of the pillars of the famous
"Dublin school of medicine" which flourished briefly in the
mid-nineteenth century. None of this, however, drew me particularly towards Corrigan. Even when I began to take an
interest in medical history as a senior registrar in cardiology
at the Manchester Royal Infirmary, Corrigan rather than
attracting me to him tended to have the opposite effect. It
seemed he lacked the grace and sensitivity of his famous contemporary, William Stokes. Even the taciturn and humourless
Robert Graves overshadowed him for his integrity if nothing
else. Then there were the lesser figures of the school —
Cheyne, Crampton, Adams and dear William Wilde, all of
whom had for me a greater appeal than Dominic Corrigan.

In contrast to these cultured, rounded men, Corrigan
smacked of the boor. It was as though he had been an irritating upstart in what was otherwise an eloquent phase of medical history. One almost wished he had not been around, and
this is, of course, exactly how many of his contemporaries
felt, but I was not to know this until much later.

If one chanced, as I had done many years earlier, upon the
biographical note on Corrigan in the *Dictionary of National
Biography*, written by a London physician Norman Moore, it
is likely that the urge to search further into Corrigan's life
would have been quenched promptly. He denied Corrigan
any priority in describing the disease and pulse that bear his
name. This is the very best he can say on his behalf: "His
paper shows that he had made some careful observations, but
he cannot have made many." Even Corrigan's success as a
practising doctor can, in Moore's view, be explained without
having to bestow any personal credit: "He had received little
general education, and had no knowledge of the writings of
his predecessors, but he was the first prominent physician of
the race and religion of the majority in Ireland, and the

populace were pleased with his success and spread his fame through the country, so that no physician in Ireland had before received so many fees as he did." His career in politics fares no better under the denigratory pen of his English biographer: "He supported the popular principles of the day, but had no knowledge of politics, and failed to command attention in the House of Commons."

There can be few biographical notes in the *Dictionary of National Biography* that attempt to destroy so utterly their subject. And yet a discerning reader could not fail to notice the extreme sentiments and sectarian undertones that in effect speak more of the writer's character than of Corrigan. However much one might have wished to examine the veracity of Moore's opinions, it would not have been easy to do so. Corrigan had faded into the mists of time without exciting more than a few laudatory obituaries, and a handful of essays that relied more on anecdote than fact.

In 1980, the centenary year of Corrigan's death, as President of the Section of the History of Medicine, (one of many specialist sections of the Royal Academy of Medicine), I chose the life of Dominic Corrigan as the subject of my presidential address. For this I required new material that might shed more light on his life and personality. There was not much to be found; not many had gone in search of Corrigan after Moore's death-blow to his ghost. I gathered what I could, and remembering that the former librarian of the Royal College of Physicians, Gladys Gardner, had once mentioned some papers on Corrigan, possibly bequeathed by the family, I sought the help of her successor, Robert Mills. We found a trunk of Corrigan's personal and business letters, note books, diaries, pamphlets and memorabilia given by one of his descendants, the late Francis Cyril Martin to the College in 1944, where they had remained undisturbed until the centenary year of his death.

These documents convinced me that there was a great deal more to Corrigan than anyone in this generation, and possibly in his own, realised. It was intriguing to discover how coming from an artisan Catholic background, he rose from being a dispensary doctor in fever-stricken Dublin in 1828 to attain an appointment to The Charitable Infirmary where he achieved international eminence in medicine, and then went on to become President of the Royal College of Physicians of Ireland, physician-in-ordinary to Queen Victoria, a baronet of the Empire, a commissioner for national education, a senator of the Queen's University, and a Liberal member of parliament for the City of Dublin.

Beneath the surface of this glistening career there were many conflicts; the personal struggle against social and sectarian prejudices; the turmoil between personal aggrandisement and humanitarian considerations for the plight of his fellow citizens; there was his intense loyalty and devotion to his church that was to sustain him through many a struggle but leave him ultimately disillusioned.

Along with this there was the story of nineteenth century Dublin and of Ireland passing through one of its more turbulent and progressive phases of history. The squalor, misery and disease of the Liberties in pre-emancipation Dublin are now nightmares of the past. Corrigan's intense involvement with the great famine of 1845 shows the ineptitude of bureaucracy (and medicine) in dealing with the catastrophe. The development of nineteenth century medicine with its Dublin school gave Irish medicine a place in the history of achievement, which is unlikely to occur again. The political vicissitudes of the period and Corrigan's views on Fenianism show that little is new in the history of this island, and that not as much has changed as some might wish to think.

EOIN O'BRIEN
Seapoint
Co. Dublin
July 1983

1

Childhood and Youth

Dominic John Corrigan was born on the first day of December in 1802. The exact place of his birth is not known but it was either above his parent's shop at number ninety-one Thomas Street, or at the small family farm named "The Lodge" in Kilmainham, then a village on the outskirts of the city.

Of his parents few facts are known. John Corrigan might be best termed a merchant; he appears to have been a man of many parts – farmer, shop-keeper, dealer, chapman, and collier-maker.[1] He made a good living providing farm implements for Irish country labourers passing through the city on their way to work the English harvest. The German traveller J.G. Kohl has left a melancholy description of these migratory Irish labourers in the early nineteenth century:

> "Every year numbers of these labourers wander away from the western parts of Ireland, particularly from Connaught, to assist the English farmers in getting in the harvest ... Wages in England, on an average are twice as high as in Ireland, and the Irish harvesters, accustomed to the cheapest food, are generally able to bring back the greater part of what they earn. The men have usually a bit of ground in Donegal, Clare, Mayo, Connemara, or somewhere among the bogs and mountains of the west, and as soon as they have put their own fields in order, they ... cross over to England, leaving their families at home. Their little harvest is often attended to by their wives, or, as among the mountains of Connaught the harvest is generally later than in England, the men are often at home again quite in time to attend to the getting of their own produce."[2]

John Corrigan's shop in Thomas Street was on illustrious ground. From a lease of 1799, we find that John Corrigan took possession of the "Castle of St John the Baptist commonly called or known by the name of St John's Castle in the precincts of St John Without Newgate." This castle had been built on the site of the ancient Priory of St John the Baptist, Dublin's first hospital in the twelfth century.[3] Thomas Street was even then an historic thoroughfare. Not far down the street on the same side as the Corrigan shop Major Sirr had arrested and wounded fatally Lord Edward Fitzgerald, and a year after Dominic's birth Robert Emmet was executed outside St Catherine's Church.

John Corrigan's wife was Celia O'Connor descended from the clan O'Connor and of royal Irish blood.[4] With her husband she gave her children a comfortable home which was, to judge by the future religious choosing of children and grandchildren, intensely Catholic. There were three boys, Patrick, Dominic and Robert, and three girls, Mary, Celia and Eliza. In Thomas Street the children witnessed sadness, mingled with short-lived flashes of hectic happiness smothered all too quickly by the ever-present misery of poverty, neglect and disease. They must have realised soon how fortunate they were with a roof over their heads and shoes on their feet. Yet despite the misery there was sparkle to Thomas Street. Though not a wealthy thoroughfare it served the commercial needs of the poor in the Liberties of the city, and was always bustling. Country labourers and farmers would come to the Corrigan shop often bargaining in Irish, the only tongue they knew. In the street heavy carts trundled by on wooden wheels; barefoot women in brightly coloured shawls and petticoats moved among the throng, the faces of the older ones showing the ravages of poverty and childbirth; half-naked urchins clinging to carts; hawkers crying their wares, and beggars pleading with those wealthier than they to part with alms, all formed this colourful if tragic scenario. Ballad singers were the entertainment of the day and the Corrigan children must have listened to the most famous of these — the blind Michael Moran, better known as Zozimus.

How much time the family spent on the farm at Kilmainham we do not know, but it might not be unreasonable to assume that the summers at least were passed there. We do know from one of Corrigan's daughters that it was here that he showed himself to be fearless on a horse, and it was not long before he was riding bareback over the fields of county Dublin.[5]

In pre-emancipation Ireland the choices open to John and Celia Corrigan for their children's education were very limited. We do not know whence their own education, such as it may have been, derived, but there is little doubt about their determination to see their own children educated. This desire, often pushed to limits of extraordinary self-sacrifice, was characteristic of Irish families up to a generation ago.

The Corrigan's would have experienced the degradation of the Penal Code system which had had a disastrous effect on Irish education.[6] Although the Penal Laws were relaxed towards the end of the eighteenth century, any schoolmaster educating a Catholic did so at great risk. To overcome this proscription of education, as the Protestant historian Lecky was to call it,[7] teaching was conducted surreptitiously by free-lance teachers, many of whom had little or no qualification, in the open on the sunny-side of a hedge. These hovels of learning became known as hedge schools —

> ". . . crouching 'neath the sheltering hedge,
> or stretch'd on mountain fern,
> The teacher and his pupils met
> Feloniously to learn."[8]

With the abolition of the Penal Laws by Grattan's Parliament in 1782, a number of Catholic schools and colleges came into existence.[9]

Dominic was sent first to Mr Lyon's day school and then to the Reverend Mr Dean's at Blanchardstown.[10] No records are extant for either institute, but neither are likely to have provided a Catholic education and so John Corrigan turned to what was then one of the few and undoubtedly the best of Catholic schools in Ireland, the Lay College at Maynooth.

St Patrick's College, Maynooth, was founded in 1795 as an ecclesiastical college by an act of George III "to prevent the mischief of young men destined for the gospel ministry being sent abroad for that education which the impolicy of the laws had so long prevented them from receiving in their own country." Or put in another and less ambiguous way "it was at least certain to all but the most obtuse, that a rebellion was imminent in Ireland, and this seemed a probable means of enlisting the Catholic clergy on the side of England."[11]

On May 1, 1800 the Lay College was opened and two years later it was housed in the elegant house and demense known as Riverstown Lodge, "where none were to be educated but the sons of nobility and gentry of Catholic Persuasion."[12] The prospectus for the college read thus: "Young Gentlemen are admitted from the ages of ten to fifteen years; each to provide two pairs of sheets, two pillow cases, six towels, a knife, fork and silver spoon, which he is at liberty to take away on his departure from the college. The holy day dress is uniform and consists of a coat of superfine blue cloth, with yellow buttons; waistcoat, buff. Terms — ten guineas on admission of which Five will be returned on departure, and thirty guineas per annum; to be paid half yearly in advance: three guineas washing and repairing".[13] The educational programme included the Latin, Greek, French and English languages; history, both sacred and profane; geography, arithmetic, book-keeping and mathematics. For those judged capable of proceeding to an university education, the Lay College would provide the necessary instruction for the examinations of the non-sectarian Royal colleges: "Students who are sufficiently advanced, and who wish to profit of the Royal College course, and continue their education through the higher classes of literature and the sciences, pay two guineas to the professor whose class they attend. Music, drawing, dancing and fencing are extra charges . . . The president and masters dine at the same table with the students. During the hours of recreation a master will constantly attend, to prevent irregularities, and enforce an exact observance of order and gentlemanly deportment."[13] The authorities were not always successful in the latter resolve and we learn from a contemporary newspaper that on a winter's night in 1807 a number of the lay students returning from a visit to their late president, then resident in Celbridge some distance from the college, found the weather particularly inclement and sought refuge in a tavern in Maynooth. The punch soon elevated their spirits and when ordered back to the college by the master, they did so reluctantly and in a mood that was "elate, volatile and giddy," and then proceeded to throw down and break various items.[14] Nor were excesses of alcohol confined to the lay students; in one year eighteen ecclesiastical students were found guilty of drinking, and on one occasion a gentleman notorious for irregularities had to be lifted "at full length" to his room.[15]

Dominic Corrigan's first journey to Maynooth from Dublin would have been by coach, probably in the company of his father. The sixteen mile ride would have taken them along the River Liffey through some of Ireland's loveliest countryside. Later he would probably make the journey along the Royal Canal in the company of lay and clerical students.

Unfortunately the register of the lay school no longer exists and we cannot be sure who Corrigan's school fellows would have been. What we do know is that in its brief seventeen years the Lay College at Maynooth had an influence, on many notables of the period,[16] among whom were the Lords Fingal and Killeen; Stephen Woulfe, barrister, Solicitor General and Attorney-General for Ireland, Chief Baron of the Irish Exchequer, and Member of Parliament; Richard Lalor Sheil, playwright, Member for Parliament and Master of the Mint; Joseph de Courcy Laffan, physician-in-ordinary to the Duke of Kent, and a baronet. Among Corrigan's school fellows there were Lord Fingal, Dean Myler, Daniel Clancy of Charleville, county Cork, later prominent in the O'Connell agitation, Francis Codd, and two who would later join him in medicine — Christopher Fleming, a future surgeon to the House of Industry Hospitals and President of the Royal College of Surgeons, and John Lentaigne.

The Lay College closed its doors in 1817 at which time Dominic Corrigan was fifteen years old. It closed not for lack of success (the contrary was in fact the case), but because "it became, however, apparent, that the different system of education which is deemed necessary for those who are to undertake the duties and obligations of the priesthood and the additional restraints to which they are subject, rendered the Lay College an inconvenient appendage."[17] The college presumably honoured its commitment to the students already enrolled, and as Corrigan did not begin medicine until 1820 he probably spent three years studying the course in humanities for the Royal Colleges. We know from his daughter that he was "an efficient, profound Latin Scholar," and when on holidays in Italy thirty-five years later he was able to carry on a fluent conversation in Latin with a priest of a small chapel in which he had earlier assisted at Mass.[18] We learn also from the diaries of his daughter Mary that the reason he became proficient in Latin was to prepare himself for his medical studies in Sir Patrick Dun's Hospital where he knew the lectures would be delivered in that tongue.

It seems that medicine had been chosen as a career either by Dominic, his father or one of his mentors at a fairly early stage. The most likely source of influence was Dr Cornelius Denvir who taught mathematics and natural philosophy at the Lay College. Perhaps it was his experiments in hydro-statics and pneumatics that initiated his protégé's mind for the scientific reasoning and experimentation that was to lead him to international fame in medicine. Again Mary tells us[19] "the foundation of Sir Dominic's life-long love for and inter-est in natural history were laid by Dr Denvir." At the time of his graduation from Edinburgh Corrigan paid tribute to his teacher: "Happening and indeed principally on account of my intimacy with Dr Denvir, professor of natural philosophy in Maynooth, to have been well prepared in chemistry, I answered pretty well on that subject. This pleased the pro-fessor . . . and he told me it would be very pleasing to all the professors if all my countrymen came as well prepared before them."[20]

Once medicine had been decided upon as a career, an un-usual course was followed. Both Denvir and John Corrigan would have been anxious for Dominic to have a further edu-cation, and moreover as they may have wished to keep him under the Catholic influence of Maynooth a little longer, it was not therefore unreasonable to enter him for the university course. What was unusual, however, was the decision to apprentice him to Dr Edward Talbot O'Kelly, who was physician and apothecary to the college, and a local prac-titioner with a reputation that extended beyond Maynooth. Again we can perceive, without drawing too much on fancy the guiding hand of Cornelius Denvir, who recognising his

pupil's prodigious appetite for work, saw advantage in expos-
ing him to medical practice with a physician who would
teach him not only the rudiments of medical therapy, but the
philosophy of illness as well. A further explanation for this
arrangement may be sought in the character of John Corrigan.
Being a cautious businessman he may have considered it
wise to determine his son's suitability for medicine before
committing himself to the expense of a medical school education. If such was his reasoning he must have been com-
forted by the opinion of Dr O'Kelly who declared himself
convinced that his pupil would rise to the very summit of
the profession, and he urged that he be given the very best
medical education possible.[21]

In his apprenticeship young Corrigan would have acted as
dresser and clerk for Dr O'Kelly accompanying him on his
rounds in rural Kildare and Dublin, and, of course, tending
to the illnesses of the staff and students of the college. He
would have learned the importance of observation in diagnosis,
the pallor of anaemia, the hectic flush of pneumonia, the
emaciation of cholera, the ravages of famine fever. He would
have been taught to examine the pattern of fever so as to be
able to predict its outcome, to palpate the quality of the
pulse, and to listen carefully to the heart with his ear pressed
to the patient's chest. He would have learned how to diagnose
the complications of pregnancy and childbirth and he would
have become an accomplished *accoucheur* by the end of his
apprenticeship. He would have observed and become practised
in the few empirical therapeutic procedures then available.
He would have been able to apply a heated cup to the skin so
that the vacuum raising up the skin would cause a blister; he
would have practised blood-letting by opening a vein with a
scalpel, or he would have applied leeches to achieve the same
effect. He would have learned how to administer purges and
emetics. He would not yet have been of an age to question
the dogma of medical practice as he was to do in later years,
nor would he have been aware that these procedures depleted
an already ill patient. His apprenticeship at Maynooth impressed the clergy as one was to recall many years later: "I
recollect well and with great satisfaction the years you spent
in Maynooth under the guidance of my worthy friend Doctor

Kelly. I remember the zeal and alacrity with which you daily discharged the duties of your then subordinate situation, as well as the prudence and discretion you manifested in your constant intercourse with every grade in the Community."[22]

Dominic Corrigan departed from Maynooth for medical school possessing a good general education and a basic knowledge of medical practice. Not all his contemporaries would be so fortunate. He was to put his advantage to good use.

2

A Medical Student

The choice of medical schools for the aspiring doctor in the early nineteenth century was, to say the least, bewildering. The oldest teaching institute was the School of Physic at the University of Dublin, more popularly known as Trinity College. The university had been established in 1591 by Elizabeth I, and though its charter included provision for the granting of medical degrees, it did not do so until 1674, and a medical school was not established until 1711.[1] This School of Physic, as it was known, required its students first to take the degree of Bachelor of Arts, and then to proceed to the degree of Bachelor of Physic, the conferring of which was under the control of the College of Physicians.[2] This body, founded in 1654, exercised a considerable degree of control over the practice of medicine at this time.[3] The possession of the degree of the University of Dublin and the College of Physicians admitted the bearer to the highest rank in the profession; he could call himself physician, a title that gave him social, financial and cultural status. In 1808, Sir Patrick Dun's Hospital was opened for the teaching of clinical medicine to students at the University School of Physic.[4]

Until the nineteenth century surgeons had been a very lowly species within the medical hierarchy; they were forced by charter to keep company with apothecaries, barbers, and periwig-makers. In 1784, they established their own college, the Royal College of Surgeons in Ireland, which erected its school in Stephen's Green in 1810.[5] Had Dominic Corrigan chosen to be a surgeon he would have attended this institute.

Besides these major teaching establishments, there were five private schools at which Corrigan could have attended for tuition — the Jervis Street Hospital School, Kirby's School, known officially as the Theatre of Anatomy, or the Peter Street School, the Medical School of the House of Industry Hospitals, the Theatre of Anatomy at Moore Street, (which specialised in skin diseases) and the Apothecaries Hall.[6] These private schools were a feature of nineteenth century Dublin medicine, when no less than eighteen flourished in the city. The schools were founded usually by eminent teachers, and served to supplement the formal courses of instruction at the University, or College of Surgeons as well as providing a lucrative source of income for their owners. They did not, of course, grant qualifications (with the exception of Kirby's School which did have a small hospital attached to it and was therefore entitled to grant diplomas acceptable by the navy and army authorities, and by the London and Edinburgh colleges of surgeons.)[7]

We are fortunate that Corrigan has left us an almost complete set of enrolment tickets for the courses he attended as a medical student, and also many of the certificates he received on completion of each.[8] We can determine easily, therefore, how he spent these five years. Perhaps of even greater value to us is an article written by Corrigan (anonymously in the *British Medical Journal*) when he was advanced in years recounting his student experiences.[9]

Dominic Corrigan commenced the study of medicine at the School of Physic, of the University of Dublin (where he matriculated on November 29, 1820)[10] with the study of chemistry under Francis Barker, the energetic professor of chemistry, who with his predecessor, the famous Robert Perceval, had established the laboratory in the University.[11] He chose also to attend Kirby's School at Peter Street, where he began the study of anatomy in October 1820. Under the tuition of John Timothy Kirby and his assistant lecturer Michael Daniell, the young student was introduced to not only anatomy, but also to physiology and surgery. He attended didactic lectures and a practical course in dissection in the famous Theatre of Anatomy.

Corrigan's second year as a student was again divided between Kirby's School where he continued to study anatomy and dissection, and the University School of Physic where he began the study of the practice of medicine under Professor

Martin Tuomy. In this year he sat a course of lectures on the anatomy, physiology and diseases of the eye delivered by the young Arthur Jacob, who, in what for the times was an unprecedented occurrence, had been invited to lecture in this speciality by the Professor of Anatomy and Surgery, James Macartney.

His third year was devoted entirely to the study of anatomy, physiology and surgery at the University where he came under the dynamic influence of James Macartney.

In his fourth year (1823-24) he attended a course in *materia medica* and pharmacy given by Michael Donovan at the Apothecaries Hall. He continued at the University under Macartney who now began to teach him how illness affected the anatomy and physiology of the body, (known as morbid anatomy or pathology), and the teaching of medicine was conducted by Professor John Boyton.

Corrigan's final year (1824-25) was a hectic one. He probably went to Edinburgh University sometime in the free summer months of 1824, where he would have found digs, and perhaps started to walk the wards of the Royal Infirmary. At any rate he registered at the university on October 12, 1824, but he could not have remained there much after that date, as we find him back in Dublin at the School of Physic in November 1824, attending a course in *materia medica* from Professor John Crampton, lectures in anatomy, physiology, and surgery, morbid anatomy and pathology as well as a course in dissection from James Macartney, and lectures in medicine from John Boyton; he also attended the wards of Sir Patrick Dun's Hospital for clinical teaching again under the guidance of Boyton. Having, no doubt proved himself to be a diligent and arduous student, he would have been able to obtain release from these courses in March or April of 1825, for we know that he was back in Edinburgh in May 1825, attending a course of lectures in botany from Robert Graham. He sat his final examination in July and graduated as a doctor of medicine (MD) of Edinburgh University in August 1825.[8]

So much for the scaffold of Corrigan's medical education. What were the influences and who were the personalities that prepared his intellect and hardened his spirit for the achievements and tribulations that lay ahead?

When we consider that medical education in the early nineteenth century was a haphazard and poorly organised affair, we must look with some admiration on the course of instruction that Corrigan planned for himself. We may assume that he received good advice from his mentor Dr O'Kelly at Maynooth and from Dr Rooney, an old friend of his father. [12] One might ask why he did not take his doctorate in medicine at the University of Dublin, especially as the lack of this degree was to prove a considerable barrier to his later advancement. To do so he would have had to also study for his Bachelor of Arts, which would have taken more time and perhaps more importantly would have involved John Corrigan in considerably greater expenditure. Medical education was an expensive investment and an MD from the University of Dublin was estimated by one contemporary opinion to be three times greater than the equivalent degree at Edinburgh. [13] The Edinburgh school had attained an unique reputation in the early years of the nineteenth century. [14] For the five years ending 1781, 128 students had graduated there, and for the five years ending in 1826 the number had increased to 574, and of all the graduates (2,792) during this period 819 were Scottish, 706 were English, 848 Irish, 225 from British colonies, with 193 "foreigners of all descriptions." [15] The rise of the Edinburgh school had been brought about by Provost Drummond, the all-powerful ruler of Edinburgh University who took three initiatives from which nearly all else flowed. First, he made the Edinburgh school non-denominational both as regards staff and students. Second, he encouraged teaching through English rather than Latin, and this did much to increase its popularity among the American colonies and later the United States of America. Third, through his patronage of the chairs of Edinburgh University and appointments to the Edinburgh Royal Infirmary, he broke nepotism and made appointments entirely based on ability, often of people from outside Edinburgh. These initiatives occurred at a time when Edinburgh was declining as a centre of government (after the Union with England of 1707) and many of the nobility, the rudimentary civil service and the courtiers were leaving for London. [16]

Not all who visited Edinburgh sung its praises. Robert

Graves graduated from the University of Dublin but studied at Edinburgh, and wrote an account of teaching at the Royal Infirmary in 1819:[17]

> "At his daily visit the physician stops at the bed of each patient, and having received the necessary information from his clerk, he examines the patient, interrogating him in a loud voice, while the clerk repeats the patient's answer in a tone of voice equally loud. This is done to enable the whole audience to understand what is going on; but, indeed, when the crowd of students is considerable, it is no easy task; it required an exertion almost stentorian to render this conversation between the physician and his patient audible by the more distant members of the class; while the impossibility of seeing the patient obliges all who are not in his immediate vicinity to trust solely to their ears for information."

Critical though Graves was of the system in Edinburgh, he recognised the presence of the academic spirit, so necessary to any institute of learning: "I am bound in candour to acknowledge the very great advantages which Edinburgh, in other respects, offers to her students; they find themselves surrounded by so much diligence, enthusiasm, and zeal, that they can scarcely resist the impulse of improvement, and consequently may learn there to think and to labour, who had been previously careless idlers."

The satirical writer Erinensis whose knowledge and understanding of medical education in Ireland and Great Britain was second to none,[18] attributed most of Edinburgh's success, at least in so far as Irish graduates were concerned, to the stupidity of the University of Dublin and the College of Physicians in making the cost of medical education prohibitive in Dublin. He claimed that there were two classes of student who left Ireland annually to graduate at Edinburgh:

> "The first class consists of pupils who have graduated in arts, and intend to become members of the College of Physicians, and finally, Doctors of the University of Dublin; but who, wishing to anticipate the emoluments of their profession, put their half dozen of tickets in their pockets, cross the Channel, and immediately on

their return commence practice, which they could not have done for many years had they awaited the tardy arrival of a degree in their native University. To this respectable class of students also belong the pupils of the Royal College of Surgeons, who, for no other reason than to qualify them to meet physicians in consultation, and to evade certain restrictions imposed on them by that body, take out the necessary tickets during their surgical studies, and having taken 'letters testimonial' as surgeons at home, pass over to Edinburgh, and return with a medical degree in their pocket, and their tongue in their cheek, at the absurdity of the College of Physicians . . . The second, and by far the more numerous class of pupils, is made up of aspiring apothecaries, and other victims of ambitious poverty, who, unable to meet the expense of a medical education in Dublin . . . embark in the desperate adventure of living on salt herrings and taking a degree at Edinburgh. These are the heroic martyrs of abstinence and study, who swell up the Irish department (of Edinburgh University), and intend to practice in the Irish villages, where 'dead men tell no tales' of their academic proficiency in science."[13]

Corrigan may have been influenced to choose Edinburgh through his friendship with a remarkable fellow-student, William Stokes. Together with Robert Graves, these two men were to found and sustain a renaissance in Irish medicine that was to develop into an international phenomenon known as the "Dublin school". Both men were to influence each other in a long friendship that was not to be without its vicissitudes. They probably became acquainted in their first or second year (1820-21) in the School of Physic at Trinity College. Stokes was in a privileged position by comparison with Corrigan. His father, Whitley Stokes, had held the chairs of both the practice of medicine and of natural philosophy at the University, and at the time of his son's studentship he was professor of medicine in the College of Surgeons, and physician to the Meath Hospital.[19] He was well positioned to give his son good advice which may not have passed unnoticed by Corrigan. In 1823 Whitley Stokes sent William to continue his medical education at Glasgow and later at

Edinburgh, and he is likely to have reported favourably to Corrigan on the system of teaching there.

Stokes's background and his future prospects are in such contrast to those of Corrigan that we should pause to learn a little more about this talented student. William Stokes was born in Dublin in July 1804. His father Whitley was a descendant of a Gloucestershire family that had come to Ireland four generations earlier. He was a scholar and senior fellow at Trinity College, where as we have seen he held two chairs. His early career had been put in jeopardy when he was ordered before the vice-chancellor, Lord Clare, for being a member of the United Irishmen. He had in fact dissociated himself from membership when the society's ideals became revolutionary, but he continued to give medical attention to its members, and had subscribed to a fund in aid of the families of two members who were in prison. He was banned from acting as a college tutor, disqualified from sitting as a member of the board, and from senior fellowship. He had the satisfaction, however, of earning the fullsome admiration of Theobald Wolfe Tone who regarded him as "the very best man" he had ever known.[20]

He published at his own expense a translation of the New Testament into Irish and wrote a reply to Paine's "Age of Reason." On the subject of general education Whitley Stokes had very strong views. He believed that private education at home would be to his son's moral and academic advantage, and so John Walker a senior fellow and scholar at Trinity was enlisted to teach William Greek, Latin and mathematics, and later James Apjohn, a celebrated scientist taught him chemistry. Whitley Stokes himself determined to look after his son's general cultural well-being, and he instilled in him from an early age a love of music, poetry, painting and literature. However, it appears that these educational efforts were not at first successful. William was, we are told, "by nature indolent and apathetic as regards both physical and intellectual effort," although he did show an early love and aptitude for romantic literature, Walter Scott's *Scottish Border Ballads* being one of his favourites. It is related that one day his mother finding him asleep in a retreat that he had made in a thick beech hedge when he should have been studying, wept over him, and young William awakened by her tears was "stung with remorse at having been a cause of so much sorrow." Such was the effect on the youth that, "his nature appeared to undergo an immediate and salutary change and the dreamy indolent boy suddenly became the ardent enthusiastic student." However reasonable his father's educational views may have been at that time William resented the fact that he had been denied a general schooling and in particular a university education.[21]

Apart from William Stokes and one or two others, such as John Creery Ferguson, Corrigan's student colleagues at the university and at Kirby's School would have been a mixed lot. There were the army students whose only ambition was to get through the course as quickly as possible and then to survive the wars and return to civilian practice through the back door. There were children from families of the Anglo-Irish ascendancy class. They were well-educated and wealthy. They would not be dependent on medicine for a livelihood. Medicine and law were for them alternatives to the army and the church, but perhaps more importantly they saw in the science of medicine the potential for intellectual fulfilment, and many were to enrich not only medicine but also science and the arts. Though their number was small, their influence was to be considerable. Most were destined for the higher ranks of the medical profession. Then there were the sons of poorer but prospering Catholic families. For these to achieve professional status in society was a significant step forward. Medicine would be their sole means of livelihood and the most they could aspire to was a dispensary practice from which the rewards were few, and the risks of death from fever considerable. Corrigan would of right have belonged to this group.

The medical student of the day did not escape the satirical wit of Erinensis:

"Their mere appearance is our present concern, and as they sit in the living panorama before us, they do not much accord with the notions which might be formed of a body of medical students. The same number of young men taken from the various counting-houses, or haberdashers' shops, through town, would present as

*1. The Liberties of Dublin. "St. Patrick's Close", by Walter Osborne.
By courtesy of the National Gallery of Ireland.* (see p. 18)

2. St. Patrick's College, Maynooth. Photograph by J. Hall.   (see p. 19)

3. Riverstown House, Maynooth. The location of the Lay College.
Photograph by E. O'Brien.   (see p. 20)

This Ticket

Will admit *Mr. D. J. Corrigan*
to the LECTURES on ANATOMY, PHYSIOLOGY, and
SURGERY, to be given in the University of Dublin,
from November, 1822 until May, 1823

The above Gentleman, having conformed to the
regulations of the School, and attended the Lectures with regularity and diligence, will receive, on
the last day of the course, a CERTIFICATE.

Signed, *James Macartney*
Profr.

4. *Admission Ticket to Lectures in the University of Dublin, 1822-3. By courtesy of the Royal College of Physicians of Ireland. Photograph by J. Hall.*

Mr. D. J. Corrigan has
diligently attended a Course of
Lectures on Anatomy, Physiology,
and Surgery in the University
of Dublin. Dated the first of
May Eighteen hundred & twenty
three
Signed
James Macartney
Prof.r of Anat.y & Surgery.

5. *Certificate of Attendance at Lectures in the University of Dublin, 1823. By courtesy of the Royal College of Physicans of Ireland. Photograph by J. Hall.* (see p. 26)

6. *The Library and Anatomy House, Trinity College, 1753.*
Photograph by J. Hall.   *(see p. 26)*

7. *Sir Patrick Dun's Hospital, Grand Canal Street, Dublin. From a print*
in the Royal College of Physicians of Ireland. By courtesy of the Royal
College of Physicians of Ireland. Photograph by D. Davison.   *(see p. 27)*

8. Whitley Stokes (1763-1845). Portrait by Charles Grey in Trinity College, Dublin. By courtesy of Trinity College. Photograph by D. Davison. *(see p. 30)*

9. *John Timothy Kirby (1781-1853). Bust by Thomas Kirk in the Royal College of Surgeons in Ireland. By courtesy of the College of Surgeons. Photograph by D. Davison.* *(see p. 49)*

10. *James Macartney (1770-1843). An engraving in the Royal College of Physicians of Ireland. By courtesy of the College of Physicians. Photograph by D. Davison.* *(see p. 51)*

11. *Arthur Jacob (1790-1874). From a photograph in the Royal City of Dublin Hospital, Baggot Street, Dublin. By courtesy of the hospital. Photograph by D. Davison.* *(see p. 58)*

12. Edinburgh University 1829. An engraving of a drawing by Shepherd. By courtesy of the University. *(see p. 59)*

13. The Royal Infirmary of Edinburgh. This building, designed by William Adam, opened in 1741 and was demolished in 1879. By courtesy of Edinburgh University. *(see p. 59)*

14. Robert Graham (1786-1845). Lecturer in Botany at Edinburgh. Portrait in the Royal Botanic Garden, Edinburgh, of which Graham was Regius Keeper from 1819 to 1845. By courtesy of the Royal Botanic Garden. *(see p. 27)*

15. William Pulteney Alison (1790-1859). Emeritus Professor of the Practice of Physic in the University of Edinburgh. Chalk drawing by George Richmond. By courtesy of Edinburgh University. *(see p. 59)*

DISSERTATIO INAUGURALIS

QUAEDAM DE

SCROFULA,

COMPLECTENS.

AUCTORE DOMINICO JOHANNE CORRIGAN.

SAEPE creditum est, Scrophulam venenum specificum esse, in sanguine existens, a parentibus ad prolem descendens, et corporis habitui inhaerens.

CULLEN de Diathesi Scrophulosa, et ejus characteribus loquens, haec habet verba. " It " most commonly affects children of soft and " flaccid habits, of fair hair, and blue eyes." Haec descriptio ad omnes fere infantes pertinet; nam si infantes diligenter scrutemur, inveniemus, numerum eorum majorem haec signa

16. *First page of Dominic Corrigan's thesis submitted for his final examination in 1825. By courtesy of Edinburgh University. Photograph by J. Hall.* *(see p. 61)*

17. **William Stokes (1804-1878).** *A graduate of Edinburgh University in 1825. A drawing in the Royal College of Physicians of Ireland. By courtesy of the College of Physicians. Photograph by D. Davison.*
(see p. 62)

18. *Dominic John Corrigan (1802-1880). A graduate of Edinburgh University in 1825. A print in the Royal College of Physicians of Ireland. By courtesy of the College of Physicians. Photograph by D. Davison.*
(see p. 62)

19. *John Creery Ferguson (1802-1865). A graduate of Edinburgh University in 1825. A photograph presented to the Ulster Medical Society by Professor J.H.M. Pinkerton. By courtesy of the Ulster Medical Society.* *(see p. 62)*

20. *James Leahy (1780-1832). A graduate of Edinburgh University in 1825. Unsigned portrait in the Royal College of Physicians of Ireland. By courtesy of the College of Physicians. Photograph by D. Davison.*
(see p. 62)

much of the elements of genius, as much of the deep traces of thought, and as much of everything else which gives a studious character to the countenance, as this blue-frocked, black-stocked, Wellington-booted assemblage of medical dandies. Gold rings, broad and bright, glitter here and there among the artful labours of the friseur, as the hand supports the head, thrown into the attitude of mental abstraction, steel guard-chains, often without watches to protect, sparkle almost in every breast, and quizzing glasses hang gracefully pendant from every neck; in short, the whole paraphenalia of puppyism are displayed here in the greatest possible profusion."[22]

Both Stokes and Corrigan were fortunate in their teachers in Dublin and Edinburgh, some of whom shine through the mists of time as influential figures. John Timothy Kirby, anatomist, surgeon, teacher and dandy, was a flamboyant figure of the period. He began his teaching career as demonstrator in anatomy to Professor Abraham Colles in the Royal College of Surgeons, but following a disagreement the basis of which seems to have been financial, he branched out on his own and after a number of ventures opened his Theatre of Anatomy at the rere of his house, number twenty-nine Peter Street. This street was then one of the most fashionable in Dublin boasting the resplendent Molyneux mansion built by Sir Thomas Molyneux, Ireland's first medical baronet and sometimes known as "the father of Irish medicine." Kirby did nothing to let the style of the area down. He dressed in remarkable finery and drove to his patients in an elegant chaise driven by a coachman clothed in bright azure livery and silver lace; to cap it all a boy with military shoulder knots perched on the box behind.[23]

Corrigan has not left us a pen-portrait of Kirby, but he was critical of one aspect of medical training with which Kirby was much involved. In wartime the need for doctors for the army and navy was great and courses were established the aim of which was to produce doctors of modest skill quickly; one of these was run by Kirby. Corrigan illustrates the inferior standard of these doctors by relating how in one instance a student was warned by his examiner, "You are wanted immediately for a transport to go with troops to Spain. I will sign the certificate for you, but only on condition that you will now take your oath on the Bible that, whether an accident occur or a man get sick, you will order nothing more than a poultice or a dose of salts between this and landing." On another occasion the celebrated surgeon Sir Astley Cooper made a brave effort "to comply as far as he conscientiously could with the tone of the time" by putting a nice easy question to a very dull student:

"What is a simple, and what is a compound fracture?"

"A simple fracture is when a bone's broke, and a compound fracture is when it's all broke."

"What do you mean by 'all broke'?"

"I mean broke into smithereens to be sure."

"What is 'smithereens'?"

The student turned to his examiner with "an intense expression of sympathy on his countenance," and commented in dismay —

"You don't know what is 'smithereens'? — Then I give you up."[9]

Corrigan observed sadly that to these doctors were consigned "the best blood of our country, and our best bones and sinews."

Kirby's course for the army was popular and for a time his certificates were forged and sold in London. According to Corrigan there was a drinking house in one of Dublin's suburbs called "The Grinding Young" which attracted its clientele by a huge gaudy sign of a miller turning the wheel of a coffee-mill down one side of which old men and women on crutches tumbled in only to appear out the other side rejuvenated by the wonderful beverage administered within. In a famous caricature of the day the miller was replaced by Surgeon Kirby. "At one side, numbers of country boys, with hay-ropes for stockings, stood waiting for their turn of admission to the hopper, while at the other side they came out of the hopper from the grind as full-blown army and navy surgeons. This caricature had immense sale in Ireland and England, and much helped to turn attention to the sad state of medical education."[9]

We may presume that if Corrigan did not actually attend

one of Kirby's notorious firearm lectures, he would at least have heard of them. These lectures were conducted mainly for the army students and the theatre was always full to capacity. Erinensis has left us this account of Kirby's lecture:

"For the purpose of demonstrating the destructive effect of firearms upon the human frame, Bully's Acre (a pauper's graveyard) gave up its cleverest treasures for the performance of the experiment. The subjects being placed with military precision along the wall, the lecturer entered with his pistol in hand, and levelling the mortiferous weapon at the enemy, magnanimously discharged several rounds, each followed by repeated bursts of applause. As soon as the smoke and approbation subsided, then came the tug-of-war. The wounded were examined, arteries were taken up, bullets were extracted, bones were set, and every spectator fancied himself on the field of battle, and looked upon Mr Kirby as a prodigy of genius and valour for *shooting dead men*."[24]

In the anatomy theatre of the School of Physic Corrigan attended lectures and received instruction in dissection from one of the greatest anatomists of the era, James Macartney. Corrigan may have been amused by Kirby's antics, but he could not forgive him for compromising the quality of doctors in his training. Macartney, however, could not fail to impress him, and the fact that Corrigan had in his possession a signed engraving of his teacher suggests a friendship in later years.[25] Macartney, whose name Kirkpatrick says, "must ever be remembered with honour in Trinity College" was born in Armagh in 1770.[26] Like Whitley Stokes, and indeed many doctors of the period, he was active for a time in the Society of United Irishmen. After an unhappy love affair, he determined to become a surgeon so as to harden his heart against any further amorous encounters. He attended the College of Surgeons in Dublin for a time and then completed his studies in London where he qualified in 1800. He was soon appointed to the chair of comparative anatomy at St Bartholomew's School, and in 1811 was elected a fellow of the Royal Society. He left London two years later to become professor of anatomy and surgery at the University of Dublin where he became a dominant force in academic medicine. He was unfortunately petulant by nature, and resigned his chair in 1837 following a dispute with the university authorities over the time of delivery of his lectures. The following year he published his classical work on *Inflammation*, and he died in 1843.[27]

Anatomy was at this time the cornerstone of medical education and Corrigan spent long hours dissecting in the anatomy room. There was, however, one major obstacle to the keen student of anatomy -- bodies for dissection were very scarce indeed. The universities and colleges, and the army and navy authorities demanded a knowledge of anatomy from those training for medicine and surgery. The law, however, only permitted the dissection of the bodies of criminals executed for murder, and this was not nearly enough for the medical schools' needs. The only alternative was to acquire bodies for dissection from the graveyards. Of course, this was illegal and anyone caught in a churchyard was liable to indictment for trespass, and if caught in the possession of a shroud (the body itself did not constitute "property" at law) the charge was the more serious one of robbery. For some years the medical students themselves aided and abetted by their teachers procured sufficient bodies from the Dublin graveyards for their needs, but soon they were being assisted by the "sack-em-ups" or "resurrection men," a disreputable bunch who set about their nefarious business with macabre indifference.

Corrigan did not approve of either body-snatching or the dissection of executed criminals:[9] "I well remember — what a horrid aggravation on capital punishment! — the bodies of two young men executed for a trades' union murder, carried in an open cart from the prison, Newgate, where they were hanged, to the College of Surgeons followed by a crowd of howling and yelling relatives and friends."

Joseph Naples, a London body-snatcher, was almost illiterate but he did keep a diary, *The Diary of a Resurrectionist*,[28] a remarkable journal that does convey the gruesome attitude so necessary for one following his avocation, and yet there is poignancy and humour to the man:

> "*Tuesday 10th*. Intoxsicated (*sic*) all day: at night went out and got 5 (bodies, at) Bunhill Row. Jack all most buried.

Thursday 12th. I went up to Brookes and Wilson (anatomists), afterwards me Bill and Daniel went to Bethnall Green, got 2 (bodies); Jack, Ben went got 2 large (bodies) and 1 large small . . .

Wednesday 18th. At Home all day and do. night. Remember me when far away.

Tuesday 31st. Met at the Harty Choak (Artichoke Public-house), had dispute about the horse.

Friday 17th. Went and look out: came home met at 11, party except Dan., Went to the Hospital Crib (slang for a burial-ground) and got 4, was stopt by the patrols, Butler, Horse and Cart were taken.

Friday 7th. Met together me and Butler went to Newington, thing bad (Body putrid, and therefore of no use for anatomical purposes).

Tuesday 25th. At home all day, at Night met Jack to go to Harps (probably short for name of keeper of a burial-ground). the moon at the full, could not go. (A full moon would expose the resurrection-men at work; this was of great importance and the Diary has on one of the pages copied out the "Rules for finding the moon on any given day.")

Wednesday 18th. Went to the Big gates (probably the entrance to a burial-ground) to look out. Came home, at home all night which was a very bad thing for us as we wanted some money to pay our debts to several persons who were importunate.

Friday 3rd. Went to look out and distribute the above, met at Jack's at night, Ben being Drunk disappoint'd the party.

Wednesday 2nd. Went to the London Hollis got Canines £8 8s 0d, Bill got paid for 1 large M. (male) £4 4s 0d. I rec. £4 4s 0d for 1 large size small, Bill Rec. £1 0s 0d for the F. (foetus) that came from St George 1 Small came Wiegate went to Wilson. Rec. £2 0s 0d for 1 large Small came from Weigate, went to St Thomas' not sold being putrid: at night the party met and divided, me and Hollis went to Harp's workd. the thing (body), proved to be bad, Jack Bill and Tom Light went to Westminster."

The job of a "sack-em-up" though aesthetically unattractive was reasonably lucrative. The average price for a body was about four guineas, but in times of shortage a good body could fetch sixteen. The export market was particularly attractive, and one consignment of Irish bodies innocently labelled "Irish Cheddar" was intercepted at Liverpool. There was also a lucrative trade in what might be termed the by-products, teeth and hair. Macartney, in an effort to gather support for legal dissection wrote a letter to the papers pointing out that "very many of the upper ranks carry in their mouths teeth which have been buried in the Hospital Fields."[29] Some body-snatchers stooped so low as to use human fat for the manufacture of candles — "I have made candles of infants' fat."[30] Over and above the price paid for each body, the medical school had to pay retainer fees to the gang that supplied it, and the anatomist often found himself supporting the family of a resurrectionist who had been caught and jailed.

Not all bodies supplied to the schools were exhumed; many were snatched from the coffin whilst awaiting burial. There is an account of the trial of one, Clarke, whose ears were described as "quick to the toll of the passing bell;" on one occasion he drugged the nurse of a recently deceased child, and then leaning through a parlour window he hooked the corpse of the child with a stick, but was apprehended sometime later by the constabulary, and imprisoned for six months. A popular method of procuring bodies was for the female members of the gang to pose as the relatives of those who had died in workhouses, or by accident or suicide, so that they would be entrusted with the burial.[31]

Understandably relatives often went to considerable expense and effort to protect their dear ones from the body-snatchers. Custodians of the cemetery could not be trusted as they were usually in league with the resurrection men, and armed guards were sometimes employed. In 1830 a full-scale gun battle took place in Glasnevin Cemetery, Dublin, between guards and a gang of "sack-em-up" men, and after the exchange of many rounds and some casualties victory was hailed for the virtuous. Mort-safes (strong iron guards), iron coffins, spring guns and even land-mines were used to deter these gentlemen, but perhaps the most effective means was to delay burial until decomposition of the body was well advanced so that the subject would be of no use for ana- tomical dissection.[32]

During Corrigan's student days in Dublin, the resurrection- men were only allowed to act with the approval of the medi- cal schools, and more often than not the students themselves procured the bodies for dissection. Their principle source of supply was the pauper's graveyard known as 'Bully's acre' adjoining the Royal Hospital at Kilmainham,[33] although occasionally the demand exceeded the supply and they were forced to raid other graveyards, a popular alternative being that known as the "Cabbage Garden" at the end of Cathedral Lane.[34] Little was left to chance in the planning of a body- snatching mission. A dissecting-room porter clad in obsequial garb spent the day at the graveyard mingling with the bereaved so as to ascertain the age and illness of the deceased. Having determined the suitability of the subject for dissection, he marked the appropriate graves. At nightfall an old pensioner in the pay of the students gave the all clear signal by lighting a candle in the window of the gatehouse, and the students then entered the graveyard and selected their prey.[9]

As Corrigan tells us: "We moved with our hands the recently deposited clay and stones which covered the head and shoul- ders of the coffin – no more was uncovered; then a rope about three or four feet long was let down, and the grapple, an iron hook with the end flattened out attached to the rope, was inserted under the edge of the coffin-lid. The stu- dent then pulled on the rope until the lid of the coffin cracked across. The other end of the rope was now inserted round the neck of the dead, and the whole body was then drawn upwards and carried across the churchyard to some convenient situation, until four or six were gathered together awaiting the arrival of the car that was to convey them to some dissecting theatre. What added to the ghastly character of the moonlight scene was, that the bodies were stripped stark naked, for the possession of a shroud subjects us to prosecution."[9]

Worse experiences were to follow, as Corrigan goes on to relate:

"On the first occasion of my joining our night excursion, an incident occurred sufficient to awaken in me at least momentary alarm. My lot fell to opening a grave in which the internment of a poor woman had taken place. I worked vigorously, and on reaching the frail coffin had no difficulty in breaking back its upper third; but, on stooping down in the usual way, with my head downwards and my feet slanting upwards, I had to support myself by resting my hands on the chest of the dead; when what was my horror to hear a loud prolonged groan from the corpse. I suddenly drew myself upwards, but there was no repetition until I again supported myself on my hands resting on the chest, when another prolonged groan was audible. The cause, on a little examination, became then explicable. The body was an impoverished weakly skeleton, and the pressure of my weight forced the air in the chest up through the trachea and larynx, and produced the sounds which had momentarily terrified me."[9]

On another occasion the students on entering the churchyard noted a white floating object on one of their marked graves. They had little fear of friends watching after midnight, "for between terror and cold and whiskey their watches were terminated." On approaching the grave they found the widow of the deceased, a labourer who had died on his way home from work on the harvest in England, keeping watch over his remains. "It need scarcely be added," writes Corrigan, "that we pledged ourselves to respect the remains for her sake, that we kept our word, and that we made up a small collection to afford her some aid."

The journey home after robbing the graves was not without risk either. There was always the danger that "some meddlesome young watchman, not fairly bribed, or busy passer-by," would raise a warning shout and they would have to make a run for their destination, using stout sticks to beat off the angry mob.

The dissection of bodies was a controversial topic not only among doctors but also with the public, and many alternatives were proposed. A writer to one of the newspapers suggested that "As prostitutes had by their bodies during life, engaged in corrupting mankind, it was only right that after death those bodies should be handed over to be dissected for public good."[35] There were proposals that the bodies of all unknown persons should be dissected and that all medical-men should donate their bodies for teaching. In fact, ninety-nine gentlemen of Dublin signed a document in which they expressed a wish, that their bodies should be devoted "to the more rational, benevolent, and honourable purpose of explaining the purpose, functions, and diseases of the human being."[36] A Mr Boys, wished to be made into "essential salts" for the enjoyment of his female friends, "When my breath or spirit shall have ceased to animate my carcase, perform the operation of vitrifying my bones, and sublimating the rest, thereby cheating the Devil of his due, according to the ideas of some devotees among Christians. And that I may not offend the delicate olfactory nerves of my female friends with a mass of putridity, if it be possible, let me rather fill a few little bottles of essential salts therefrom, and revive their drooping spirits."[37]

Despite all its short-comings, the system worked reasonably well until the resurrection-men formed partnerships, and sold bodies directly to the anatomy lecturers. Further problems developed as the resurrection-men fell out among themselves, fought for their spoils in the neighbourhood of the churchyards and stole from one another. But a more sinister development was to take place. In overcrowded cities with many unfortunate paupers, it was inevitable that before long murder would be seen as an easier and more lucrative means of supplying the demands of the medical profession. In one year two Irishmen, Burke and Hare, murdered sixteen persons in the city of Edinburgh. They chose unfortunates who were homeless and adrift, but they were brought finally to trial in 1828. Hare saved his neck by turning king's evidence. Burke was hanged and publicly dissected and his skeleton is preserved in the anatomical museum of Edinburgh University.[38] As a result of public indignation parliament in 1832 brought in the Anatomy Act which laid down strict conditions for anatomical dissection and permitted executors or other parties having lawful possession of a body the power to give it up for anatomical purposes provided the deceased had not objected either in writing or verbally during his lifetime, and that the next of kin did not object. In effect this meant that the bodies of persons dying unclaimed in public institutions were given to anatomy schools. The act also made provision for those wishing to donate their bodies for dissection, and repealed the statute that had legalised the dissection of hanged criminals. With the Act came the end of the body-snatching era — the "sack-em-up" man was no more.

Another teacher at the School of Physic was Arthur Jacob, who with William Wilde was one of the first doctors to make a special study of diseases of the eye. It is to Macartney's credit that in order to improve the educational facilities for his students he invited Jacob to lecture on diseases of the eye. Jacob was an outspoken champion of medical education and reform. His most original discovery was the layer of rods and cones in the retina of the eye known for many years as *membrana Jacobi*.[39]

Of Corrigan's other teachers in Dublin not much need be said, with the possible exception of John Crampton, professor of *materia medica* at the School of Physic, to whom Corrigan dedicated his thesis for his MD. He appears to have been a competent physician (Corrigan was destined to succeed him on the staff of the House of Industry Hospitals when he died in 1840), and a man who was prepared to state his case however unpopular it might prove to be. He alone of the three King's professors in the University supported Macartney when he tried to substitute English for Latin in the examinations.[40] Macartney held the view quite reasonably that as Latin was poorly learned by many students it proved an obstacle to the student expressing his knowledge, and indeed to the examiner in determining the extent of his ignorance. Both Crampton and Macartney were opposed by John Boyton and Martin Tuomy, two of Corrigan's professors, in their resolve to introduce the English tongue. As we have seen Corrigan became proficient in Latin at Maynooth knowing that he would need it in medicine. At the ward classes in Sir Patrick Dun's Hospital the teacher having examined the patient, would convey his findings to a clerk who in turn passed on these in indifferent Latin to a large crowd of students many of whom could not even see the patient. Indeed, many of them would graduate without having ever examined a sick patient. The School of Physic Act of 1800 required that lectures be given in English rather than Latin, but because English was regarded as injurious to the character of the medical profession and because examinations were conducted in Latin, the classic tongue continued to be used and abused as Robert Graves discussing the subject commented laconically, "I have called the language Latin in compliance with the generally received opinion concerning its nature."[41]

At Edinburgh it is likely that both Stokes and Corrigan came under the influence of the magnetic Professor of Medicine, William Pulteney Alison.[42] We know for certain that Stokes was greatly influenced by him, not only for his medical ability and clinical acumen, but also for his immense dedication and charity towards the sick and destitute. Stokes has described his first meeting with Alison. One wet night he was walking down the old Cowgate when he saw a crowd at the entrance of a dark passage. Curious, he walked through the gathering and entered a low room filled with the sick poor and seated in their midst was Alison who had just examined a young man ill with fever. Stokes introduced himself as one of Alison's pupils, and offered to take the poor patient to his home. The two later became good friends, and Stokes wrote of his mentor, "Alison was the best man I ever knew. I wonder how it has happened that men should forget what reverence is due to his memory — whether we look on him personally as a man of science and a teacher, or at his life as that of an exemplar of a soldier of Christ. It was my good fortune to be very closely connected with him during my student days in Edinburgh, and to attend him by day and more often far into the night in his visits of mercy to the sick poor of that city whom he was for many a dear physician, friend, and support."[43]

Alison was an authority on fever and scrofula (tuberculosis), which was to form the subject of Corrigan's thesis, and much of his later interest and publications in medicine were to be directed towards the diagnosis and management of fever.

Another influence was to affect the lives of each of these young men. From France came the news of a new invention — a medical instrument known as a stethoscope. In the Necker Hospital in Paris, Rene Theophile Hyacinthe Laennec published in 1818 *A Treatise on the Diseases of the Chest and on Mediate Auscultation.*[44] Up to this time the sounds in the lungs and heart were listened to by placing the ear directly against the chest, a technique known as immediate auscultation. This method, apart from being inconvenient did not give satisfactory results. Laennec summed up the disadvantages: "It is always inconvenient both to the physician and patient, and in the case of females it is not only indelicate, but often impracticable, and in the class of persons found in hospitals it is disgusting." He goes on to tell us how he arrived at his invention. "In 1816 I was consulted by a young woman labouring under general symptoms of diseased heart, and in whose case percussion and the application of the hand were of little avail on account of the great degree of fatness. The other method just mentioned (immediate auscultation) being rendered inadmissible by the age and sex of the patient, I happened to recollect a simple well-known fact in acoustics, and fancied it might be turned to some use on the present occasion. The fact I allude to is the great distinctness with which we hear the scratch of a pin at one end of a piece of wood on applying our ear to the other. Immediately, on this suggestion, I rolled a quire of paper into a kind of cylinder and applied one end of it to the region of the heart and the other to my ear, and was not a little surprised and pleased to find that I could thereby perceive the action of the heart in a manner much more clear and distinct than I had ever been able to do by the immediate application of the ear." This moment of serendipity gave to medicine one of its most valuable instruments.

Stokes read Laennec's paper and was fascinated. He was the first outside of the mainland of Europe to recognise the importance of the stethoscope in the diagnosis of heart and lung disease. He began to use it on the patients he examined at Edinburgh and he recorded his observations. In 1825 shortly before qualifying he published the first treatise in English on the stethescope for which he received the then handsome sum of £70.[45] This singled out the young student as a future doctor of great promise.

Corrigan worked hard at Edinburgh, but he was not happy: "Since I have come to Edinburgh has been one of those few periods of my life in which the Blue Devils have a good deal annoyed me, removed from all my old friends and my examination each day drawing nearer, most of my time passed uncomfortably enough . . . Coming before the professors here, a perfect stranger to them, I dreaded that they might be more strict, and reasonably so, on me than on one of their pupils. This had at least the effect of making me study much harder than otherwise I might. My examination lasted about two hours, and was I think as fair as if I had studied under themselves."[46]

Corrigan, happily for history, collected personal memorabilia especially those relating to important events in his life. He kept his final exam papers in Latin,[47] and these were given to the College of Physicians together with his other papers in 1944, over a hundred years later. We need not dwell on the technical content of these papers but a few features are worth noting. The format of the examination was a brief presentation of a case history, on which the student was asked to write an essay on the cause of the symptoms, the likely diagnosis, and his approach to treatment. Corrigan's reasoning was sound, and he displayed a good knowledge of pathology and clinical medicine. He quoted freely from the literature showing that he had read contemporary advances. The most interesting feature of his dissertation relates to treatment. It was common practice in the nineteenth century to deplete the strength of already debilitated patients by purging, vomiting, blistering and leeching, but in Corrigan's final exam papers we find evidence of the iconoclasm which was later to become one of the featues of the "Dublin school" when Graves, Stokes and Corrigan rebelled against this nonsensical practice. He stressed the importance of building up the system, and of stopping vomiting "so that strength is not broken down and . . . prescribed medicaments are not rejected." For his doctorate Corrigan chose to write his thesis on scrofula, a disease of the glands of the neck now known to be due to tuberculosis, but then thought to be due to a variety of causes. He reviewed the history of the different cures that had been tried over the ages and came closer than most medical students would dare to criticising the profession by inferring that doctors did more harm than good with their efforts at treatment. He advocated the royal touch employed by Charles II in 92,107 persons over a number of years as the most efficacious form of therapy: "Amongst all the ancient methods of treatment, the royal touch was the best, not on account of the touch itself but of the conditions which accompanied it. Those who used the royal touch were freed from the application of specifics which were often harmful and very rarely useful."

Dominic Corrigan graduated as a doctor of medicine from Edinburgh in August 1825. One hundred and thirty-nine others graduated with him of whom 47 were English, 28 Scottish, and 44 Irish.[48] Among these was William Stokes, and of the others only a few merit mention. John MacDonnell was destined to be the first in Ireland to perform surgery under anaesthesia in the Richmond Hospital in 1847.[49] James Leahy was to become a future president of the Royal College of Physicians. John Creery Ferguson would become the first professor of medicine at the Queen's University of Belfast, but it was his use of the stethescope in diagnosing pregnancy that makes him noteworthy today.[50] Another contemporary at Edinburgh was the Englishman, James Hope who like Stokes and Corrigan went on to study cardiac disease; he and Corrigan were to cross swords on more than one occasion in the pages of the medical journals.

After qualification at Edinburgh, Stokes and Corrigan returned to their native Dublin.

3

Practice in Pre-Emancipation Dublin

The future prospects for these young doctors on their return to Dublin from Edinburgh in August 1825, were, at first glance, very different. Corrigan's ambitions, if reasonable, would not have extended further than a dispensary, preferably in Dublin, where with the help of his family contacts he could hope to establish a prosperous practice. Here he would gain a reputation as a capable and conscientious doctor. The multitudinous poor would form the majority of his patients, but for his livelihood he would depend on the prospering Catholic artisan and merchant classes of the city. He could be assured an arduous existence which would see him comfortably off but not wealthy.

For his confrère William Stokes the outlook was altogether brighter. Being of the established Church and having a father in a position of considerable medical and academic influence, he could look forward to a hospital appointment as a matter of course. It might be anticipated that here he would achieve eminence and wealth as a physician and teacher. In time the promise he had shown as a student would in all likelihood mature into academic fulfilment with his elevation to a chair of medicine.

Both physicians would have been aware, albeit from differing vantage points of the vagaries of fortune which in the apportionment of the benefits of birth, and more especially religion, had secured for one a privileged position in both the medical profession and society that was to be denied the other. But destiny had tempered each to her liking for their respective roles. Whereas Corrigan was tough, tenacious, and as we shall see, ruthless when necessary, Stokes was of a gentle and more sensitive temperament. As a contemporary was to put it, Stokes would become the "poetry" and Corrigan the "prose" of Irish medicine.[1] Corrigan's ambition to succeed arose not from necessity as much as from pride — a pride that was in its origins Irish and hence rebellious and stubborn. He determined early on in his career that he would reach the top of his profession regardless of what the obstacles might be. His personality was well suited to adversary, and his spirit was stimulated by controversy, all the more so when he was the centre of it. His capacity for work was, even by Victorian standards, voracious. Failure did not discourage him, or if it did, it certainly never deterred him; in fact, the greater the reverses the more determined he became to succeed. Achievement was what Corrigan admired most and there was little room for jealousy in his soul. He would have wished his friend Stokes every success, but to see him succeed his father as physician to the Meath Hospital within a year of his return to Dublin must have made him acutely aware of his own shortcomings. A practice among the sick poor of the Liberties in rented rooms in number eleven Upper Ormond Quay hardly bears comparison with a staff appointment to the Meath hospital and a practice in then fashionable York Street.[2]

Stokes for his part could never tolerate religious discrimination, and he may well have given advice and support to Corrigan. As against this, he may not at this stage have been aware of his friend's ability, whereas, he had as a student marked himself for distinction with his book on the stethoscope. His father, Whitley, a sagacious and tolerant man, would have anticipated the effects of Catholic emancipation, and he might have sensed the ability to succeed in his son's colleague; if he did, and we have no evidence that this is so, he would have been generous with his advice and guidance through the long wait that lay ahead.

We can see, without calling excessively on imagination, the shy, rather gauche young doctor from Thomas Street thrown among the elite of Georgian Dublin's society at a soirée in the Stokes house. How would he fare with the nobility, the divines, his peers in medicine, the officers of the army, and the artists and writers of the day? Perhaps knowing that it is easier to achieve dismissal from fashionable society than gain access to it, he would not have said much preferring to watch, listen and think. And of what would his thoughts have been? Mapother writing in 1880 captures the mood: "Pre-eminence may be claimed for Graves and Stokes; but illustrious as were their talents, and popular and enduring as are their writings, these well-born men owed much to fortune and to the aid they generously gave each other."[3]

On his return to Dublin Corrigan began practice in Upper Ormond Quay. There would have been no shortage of work in the adjoining densely populated city streets, and not all his patients would have been poor. There was a prospering Catholic merchant class with whom we may assume he would have been popular. The population of Dublin in the early nineteenth century was a little over 175,000.[4] The Liberties of Dublin was remarkable for its poverty and the extreme misery of its inhabitants. The Rev James Whitelaw, vicar of St Catherine's "undeterred by the dread of infectious diseases, undismayed by degrees of filth, stench, and darkness inconceivable by those who have not experienced them . . ." conducted a house-to-house census of the city.[5] He has left us a picture of the city in which Corrigan practised, so awful in the extent of its wretchedness, that we can today scarcely credit the degree of degradation of the inhabitants. We can do no better than read Whitelaw's account:

> "The streets . . . are generally narrow; the houses crowded together; the rears or back-yards of very small extent . . . of these streets, a few are the residence of the upper class of shopkeepers or others engaged in trade; but a far greater proportion of them, with their numerous lanes and alleys, are occupied by working manufacturers, by petty shopkeepers, the labouring poor, and beggars, crowded together to a degree distressing to humanity."[6]

To this assortment of tenements might be added "brothels, soap manufactories, slaughter-houses, glass-houses, lime-kilns, distilleries etc." The extent of overcrowding, and the lack of even rudimentary hygiene combine to create so repugnant an atmosphere, that one can only marvel at Whitelaw's perseverence:

"I have frequently surprised from ten to sixteen persons, of all ages and sexes, in a room not 15 feet square, stretched on a wad of filthy straw, swarming with vermin, and without any covering, save the wretched rags that constituted their wearing apparel. Under such circumstances it is not extraordinary that I should have frequently found from 30 to 40 individuals in a house . . ."

From Whitelaw's vivid account of the filth of these houses we can readily appreciate that Corrigan found no shortage of patients in whom to study the effects of epidemic fever:[7]

"Into the backyard of each house frequently not 10 feet deep, is flung from the windows of each apartment, the odure and other filth of its numerous inhabitants; from which it is so seldom removed, that I have seen it nearly on a level with the windows of the first floor; and the moisture that, after heavy rains, oozes from this heap, having frequently no sewer to carry it off, runs into the street, by the entry leading to the staircase."[8]

Less this description should fail to depict the extent of the filth in the city, Whitelaw, goes on to give in detail an account of one particular visit:

"When I attempted in the summer of 1798 to take the population of a ruinous house in Joseph's Lane near Castle Market, I was interrupted in my progress by an inundation of putrid blood, alive with maggots, which had from an adjacent slaughter yard burst the back door, and filled the hall to the depth of several inches. By the help of a plank and some stepping stones which I procured for the purpose (for the inhabitants without any concern waded through it) I reached the staircase. It had rained violently, and from the shattered state of the roof a torrent of water made its way through every floor, from the garret to the ground. The sallow looks and filth of the wretches who crowded round me indicated their situation, though they seemed insensible to the stench, which I could scarce sustain for a few minutes. In the garret I found the entire family of a poor working shoemaker, seven in number, lying in a fever, without a human being to administer to their wants. On observing that his apartment had not a door, he informed me that his landlord, finding him not able to pay the week's rent in consequence of his sickness, had the preceeding Saturday taken it away, in order to force him to abandon the apartment. I counted in this style 37 persons; and computed, that its humane proprietor received out of an absolute ruin which should be taken down by the magistrate as a public nuisance, a profit rent of above £30 per annum, which he exacted every Saturday night with unfeeling severity."

Nor was this misery confined to the Liberties of the city. Whitley Stokes has recorded that conditions similar to those encountered by Whitelaw were to be found in the neighbourhood of College Park, and, *mirabile dictu*, even in the environs of fashionable Merrion Square:

"I have seen there, three lying ill of a fever in a closet, the whole floor of which was literally covered by a small bed, and when I opened the door, an effluvia issued, from which accustomed as I am to such things, I was obliged to retire for a moment. The inhabitants of Merrion Square may be surprised to hear, that in the angle behind Mount Street and Holles Street, there is now a family of ten in a very small room of whom eight have had fever in the last month."[9]

Amidst this poverty and misery Dr Corrigan of Upper Ormond Quay began to establish a practice, and to study carefully the symptoms and effects of two diseases rampant among the poor — epidemic fever and rheumatic fever. Shortly after his return he was appointed medical assistant to his native parish of St Catherine, and in 1826 he became Physician to the Sick-Poor Institution of Dublin in Meath Street, also known as the Charitable Institution or Dispensary.[10] This appointment must have given Corrigan at least a little encouragement. The position was one of some eminence which had been occupied for a time by one of Dublin's most famous surgeons, Abraham Colles. It would, moreover, expose him to the nepotism that was (and still is to a lesser degree) so much a part of Irish medical appointments; he would learn how to defeat and utilise this system in the years ahead. Though Corrigan lacked the advantages that Stokes had in religious and political influence, his family was prepared to give him whatever financial backing was needed to secure his advancement. A candidate for an appointment might have to canvass, as we shall see later, hundreds of interested parties and if this did not necessitate a direct financial inducement, as indeed it often did, it called for many a *quid pro quo*. A case in point occurred when Corrigan in seeking support for the Sick-Poor Institution approached a shopkeeper in the Liberties for his vote; he was outlining his qualifications when the shopkeeper had to excuse himself to attend to a lady who Corrigan noted with satisfaction, was his mother's cook and that vote Corrigan recorded gleefully, was obtained without further difficulty.[11]

The Sick-Poor Institution was, according to Corrigan, "the largest dispensary in the city" and he thought highly of his appointment.[12] It was founded in 1794 to dispense medical relief, which was of little avail when the real need was food. Corrigan realising this was impressed by seven ladies of charitable mind who met at the Sick-Poor Institution in 1816 and established the Dorset Nourishment Dispensary which functioned from voluntary subscription for over 30 years and provided the people with food. He has left this description: "The medical attendants of the dispensary who visit the sick poor at their homes, are provided with tickets . . . which they distribute at their discretion, and which remain in force for as many days as they think necessary. These tickets presented at the dispensary entitle the holder to receive daily for the time specified so many pints of whey, gruel or girth, as may be ordered, each pint of gruel being accompanied by half a pound of bread, and each quart of broth with one-fourth of a pound cut up in it." Corrigan arranged that the food should be given cooked as many could not afford the means for doing so. Believing that something given for nothing could be demeaning he advocated that those who could pay one penny should do so, and within six months of this scheme being introduced £277 were collected in pence.[13]

Corrigan's appointments to St Catherine's parish and to the Sick-Poor Institution did not give him access to a hospital, nor are they likely to have earned him much income but he did at least have some status. More importantly a large portion of the city's sick-poor was now under his care and he was well placed to observe and record the awful fever epidemic of 1826-27 which he said was "of unparalleled extent and severity."[14] He had at his disposal one of the largest laboratories of human misery in the world.

The great famine of 1845, one of history's major calamities overshadows the frequent and devastating famines that occurred regularly in Ireland. As one observer put it, "For a hundred years the story had been the same, usually owing to the failure of Raleigh's gift (the potato), which has been to poor Ireland a root of much evil. In the epidemic of 1817-18, one quarter of the population (then six millions) took fever."[15]

Stokes wrote vividly from the Meath hospital of the horrors of the 1826-27 famine:

"They are literally lying in the streets under fever, turned by force out of their wretched lodgings, their bed the cold ground and the sky their only roof. We now have 240 cases in the Meath Hospital of fever and yet we are daily obliged to refuse admittance to crowds of miserable objects labouring under the severest form of the disease. God help the poor! I often wonder why any of them who can afford it should remain in this land of poverty and misrule. Government has now opened in different parts of the town hospitals with accommodation for 1,100 patients, and yet this is not half enough. I walked out the other night, and in passing by a lane my attention was arrested by a crowd of persons gathered in a circle round a group which occupied the steps of a hall door. This was a family consisting of a father, mother, and three wretched children who had been just expelled from their lodgings as having fever. The father was in high delirium, and as I approached him started off and ran down the street; the mother was lying at the foot of the door perfectly insensible, with an infant screaming on the breast, whence it had sought milk in vain; and the other two filled the air with their lamentations. It was a shocking sight indeed. No one would go near them to bring even a drop of cold water. In a short time, however, I succeeded in having them all carried to the hospital, where they have since recovered . . . It is calculated that should the epidemic go on in this way for a year, one-third of the inhabitants will have suffered fever. There are at present 1,414 beds in different hospitals open for fever patients, but this is a mere drop in the bucket. Were there five times the number open they would be filled in a day."[16]

The dangers for doctors working among fever patients were great. Stokes assured his fiancée that he was not in danger: "It is a great comfort that constant exposure to the infection diminishes the probability of taking this fever, and I now do not fear it in the slightest degree." His composure in the face of virulent infection was not justified. He did become infected from one of his patients and nearly died from the illness.

Corrigan's other interest, rheumatic fever commonest in overcrowded unhygienic conditions, abounded in his practice. This illness causes thickening and roughening of the valves of the heart which become obstructed or incompetent, and the blood flowing through the diseased valves produces a turbulence giving rise to murmurs that can be heard with a stethoscope. Cardiac murmurs were poorly understood in the early nineteenth century, but Corrigan realised that with the stethoscope it should be possible to record them more accurately and to relate their cause to the pathological changes in the heart at post-mortem examination – an event that was all too frequent. He appreciated the limitations in attributing dynamic events to the morbid changes in the dead, so he decided to study the heart's action in animals. He set up a small laboratory in Ormond Quay, and in the evenings when his rounds were over he recorded carefully the observations he had made on his sick patients, and then designed experiments on frogs and other cold-blooded animals by which he attempted to explain the cause of the murmurs he was hearing with the stethoscope.

It has already been noted that a fellow-student at Trinity College, John Creery Ferguson, graduated at Edinburgh with Stokes and Corrigan. He had not returned directly to Dublin but had spent some time in Paris where he had met Laennec and Kergaradec, who had applied Laennec's discovery to the auscultation of the foetal heart in pregnancy. Back in Dublin Ferguson developed his interest in the auscultatory signs of pregnancy, and in 1829 we find Corrigan and Ferguson, together with Dr Percival Hunt performing an experiment on a goat. Just before opening the abdomen Ferguson "casually applied the stethoscope to its abdomen without the slightest knowledge of its pregnancy and was surprised to detect almost immediately the distinct double pulsations of the foetal heart."[17] His two friends also satisfied themselves as to the veracity of Ferguson's finding, and an hour afterwards confirmed their observation by removing a foetus with a heart no larger than a hazelnut. Ferguson became, in fact the first man in these islands to hear the human foetal heart, an event that occurred in the Dublin General Dispensary in 1827. He regarded auscultation of the foetal heart as the only unequivocal evidence of pregnancy: "A blind man," he wrote, "who hears the foetal heart *in utero* is as morally certain of its existence as he who sees it after birth." The Rotunda Hospital was quick to see the importance of this innovation, and it soon became routine practice there, though it was to be many years before the British and continental obstetricians overcame their prejudices to the stethoscope, "this new fangled and ridiculous plaything."[17]

Apart from animal experiments Corrigan was afforded ample opportunity to observe the effects of rheumatic fever on the heart at post-mortem examination. Here he correlated the pathological changes in the valves of the heart with the murmurs he had heard with the stethoscope during the unfortunate patient's last illness. Slowly the facts accumulated over three years, and painstakingly he began to make conclusions. He must have contemplated many times how he might rise from his humble station in the medical fraternity. He was prepared to work hard, extremely hard, but the gratitude of the sick-poor of a city, however fulfilling, does little to hasten advancement within the medical profession. How was he to prove to the elite hierarchy of the profession that he, Dominic Corrigan, a Catholic, practising in Upper Ormond Quay, was worthy of joining them? The competition for hospital appointments was such that even if his background and religion were favourable, he would be hard put to succeed. Ability was no match for political and social influence. It is tempting in evaluating history to discount the vagaries of chance (the existence of which may be denied more easily than it is explained) and to seek in every occurrence a causative pattern of events. Nonetheless, when the futility of Corrigan's position after his return from Edinburgh is viewed against his subsequent success, it becomes difficult not to credit him with a carefully executed campaign, the purpose of which was to bring himself forcefully from obscurity to the attention of the medical establishment.

In 1828, when Dominic Corrigan published his first paper in the *Lancet* on the use of the stethoscope in diagnosing murmurs of the heart from the humble address of "11 Upper Ormond Quay" the medical fraternity was unaware of his existence.[18] We need not concern ourselves unduly with the medical details of this paper in which he advocated the use of the stethoscope then being scoffed at by so many, and described erroneously a visible pulsation that he believed to be diagnostic. There are, however, two characteristics that we should note – his ability to describe the signs and symptoms of disease, a talent that was to become his outstanding contribution to the Dublin School, and his arrogance in believing even at this early stage in his career that he could be right and his peers might be wrong. He described how a man with chest discomfort came to see him:

> "After having tried, without avail, all the usual domestic remedies, he had recourse for advice to several eminent practitioners in the city, who did not use the stethoscope. When he came to me, his breast was covered with the marks of recent cupping, and between his shoulders, the back was bare from blister; he had been repeatedly bled. The obstinacy in resisting the exhibition of active remedies for what seemed, at first sight, an attack of simple bronchitis, attracted my attention. On stripping him, the first remarkable appearance that caught the eye, was a singular pulsation of all the arterial trunks of the upper part of the body. As his arms hung by his side, the whole tract of the brachial and carotid arteries was thrown out in strong relief, at each impulse of the heart, as if the vessels, from having been previously comparatively empty, had become suddenly filled."

The tone in which he concluded this first major paper betrays his polemical nature: "Whether my observations and opinions be disproved or supported, I shall be equally satisfied. Truth is the prize aimed for; and, in the contest, there is at least the consolation, that all the competitors may share equally the good attained."

With each successive paper he became a little more critical of his peers, a little more audacious, and the fearless Thomas Wakley, editor of the *Lancet*, the most outspoken medical journal ever to be published, was we can assume, delighted with his critical tones.[19] Certainly he did not deny him a platform from which to declare his views, and from time to time he gave him the additional trumpetry of a pithy editorial.[20]

In a major work describing the results of his animal experiments he made some interesting but incorrect assumptions on the heart's action in humans, and concluded in a tone that could not fail to raise a mighty storm:

> "We now offer the views embraced by us to the profession. On the motions of the heart, we stand at issue with all the physiologists of the day. On the modes in which the sounds of the heart are produced, and the actions which those sounds indicate we are equally at variance with Laennec, and all who have made mediate auscultation their study. If our views and opinions be found to be correct, the whole pathology and semeology of heart disease must undergo revision."

And in anticipation of the trouble which must surely follow he continued, "We differ from great men of the past and present day, and our subject has obliged us to criticise closely the labours of others. It is perhaps under these circumstances to be expected, that there may be strong prejudices against us."[21]

The paper did indeed attract "strong prejudices." Its provocative style can only have been calculated to do so. Had anyone ever dared before to criticise the mighty Laennec — discoverer of the stethoscope? James Hope, who had graduated with Corrigan and Stokes from Edinburgh was writing at this time a text book on heart disease which was to be widely acclaimed.[22] He repeated Corrigan's experiments and wrote criticising quite reasonably his conclusions.[23] However, an anonymous reviewer made a personal attack on Corrigan and the *Lancet* which was not held in high esteem in academic circles because of its outspoken criticism of the profession:

> "Pretenders will start up who will prostitute the stethoscope to their own vile ends, or who knowing nothing of auscultation will bring it into odium by their quackeries and blunders . . . It seems that Dr Corrigan was hardy enough to publish a memoir on the *bruit de soufflet* in the *Lancet*, and what is yet more worthy of admiration, he is sufficiently simple or confident to refer to it. We know not what Dr Corrigan may think, nor do we particularly care, but this we will say, that such a mode of coming before the public is not calculated to win the ears of the respectable part of the profession in England. The acquaintance of the costermongers of St Gile's is not a good passport to society in St James's and so such writers as Dr Corrigan will discover."[24]

The *Lancet* could stand no more. After all Corrigan was now a protégé of the journal: "The name of Dr Corrigan is already familiar to our readers . . . In the paper now before us, he has put forward novel and extraordinary doctrines, startling in their kind, and of immense importance, as far as regards the decision which the profession may ultimately form of their merits."[25] The *Lancet's* vitriol was then directed at the anonymous reviewer, a genre it found particularly offensive: "Habituated to rust and rubbish, they (the reviewers) gradually conceive antipathies to everything not so stupid as themselves, and especially they become the enemies of originality, in order to save themselves the trouble of properly investigating the merits of a proposed innovation." As for the *London Medical Gazette* which had written in such derogatory terms about the *Lancet*, the latter was brief in dismissing it's rival: "the filthiest vehicle that ever sprung from the prostitution of typography."

So by 1830 the unknown Dr Corrigan of Dublin had achieved quite a reputation for himself. Apart from his contributions on heart disease there were two papers (again in

the *Lancet*) on the fever epidemic of 1826-27 in which he
warned the government that if the Irish peasants' dependency
on the potato was not altered a major pestilence would follow.[26, 27] He was, in fact, forecasting the Great Famine and
the *Lancet* again gave his strictures editorial force.[28]

What sort of man was this young Dr Corrigan of Dublin?
In appearance he was tall, erect, of commanding figure, not,
it was said, unlike Daniel O'Connell. He had the countenance
of an intellectual, "which when he rose to the full height on
the occasion glowed with enthusiasm and conscious power,"
and his face "beamed with kindness."[29] He was a man of
great physical energy and was "a splendid horseman, and a
famous rider to hounds."[30] In temperament his distinguishing traits were kindness and tenderness towards the sick, and
the ability to make a bold decision. His manner "if a trifle
brusque, was most fascinating, and a sturdy manner of asserting opinions bore down opposition."[31]

In these early days Corrigan was not earning much money.
At the best of times private practice is slow to flourish; it
takes patience and some luck to establish a reputation.
Corrigan's determination to forge himself an academic career
must have left him with little time to devote to the development of his practice. But he had confidence in his ability and
the maturity of mind to bide his time in the assurance that
success would ultimately come. He realised that though he
might achieve professional approbation, it was quite a different matter to gain public recognition. Indeed the latter is
quite unpredictable and is not necessarily related to a doctor's
scientific ability. Corrigan had this to say on the topic: "The
public often wonder when they see a man, to them as it were,
suddenly bursting into high position and great emoluments,
and are prone to attribute it to some ridiculous cause or
chance, or accident, but the public had not seen the long,
silent, and continuous hard years of labour in hospital, lecture room, and study. These labours have been laying the sub-
structure on which the foundation of the ediface of fame and
wealth at length arose, which arrested the public eye, and at
which it ignorantly wondered."[32]

Corrigan recalled with humour in later life the advice he
received from his colleagues at this early stage of his career:

"When I was in the very beginning of my professional life I received from numerous acquaintances and friends an abundance of what none of them then would take from me, namely, advice; and that on a point of great consequence to me *vis*: how I was to get on in life; how I was to attain eminence and competence.

"The first of the advices I got, as I recall them, was to take the house of an eminent physician, who was just then deceased, and try to step into his shoes; but however applicable that advice might be to succession in trade or business, I felt that in our profession it was the man and not the house that was sought, and therefore I did not act on that advice.

"The next advice I got was to frequent 'flower shows,' 'charitable bazaars,' 'matinee musicales,' and 'afternoon teas,' and perhaps learn to twang a little on the 'zither' or 'guitar.' This advice did not suit me; I had 'no music in my soul,' and I felt, like Richard, that I was 'not shaped for sportive tricks;' and moreover, I felt sure that such accomplishments, however suited for festive scenes, could not be the qualities which the sick would lean on for relief. The advices I got did not end there.

"Some of my kind friends assured me the very best way to get business in my profession was to pretend to have it; to put on the appearance of being overpowered with it. They assured me they knew for certain some who succeeded by having themselves frequently called away from Church and from the dinner-tables of their friends by urgent summonses to sudden and important cases. They considerately, however, added that the note marked 'immediate and pressing,' while ostentatiously handed to me should, however, always be at a suitable time for my own comfort, so that I should not lose the good things of the table.

"The next kind friend recommended me to take to driving hard in a carriage, particularly on wet and muddy days, so as to bespatter pedestrians and endanger lives at crossings, and make every passer-by inquire who I was. That did not meet my views or my pocket, and I thought of the lines applied to one of the profession,

who was said to have so acted. I did not desire to have
them applied to me:

> 'Thy nag's the leanest thing alive,
> So very hard thou lovest to drive;
> I heard thy anxious coachman say
> It cost thee more in whips than hay.' "[33]

All of this depressed the young doctor and he admitted to a
distaste for the profession's greater interest in matters fiscal
than medical, but he took solace from reading the lives of the
great physicians of whom he observed: "Whether they were
polished in manners like Linacre and Meade, or boorish like
Radcliffe, a staunch royalist like Harvey, or a roundhead like
Sydenham, a very martinet in dress like Jenner, or plain as a
Quaker in costume like Sir Thomas Browne, there was one
quality which all possessed in common, and that it was
which placed fortune at their feet — unremitting hard work
in their early days. They were never the playthings of fortune as Dr Johnson foolishly ventured to say — they commanded fortune."[34] Of these Sir Thomas Browne was to
impress him most. To his students, or "young friends" as he
preferred to call them he was later to say: "Remember the
celebrated saying of Sir Thomas Browne, the author of
Religio Medici, one of the most extraordinary men, next to
Bacon, who ever lived, who held a high position, was a practising physician, with a world-wide reputation as a philosopher.
He used often to say 'I never could be doing nothing.' "[35]

In 1829, at the age of twenty-six years, Dominic Corrigan
married Joanna Woodlock, the twenty-one year-old daughter
of a wealthy Dublin merchant. We know little of the couple's
early days. The marriage appears to have been founded on
good Victorian romanticism to judge from a poem written
to Joanna by Dominic just before their wedding:

> "So be thy life, — when Memory's power
> In days to come shall make each hour,
> And long passed scenes of life arise
> Again in all their varied dyes
> And while reflection dwells to see
> The magic work of memory,
> May each scene opening on thy sight

> Be theme to pause on with delight,
> And be again as fair to view,
> As when, first, Fancy's pencil drew
> The self same scene in earlier hours
> While Hope in thousand lovely colours
> Played oer it, like a morning beam
> Of Sunshine on a sparkling stream
> So be thy life."[36]

Though Joanna was to remain, as far as the records go, a background and retiring figure, we are told by Mary in later years that theirs was an affectionate and loving partnership.[37] For many years they spent their summer evenings on the farm with Dominic's parents at Kilmainham. There were to be six children in the family — three boys, John, Robert who died in infancy, and William, and three girls, Joanna, Mary and Cecilia Mary.

4

Hospital Appointments

By 1830 Corrigan had published no less than seven papers,[1] a number of which had attracted the attention of research workers in Britain, and as we have seen Thomas Wakley, the editor of the *Lancet*, had been fascinated by Corrigan's courage in stating what he believed to be the facts, even if as happened on more than one occasion, he was in error. An aggressive honesty was, in Wakley's view, fundamental to scientific advancement, and he abhorred the hypocrisy and humbug of the medical establishment which he saw as a deterrent to progress. Corrigan's next step had to be an appointment to an hospital.

The Catholic Emancipation act was passed in 1829, but this is unlikely to have influenced Corrigan's position greatly. Though restrictions on Catholics in Ireland had been relaxed considerably in the latter part of the eighteenth century, the full benefits of emancipation were not to become effective for some years. Corrigan, was nonetheless faced with a formidable task in achieving an hospital appointment because of his religion. Sir Francis Cruise, himself a Catholic, and younger contemporary of Corrigan, appreciated the difficulties facing a Catholic: "I believe it would be impossible for anyone who did not live and struggle for success in the medical profession at the period when Corrigan commenced to form an idea of the difficulties which beset a Catholic in the effort to attain it in Dublin."[2] Certainly Corrigan was aware of the disability under which he laboured. Indeed, there is evidence that because of it he tended at times to over-react, or to use modern parlance, he carried a chip on his shoulder.

To understand the repressive measures with which Catholics had to contend in the early nineteenth century it is necessary to reflect on a piece of legislation known as the Penal Code, passed at the end of the seventeenth century. These laws were devised with only one brutal aim, and that was simply to deprive the Roman Catholics, referred to scornfully as "Papists," from holding any positions of authority under the Crown. The Irish aristocracy was dispossessed and driven into exile, leaving behind a Catholic populace without leadership. The clergy and bishops were forced to live in hiding in peril of their lives. No Catholic could be educated in Ireland, and the families of those who sent their children abroad did so at the risk of the death penalty. Catholics were denied the franchise, and could not themselves seek election. They were forbidden even to take a reasonable lease of land, or to own a horse worth more than five pounds; their participation in industry and the professions was restricted greatly and without education their involvement where permitted (as it was to a certain extent in medicine) was limited.[3] Writing of the "vicious perfection" of the Penal Code, Edmund Burke, put it thus in his own inimitable and eloquent style: ". . . it was a complete system, full of coherence and consistency; well-digested and well-composed in all parts. It was a machine of wise and elaborate contrivance; and as well fitted for the oppression, impoverishment, and degradation of a people, and the debasement in them of human nature itself, as ever proceeded from the perverted ingenuity of man." It was in its almost complete perfection that Burke perceived quite correctly its inherent weakness: "My opinion ever was (in which I heartily agree with those that admired the old code) that it was so constructed that if there was once a breach in any essential part of it, the ruin of the whole, or nearly the whole was, at some time or other, a certainty."[4]

The weakness in the Penal Code was exposed by men like Henry Grattan, a member of the bigoted Protestant ascendancy which enforced so ruthlessly the code, and finally by Daniel O'Connell who won emancipation for Ireland's Catholics (three-quarters of a population of somewhere around five to six million) in 1829. But emancipation was earned at a price, a very high price — the Act of Union of 1801. Prior to this act Ireland had its own parliament which met in the House of Parliament (now the Bank of Ireland) in

College Green. Pitt, as prime minister of England, promised the Irish Catholics immediate emancipation if they did not join with the Protestants in resisting union with the British parliament. The young Daniel O'Connell saw the dangers in this agreement and just before the last session of the Irish parliament, in which the Act of Union was carried had appealed to "every Catholic who feels with me to proclaim that if the alternative were offered to him of Union or the re-enactment of the Penal Code, in all its pristine horrors, that he would prefer without hesitation the latter, as the lesser and more sufferable evil; that he would rather confide in the practise of his brethren, the Protestants of Ireland, who had already liberated him, than lay his country at the feet of foreigners."[5] Pitt achieved Union, and the Irish parliament passed out of existence. The nobility and aristocracy departed Dublin for London and the course of Irish history was changed irrevocably. Pitt reneged, as might have been anticipated, on his promise of immediate emancipation and the Catholics of Ireland had to await the exertions of O'Connell before their ambition was fulfilled. Many of the laws of the Penal Code became inoperative in the latter part of the eighteenth century, but they remained on the Statute Book, and the Church of Ireland remained the established church. The extent of the relaxation in the Penal Code may be appreciated, however, when it is realised that the Catholics had begun to actually erect cathedrals where, "a generation earlier, the clergy had been compelled to conduct religious services in obscure places."[6]

Corrigan would have watched carefully the vacancies brought about by the death or retirement of members of the staff of the city's hospitals. He would, moreover, have listened to the advice of his friend Stokes, and perhaps to that of his father Whitley and he would have had also the guidance of his own father, and of the powerful Catholic members of his wife's family, the Woodlocks.

On January 12, 1831, Dr Thomas Lee, physician to The Charitable Infirmary, Jervis Street wrote to the hospital's managing committee: "Gentlemen, I resign the situation of physician to Jervis Street Hospital, and avail myself of this opportunity to assure you of my increasing good wishes for the prosperity of that valuable institute."[7]

No trace can be found of Dr Lee. We do not know if he retired because of age, ill health, or an appointment elsewhere. It does appear certain, however, that Dr Lee was well acquainted with Dominic Corrigan, for on the day after his resignation the accounts credited to The Charitable Infirmary include subscriptions from John Corrigan (two guineas), William Woodlock (two guineas), Thomas Woodlock (two guineas), William Woodlock (two guineas), his friend Dr Percival Hunt (who had with Ferguson and Corrigan auscultated the foetal heart of the goat — thirty-one pounds ten shillings for fifteen persons), and "Doctor Corrigan" (forty-two pounds for twenty persons).[8] These subscriptions secured the election of forty governors to the hospital, and on Tuesday, February 8, 1831 when seventy-seven governors of the hospital assembled for "the purpose of Electing a Physician in the place of Doctor Lee who has resigned," we learn that "on casting the Ballot, the entire of the votes was in favour of Dominick (*sic*) John Corrigan."[9]

It is not clear how exactly Corrigan's election was decided. The post of physician would have been advertised inviting applications from suitable candidates. There is no record of an interview, nor of a meeting to select candidates for the ballot of governors. The Charter of 1820 states that "the said corporation at large (i.e. the governors) shall have the exclusive power and authority to elect and appoint by ballot to all vacancies which shall or may occur in the situation of physicians, surgeons, apothecary and officers of the said institution."[10] The same charter permits any paid-up subscriber to vote at such elections, but a Supplemental Charter of 1888 removed this facility by ordaining "that no annual member shall be entitled to vote at any elections of Physicians or Surgeons unless he shall have been an Annual Member for the year ending 31st of December immediately preceding the meeting at which he shall claim to vote."[11] It is unlikely that Corrigan was the sole applicant for what would have been regarded as a prestigious post. His selection presumably took place at the meeting of the governors who voted unanimously in his favour. An interview of the candidates was not conducted as is the practice today. This would have been considered superfluous as all candidates would have approached personally each governor in an effort to secure his vote.

Corrigan's appointment to The Charitable Infirmary may be regarded as the most significant step of his career. His success may be attributed to three factors. The first and most important was his record of achievement in the five years following his graduation from Edinburgh. With seven publications to his credit, none of his competitors would have been likely to rival his academic achievements. Moreover he would have produced ample evidence of his administrative ability in coping with the fever epidemic in the city in 1826. Second, he had studied carefully the nepotic rules governing hospital appointments, and was able to gather the necessary financial and political support to secure his election. Third, and of less importance was the granting of Catholic emancipation in 1829, after which the medical establishment may have been more receptive, but not fully resigned to the admission of a well-educated and experienced Catholic doctor to its ranks. Such an occurrence did not necessarily poise a threat to the Protestant ascendancy in the profession, as the numbers capable of success were small. There were then men like Whitley Stokes who condemned all forms of discrimination, and these would have welcomed Corrigan's achievement.

Biographical essays on Corrigan often state that he had to pay a sum of money for the purchase of beds when he was appointed.[2] Indeed in a debate on the most appropriate means of selecting doctors for appointment to hospitals in 1869 it is stated that the price in that year was £500 of which £300 went to the hospital and £200 to the retiring doctor. Fortunately for historical accuracy Corrigan was there to deny this and to explain the rather strange system that then existed. The Charitable Infirmary, he tells us, "was a county infirmary, subject to the infirmary acts. There might be 100 governors this year, 400 another year. There might be an agreement as to the appointment, but there was no arrangement by which a man paid £400 or £500 for the situation." When Corrigan applied, there were between three and four hundred governors most of whom had to be canvassed. Some of these might wish to be seen as benefactors of the poor at the candidate's expense, and would take (as in one instance) as

much as £200 to go to the support of the hospital in exchange
for a vote. A more effective, and less expensive way of gathering support was to ensure that a number of favourably disposed citizens became governors at a cost of two guineas
each. Corrigan later commented on this system with humour,
"it was a very curious thing" he said, "that whatever might
be the evils of contested election in large popular bodies,
whether in regard to politics or hospitals, it was curious the
development of latent philanthropy that came out . . . On
the eve of a contested election men went about seeking whom
they might deliver from prison, and on the eve of a medical
election men rushed in to subscribe their money for the good
of the public."[12]

Not only did money change hands in the jostle for support,
votes were also exchanged in return for favours in business.
Corrigan was not without friends in influential places. When
he told one of his advisors in the Chamber of Commerce that
a certain individual whom he had approached had denied
him support, he was given a note which had the desired effect
on the reluctant voter who then said to Corrigan: "Since
yesterday I have inquired into the relative merits of the
candidates and your qualifications are of such a high order
that I must break my promise to the other candidates."

Corrigan approved of this system of election because he
saw even greater evils in election by a medical board that
might itself indulge in nepotism leading to the appointment
of inferior men: "It was," he said, "perfectly impossible for
five or six men, no matter how pure their motives might be
in the hospital, not to prefer any one of the young men they
had known themselves — their own relatives for instance — to
strangers." He realised that no system was perfect and that
a purchase system was open to abuse, but with a prospering
Catholic community he probably saw this as a lesser threat
than a closed system based on religious discrimination. "In
the medical profession foreign corn was let in by the purchase
system to compete with the native grown corn," and he cited
the late Dr Cheyne of Scotland as an illustrious example.[12] It
is of interest to note in passing that as yet there is no uniformly satisfactory system for hospital appointments in
Ireland.

Not only did Corrigan have to organise support among the governors, but he had also to secure the backing of the medical staff in the hospital. We do not know how he did this, but from a letter written some years earlier to his mentor Dr O'Kelly of Maynooth in which he explained the futility of supporting a family friend, a Dr Roney, we can come to appreciate the internal machinations that must have applied also to his own appointment:

"At the last election when Stapleton was returned O'Reilly's interest was opposed to him. Harrison had promised Stapleton his support. Harrison himself is a life governor, and has many personal friends among the governors. O'Reilly proposed to Harrison to become a candidate, so that by joining his Catholic interest with Harrison's Protestant interest, Stapleton would certainly be thrown out. Harrison refused to break his word to Stapleton and Stapleton in return pledged himself to support Harrison on the next occasion. Harrison also had the Presbyterian interest of Mr Denham who stood last time in O'Reilly's interest and who gave over his support to Harrison. The occasion for Stapleton to fulfill his promise to Harrison has now come and thus the contending interests stand. There are about ninety votes. Of these Harrison goes to the poll with the Presbyterian interests secured to him, his own interest among them, and Denham's resignation in his favour."[13]

Calculating this support at the lowest Corrigan concluded that Stapleton would secure fifty-four votes to which must be added the votes of those governors, "who caring neither about religion nor politics look for the best qualified man, and are at once secured for Harrison by his high character." He goes on to predict the votes the other candidates are likely to attract and concluded: "What use would there be in keeping for him the twelve or fifteen votes I might influence . . . It would not only be silly on my part but it would be positively injurious to Roney's chances on a further occasion for it would be putting him and me in fruitless opposition to influence, what I might at a future time work up for him." This correspondence gives us insight not only into the complexi-

ties of hospital staffing at the time, but we may detect also
a political awareness in Corrigan who was learning to work
the system to his advantage from an early stage in his career.

What sort of an institute was this hospital, The Charitable
Infirmary, to which Dominic Corrigan had been appointed?
It had been founded by six Dublin surgeons in a small house
in Cook Street in 1718 and has the distinction of being the
first voluntary hospital in Great Britain and Ireland. Dublin
had been without a hospital since the dissolution of the
monasteries nearly two centuries earlier, and the condition
of the sick-poor of the city was such that one may well wonder how it was that a hospital had not been founded earlier.
Be that as it may the philanthropic founders of The Charitable
Infirmary were the first to try and ameliorate the neglect of
those who were ill in the poor quarters: "the City of Dublin
abounds with a great number of poor, who when they happen
to be maim'd, or meet with any accidents that require the
assistance of surgeons, perish in a miserable manner for want
of help and other necessaries."[14] The hospital subsequently
moved from its humble beginnings in Cook Street to Anderson's Court in St Michan's parish where eight or nine beds
supported by voluntary contributions were administered by
twenty trustees. In 1732 a piece of ground was purchased in
St Mary's parish in the hope of building a hospital with
thirty-two beds, but the trustees depending "on the Providence of God and the Charity of good Christians to raise a
sum sufficient to build same" were disappointed on both
counts, and had to make do with a larger house on the Inns
Quay. Though dilapidated and in need of repair it had the
advantage of being in the heart of the city and close to the
shops, one of which was a wine cellar, at which could be purchased "right good French claret and white wine at eleven
shillings a dozen, good sack at four shillings and fourpence
per gallon, and French brandy at the rate current." Two of
the founder surgeons were not slow to make known their
talents in the newspapers, "Both professed surgeons do by
the blessing of God, perfectly cure all manner of ruptures in
any age or sex, by a very easie, safe, and speedy method (far
different from any that ever was practised hitherto) . . .
without either truss or bandage. The poor cured gratis."[14]

Apart from voluntary subscription the Infirmary was supported from lotteries and entertainments. The most famous of these was the first production by Handel of the Messiah in the New Music Hall in Fishamble Street, an occasion which the press happily acknowledged, "It is but justice to Mr Handel, that the world should know, he generously gave the money arising from this performance to be equally shared by the Society for Relieving Prisoners, The Charitable Infirmary, and Mercer's hospital, and that the gentlemen of the Choirs (of the two cathedrals), Mr Dubourg, and Mrs Cibber, who all performed their parts to admiration, acted also on the same disinterested principle, satisfied with the deserved applause of the publick, and the conscious pleasure of promoting such useful and extensive charity."

In 1786 the Inns Quay was designated for James Gandon's Four Courts and the Kings' Inns removed to Henrietta Street, with The Charitable Infirmary going to the former town house of the Earl of Charlemont, at number fourteen Jervis Street. We may in passing note that the pernicious tendency to call this venerable institute Jervis Street hospital does little credit to its origins, and worse it elevates it to a pinnacle of remembrance the name of Lord Humphrey Jervis, a speculator who sacked one of Dublin's most precious historical institutes, St Mary's Abbey, to build a bridge across the River Liffey for the pleasure of Lord Essex and his own aggrandisement.

Following the granting of a charter in 1792, substantial funds were collected, and in 1804 a new hospital was built.[15] A double flight of granite steps led to the ground floor on which there was a surgery, board room, and apothecary's department. The wards were in the upper floors together with the matron's room and a room for performing operations. A curious feature for the period was provision for semi-private patients, and the hospital was in the historian Widdess's view unique in that it "appears to have been the first of Dublin's hospitals to recognise that there were others of small means, unable to afford medical treatment, but whose sensitivity made repugnant exposure in the public ward."[14] These patients had to provide themselves with food, but they received advice and medicine free of charge and had "all the comforts of fire, candle-light, warm shelter, regular attendance, and medicine." Until this time the hospital, which had been founded by surgeons, was devoted almost exclusively to surgery and though two physicians were appointed to the staff in 1738, they could not admit patients, and only attended in consultation on patients admitted for surgery.[16] After 1803, patients with any illness other than an infectious one were admitted. It then became necessary, not only to have physicians on the staff, but to provide teaching in medicine, and in 1808 The Charitable Infirmary became a teaching institution. When Corrigan joined the staff, the Infirmary boasted about sixty beds of which only four were for use by the physicians, and perhaps as many as forty thousand patients attended as externs each year.[17]

Though few the beds at his disposal, Corrigan, who for so long had been denied a means of observing closely the progress of disease and the effects of treatment, did not complain — at least not immediately. In fact he put his beds to very good use and concentrated on studying a particular form of rheumatic heart disease that had fascinated him in his experimental researches. On April 1, 1832 a paper by Corrigan entitled "On permanent patency of the mouth of the aorta, or inadequacy of the aortic valve" appeared in the *Edinburgh Medical and Surgical Journal.*[18] This paper was to secure for Corrigan not only international fame, but also eponymous immortality. Now renowned as a classic in medical literature it opens: "The disease to which the above name is given has not, as far as I am aware, been described in any of the works on diseases of the heart. The object of the present paper is to supply that deficiency. The disease is not uncommon. It forms a considerable proportion of cases of deranged action of the heart, and it deserves attention from its peculiar signs, its progress, and its treatment. The pathological essence of the disease consists of inefficiency of the valvular apparatus at the mouth of the aorta in consequence of which the blood sent into the aorta regurgitates into the ventricle." The paper describes in great detail the symptoms, the clinical signs, and the treatment, and the findings at post-mortem examination are illustrated with engravings. He described in a characteristically clear and lucid style the three diagnostic signs of the disease — the visible pulsation of the arteries of the head and superior extremities, a murmur in the heart that may be heard with the stethoscope (*bruit de soufflet*), a rushing thrill felt by a finger placed on the carotid arteries (*fremissement*) and the peculiar collapsing quality of the pulse when the arm is elevated. Corrigan certainly knew that he had produced a good paper, although he can have hardly guessed that it would become a masterpiece, for shortly afterwards when sending a paper on catarrh to the newly founded *Dublin Journal of Medical Science*[19] he wrote apologetically to the editor, "had I known at an earlier date of the forthcoming of an Irish periodical, I might have had a better offering to present."[20]

To claim priority of description in medicine, or for that matter any science, is always risky, but Dr Corrigan, never one to be unduly modest in such matters was confident that his claim was justified. He was quickly taken to task once again by James Hope, who protested that he had described aortic insufficiency as far back as 1825.[21] In fairness there is some justification in Hope's claim, but his description of the disease is neither as comprehensive nor as accurate as that of Corrigan. In fact, a careful study of the medical literature[22] does show that the disease had been described previously by William Cowper in 1706, Raymond Vieussens in 1715, and by Thomas Hodgkin in 1829,[23] but none bears comparison with Corrigan's account. In Dublin, Robert Graves physician to the Meath hospital, while recognising the quality of Corrigan's paper was of the opinion that the symptoms were uncertain and "too hastily established,"[24] but he later retracted this opinion: "When Dr Corrigan first published his views, I fell into the error of supposing that he intended to put this forward as a diagnostic mark between aneurism of the abdominal aorta and diseases which simulate it. This, however, is not the case . . ."[25] In the international literature the opinion of his friend and colleague William Stokes was to prevail, "We owe the diagnosis of this disease to Dr Corrigan."[26]

There is a noteworthy *apologia* by Corrigan in this famous paper for erroneous views put forward in the very first paper he had published in 1828; he says that some of the cases described by him then had led him to make an error, "for meeting the signs of permanent patency of the aortic orifice in conjunction with aneurism, I erroneously attributed to the aneurism the signs which arose from the permanent patency."[18] When the British Medical Association visited Dublin in 1835 he was invited to join a committee to investigate the physiology of the heart. Probably because of the criticism of his paper on cardiac physiology by Hope and others he declined: "I at once rose and stated that the view that I had put forward was erroneous, and arose from making the mistake into which I fell of experimenting on the heart of cold-blooded animals, fishes and reptiles, and arguing from them to the heart of warm-blooded animals. And how is this avowal received? By passing a vote of thanks to me for my communication. I do not know of any other profession at which a similar avowal of error could have been as safely made and would have been as well received."[27]

In the *Clinique Medicale de L'Hotel Dieu de Paris* the celebrated physician, Armand Trousseau was speaking of the "maladie de Corrigan,"[28] and the Corrigan eponym was first used in print in *La Lancette Francaise: Gazette Des Hopitaux* in 1838.[29] Let us move forward a few years for the purpose of recounting an interesting anecdote. Corrigan, as we shall see, liked to travel, and he often visited the major hospitals in the capital cities of Europe. On one such occasion in Paris he was accompanying the doctors and students on a round of the wards when one of the French physicians proclaimed a patient to be suffering from "maladie de Corrigan;" remembering the name of his guest, he asked him if he knew Corrigan of Dublin to which Corrigan promptly replied, "Ce moi, monsieur." He was led without further ado to the lecture theatre where he was presented to the staff and students of the hospital, and to quote Francis Cruise: "A right royal reception was given to the illustrious visitor."[2] In America writers were referring to the characteristic pulse as "Corrigan's pulse,"[22] and because the pulse bore some resemblance to the sensation given by the Victorian toy the "water-hammer" the pulse is often referred to as the "water-hammer pulse."[30]

These early years in The Charitable Infirmary were in some respects frustrating. His efforts to obtain better facilities were thwarted by his surgical colleagues who were determined to maintain their dominance over the physicians. Yet these were the most productive years of his scientific career. With only a few beds at his disposal he perfected his powers of clinical observation, and he wrote no less than seventeen major papers during the decade he was attached to the hospital. Though he was to remain a prolific writer he would never again match the originality of his contributions to medical science during this period. These papers are characterised by a lively and stimulating style which holds the readers interest, but he tends to be repetitive, and all his papers would have been improved by good editing. He goes to great lengths to acknowledge the work of his contemporaries particularly his Dublin colleagues, and we often find informal tributes such as: "To my friend and colleague Dr Hunt, to whom I am indebted for this case," or "Dr Stokes in his admirable work on diseases of the chest," etc.

In 1838 he described the fibrosis of the lung that occurs in chronic tuberculosis calling it "cirrhosis of the lung" — "This disease is in the lung what cirrhosis is in the liver; and I have, therefore, ventured to call it by the same name. A better name might be selected, but as there are already in medicine so many instances of names of diseases bearing no connexion with their nature I have thought it better to retain the name, than burthern our nomenclature with another. I would rather add an additional fact than a new name to science."[31] Little did he know that he was to add another eponym to medical science; for many years the condition he described so well was known as "Corrigan's cirrhosis," a term no longer in use.

In another paper he comes so close to describing for the first time a major heart disease that we may well wonder how his reasoning just failed him.[32] Recently there has been great interest in the effects of heart disease on the performance of the brain. Previously many patients, mostly elderly, complaining of dizziness, confusion and blackouts were thought to have degenerative disease of the brain due to narrowing of the cerebral blood vessels, but it is now known that often the cause of the symptoms is in the heart rather than the head: the specialised tissue that conducts electrical impulses in the heart degenerates and the heart escapes from normal control to become episodically rapid or very slow.

During either of these phases the blood supply to the brain may be reduced causing dizziness incorrectly attributed to senility. Of course, the concept of the heart being the cause of cerebral symptoms was not quite new in Corrigan's day. Robert Adams, a surgeon and a contemporary of Corrigan in The Charitable Infirmary, in a paper written in 1827 had suggested that "apoplexy must be considered less a disease in itself than symptomatic of one, the organic seat of which is in the heart."[33] Had Corrigan been aware of this paper he would surely have appreciated Adams's iconoclastic conclusion. He would not then have made the error when describing "epileptic palpitation" of attributing the trouble to the head rather than to the heart, and the disease now known as the "sick sinus syndrome" in which the heart may become alternately rapid or slow and so interfere with blood flow to the brain, would undoubtedly bear the eponym of Corrigan. How close he came to getting it right: "On recovering from, or on the coming on of the attack, there is fluttering and palpitation about the heart; the loss of consciousness and the staggering or fall are described by fainting, and the occurrence of fluttering or palpitation seems to point out the heart as the seat of the evil." Alas, he settled for the explanation that, "The brain or nervous system is the offending cause."

Corrigan's reputation was growing rapidly. In 1838 he was elected consulting physician to his *alma mater* the Catholic College of Maynooth, a prestigious position for which he received one hundred and twenty pounds per annum in return for one visit a month.[34] As his reputation grew so did his private practice, especially among the Catholic community and the clergy. Shortly after being appointed to The Charitable Infirmary he moved his rooms from Upper Ormond Quay to the more respectable number thirteen Bachelor's Walk.

Medical education was to become one of his dominant interests. He was an impressive teacher and was soon appointed lecturer in the practice of medicine to the Diggis Street Medical School and to the Apothecaries' Hall. There were many medical schools in Dublin at that time and competition between them was considerable.[35] Corrigan led a movement to fix a minimum fee for a course of lectures, so that an inferior standard of lecturing would not be offered at cheaper rates. At a meeting in Corrigan's house the professors and lecturers of medicine resolved, "that the present rate of remuneration is totally inadequate and that in order the better to enable us to meet the expenses incurred in preparation and requisites for courses or lectures such as the present state of medical science and the character of the Irish medical school require, we therefore feel it necessary to raise the fee for each first course of lectures to three guineas." The move was not successful because the Park Street School advertised its lectures at a guinea less and refused to meet to discuss the implementation of a uniform scale of fees. There was, however, an interesting social development. The initial spirit of goodwill among the teachers was such that they formed themselves into a "Social Medical Club to be called The Lecturers Club."[36] The object of the said club was "to keep up a spirit of good feeling and friendship among the lecturers, which will enable them the more readily to act in concert for their mutual support and the advancement of their profession." It was further hoped that social intimacy would "be the means of diffusing much useful information, of keeping up an incentive to excel in each department of teaching, of cultivating a personal intimacy, so desirable to all, with the distinguished members of the profession of other countries, and of more widely extending a knowledge of the facilities and advantages presented by the Irish schools for the cultivation of medical science." Corrigan was appointed secretary and treasurer, and the club had a membership of fifty professors and lecturers at an annual subscription of one pound. On September 6, 1837 thirty members of the club including such luminaries as Philip Crampton, Richard Carmichael, Robert Graves, Robert Harrison, Arthur Jacob, William Stokes and Robert Adams dined at "Molony's" at a total cost of £8 8s 8¼d which included candles, carriages, a hamper and alcoholic beverages costing £3 14s 9½d.

Corrigan's appointment to The Charitable Infirmary was the most significant event of his career. He would in the course of time receive many apparently more illustrious posts and honours, but none would have been possible without the first step forward. Moreover, it was at The Charitable Infirmary that he published the paper that was to establish his reputation.[18] For all this there is evidence to suggest that Corrigan did not hold his position in the hospital in high regard; he once wrote: "Since the year 1830, I have been physician to Jervis Street hospital, an hospital, it is true on a small scale, but sufficient to give me a knowledge of hospital attendance."[37] Corrigan attempted to improve his lot by acquiring more beds, but neither the surgeons who dominated the hospital, nor the management committee were impressed by the pleas of the physician. The minutes of June 7, 1831 make the position quite clear: "That the management committee do not consider it expedient to make any alteration in the by-laws relating to the duties of the physicians or to the number of medical beds in the hospital . . ."[38]

Corrigan had a large out-patient attendance but with few specific remedies for disease available, the best hope for cure would have been in hospital where at least he would provide care, adequate nourishment, and wine! To how many of the city's sick-poor did he have to deny admission because he did not have sufficient beds? In order that he could have more beds at his disposal he applied successfully for the post of physician to Cork Street Fever Hospital. The managing committee of The Charitable Infirmary supported his application: "I am requested . . . to communicate to you this unanimous resolution of approval of the diligence, professional ability, and zealous devotion of the discharge of your duties which you have uniformly evinced . . . The committee regret that the smallness of the Funds does not permit so extensive a field for your professional exertions as they could desire . . ."[39] In retrospect it is easy to criticise the hospital for not providing Corrigan with more facilities and tempting to attribute this to the intransigence of his surgical colleagues who might have released some beds for his use, but altruism within the profession is indeed rare, and The Charitable Infirmary, never a wealthy institute, was unlikely to have had funds for improving the hospital.

The Fever Hospital and House of Recovery, Cork Street, was founded in 1804 by a "few benevolent citizens" in response to the dreadful mortality from fever in Dublin in the early years of the nineteenth century. So generous were these voluntary contributions that the founders were able to enlarge the original plan from 40 to 120 beds, and the hospital was extended subsequently on a number of occasions.[40] The well-preserved minute books make a fascinating diary of the social, medical and meteorological vicissitudes of the nineteenth century.[41] The hospital was the first in Dublin to use an ambulance for transporting sick patients: "Patients were conveyed to the hospital in a carriage, hung on springs, and specially provided for that purpose, experience having proved that fatal consequences had often arisen to the health of the inhabitants of the City of Dublin from the usual practice of conveying persons labouring under contagious diseases to hospital in hackney coaches and sedan chairs."[42]

In 1837, the year of Corrigan's appointment to Cork Street Fever Hospital there were 6,595 admissions to the hospital of whom 595 died. We learn from the minutes: "Great snow early in January. Cases of modified small-pox prevailed in the City of Dublin. At the commencement of the year the typhoid fever epidemic again reappeared, and so extensively that the Government felt themselves called upon to provide additional Hospital accommodation to meet the emergency."[43]

Corrigan's publications during the period of his attachment to The Charitable Infirmary are the most significant of his career, but he was at that age when the mind is innovative and alert, and it was in this period that he devoted himself almost totally to clinical medicine. How much greater would his contribution to medical science have been, if the hospital had facilitated him with more beds? Whatever the answer, it is unlikely that he would have remained with the institute indefinitely. The Charitable Infirmary in those days was regarded as inferior to some other hospitals, and Corrigan was never one to tolerate anything short of excellence for long. He was quite frank about the system that then prevailed in Dublin: "A medical man bought the field in which he exhibited, and then the large hospitals were glad to get him."[44] Corrigan had bought "the field in which he exhibited" — The Charitable Infirmary; the question that now troubled him was to which large hospital should he seek appointment.

In June 1840, John Crampton, professor of *materia medica* at Trinity College died leaving a vacancy on the staff of the House of Industry Hospitals.[45] Corrigan applied and was successful, though he did not actually resign from The Charitable Infirmary for another three years. He was not the first to take this course; his colleague Robert Adams had made the same move some years earlier, and in 1817 John Cheyne had been attracted from the Meath Hospital to the House of Industry Hospitals.[46]

The appointments to the House of Industry Hospitals were the prerogative of the lord lieutenant, and Corrigan in seeking the post had to secure political patronage. Lord Morpeth, then chief secretary of Ireland was a staunch ally.[47] Like his father he favoured the removal of Jewish and Catholic disabilities and during his term as chief secretary a number of important bills were passed. Another supporter was Sir Michael O'Loghlan, the first Catholic judge in Ireland since the reign of James II, who held the influential positions of solicitor general and attorney general for Ireland. Corrigan also knew Daniel O'Connell but not it seems well enough to approach him directly, but his espousal of the Liberal cause did persuade his son John O'Connell, then a Whig member of parliament, to use his influence on his behalf, even if he did so without much optimism: "Let me *beg and pray* of you most earnestly not to deceive yourself with expectations. I very much regret to say that ministers but too often give appointments to their enemies, or to neutrals which they owe to their honest supporters, and so strong is the conviction of this in my father's mind that he thought it worse than useless to write to Lord Morpeth, tho' he means to speak to him in the House in your favour. I fear with only too much reason that you will not succeed in your wishes and therefore I anxiously beg of you not to be sanguine."[48] In spite of this pessimistic caution, Corrigan was successful. He was appointed as physician to the Hardwicke Fever Hospital containing 144 beds, and to the Whitworth Hospital containing 82 beds.[49] To what sort of an institute was Corrigan transferring his allegiance?

An act of parliament passed in 1771 instituted the Corporation for the Relief of the Poor in the City of Dublin, and in 1772 the passing of the House of Industry Act brought into existence a workhouse known as the House of Industry in

Channel-row (now Brunswick Street).[50] This institution was empowered by the act "to seize strolling vagrants, &c., and to commit them to the House of Industry, to be kept at hard labour from two months to four years, according to circumstances, and to inflict reasonable corporal punishment, in cases of refusal to work, or ill behaviour, but never acquires, in any instance, the power of detaining a pauper for life." Draconian though these measures may now seem, they did apparently meet with some success in curtailing beggary, then a major problem. Dr Woodward, Bishop of Cloyne relates "the nuisance of beggary grievious beyond the experience of other great cities, and from its greatness esteemed to be beyond remedy was suppressed."

There was within the workhouse a degree of tolerance and ecumenicity not always present in some latter day establishments. Wages were earned for labour, but at a minimum rate based on that which would provide independent subsistence. This principle was central to the successful administration of the establishment: "No clothing is gratuitously furnished to the adult poor, the governors having found, from experience, that giving clothes indiscriminately to the poor relaxed their industry, and that such clothes not being their own property, or acquired by industry, were neither valued nor preserved, but generally commuted for spirituous liquors. There is no restraint in the exercise of religion; and there are two chaplains, a Protestant and Roman Catholic, and two distinct places appropriated for religious worship, and all children educated within the establishment, are instructed in the religion which their parents profess."

Begging in Dublin in the eighteenth century was official, only if licensed, eligibility being decided by parochial committees that submitted lists of the "helpless poor." All unlicensed begging had been banned by the lord mayor on May 1, 1773, when one thousand official badges with the names of the parishes inscribed on them were struck at a cost of eighteen pence each. A wagon, known as "the Black Cart" was driven through the streets on three days of each week accompanied by thirteen beadles dressed in livery in search of unlicensed beggars. Beadles were allowed a premium of 5s 5d for each beggar secured and brought into the House of

Industry, and a reward of five pounds was given to any one who prosecuted to conviction a person who had attempted to rescue a vagrant from the beadles. This happened often, and beadles were not infrequently killed by the angry citizens; from 1775 the attendants of the cart carried musquetoons.[51]

Within the house there was strict routine and discipline. Two meals were served daily. The men worked at a variety of industries preparing oakum, extracting dyes, and beating hemp, and the women spun flax, cotton, and wool and worsted. In addition they carried out combing, carding and other processes associated with the production of textiles. The products of these labours were sold, and of the profits one-third was given to the working inmates, one third to the instructors, and the remainder was added to the funds of the institution. Smuggling in of intoxicating liquor, and theft were punished by a period in the stocks or by whipping. Punishment was similar for both staff and inmates, the distinction between the two often being slight, as domestics and nurses were recruited frequently from the inmates.

The House had its characters; Hackball a paralysed cripple, who was driven to his stand on the Liffey in a little cart drawn either by a mule or two large dogs, resisted all efforts by the corporation to reform him, and he became known as the King of Dublin Beggars. He was celebrated in prose and verse as "His Lowness, Prince Hackball," though his real name was Patrick Corrigan. He was seized one day, but was rescued by "a riotous mob," and the corporation threatened to use the military to secure his capture. Shortly afterwards he was taken to the House, where because of his stature he was given special quarters.[52] Another notorious character who spent some time in the House was "Billy-in-the-Bowl." Billy had had the misfortune of being born legless in a poor society where survival depended on being fast of wit and fleet of limb. He compensated for his incapacity by propelling himself around the Stoneybatter and Grangegorman in a wooden bowl shod with iron. With his "fine dark eyes, acquiline nose, well formed mouth, dark curling locks, with a body and arms of Herculean power," he must have been a strange sight, striking sparks off the cobbles as he proceeded through the Liberties. There was a nasty streak to this "universal favourite," who thought little of assault and robbery in deserted parts of the city, for which crime he was finally taken prisoner and wheeled away in a barrow to be committed to Green Street Jail under sentence of hard labour for life.[53]

The workhouse had a hospital from which was to develop a lasting medical tradition. The hospital was, at first, small, cramped and totally inadequate, but in 1807 the Hardwicke Medical Hospital, named after the then viceroy, the Earl of Hardwicke was opened, and shortly afterwards became and remained until recent times a fever hospital. Two later viceroys gave their names to further developments of the hospital complex. In 1810, a Catholic convent in Brunswick Street was converted into the Richmond Surgical Hospital, and in 1813 the Whitworth Medical Hospital opened.[54] These hospitals served the workhouse and the poor from the surrounding districts until 1838 when Sir Robert Peel's Poor Law Act separated the workhouse from the hospital, which continued as the House of Industry Hospitals, known affectionately to generations of Dubliners simply as "The Richmond."[55]

Conditions in the hospital were altogether better than those to which Corrigan had been accustomed at The Charitable Infirmary. Surgeons and physicians visited daily in the morning, the former at thirty minutes past eight o'clock and the latter at ten o'clock. There were two medical and surgical clinical lectures each week and special courses on fevers and epidemic diseases, diseases of the eye, and mental diseases. There was an extensive pathological museum with about four thousand drawings, casts and preparations, with descriptive catalogues. There was a good medical and surgical library supported by the staff and by a small subscription from the students who used it, and containing about six hundred volumes. Operations were performed on Wednesday mornings only, except in urgent cases. Nine clinical clerks, interns and externs, and the dressers were selected from the best qualified students. Nurses were paid little more than ward maids — nine pounds a year, and one pound good conduct money, with improved rations.

Corrigan was active in achieving improvements for patients and staff alike. A complaint that some of the patients in the Whitworth hospital had very dirty shirts, led to the matron being reprimanded and an order for reserve clothing, shirts, shifts, caps and sheets. Corrigan requested that a book be kept by the clinical clerk for recording the names and addresses of any foreign or other professional persons of distinction who might visit the hospital. He had his wards supplied with test tubes, urinometers and glasses. Fixtures of an ordinary kind were placed in the large room opposite the hall door of the Whitworth hospital for the use of patients seeking admission, and a Kidderminster carpet was provided for the room in which the physicians examined these patients.[56]

Corrigan found himself among colleagues who kept abreast of medical change. In 1847 the first operation in Ireland under anaesthesia using ether was carried out by John MacDonnell.[57] This was a remarkable event carried out only days after the technique of Jackson and Morton had been published in the *British and Foreign Medical Review*. With the advent of anaesthesia one of the two major barriers to surgical progress was removed; the other, namely the control of sepsis, was introduced by the great surgeon Joseph Lister in 1865.[58] Whereas the Richmond surgeons were among the first to use anaesthesia, they were slow to apply Listerism, as antisepsis was known, to the practice of surgery. A possible explanation for their reluctance to adopt antiseptic techniques (they did not do so until 1885) was their remarkably low mortality for amputation of only 6.6 per cent: "By insisting on free ventilation, by removing the night-chairs from the wards, and having water-closets erected, by stimulating the nurses to cleanliness by rewards . . . by repeatedly impressing, however on the more intelligent patients, and on the nurses, the importance of cleanliness, a plentiful supply of the vital breath of heaven, and by the valuable aid of our resident pupils, we have succeeded in preserving our hospital from the visitation of the epidemic diseases common in ill-aired institutions . . ." So claimed the surgeon John Hamilton.[59]

Among Corrigan's colleagues there was also Robert Adams, and the famed teacher Richard Carmichael, who with Ephraim McDowell founded the school of anatomy, medicine, and surgery of the Richmond hospital. Carmichael was a founder member of the Medical Association of Ireland, and was president from its inception in 1839 until his tragic death in 1849.

Riding from Dublin to his seaside house at Sutton, he was caught by a treacherous tide and both horse and rider were drowned. The medical school at the Richmond was subsequently named after him.[60]

When Corrigan was appointed he was given charge of the Hardwicke hospital with 144 beds "devoted to fever and to contagious disease."[61] In the first five months of office 297 patients were admitted of whom twelve died from a variety of infections.[62] However, only one patient died from the disease known as "maculated fever" which affected most of the remaining patients. This illness was typhoid fever and Corrigan has left us a vivid description of a patient named Murphy, a policeman:

> "He was very ill in maculated fever — so violent that it was necessary to put a strait-waistcoat on him. His delirium was furious; his tongue was dry and brown; his pulse beating above 130; his skin covered with both maculae of fever and petechiae of purpura. He had not slept, and his eyes were suffused: he passed faeces in the bed, and we were positively assured by the nurse that he also passed urine copiously under him. This report seemed to be confirmed on first sight on turning down the bed-clothes, for there was a strong urinous smell; the clothes were stained by the urine; and the urine was seen welling from the orifice of the urethra, and dribbling over the thigh. Notwithstanding all this I had the catheter introduced, and there were drawn off certainly not less, and I believe more, than two quarts of urine."[62]

Corrigan devoted the same energy to his work in the House of Industry as he had done in The Charitable Infirmary. With more beds at his disposal he was now able to concentrate on teaching. He held lectureships in the Diggis Street and Richmond Hospital schools. He commenced his teaching rounds in the Hardwicke Hospital each morning at eight o'clock, and there was always a large attendance of students recording and commenting upon his patients.[63] He was an excellent bedside teacher, but it was his didactic lectures on the practice of medicine that earned him a reputation as an out-

standing lecturer. These lectures were published in the major
medical journals.[64] Frequently the theatre could not accommodate the students who flocked to hear him. He illustrated
his presentation with casts or drawings from clinical
cases. He liked to do his own dissections, and his demon-
strations of these "were most lucid — always explicit, and
while using the plainest of language he never was dull or
wearisome."[65] Mapother, who attended his lectures in
1851-2 has left us this account of his prowess as a lecturer: [65]
"Although he rarely spoke for more than half an hour, he
told us more practical facts and portrayed disease more
strikingly than others would in five hours. He frequently
used the microscope — an aid to the investigation of disease
only just adopted. Many of his illustrations were homely, for
instance, to satisfy ourselves that the impulse of the heart
against the left side of the chest is not solely due to its apex,
he would tell us that night to take the cat on our lap and
feel the impulse on both sides, as the chest is so narrow in
that animal. A favourite anecdote was that soldiers had
tried to persuade him that certain round scars of skin disease
were bullet marks; he retorted that as they were never found
except on the back they did not attest to the glory of facing
the enemy."

Corrigan's addresses to the students of the Richmond are
so good as to be worthy of editing and republishing for the
benefit of contemporary students. Like Graves he was aware
how much the teacher is in debt to his patients: "In our
intercourse with the poor in hospital we never forget, and
neither will you, that the poor who come to us here are to be
treated with the same consideration as the rich. The rich can
go where they like — the poor have no choice. If the poor
obtain the highest medical aid in the hospitals of our city,
they pay a price for it. Their cases are lectured on — their
diseases are the subject of scrutiny, and their bedsides are
the places for your instruction."[66] The art of clinical medicine is acquired only by diligent application and study at the
bedside of patients. Corrigan was a firm advocate of this form
of medical instruction, and he constantly urged his students
to avail of the opportunity to study disease in the wards.

Corrigan was content in the Richmond; more so than he

had been in The Charitable Infirmary. He spoke well of the hospital and he found that it compared well with foreign institutes:[67]

> "I have had opportunities of visiting many of the great hospitals of France and Germany, at Paris, Vienna, and Berlin. I can now, with confidence, say that, in all essential particulars, our hospitals here — not alone this institution, but our hospitals generally — can fully stand comparison with their best. On the eye of the casual or unprofessional visitor, the statuary in the halls, the frescoes on the ceilings, and the waxed floors, produce an imposing effect; but these do not constitute the essentials of an hospital or give comforts to the patients. The casual visitor seldom goes beyond these, but when the professional scrutinizer enters into the details of ventilation, of cooking, of medicine, of clothing, of the numerous little, yet requisite, appliances for the sick, he then learns to value his own institutions more than before, and to find out that there is often little to be adopted from others."

He approved of the way in which it was managed by a mixed board of professional and non-professional members. "The experience of many years has shown that this is probably the best form of a board of management that could be desired. The non-professional members bring to the board all that general knowledge of finance, contracts, and books, without which no institution can be economically or satisfactorily carried on, and with which professional men are seldom familiar, while the medical officers carry into its management that intimate acquaintance with details which unprofessional personnel with the best intentions could never acquire."

He had his difficulties of course, but after a decade of tussling with the Jervis Street surgeons these would have scarcely irritated him. The governor of the hospital apprehended him shortly after his arrival for a very greatly increased consumption of wine in his wards, numbers one and three of the Hardwicke Hospital. Corrigan pointed out that the liberal use of wine in the treatment of typhus fever was essential but he did agree to see what might be done to comply with the request.[68] Wine was not the only item about which the governor had to complain. The leech, *Hirundo medicinalis* was in common use for blood-letting, a practice that was considered advantageous in many conditions. The apothecary cared for and distributed these animals, and on August 17, 1841, in applying for an extra hundred leeches, "he begged to state that the 500 leeches allowed for each month *have all been used* a fortnight before the allowed time this month — there were some bad eye cases after operation requiring application of leeches."[69] Our modern hospitals are having similar difficulties controlling the successor to the leech — drugs, which account for an exorbitant portion of our health service expenditure.

The Richmond was more flamboyant than The Charitable Infirmary, and Corrigan, at his best in front of an audience, had ample opportunity to state his views. *The Irish Times*[67] reported the opening of the academic session for 1858: "The hour announced was eleven o'clock, and long before that time the gallery of the lecture hall was filled by students in medicine and surgery, anxious aspirants to professional fame. Dr Corrigan entered the theatre at eleven o'clock, and his presence was the signal for an enthusiastic burst of applause from the youthful auditory, and this was no less enthusiastic than sincere, for we believe that in this or any other country there is not a professor or clinical lecturer more respected and beloved by his pupils than the eminent physician who then stood before those who will derive counsel and proficiency from him during the session which he yesterday inaugurated. Exclusive of the array of young men who thronged the benches in the gallery, the space or platform upon which Dr Corrigan stood was occupied, right, left and front by an assemblage of professional and non-professional men, anxious to listen to his inaugural address, and to be present at the opening scene for the season of those interesting public institutions; and amongst those present we perceived: The Right Hon. the Lord Mayor; Right Hon. Lord Naas, Chief Secretary; Right Hon. J.D. Fitzgerald, QC, MP; Colonel Dunne, Private Secretary; etc."

Corrigan ever aware of the importance of political patronage for the advancement of himself, his institute and science, made good use of the occasion: "Dr Corrigan having retired from the theatre, he conducted Lord Naas and Colonel Dunne on an inspection of several wards in the institution, with which the noble lord and gallant colonel expressed their cordial approval of the discipline and general management of the several departments; and having descended to the kitchen department, the noble lord and the gallant colonel closely inquired, and examined minutely, the process of cooking and serving the food of the patients. With all the management and discipline the vice-regal party expressed their cordial approval. Having remained for some time on the grounds, in conversation with Dr Corrigan and other professional gentlemen and visitors, Lord Naas and Colonel Dunne took leave and returned to the Vice-Regal Lodge."

At the Richmond Corrigan continued to publish regularly in the medical journals, one of his more curious contributions being a description of an instrument which when heated to dull redness in a spirit lamp was applied over an area of sciatica or lumbago to induce what he called mild counter-irritation. This was known as "cure by firing."[70] It was popular until the early part of this century and the instrument was known as "Corrigan's button."[71]

Corrigan enjoyed applying his medical knowledge to the invention of appliances for the treatment of disease. He designed a stethoscope,[72] and impressed by a report from Laennec on the beneficial effects of seaweed in chest disease, he invented an inhaler which became kι.own as "Doctor Corrigan's diffuser."[73] He believed, with good reason that this would be a more effective way of administering iodine than Laennec's method of strewing sea-wrack throughout the wards of the hospital. He also designed hospital beds — "Doctor Corrigan's adjusting bed for invalids"[74] was a primitive version of today's ripple-bed for preventing pressure sores. A series of leather straps formed the base of the bed and could be released and tightened as required so that pressure could be removed from tender areas of the recumbent patient. In 1847 he designed "an economical bedstead" for the Central Board of Health and we can presume that this became the standard bed in most fever hospitals.[75] There is mention in one review of "Corrigan's hammer"[76] which was used to tap the chest to stimulate a failing heart, but I cannot find an original publication to authenticate this invention.

In 1841 Corrigan and Stokes both applied for the King's professorship of the practice of medicine, the teaching chair at Trinity College, and each was unsuccessful, one named George Greene being appointed.[77] As sometimes happens with professorial appointments when there are two exemplary candidates, the appointing authority rather than disappoint either settles for a compromise and often inferior candidate, and in so doing renders the institute a grave disservice.

Corrigan's application for the professorship was such that even today he would do himself proud in the most celebrated universities.[78] Having presented himself as a suitable candidate on the basis of possessing "an extensive field of hospital practice," and of having contributed "to the improvement of his profession and the advancement of the science of medicine," he asserted that he had moreover "the capability of lecturing, or of conveying to others the information" which he had himself acquired. Listing his many publications he claimed to have been paid the unique distinction of having had a disease named after him: "The high compliment has occasionally been paid to a writer, of affixing his name as a specific distinction to a discovery of which he is the author." He gave further testimony to his fame by quoting Sir Philip Crampton's appraisal of his publications as containing "discoveries which must rank Dr Corrigan among the ablest pathologists of the present day," and Robert Graves who wrote to him, "I have no hesitation in asserting that your papers have been of the highest order, and that they are quoted with approbation both in America and throughout Europe as containing some important discoveries in the practice of medicine." From the mighty Andral, professor of pathology at the Faculty of Medicine in Paris came European acclaim for his work: "Je connais les différens mémoires que vous avez publiés; ils ont utilement contribué aux progès de la science; ils annoncent tous un medecin habitué a observer, à trer parti des faits et qui sait exposer ses recerces avec autant de methode que de clarté."

5

The Dublin School

Ireland holds a position of esteem in the annals of nineteenth century medical history for the remarkable contributions to clinical medicine emanating from a movement that came to be known simply as the "Dublin school." This title, correct in denoting the origins of the school and its role in the reformation in clinical medicine does not, however, convey the dynamic idealism and iconoclasm which gave to this renaissance international recognition and the approbation of posterity. The "school" has been decked with many garlands, not least being the romantic title "the golden age of Irish medicine," a tribute not undeserved, for at no time previously, nor at any time since, has Dublin had so great an influence in medicine.

Three "giants" stand out from a galaxy of lesser, though by no means insignificant, luminaries who constituted the "school" — Robert Graves, Dominic Corrigan and William Stokes. If we seek qualities common to these three Irishmen, we may discern two outstanding talents: a compelling desire to observe the pattern and effect of illness with impartiality even when their studies refuted conventional practice, and the ability to describe their observations with elegance and authority. Their courage in assailing the doctrines of established medicine was sustained by a clarity of vision cultivated in no small measure by their frequent travels abroad; they insisted on maintaining and fostering contact with their continental and American colleagues, realising as they did so clearly, that Irish medicine deprived of exposure to an active intellectual environment would sink to mediocrity and flounder. Indeed, it was the complacency arising from insularity, together with a dearth of talent to replace the founders of the "school," that brought about its ultimate dissolution with Corrigan's death in 1880. The personalities of the founders may fade into the shadows of time, but their contributions to medicine have been immortalised by eponyms with which medical students across the globe are familiar — "Graves' disease," "Cheyne-Stokes respirations," "Stokes-Adams' attacks," "Corrigan's disease," and "Corrigan's pulse." To appreciate the achievement of the "Dublin school" we need to look back to the Georgian doctors who laid the foundations on which these Victorians could build their temple to Aesculapius and to examine the state of medicine in Ireland in the mid-nineteenth century.

The standards of medicine in Georgian Ireland were deplorable, both in practice and within the organisations responsible for the regulation of the profession.[1] The overall impression of the period must be, that with a few magnificent exceptions, the Georgian doctors of Dublin concentrated mostly on their own welfare, and did little to advance the practice of medicine. Such of course, was the mood of a selfish age. The College of Physicians and the University of Dublin, must bear censure for failing to effect the reforms that were so obviously needed, though were it not for a few outstanding individuals in both institutes what little progress was made might not have happened. The surgeons stand exempted from this criticism and merit acclaim for establishing their own college in 1784, which soon became an effective force in medical education and in the practice of surgery. Outside of the establishment bodies there were doctors of altruistic temperament who could stand no longer the disgraceful sufferings of the sick-poor of the city, and together with benevolently-minded citizens they gave to Dublin its Georgian hospitals, many of which survive to this day.

Dublin, in common with much of the country had had hospitals (many of which were leper or lazar-houses) since the twelfth century, one of the oldest and most famous of which had been the Augustinian Hospital of St John the Baptist dating from 1188.[2] When Henry VIII extended the suppression of monasteries to Ireland in 1541, the monastic and religious houses throughout the country were closed, among which was the Hospital of St John the Baptist. Dublin remained without a hospital until, as we have seen, six surgeons determined to provide for the medical needs of the sick-poor, and The Charitable Infirmary was opened in 1718.[3] This was followed by Dr Steevens' hospital in 1733, Mercer's hospital in 1734, the Hospital for Incurables, in 1744, the Rotunda Lying-In Hospital in 1745, the Meath hospital in 1753, St Patrick's hospital in 1757, the Cork Street Fever Hospital and House of Recovery in 1804, Sir Patrick Dun's Hospital in 1818, and the Coombe Lying-In Hospital in 1823.[4] All these were "voluntary hospitals" meaning that they were erected and maintained by public subscription. Government involvement in providing hospital care did not match the voluntary participation of the medical profession and citizens of the city. In 1729 the notorious Foundling Hospital was opened by the government,[5] and in 1773 the House of Industry Hospitals were founded from which developed the Hardwicke Fever Hospital (1803), the Richmond Surgical Hospital (1810) and the Whitworth Medical Hospital (1818).[6] The background story to each of these hospitals is one of individual and corporate endeavour. Dr Richard Steevens bequeathed his considerable wealth to the erection of the hospital now bearing his name, but it was the tireless energy of his sister Grizel that carried his wishes to fulfilment.[7] The most remarkable philanthropic doctor of the Georgian period was Bartholomew Mosse, who by personal denial, selfless dedication, and a vision both classical and practical, raised sufficient money to build the Rotunda Hospital, a memorial to the architectural beauty of the age, which continues today to care for the lying-in women of the city.[8]

Jonathan Swift, Dean of St Patrick's Cathedral, believed that the city of Dublin had a need every bit as compelling, if somewhat at variance to that which had motivated Mosse:

> "He gave the little wealth he had
> To build a house for fools and mad;
> And showed by one Satiric touch
> No nation wanted it so much."[9]

The regulation of the practice of medicine lay with the College of Physicians, founded in 1654, which together with the

University of Dublin, granted degrees in medicine. Many aspiring doctors chose to go abroad for medical training to Edinburgh, London, Paris, Vienna, or to Leyden where the mighty Boerhaave influenced generations of European doctors.[10]

The medical school at the University of Dublin was established in 1711, but it did not become an effective force in medical education until the early nineteenth century under the influence of men of the calibre of James Macartney, Whitley Stokes and Robert Perceval. Perceval had the vision to realise that without an hospital for the teaching of clinical medicine, Irish students would continue to go abroad for medical training, and he was largely responsible for the Physic Act of 1800 which brought about the building of Sir Patrick Dun's Hospital where, as we have seen, Corrigan walked the wards as a medical student.[11]

In the hierarchy of medicine, the physicians ruled supreme, and blind to the benefits of future development of the profession they protected their privileged position with an intense chauvinism. The midwives, apothecaries and surgeons remained much the inferior members of the profession.[12] Before the founding of the College of Surgeons, surgery was treated as a trade and the surgeons were incorporated by charter in a body with the apothecaries, the barbers and periwig-makers. Training for surgery was through apprenticeship to an established surgeon, a practice that persisted until 1844.[13]

The first sign of revolt in Irish surgery is attributed to Sylvester O'Halloran, a Limerick surgeon, who, in 1765, made proposals for "the Advancement of Surgery in Ireland."[14] Shortly afterwards William Dease, a Dublin surgeon, criticised the University of Dublin for failing to teach surgery and applauded the French surgeons who "by procuring a total separation from that preposterous union with the company of barbers" had been enabled to raise the standard of surgery.[15] Samuel Croker-King, surgeon to Dr Steevens' hospital was instrumental in petitioning parliament for a charter for a College of Surgeons, which was granted on February 11, 1784. Croker-King was elected first president of the Royal College of Surgeons in Ireland, which met for the first time in the board room of the Rotunda hospital on March 2,

1784.[16] The rise of this institute, which will shortly celebrate its bicentenary, when compared to the apathetic performance of its elders the Royal College of Physicians and the University of Dublin, is quite remarkable. It was fortunate in having on its early staff men of considerable talent and energy among whom were Whitley Stokes, Arthur Jacob and John Timothy Kirby of whom mention has previously been made.

An early president of the Royal College of Surgeons was Philip Crampton (in 1811, 1820, 1844 and 1855) a leading surgeon and anatomist, who was also a keen zoologist and founder member of the Royal Dublin Zoological Gardens.[17] Fastidious in dress and elegant in appearance he did not escape the attention of the satirical Erinensis: "About six feet in height, slightly framed, elegantly proportioned, and elastic as cork wood; and if instead of the Gothic fabrics, by which his graceful figure was distorted, he had been habited in Lincoln's Green, he might doubtless have posed as the model of James Fitzjames. A blue coat, with scarcely anything deserving the name of skirts; a pair of doe-skin breeches, that did every justice to the ingenious maker; top boots, spurs of imposing longitude, and a whip, called a "blazer" in his country, completed the costume of this dandy Nimrod."[18] Indeed Crampton's appearance was the cause of a bon mot; when he first appeared at Dublin Castle resplendent in the handsome uniform of surgeon-general, King George IV inquiring as to his identity was informed, "He is the surgeon-general," to which added the witty Judge Norbury, "I suppose that is the *General* of the *Lancers*."[19] Crampton was created a baronet by Queen Victoria in 1839 and was commemorated until recently by the rather strange bronze fountain, backed by a leafy phallus that stood at College Street, and bore an inscription even odder than its design: "This fountain has been placed here — a type of health and usefulness — by the friends and admirers of Sir Philip Crampton, Bart., Surgeon-General to her Majesty's Forces."[19] He lived at number fourteen Merrion Square, a house famous for the pear tree planted in the year of Waterloo. He died in 1858, at the age of 81 years, and according to his wish, his body encased in Roman cement was interred in the cemetery at Mount Jerome, a mode of burial that must have caused some distress to his pall bearers, as Meenan observed.[20] One is put in mind of the terminal eccentricities of doctors; Jonathan Osborne of Mercer's hospital had been incapacitated by severe rheumatism and was buried standing, so that he might be first out on judgement day, and Swift's physician Robert Helsham had directed "that before my coffin be nailed up my head be severed from my body and that my corps be carried to the place of buriel by the light of one taper only at the dead of night without herse or pomp attended by my domesticks only."[21]

John Cheyne, first professor of medicine in the Royal College of Surgeons (1813-1819) was not Irish, but such has been his association with Dublin that his Scottish origins are often overlooked. After graduating from Edinburgh he joined the Royal Regiment of Artillery at Woolwich, and then accompanied a brigade of horse artillery to Ireland and was present at the abortive insurrection at Vinegar Hill in 1798. He did not regard his career in the army as altogether satisfactory, "much of his time being spent in shooting, playing billiards, reading such books as the circulating library supplied, and in complete dissipation of time." In fact, so successful was he in the pursuit of pleasure that he "learned nothing but ease and propriety of behaviour."[22] He returned to Scotland for a short time, but in 1809 we find him "as a candidate for public favour in Dublin . . . neither expecting nor indeed wishing for rapid advancement; what is easily acquired is little valued and not infrequently soon lost." Principled, and idealistic, as indeed are most young doctors, he sought an opening that would give him the opportunity of distinguishing himself rather than "securing a large income." He was given his chance in 1811 when he was appointed physician to the Meath hospital, and two years later he became professor of medicine at the Royal College of Surgeons. Four years later he was appointed Physician to the House of Industry Hospitals, where by virtue of "experience and of well-trained sick nurses, who allowed nothing to escape their observation," he was able to complete his daily visit in "little more than an hour." Before long he had a flourishing private practice, and the principles that originally motivated him to leave the army and seek a more altruistic career appear to have suffered a

21. *The Charitable Infirmary, Jervis Street, Dublin. From an engraving on a lecture certificate dated 1833-4. By courtesy of the Royal College of Physicians of Ireland. Photograph by D. Davison.* (see p. 81)

22. *The Richmond Surgical Hospital. From an engraving on a lecture certificate. By courtesy of the Royal College of Surgeons in Ireland. Photograph by D. Davison.* (see p. 96)

23. *"Billy in the Bowl". A cripple begging. A detail from an engraving by Hogarth, "Industry and Idleness", Plate 6.* (see p. 98) *Photograph by J. Hall.*

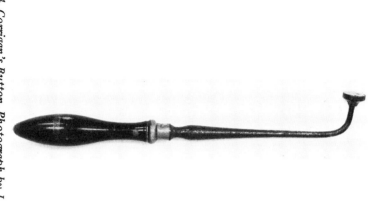

24. *Corrigan's Button. Photograph by J. Hall.*
(see p. 105)

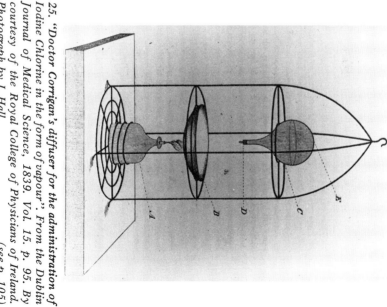

25. *"Doctor Corrigan's diffuser for the administration of Iodine Chlorine in the form of vapour". From the Dublin Journal of Medical Science, 1839. Vol. 15. p. 95. By courtesy of the Royal College of Physicians of Ireland. Photograph by J. Hall.*
(see p. 105)

26. Philip Crampton (1777-1858). From an engraving of a portrait by Stephen Catterson Smith, Snr. in Dr. Steeven's Hospital, Dublin. By courtesy of Dr. Steeven's Hospital. Photograph by D. Davison.
(see p. 111)

27. *John Cheyne (1777-1836). A porcelain relief in the Royal College of Physicians in Ireland. By courtesy of the College of Physicians. Photograph by D. Davison.* *(see p. 112)*

28. *Abraham Colles (1773-1843). Portrait by Martin Cregan in the Royal College of Surgeons in Ireland. By courtesy of the College of Surgeons. Photograph by D. Davison.* *(see p. 129)*

29. An operation in a Dublin drawing-room on July 20th 1817. A water-colour in the Library of the Meath Hospital, Dublin. The surgeon performing the operation is Rawdon Macnamara and Sir Philip Crampton, in hunting jacket and riding boots has his hand on the patient's shoulder. By courtesy of the Meath Hospital. Photograph by D. Davison.

(see p. 132)

30. *Richard Carmichael (1776-1849). An engraving by E. Finden of a drawing by Frederick Burton in the Royal College of Physicians of Ireland. By courtesy of the College of Physicians. Photograph by D. Davison.* *(see p. 134)*

31. *Robert Graves (1796-1853). A drawing by Charles Grey in the Royal College of Physicians of Ireland. By courtesy of the College of Physicians. Photograph by D. Davison.* (see p. 140)

32. "Passage of Mount Cenis" by J.M.W. Turner. Robert Graves and Turner travelled together through the Mount Cenis pass in 1819. By courtesy of Birmingham Museums and Art Gallery. (see p. 141)

33. Dominic John Corrigan (1802-1880). From a print in the Royal College of Physicians of Ireland. By courtesy of the College of Physicians. Photograph by D. Davison.

34. William Stokes (1804-1878). From a portrait by Frederick Burton in Trinity College, Dublin. By courtesy of Trinity College. Photograph by D. Davison. *(see p. 150)*

35. Robert Adams (1796-1875). From an engraving in the Royal College of Physicians of Ireland. By courtesy of the College of Physicians. Photograph by D. Davison. *(see p. 151)*

36. William Wilde (1815-1876). From a photograph in the Royal College of Physicians of Ireland. By courtesy of the College of Physicians. Photograph by D. Davison. *(see p. 158)*

37. *The Dispensary for Diseases of the Eye and Ear in Frederick Lane,*
1841-1844. From a water colour by Caroline Scally in the Royal Victoria
Eye and Ear Hospital, Dublin. By courtesy of the Hospital. Photograph
by D. Davison. *(see p. 160)*

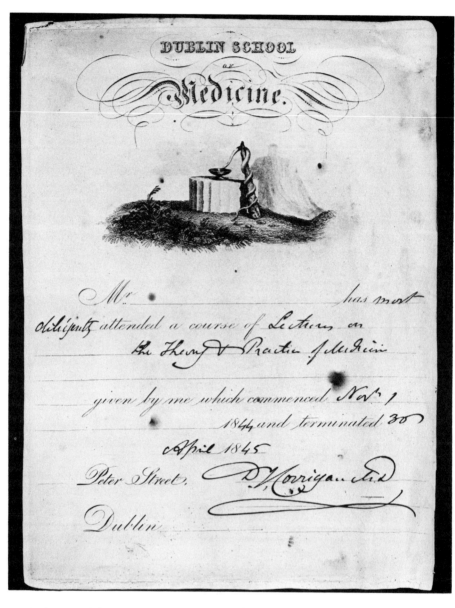

38. *"Dublin School of Medicine" Certificate, 1845. Signed by D.J. Corrigan. By courtesy of the Royal College of Physicians of Ireland. Photograph by D. Davison.* (see p. 165)

reverse: "I therefore felt it necessary to resign my professor-ship at the College of Surgeons, as well as my charge at the Meath Hospital, that my private practice, which in 1916 yielded me £1,710 might not suffer by the extent of my official duties." Indeed he appears to have become rather obsessed by money and when he was appointed physician-general to the army he assessed his achievements in purely monetary terms: "As my practice yielded £5,000, which was about its annual average during the next ten years, I felt that I had fully attained the object of my ambition . . . I am con-vinced had my health permitted me, that I could have added £1,500 a year to my income."

John Cheyne would not be of great interest to us were it not for the fact that in 1846 William Stokes[23] in describing a peculiar form of respiration commonly found in terminal illness recalled an earlier description by Cheyne,[24] the con-dition now being known as "Cheyne-Stokes respiration." In 1825 Cheyne's health began to deteriorate and he returned to England where he worked in general practice in the village of Sherrington, and wrote some rather eccentric essays reflect-ing a deep obsession with religion. He died in 1836 leaving instructions for the erection of a monument which bore quotations from the scripture and exhortations to passers-by: "Reader! the name, profession and age of him whose body lies beneath, are of little importance; but it may be of great importance to you to know that by the grace of God, he was brought to look to the Lord Jesus as the only Saviour of sinners and that this 'looking into Jesus' gave peace to his soul."[22]

The most illustrious member of the new College of Sur-geons, and one who could, at least in terms of eponymous recognition, be counted part of the Dublin school was Abraham Colles. Born in Millmount in Kilkenny in 1773, he graduated like so many of his contemporaries at Edin-burgh, which he found a rather strange and frightening place: "Since my arrival here I had not made the acquaintance of any Irishman, or one of any other nation, indeed, I am afraid to get acquainted with men to whose character I am an utter stranger."[25] Such shyness in the Irish when first venturing abroad is a common and often appealing characteristic, which

secured for young Colles the friendship of his landlady: "She
is positively afraid that I shall read myself into a coffin, and
actually comes to keep me idle at different times, out of her
desire to keep me in health." As the same good landlady had
previously alluded to her charge as "a very spry buck," we
may wonder a little at those "idle" study periods. Colles
returned to Dr Steevens' hospital in 1799 at a salary of fifty-
five pounds per annum, with five pounds in lieu of furniture.
In his first year he earned £8 10s 7½d, but this rose to
£6,128 in 1826. He was by nature thrifty, and kept a meticulous accounts book in which we may detect a humorous
lack of scruple: "For giving ineffectual advice for deafness,
£1 2s 9d; another fee for I know not what service, unless he
may have thought the last fee too small." Though his publications are fewer than those of his later contemporaries, the
quality and content are exceptional. "Colles's fracture" was
described in 1814, and in his work on *Venereal Disease*
he challenged the well-established Hunterian view that secondary syphilis was not contagious, by stating what was once
known as Colles's law — "One fact well-deserving our attention
is this; that a child born of a mother without any obvious
venereal symptoms, and which without being exposed to
any infection subsequent to its birth, shows the disease within a few weeks old; this child will infect the most healthy
nurse whether she suckle it or merely handle it; and yet this
child is never known to infect its own mother, even though
she suckle it while it has venereal ulcers of the lips and
tongue."[26] What Colles did not realise was that the mother
had previously been infected, but nonetheless his deductions
were for the time prescient. Dr Steevens' hospital then as
now had a reputation for the treatment of venereal disease.
In the "fluxing" or "salivating" wards patients were given
under special nursing care courses of mercury, which is highly
poisonous if given in excess. It was administered either as a
medicine by mouth, or was applied to the skin as an ointment.
To improve absorption of mercury by the skin the patient
was placed in front of a good fire and the area for application
was rubbed with a dry hand until red; then the ointment,
often containing turpentine and fresh hog's lard in addition
to mercury, was applied. An alternative treatment was the

inhalation of mercury vapour by stoving or fumigation, a technique regarded as quite hazardous. Patients were prepared for mercury treatment by bleeding, purging and the administration of emetics to induce vomiting. One of the effects of mercury is to stimulate the production of saliva, and the efficacy of treatment was judged by the quantity of saliva produced each day; each patient had a pewter mug in which the saliva could be collected and measured. A satisfactory response or "ptyalism", as it was known, was three to six pints of saliva in the twenty-four hours, and a course of salivation generally lasted about one month.[27]

Colles was a skilled surgeon but surgery in these early days before anaesthesia and antisepsis was to say the least, primitive and often terrifying. In one of his papers there is a vivid description of an operation in which he attempts to tie off one of the main arteries in the chest to cure an aneurism or swelling of the artery: "And now it was found that the aneurismal tumour had extended so close to the trunk of the carotid as to leave it uncertain whether any portion of subclavian artery was free from the disease . . . the majority (of assistants) appeared disposed to abandon the operation altogether . . . Prior to tightening the noose (around the artery) the breathing of the patient had become more laboured and he complained of much oppression of his heart . . . his countenance grew pale and indicative of instant dissolution . . . some of the assistants were so strongly impressed with the idea of his danger that they quitted the room lest he should expire before their eyes." Such hopeless efforts at heroic surgery were not uncommon and the outcome was almost invariably fatal.

Colles was a magnificent teacher, and in his lectures he attempted to inspire integrity as well as knowledge in his students: "Be assured that in this, more than in any other walk of life, public benefit and private advantage are so blended together that the most certain means of advancing your private interest is to promote the public good."[25] He was devoid of political ambition and in 1839 he declined a baronetcy. In 1841 anticipating his death, he requested his friend Robert Harrison to have his body examined "carefully and early . . . to ascertain by examination the exact seat and nature of my last disease." When he died, William Stokes in accordance with his last wishes published *Observations on the case of the late Abraham Colles*[28] in which the cause of death was attributed to a weakened and dilated heart, chronic bronchitis and emphysema of the lungs, as well as congestion of the liver, all occurring under the influence of a gouty constitution.

It is difficult, indeed almost impossible for us today to appreciate the barbarism of surgery, and the paucity of medical remedies in the nineteenth century. Many accounts of surgery in contemporary journals bear testimony to the cruelty of the operations attempted without anaesthesia, but none convey the hopelessness as vividly as the drawing by a student who was present at an operation for the removal of a malignant tumour from the left breast and armpit of one named Richard Power in a Dublin drawing room on July 20, 1817. The surgeon performing the operation is Rawdon Macnamara (president of the Royal College of Surgeons in 1813),[29] who was at the time only two years qualified and most probably apprenticed to Sir Philip Crampton depicted in blue coat and hunting boots. Even if patients survived the pain and calamity associated with major surgery, infection almost certainly claimed the victim, as it did the unfortunate Power within days.

To appreciate further the state of surgical practice we can do no better than turn to one whose claim to have read every surgical paper published in Dublin between 1808 and 1848 qualifies him as no other to portray this period. William Doolin in a delightful essay *Dublin's Surgery 100 Years Ago*[30] describes practical surgery as the cinderella of the healing art. "In the absence of anaesthesia these men had developed a manual dexterity swift as a sword in the juggler's hand . . . one searches in vain through their writings for any hint of 'principles' on which they based their surgical treatment: such as appeared to guide them were derived from the accumulated experience of individuals through the centuries that had gone before." And yet the accumulated experience of the ages restricted them but little in their attempts to perform the impossible. Overwhelming evidence pointing to the inevitable mortality of an operation served more often to encourage the surgeon to enhance his reputation on the slim chance of being successful than to desist from hopeless intervention. He was ready to treat all forms of injury, such as fractures and dislocation, and he would have had a go at removing any lump or bump be it a tumour, malignant or innocent. There were a number of "capital operations" which were almost invariably fatal. These included the release of the strangulated hernia, the major amputations, the ligation of the larger arteries for aneurism, and removal of kidney stones known as lithotomy.[30] Surgical skill was often judged by the speed with which a stone could be removed, and William Dease was reputed to carry a stone in his pocket ready to slip into the bladder should none be found there.[31] Another "capital operation" terrible to even contemplate was the use of the trephine for head injury. This consisted of boring a hole in the skull and was as William Porter declared "a dread ordeal, cruel and fearful to behold" in the conscious patient. It generally took place with the unfortunate victim sitting in a chair with two or more assistants holding him down. Hernias were fair game for the surgeon who, if he failed to reduce it by manipulation, would then "throw up a smoke enema," as was advocated by Colles, among others:[30]

"Tobacco injections are the very best thing after bleeding. Formerly the smoke of tobacco was used for the purpose, but the objections to it were the difficulty there often was to get the machine to work well, and the distension it caused was distressing; the infusion is therefore now substituted. You get a drachm of tobacco leaves and infuse it for 10 to 15 minutes in a pint of boiling water; when cool, inject one half and if in a quarter of an hour you observe no effect from it on the system, inject the other. The effect you look for is fainting, depression, cold perspiration, etc. I have seen many cases where the surgeon worked for a considerable time to try to put up the hernia by taxis without success, and which went up of its own accord after the tobacco enema."

For those interested in the *materia medica* of this strange practice, Doolin informs us that one practitioner found "the

tobacco sold under the name of *Shag* . . . more efficacious
than the *Pigtail*."

Undoubtedly the most distressing account of surgery in
nineteenth-century Dublin was that submitted to the *Lancet*
by a "pupil of the College of Surgeons in Ireland."[32]

"On Tuesday last hearing that the operation of removing
a portion of the lower jaw, on account of an osteosar-
comatous disease, was to be performed at the Richmond
Surgical Hospital, I made my way with many others,
uninvited into the operating theatre of that institution.
This room, though larger than any of the theatres of the
London hospitals, was nearly filled with pupils and
surgeons; the former seated on the benches, the latter
standing on what may be termed the stage, and obstruct-
ing and mobbishly closing up its whole area. The patient
was a boy about fourteen — the operator, Mr Carmichael.
The patient was placed on the lap of an able assistant,
but on the first incision screamed and struggled with so
much violence that it required much more than the
strength, applied as it was, of the many broad-shouldered
gentlemen surrounding him to keep him on his seat, but
as to securing his head, the more hands that attempted
it the worse they succeeded. A regular confusion now
ensued; the operator supplicated for light, air, and room;
his privileged brethren thronged but the more intensely
about him, the pupils lost altogether a sight of the
patient, the operation, and even of the operator. The
patient was shifted to a table but still remained invisible;
his continued screams, however, and the repeated remon-
strances of Mr Carmichael insisting for elbow room,
assured us that the operation was still going on . . . This
scene . . . continued for upwards of half an hour, when
at length the pupils were gratified with a view of the
piece of the jaw-bone which had been removed, and
which exhibited an interesting specimen of this disease
. . . We also saw the boy walk stoutly out of the operating room, notwithstanding his sufferings and loss of
blood, without deigning to avail himself of the assistance
which was proferred to him on all sides."

If such was the state of surgery, the practice of medicine was little better. The actions of such drugs as were available were poorly understood, and most therapeutic remedies were directed towards counteracting the effects of inflammation, both general and local. With fever and suppuration accounting for the great majority of illnesses, the antiphlogistic methods of treatment had an almost universal application. These remedies consisted of bleeding, purging and starvation, and were often combined with techniques of counter-irritation, such as blistering, and the application of heat and cold.[33]

The oldest of these techniques was blood-letting, which has been practised in one form or another by almost all cultures and societies.[34] One method employed was phlebotomy or venesection whereby a vein was opened with a lancet or fleam, the blood then being collected in a bowl; alternative techniques were the local removal of blood by means of scarification, cupping, or the use of leeches. Large quantities of blood can be removed from a vein and the practice was often carried to extremes causing the death of the patient. This was hardly surprising if the advice to "bleed to syncope" was taken literally, or if credence was placed in the dictate: "as long as blood-letting is required, it can be born; and as long as it can be born, it is required."[35] The rationale of the technique was based on the fallacious belief that by turning the circulation of the blood from the centre of the body to the surface, the patient's illness would be dissipated.[36] The physician's reputation depended not only on his dexterity and grace in employing the lancet, but also on his judgement in determining the amount of blood to remove. Quite apart from the dangers to the patient, Robert Graves was aware of the damage injudicious bleeding might do a doctor's reputation. In his *Lectures* he recounts his treatment of a patient with a stroke:[37] "the face was flushed, his temporal arteries were dilated and pulsated violently, and his pulse was hard, while the heart pulsated with great strength. This attack came on during our visit, and I ordered a vein to be opened immediately. The blood flowed freely. When about fourteen ounces were taken the pulse flagged and grew extremely weak, and never again rose. He died in about two hours, and an ignorant person would have ascribed his death to the bleeding." Graves exonerated the venesection because post-mortem examination had shown a large blood clot in the brain from which the patient would have died, but perhaps the blood-letting hastened his end and caused discomfort without the merit of benefit. At any rate Graves did warn his students: "Had such a case as this occurred to any of you in private practice, it would be almost fatal to your reputation."

Leeches were used as an alternative to phlebotomy for blood-letting. The species used for bleeding was *Hirundo medicinalis*, found in the streams and swamps of Central and Northern Europe. The leech was usually between fifty to seventy-five centimetres long with a dull olive-green back and four yellow longitudinal lines.[38] A large sucker at one end of its worm-like body is used for anchorage and at the other end a smaller sucker with a mouth is used to puncture the skin. Leeches were gathered in the spring months with a net, or leech fishers themselves waded into the water allowing the leeches to fasten onto their legs. Alternately cattle and horses were used as bait for the leeches. Leeches could be applied to almost any area of the body, including the eyes, the mouth, nose, ear, vagina and even the rectum. In preparation for the procedure the leech was dried with a piece of linen, and the skin was washed and shaved.[39] The leech was often confined to the area for bleeding by an inverted small wine glass. Sometimes the leech had to be enticed to feed with a little milk or blood. Leeches generally fed until satisfied for an hour or so when they would drop off; sometimes the tail was cut off so that it would continue to suck. A good leech could be expected to remove about an ounce of blood. Once used a leech could not be reused for several months, unless it was made to disgorge its meal in salt water or weak vinegar. The number of leeches used varied according to the illness, the size of the patient, the whims of prevailing practice and the availability of leeches. For small children only one or two might be necessary, whereas in adults twenty or even fifty leeches might be applied at once. Graves preferred to use "relays" of six or eight leeches at a time, a practice which permitted him to maintain "a constant oozing of blood from the integuments over an inflamed organ for twenty-four, or even thirty-six hours."[40]

Of all the skills employed by the physician, that of cupping called for the greatest show of dexterity and professional aplomb. Cupping is one of the oldest medical procedures, and one that is not yet extinct even in Britain.[41] The technique is performed by heating a glass cup to exhaust it of air, and then placing the cup on the skin which is sucked into the mouth of the glass and after about 10 minutes the capillaries in the skin burst giving a painless bruise. This procedure is called dry-cupping, which may, if indicated, be supplemented by wet-cupping whereby the bruised area is scarified by several incisions (made with a special scarificator containing several small blades), and the cups are then reapplied to draw off blood. One glass could extract as much as four ounces of blood[42] and it was common practice to place four or six cups on the back or abdomen, though most areas of the body capable of supporting a glass were cupped by practitioners of this art. The area selected was first fomented with hot water, then a torch dipped in alcohol was lit and inserted in the cup for a few seconds, after which it was placed on the skin and allowed to sink under its own weight. While the skin was tumefying under the cup the scarificator was warmed in the palm of the hand in preparation for the most difficult part of the operation. The skilled cupper could, with grace and dexterity lift the cup, scarify the chosen area, reheat the cup and reapply it before the tumefaction had subsided and without spilling blood on the bed-linen. However, even in the most experienced hands the procedure could be unsuccessful. When Baron Larrey, Napoleon's surgeon, visited Dublin in 1826, he was conducted to Mercer's Hospital to exhibit his mode of cupping:

"His method has at least the merit of being extremely simple. He first marked out the place of the operation by burning some tow under a glass, and taking an instrument out of his pocket, resembling a horse phleme, scarified the part within the circle, with a lightness of touch and velocity of movement that indicated great manual dexterity. The blood, however, not coming freely on the reapplication of the ignited tow and receiver, he observed, that the subject of the experiment was too fat."[43]

Dry-cupping was one of many forms of counter-irritation, a term which according to a contemporary writer "implies any irritation artificially established with a view to diminish, counteract, or remove certain morbid processes which may be going on in a more or less remote part of the system."[44] Other methods of inducing counter-irritation included the use of rubefacients (such as linaments or mustard poultices), setons (the placing of silk thread under the skin to maintain a free discharge from an incision), moxas (a most painful technique whereby an impregnated wick was allowed to burn slowly down to the skin to produce a sore), pustulants (the application of croton oil or nitrate of silver to induce an infected sore on the skin), and issues (the production of chronic suppuration by placing a pea in a sore induced by caustic potash).[44] The most popular methods of counter-irritation were dry-cupping and blistering, whereas the one causing the least pain and injury was the method described by Corrigan in which a small flat iron was heated and applied to the skin until redness was produced; the instrument used for this form of counter-irritation was known as "Corrigan's button"[45] and was popular until the early part of this century.[46] Blistering was accomplished by placing a solution of cantharides (Spanish fly) or glacial acetic acid on the skin to produce intense redness and pain. The effect of blistering was often considerable, and it is not difficult to appreciate its efficacy as a means of counter-irritation: "Such persons, when blistered, will often have profuse discharges, first of serum and afterwards of sero-purulent matter, from the denuded surface, accompanied by torturing pain, loss of rest, and considerable irritation of the general system. I have seen the discharge continue to flow profusely for five or six days; in fact, to such an extent as to wet several napkins in the course of a day."[47]

Other antiphlogistic measures consisted of purging with laxatives or emetics sometimes given to maintain a state of continuous nausea, and finally starvation.[48]

The drugs available were few and their actions poorly understood. Digoxin, morphine and quinine, which are still in clinical use, were available in the nineteenth century, but so also were strychnine and mercury, and there is evidence

that all were used to excess.[49] Doctors had not yet considered the concept of assessing the efficacy of treatment
by controlled studies.

It was from this state of medical practice that the "Dublin
school" was to arise. Is it possible for us from this distance
in time to detect its origins? A surprising feature of the
school is that its appearance was anticipated. Erinensis wrote
of the beginnings of a school as early as 1827.[50] He castigated
the College of Physicians and the University School of Physic
for failing to establish a "national school of medicine" by the
joining together of medical and surgical interests. However,
on reflection, he despaired of any good coming from this
ideal:

"Scarcely less ridiculous is the idea of assisting by the
new regulations the progress of Dublin into a great
school of medicine, with which they have at least been
associated in conversation. If by a multitude of pupils,
cheap licences obtained without qualifications, dear
pathology and consequent ignorance, it is meant to
establish a great school of medicine, then, indeed, these
measures are admirably adapted to produce such a happy
combination of circumstances; but such a great school
would undoubtedly be, like a great book, a very great
evil. Dublin possesses some reputation in medical science;
but if it be contemplated to extend its fame, by convert-
ing it into a mart for the sale of diplomas, like London
and Edinburgh, then let Dublin remain as it is at present."

However by 1834 Robert Graves was in no doubt but that
there was a movement of some consequence underway.
Talking to his students, he lamented the fact that Ireland did
not have a place on the international stage of medicine:

"It is not unusual to find the publications of France,
Germany, Italy and England, simultaneously announcing
the same discovery, and each zealously claiming for
their respective countrymen an honour which belongs
equally to all. I am sorry to say that, with some splendid
exceptions, this interesting and innocent controversy
has been carried on by other countries, while Ireland has
put no claim for a share of the literary honours awarded
to the efforts of industry or genius."[51]

Graves in assuring his students that recent years have seen the names of many members[52] of the Irish profession "spread abroad," makes special mention of two of his younger colleagues: Corrigan and Stokes; of the former he writes:

> "Neither have we, at present leisure to enter into the no less interesting field of investigation which Dr Corrigan has opened, by the publication of his experiments on the sounds and motions of the heart – experiments leading to conclusions so novel, that most physiologists were at first incredulous and many even ventured boldly to call into question their accuracy. Without, at present, venturing to decide whether Dr Corrigan's opinions be in every respect correct, I may assert that his paper is written in the true spirit of philosophical enquiry, and that he deserves opponents of a far higher grade than those who have endeavoured to refute his arguments in the English periodicals."

Of his junior colleague at the Meath hospital, he has this to say:

> "Concerning . . . my colleague, Dr William Stokes, I shall impose upon myself an unwilling and constrained silence, partly because his merits claim a warmer and longer eulogy than would suit this time and place, but chiefly because his labours have placed him in a position, as far elevated above the necessity of praise, as above the fear of censure."

Having thus, diplomatically singled out at this early stage his most dynamic colleagues in the creation of the "Dublin school," he closes his lecture with prophetic accuracy: "They all rank high among the successful cultivators of some of the most useful departments connected with our art; their names . . . form a catalogue the subject of congratulation for the present, of happy augury for the future . . ."[53]

The international reputation of the "Dublin school" can fairly be stated to have had its very foundations in Robert Graves. He was born in Dublin in 1796 to a family whose antecedents had come to Ireland with the Cromwellian army.[54] His father Richard, a scholar and divine, was twice

Donellan lecturer, Archbishop King's professor of divinity, professor of laws and regius professor of Greek and divinity at Trinity College, and Dean of Ardagh. Having spent some-time at Edinburgh, Graves graduated from Trinity in 1818 at the age of twenty-two, and promptly set off to study at the famous European centres of Berlin, Göttingen, Vienna, Copenhagen, Paris and Italy. His travels were not without interest and excitement. A facility for foreign languages landed him in an Austrian prison for ten days on the suspicion of being a German spy. While travelling through the Mount Cenis pass in the Alps in the autumn of 1819 he met a young artist and the pair travelled together for some time neither seeking the other's name. Graves and his companion, who he described as looking like "the mate of a trading vessel," had a common interest — sketching; together they painted and sketched as they travelled through Turin, Milan, Florence, and Rome. "I used to work away," Graves later recalled to Stokes, "for an hour or more, and put down as well as I could every object in the scene before me, copying form and colour, perhaps as faithfully as possible in the time. When our work was done, and we compared drawings, the difference was strange; I assure you there was not a single stroke in Turner's drawing that I could see like nature; not a line nor an object, and yet my work was worthless in comparison with his. The whole glory of the scene was there."

Graves sailed from Genoa for Sicily on a poorly-manned and unseaworthy vessel which soon ran into difficulties in a storm. The Sicilian crew promptly prepared to abandon ship, leaving Graves and his one fellow-passenger, a Spaniard, to their fate. Graves was lying "suffering from a painful malady" on his bunk when the terrified Spaniard brought him the news. He rose, and with an axe concealed under his cloak rushed on to the deck where he pleaded unsuccessfully with the captain who continued the preparations to abandon the ship. Graves then stove in the only lifeboat with the axe declaring to the captain and the crew: "Let us all be drowned together. It is a pity to part good company." The irate sailors seeing little wisdom in throwing Graves overboard, and per-haps being afraid to advance on him because of the axe instead permitted him to help them reach safety. He repaired the leaking pump valves with the leather from his boots, restored general morale, and happily for medicine the vessel eventually reached land.

Graves was appointed physician to the Meath hospital in 1821 at the age of twenty-five years. His opening lecture did little to endear him to his seniors. He claimed that many fatalities resulted from indifferent treatment, and he deplored the attitude of medical students who walked the wards in pursuit of entertainment rather than medical knowledge. William Wilde has left us a description of the method of clinical teaching that Graves so despised: "Hitherto under the old system when the student *walked* or to speak more correctly, *ran*, the hospitals, and hurried from ward to ward in order to keep pace with the rapid strides of his teacher, and when his object was, chiefly by his presence to become entitled to the semestral certificate of 'diligent attendance,' he considered himself fortunate if in his morning's walk he heard the remedies prescribed, often without knowing for what; he was never once questioned as to his practical knowledge of disease, at the place where information derived from books would avail him little; he *crammed* for his examination and was perhaps called upon the day after he obtained his 'licence to practise' for the first time in his life, properly to examine his patient; to exercise for the first time, his own judgement upon the issue of life or death, and best mode of treatment for a valuable member of society — then, indeed, experience often was gained at the sacrifice of life." Graves had been much impressed by the method of bedside clinical teaching on the continent especially in Germany. He praised the gentleness and humanity of the German physicians, who unlike their Irish and English colleagues, did not have "one language for the rich, and one for the poor," and whose practice it was to put unpleasant diagnoses into the Latin, rather than upset their unfortunate patients.

Dr Arthur Guinness, one of Graves' students has described the new form of intimate bedside teaching being cultivated by Graves: "As he had a very large practice he used to come in winter time, when I was resident, about seven o'clock in the mornings when it was quite dark to visit the wards, and many a time have I walked round with the clinical clerk,

Hudson, and often carried a candle for Dr Graves ... Dr Graves had a rather deep-toned voice, which caused 'Old Parr,' the apothecary, who was a regular joker and punster, to say: 'Graves always speaks in a sepulchral tone.' And one day when doing his rounds of the wards he said in this tone to a poor man dying of phthisis, 'How are you today, my poor fellow?' The patient answered, 'I am very bad your honor.' 'You are doing well my poor fellow,' answered Graves, but turning to the class he said, 'Gentlemen, moribundus,' and passed on."

Graves introduced to Dublin a system of teaching that was unique to Ireland and Britain; it had its origins in the German schools as Graves acknowledged:

Each school has three distinct medical clinics attached to it, by which means the labour of teaching is divided among the professors, and the number of students attending each is diminished ... when a patient is admitted, his case is assigned to one of the practising pupils, who, when the physician is visiting the ward, reads out the notes he has taken of the patient's disease, including its origin, progress, and the present state. This is done at the bedside of the patient, and before he leaves the ward, the physician satisfies himself whether all the necessary particulars have been accurately reported by the pupil. After all the patients have thus been accurately examined, the professor and his class proceed to the lecture room ... the cases admitted that day are first enquired into, and the pupils are examined as to the nature of their diseases, their probable termination, and the most appropriate method of treatment, – each student answering only concerning the patients entrusted to his special care. During their examination the pupil's diagnosis and proposed remedies are submitted to the consideration of the professor, who corrects whatever appears to be erroneous in either, and the student retires to write his prescription while the next of the cases and pupils undergo similar examination."[55]

A feature common to the personalities of Graves and Corrigan was a willingness to claim credit for their contributions to medicine. Graves was in no doubt as to the value of his reforms in clinical medicine:

> "It is extremely satisfactory to me to find that the mode of clinical instruction which I introduced at this hospital in 1822, has been adopted in most of the Dublin hospitals, and in many of the medical institutions of Great Britain ... It is recommended at once by its simplicity, and by its admirable fitness for fulfilling the purposes which it is intended to accomplish. A card is suspended over each patient's bed on which is recorded the date of his admission, the history of his case and the daily treatment, dietetic as well as medical. These cards remain in the wards until the patient leaves the hospital, and in this way any gentleman who wishes to observe the progress and termination of any particular case, can easily make himself master of its principal features and the different remedial agents employed for its alleviation or removal."[56]

He was determined to reform the teaching system then practised in Dublin and Edinburgh, whereby students could qualify without ever examining a patient. Clinical teaching was often little more than an interrogation of the patient by the physician, with the results of the interchange delivered in poor Latin by a clerk to a crowd of students, most of whom could not even see the patient. "The impassible gulf which in that aristocratic era lay between the student and his so-called teacher, was by Graves made to disappear and for the first time in these countries was the pupil brought into a full and friendly contact with a mind so richly stored that it might be taken as an exponent of the actual state of medicine at all time."[57] Together Graves and Stokes taught Auenbrugger's method of percussion, and both were experts with the stethoscope. They encouraged the student to take a history directly from the patient, then to examine the patient, to make notes and finally to discuss the diagnosis, pathology and treatment. Graves never forgot the patient: "Often have I regretted that, under the present system, experience is only to be acquired at the considerable expense of human life ... The victims selected for this sacrifice at the shrine of experience generally belong to the poorer classes of society."

These revolutionary methods caused some resentment, but it is to the credit of the Meath hospital that it permitted its young physicians to effect their reforms. It was not long before Graves and Stokes had an international reputation that was later acknowledged by the great William Osler, who said: "I owe my start in the profession to James Bovell, kinsman and devoted pupil of Graves, while my teacher in Montreal, Palmer Howard, lived, moved and had his being in his old masters, Graves and Stokes."[58]

In 1843, Graves published his famous *Clinical Lectures on the Practice of Medicine*,[59] which were subsequently translated into French, German and Italian. In this book we find evidence of the gift that was common to these Victorian masters of clinical expression — the ability to describe their observations in clear and lively prose. Hale-White[60] put it rather nicely: "The lectures are unlike a modern textbook in that they can be read with enjoyment in front of the fire." The famous French physician Armand Trousseau regarded Graves's book as a masterpiece: "For many years I have spoken well of Graves in my clinical lectures. I recommend the perusal of his work; I entreat those of my pupils who understand English to consider it as their breviary; I say and repeat that of all the practical works published in our time, I am acquainted with none more useful, more intellectual." In his preface to the French edition he wrote: "I have become inspired with it in my teaching . . . when he (Graves) inculcated the necessity of giving nourishment in long continued pyrexia, the Dublin physician single-handed assailed an opinion which appeared to be justified by the practice of ages." Here he was referring to Graves's revolutionary treatment of patients with fever, in whom he advocated supportive therapy rather than starvation, bleeding and blistering. The story goes that one day on his rounds, he was struck by the healthy appearance of a patient recently recovered from severe typhus fever and said to his students: "This is the effect of our good feeding, and gentlemen, lest when I am gone, you may be at a loss for an epitaph for me, let me give you one in three words: 'He fed fevers'." Graves had made the logical observation that a healthy man starved for weeks became weakened, but that oddly the medical profession expected a man ill with fever to improve when denied food and continuously bled. He attributed many fatalities to this form of therapy and advocated frequent meals of steak, mutton or fowl, washed down with wine and porter.[61]

Though he did practice bleeding, cupping and blistering, he called for moderation in the application of these techniques and horrified by the excesses of blistering he introduced what he called "flying blisters,"[62] whereby rather than protract the blister he kept up "a succession of blisters along the inside of the legs, and over the anterior and inner parts of the thighs."[63] He was quite proud of the acceptance of this modified technique: "If I have done nothing better, I think I deserve some merit for being the first to reprobate the practice of keeping on blisters for twelve, eighteen and twenty-four hours, and for having shown by numerous experiments that a much shorter period of time was required to ensure the full effect of these remedies."[64]

Corrigan was preaching a similar philosophy on the north side of the city. He disapproved strongly of treatment that weakened and depleted the patient. Discussing a child suffering from episodes of palpitation he commented: "In some of those cases there is a disposition to bleed from the nose, and the haemorrhage is occasionally very profuse, and this, coupled with pain of the side, which is occasionally present, leads to treatment not calculated to amend the symptoms. The boy is denied animal food. He is sent to the infirmary of the school, and given tartar emetic and bled, or lowered in other ways by purgative or nauseating medicine."[65] Corrigan's alternative was sea air, sea-bathing, a full diet, wine and iron. On another occasion he took the French physician Bouillaud to task for his treatment of acute rheumatism.[66] "A patient treated on Bouillaud's plan has to recover from what is worse than the disease, the debility, which is the necessary result of the frequent bleedings *coup sur coup*, of cupping, tight bandaging, blisters and mercurial cerates, for he uses all those adjuvants as he calls them." Corrigan advocated opiates in generous dosage together with local measures to relieve the pain and swelling of the inflamed joints. Whether or not this resulted in much opium addiction is debatable, but at least "the patient cured by opium has neither bleeding, blistering, nor mercury, to recover from in his convalescence." An interesting account of the effect of this treatment has been left to us by one of Corrigan's patients, a Dr J. Aldridge who was wary of his physician's liberal prescription: "I confess that I was somewhat afraid of what appeared to me very large doses of this powerful drug, especially as my head always had a tendency to be affected whenever I had fever of any kind. It was therefore with some misgiving I obeyed you, but soon had reason to congratulate myself on the effects of your advice, for during the remainder of my illness, i.e., from the second day after being forced to succumb, the pains, although they visited me occasionally, were by no means so intolerable; I slept much, my intellect remained clear, except when occasionally I took an overdose of the opium, (for as soon as I began to experience its good effects, I became quite enamoured of it) and, in time, I was enabled to walk down stairs the fourteenth day after taking to bed. During another week I rubbed such joints as were occasionally painful with a linament made with sulphur and camphorated oil, and took internally quinine and guaiacum; but since then, now during a period of four months, I have not had the slightest return of the disease. As nearly as I can recollect, I swallowed during my illness about two hundred grains of opium."[67]

Corrigan's treatment of fever was remarkably successful due, he believed, to a conservative approach: "There are three active remedies which I have found it necessary to abstain from — general bleeding, sudorifics (*to induce per-spiration*) and catharetics (*for purging*)." This is not to say that Corrigan did not advocate what he called local depletion with leeches, especially when there was delirium an occurrence that he considered ominous: "After having the head shaved, wait for no other symptom of derangement of the cerebral function than the want of rest. Apply some leeches to the forehead; the number may be few; we seldom use more than four to six. The result is almost always gratifying: in some cases there is good sleep at once procured, in others only a snatch the first night; the repetition of the leeches is again made the next day, and there is again rest: it is seldom neces-sary to repeat them more than a third time." Corrigan's fever reports are characteristic of his style, he holds his readers attention by referring now to one case, then to another:[68] "You remember the case of Toner. He was admitted on 25th February, on the eighth day of maculated fever, with suffused eyes and dark maculae, his pulse 108, very weak. He was put on wine. Now what was the result? That under the administration of wine, in very large quantities, on the thirteenth day the suffusion of the eyes began to disappear, and, on the sixteenth day, he was convalescent." But in the case of Matthews in whom the maculae "were very dark in colour, and his eyes, too, were congested" sixteen ounces of wine was without effect and blistering had to be resorted to. "Hence it is, as in such a case as Johnson's or Harrington's, or many others, blister after blister was applied for days in succession, now to the chest, then to the legs, then to the thighs, again to the chest, leaving each blister on long enough only to produce increased action, but keeping it up by a continued succession."

Dissection of the human body had been used for centuries as the principal means of providing practical instruction for medical students. As we know from Corrigan's student days anatomy was the cornerstone of medical education. Pathology was demonstrated also by dissection of cadavers but this was done without reference to the terminal illness and often long after death by which time post-mortem changes rendered it only a crude guide to the disease process during life. One of the major contributions of the "Dublin school" was the study of disease during life and after death. Stokes, Corrigan and Graves observed carefully the signs of illness in life, and then performed detailed post-mortem examinations (often lasting four hours or more[69]) observing the changes that had been induced on the affected organ by the disease.

One of Graves's students has left a touching memoir of the master in the dead room:

> "There were few of us who like to be inhaling the emanations from a body recently dead from fever, or other such ailments on empty stomachs, and often I have been busy for hours, until the afternoon, and alone, when he (*Graves*) would return to the dead room where I had been making careful dissections of the diseased

parts. Graves would say, 'This is the true way to study pathology. Here we see the changes which caused the symptoms we watched at the bed-side with so much anxiety, and which are still fresh in our memory; and we can mentally follow each in its progress, until death resulted. This is infinitely more instructive than what we occasionally see in the dissecting room. There we know nothing of the patient, his calling, or his disease. The body has been dead (buried possibly) for somedays, and of his symptoms or sufferings we are in total ignorance; whereas here we know all we require of the poor fellow . . . Now run home and take your breakfast.' "[70]

We may detect in this anecdote the same kindliness that was shown by Graves to his patients. He warned against early discharge of patients from hospital after a serious illness, a practice that might improve the hospital returns but at a cruel price: "How injurious to persons so debilitated the change from the warmth and comfort of a hospital to the cold and desolation of a damp garret or cellar!"[71]

It was Trousseau who proposed that the illness exophthalmic goitre, described in the *Lectures* be named "Graves' Disease." The original description is masterly:

"I have lately seen three cases of violent and long continued palpitations in females, in each of which the same peculiarity presented itself, *viz* enlargement of the thyroid gland; the size of this gland, at all times considerably greater than natural, was subject to remarkable variations in every one of these patients . . . The palpitations have in all lasted considerably more than a year and with such violence as to be at times exceedingly distressing, and yet there seems no certain grounds for concluding that organic disease of the heart exists . . . She next complained of weakness on exertion, and began to look pale and thin . . . It was now observed that the eyes assumed a singular appearance, for the eyeballs were apparently enlarged, so that when she slept or tried to shut her eyes, the lids were incapable of closing. When the eyes were open, the white sclerotic could be seen, to a breadth of several lines, all around the cornea."[72]

Graves was King's professor in Trinity College from 1827, until he was elected president of the Royal College of Physicians of Ireland in 1843, and in 1849 he was elected fellow of the Royal Society of London. During his professional career he received many honours, including an honorary membership of the medical societies of Berlin, Vienna, Hamburg, Tübingen, Bruges and Montreal. He died in 1853 from cancer of the liver at the age of 57. In the following year, Stokes in a discourse on the life and works of "his teacher, colleague and friend" wrote thus: "His active mind was ever seeking for and finding analogies, and this led him to the discrimination of things similar, and to the assimilation of things dissimilar in a degree seldom surpassed by any medical teacher."[73]

William Stokes (1804-1878) differed from other members of the school, in being not only an astute and successful clinician, but also a man of learning with a deep appreciation for the arts. When he returned from Edinburgh to join Graves at the Meath hospital he brought with him the stethoscope, which caused quite a stir: "There was much surprise and no little incredulity, with a shade of opposition, shown by sneering, or as we say now, 'chaffing' in its first introduction. The juniors looked at it with amazement, as a thing to gain information by — it so put them in mind of the pop-gun of their school-boy days; the seniors with incredulity . . . the first instrument of the kind I saw was a piece of timber (elm, I think) three inches in diameter from twelve to fourteen inches long, having a hole drilled through it from top to bottom, no ear-piece, and no attempt at ornamentation. It was amusing to watch the shakes of the head as this bludgeon was passed from hand to hand among the pupils, and to listen to the comments made by them."[74]

Stokes published two papers that earned him eponymous fame. As we have seen he described a form of breathing often seen in terminal illness, which had been previously described by John Cheyne.[24] Stokes's description of this condition now known as "Cheyne Stokes respiration" is word perfect: "The inspirations become each one less deep than the preceeding until they are all but imperceptible, and then the state of apparent apnoea (no breathing) occurs. This is at last broken by the faintest possible inspiration, the next effect is a little stronger, until, so to speak, the paroxysm of breathing is at its height, again to subside by a descending scale."[23] Few could rival him with the stethoscope, but the wise patient having received his diagnostic deliberations, might do best to decline his advice on treatment. In bronchitic children he advocated that the gums should be "freely and completely divided to allow the teeth to appear." He supported the common practice of bleeding in most illnesses, but he found that the application of leeches "applied to the mucous membrane, as near as possible to the epiglottis" was particularly efficacious: "The child's breathing becomes easier, the face less swelled, and the skin cooler." Emetics were also considered advantageous: "I would advise that the medicine should be so exhibited as to produce free vomiting, at least once every three-quarters of an hour," but he later modified this form of treatment so that it was possible "to keep up a state of permanent nausea, without vomiting."[75]

As William Stokes had rescued from obscurity the work of John Cheyne, so too was he to do for his colleague Robert Adams (1796-1875) another member of the "Dublin school." In 1846 Stokes published a paper describing how a slow heart could interfere with consciousness,[76] and he drew attention to an earlier paper by Adams in which he suggested that "apoplexy must be considered less a disease in itself than symptomatic of one, the organic seat of which was in the heart."[77] The disease is today known as "Stokes-Adams' disease."

Adams was a successful teacher, and was one of the founders of the Peter Street School of Medicine, and later of the famous Carmichael School of Medicine and Surgery. His first appointment was to The Charitable Infirmary where he was a contemporary of Corrigan. In 1835 a vacancy occurred in the staff of the Richmond hospital on the death of Ephraim McDowell. Robert Adams and John MacDonnell contested the post, and such was the stature of both candidates that Richard Carmichael resigned rather than deny "the institute the benefit of their talents." Adams became surgeon-in-ordinary to Her Majesty Queen Victoria, regius professor of surgery in Trinity College, president of the Royal College of Surgeons in Ireland and a member of the senate of the Queen's University.[78]

Apart from these two famous papers, Stokes published many clinical works, among which were two important books one on disease of the chest, and another on the heart.[79]

In medical education Stokes was ahead of his time: "The chief, the long-existing, and I grieve to say it, the still prominent evils among us are the neglect of general education, the confounding of instruction with education, and the giving of greater importance to the special training than to the general culture of the student . . . Let us emancipate the student, and give him time and opportunity for the cultivation of his mind, so that in his pupilage he shall not be a puppet in the hands of others, but rather a self-relying and reflecting being." He would be saddened by medical training today, and in particular he would deplore the neglect of the humanities, and the suppression of cultural development with the emergence of the narrow-minded super-specialist: "Do not be misled by the opinion that a university education will do nothing more than give you a certain proficiency in classical literature, in the study of logics and ethics, or in mathematical or physical science. If it does these things for you, you will be great gainers, for there is no one branch of professional life in which these studies will not prove the most signal help to you."[80]

The "Dublin school's" greatest achievement in medical education was the introduction of bedside teaching in the instruction of doctors. Graves and Stokes inculcated this method to generations of their own students and to many from Europe and America, while Dominic Corrigan did likewise with no less enthusiasm in the wards of the Hardwicke hospital. In one of his lectures Corrigan said: "Let me earnestly impress upon you the absolute necessity of accustoming yourselves to the practical investigation and note-taking of cases . . . Is not one glance worth pages of description? Numerous associations fix in your mind, and for ever, the appearance and symptoms of a living case of disease which you have examined, and on which you brought your senses of sight, touch, and hearing, to bear . . ." To emphasise this he was fond of quoting the famous French teacher Bichat to his sometimes none too eager students: " 'You ask me,' said he (Bichat), 'how I have learnt so much. It is because I have read so little. Books are but copies – why have recourse to copies when the originals are before me? My books are the living and the dead: I study these.' "[81]

His advice to students on the art of observation in clinical medicine cannot be improved, and though he was speaking of fever of a type not often seen today, his words capture, as few have ever done, the art of clinical observation:[82]

"Let me suppose you now at the bedside of a fever case; stand there quietly, don't disturb the patient, don't at once proceed to examine pulse, or chest, or abdomen, or to put questions. If you do, you may be greatly deceived, for under a sharp or abrupt question a patient may suddenly rouse himself in reply, answer your questions collectedly, and yet die within three hours. Look at your patient as he lies when you enter the ward or sick room; his very posture speaks a language understood by the experienced eye. It is not unusual for the anxious and young resident to draw the earliest attention of the physician in his morning round to some patient who had appeared to him to be in a most dangerous state all night, and for the physician to take a single glance at the patient, and say in reply, 'Never mind him, he is all right; come to the next case, it is a bad one.' What is the difference between the two? Merely that of posture. The first patient, or apparently very bad case, had gone through the agitation of crisis during the night, but at morning visit was asleep, lying three-quarters on his side or half on his face, in the posture instinctively chosen to relieve the diaphragm from abdominal pressure, and with muscular strength enough to retain that posture; while beside him lies the serious case, the man who gave no disturbance during the night, who did not complain, but lies on his back without the preservative instinct and without the strength to change it, and with the abdominal viscera like a nightmare on the diaphragm."

How wonderful it is to hear an experienced practitioner voicing so eloquently the knowledge acquired through years of observation:

"In the child in fever there is another sign revealed to you from merely looking at the countenance, and always to be dreaded — it is frowning, however slight. A frown is not natural to a child, and it is often the first sign of commencing mischief in the child's brain. Wakefulness, headache and frown are of more serious import in the child in fever than in the adult. There is an apparently trivial sign about the eye of a fever patient, which you will lose if you rudely disturb the patient or question him. It is the passage of the tear. If the secretion of the lachrymal gland flow on in its natural course and pass out through the nasal duct, having performed its office of washing the eyeball and keeping it moist, it is a good sign, for it indicates that the instinctive functions of organic life are still performed; but if the eyelids cease to act, and the tear-drop falls over the outer angle of the eye, it is a sign that the functions of organic life are beginning to give way."

He was aware of the student's irresistible urge to examine the patient, and his desire to use the stethoscope all too precipitously: "In reference to the examination of the system of circulation, on the sustainment of which so much depends in the treatment of fever, I would impress on you in judging of the strength of the heart's action, to depend on the pulse, radial or carotid, not on the examination of the heart's sounds or impulse by the stethoscope."

Corrigan realised from his own student days that it was possible to study and learn the theory of medicine from textbooks and lectures. He knew that an intelligent student could pass his final examinations without being skilled in clinical technique, without in effect having examined many patients. At this time the final examination comprised an oral exam and usually a written paper. Corrigan saw the deficiency in this assessment of competence. In 1840 he announced a new form of examination for the students of the Richmond:[83] "We trust to no verbal examination; but for the last four months of the session, commencing at any time after the 1st January, we shall, without any previous notice, select cases as we shall deem proper for our purpose on admission into hospital, and require the candidates for our prizes to take those cases, writing down the symptoms, diagnosis, prognosis, and principle treatment, and giving to each candidate from a quarter to half an hour for his examination of the case; requiring his notes, however, to be written on the spot."

Later even this competitive clinical examination was not in itself enough to satisfy the Richmond teachers as to the quality of their trainees, and Corrigan instigated a term of apprenticeship during which the student would be permitted the opportunity of showing his worth, while at the same time his teachers could assess his development as a doctor:

> "For more than mere professional knowledge is required in the resident pupil of an hospital; we required other qualities — we required steadiness, attention, propriety of conduct, good temper and kindliness of disposition and manner in dealing with the sick. Competitive examination gave us no insight into the possession of these qualities, and we knew — what will be admitted, I think, without question — that the possessor of these personal qualities, with a very moderate portion of professional knowledge, was of far more value than the possessor of the highest but purely professional attainments without these qualities. Hence, we felt ourselves obliged to discard mere competitive examination. Still it remained necessary to ascertain that the candidate possessed a competent degree of professional knowledge. The mode we have acted upon for a long time is this — We give abundant opportunities to all such students as desire to become extern clinical clerks. This is a probationary stage, and it affords us the opportunity of judging if, along with a competent degree of professional knowledge, the candidate presents the possession of those other qualities to which I have referred."

In the Meath hospital Stokes was stating the same policy but was prepared to go further; he thought it might be possible to dispense altogether with a final examination, "by simply affording to students full opportunity for every branch of medical study and observation coupled with tutorial teaching."[84] These Victorian teachers were more than a century ahead of their time in advocating continuous assessment rather than examination alone in evaluating medical students.

Corrigan was ever aware of the value of distinction in one's chosen career, and he urged his students to strive for excellence that would elevate them above mediocrity. His carefully chosen words to his students at a prize-giving could be delivered today without revision:[85]

> "From my heart I say, that were I a student, were I one of you, there is not an honour I know of, which I should so ardently seek for, and so proudly boast of, as the winning of one of those prizes. The possession of a mere professional degree, sinks into comparative insignificance compared with the achievement of such a distinction. The common routine industry of all suffices to obtain the mere professional diploma, and all having obtained it, are equal, but to win a prize in a society like this, requires far more than ordinary industry, and confers more than ordinary distinction. When in after years a selection is to be made, either to fill the high office of lecturer, or to promote to the charge of public institutions, which in our profession constitute the arena for the display of talent, believe me there will be no recommendation more likely to be attended to, than the possession of a prize . . ."

He had tasted the elation of success, the satisfaction of achievement; he was also only too well aware of the depression and lassitude of spirit that may come after the routine of years of caring for the ill, and he saw the medical student as having an important role in preventing this all too frequent development:

> "The physician or surgeon who has under his charge the poor in an hospital, may tire or grow cold in the exercise of his duty, and active diligence in the care of the sick, might, after a time, unconsciously degenerate into the mere listless routine of going the round of the wards: but surrounded by intelligent pupils his attention to the sick, and his treatment the subject of observation; his opinions and the grounds of his opinions closely scrutinised, his skill tested by the measure of his success on

curable cases, by the examination of the dead in incurable affection, the physician or surgeon can never flag in the discharge of his duty; his pride is kept awake, his character is at stake, and the result is, constantly increasing knowledge to himself, the undeviating exercise of humanity and skill towards the poor, and the benefit to society of the diffusion of professional information."[86]

In the Meath hospital where his colleagues Stokes and Graves were preaching similar sentiments, the system of medical education was undergoing rapid change. A dominant theme of Stokes's many discourses on medical education was the importance of providing a cultural as well as a competent doctor. He believed medicine to be derived from knowledge of many kinds: "Medicine is not any single science: it is an art depending on all sciences." He maintained that the tendency towards specialisation, evident even in his day, would "at the best, produce a crowd of mediocrities with no chance, or but a little one, of the development of the larger man."[87]

Corrigan would not have disagreed with Stokes's views but his outlook was more pragmatic. He saw the priorities of the nation more clearly than Stokes, and realised that the development of the individual was a luxury which Ireland could not yet afford:[88]

"I would not decry the terse poetry of Horace and the rounded periods of Homer; but neither will teach a man to measure his field or to drain it; neither the one nor the other will teach him chemistry, or the application of science to manufactures; neither the one nor the other will teach him natural history; and I would, if I could, divert the mind of the country into those branches which have a practical bearing on every hour of our existence and the prosperity of our country . . . The mind of the country — and the sooner we learn it the better — is as uncultivated as the barren soil of our bogs . . . The education of the middle classes — and the sooner it is known the better — is on the lowest par in Europe, and when a few men come forward and attempt to give us information it is thrown on soil which is not productive, and men who do not understand it undervalue it."

To many it may come as a surprise to find William Wilde included as a member of the "Dublin school." But then, unfortunately this great Victorian is often remembered only as the father of Oscar, or he is ridiculed and lampooned for his eccentricities and illicit amours. Too often it is forgotten that he was an innovative doctor, an accomplished archaeologist and author of some very fine books on Ireland. Moreover, he and his wife Speranza were Victorian Dublin's most colourful couple. However, let us first put his medical achievements into perspective. None is better qualified to do so than his biographer, the late T.G. Wilson, an ear, nose and throat surgeon (or as he would now be known, an otorhinolaryngologist) of repute.[89] He ranked Wilde as "one of the two greatest English-speaking aurists of his time," the other referred to being Toynbee. He considered Wilde to be "almost as brilliant an oculist as he was an aurist." The science of otology (disease of the ear) when Wilde entered the speciality was in the hands of quacks, and as Wilde developed new techniques, so did he invent suitable instruments including "Wilde's snare." "Wilde's incision" is still occasionally spoken of, although "Wilde's ointment" is no longer in use.[90]

William Wilde, the youngest of five children was born in 1815 in the village of Kilkievin in the west of Ireland. His father was a doctor and the son decided to follow in his footsteps. In 1832 "a dark ferrety looking young man below the average size, with retreating chin and a bright roving eye, boarded the coach for Dublin."[91] He was apprenticed to Abraham Colles and spent four years at Dr Steevens' hospital, and then went to the Rotunda. After his final exam he collapsed, and Dr Graves was sent for. The astute physician prescribed a glass of strong ale to be taken every hour, and the following morning the dying student was much revived and Graves found him sleeping comfortably. Collapse after finals, particularly in the somewhat rabelaisian ambiance of the Rotunda Hospital might be attributable to many causes but Wilson was of the opinion that Wilde had contracted typhus fever. Whatever the cause, he recovered and received his Letters Testimonial from the Royal College of Surgeons in the year of Victoria's accession to the throne, and in the same year we find him the father of his first illegitimate child.

The mother was reputedly a Dublin beauty with the unlikely name of Miss Crummles.[92] Sir Henry Marsh and Robert Graves decided that the young surgeon had best leave Dublin for a time, whether for health or social reasons is not clear, and on September 24, 1837 William Wilde sailed down the Solent on the ship *Crusader*, in his charge a patient with consumption on his way to the Holy Land. During his travels, he developed a keen interest in archaeology, and after witnessing the devastating effects of the eye disease trachoma, so common in Egypt, he decided to specialise in ophthalmology. He published an interesting and successful book of his experiences, and with the profits was able to spend some time on the continent.[93] In London he was introduced to society by Sir James Clark and Maria Edgeworth. The latter needs no introduction, but Clark is worthy of further mention. "Poor Clark" as Queen Victoria was later to call him had an unfortunate career. He misdiagnosed pregnancy in Lady Flora Hastings, one of the Queen's maids of honour when in fact the poor lady was virginal and unfortunately suffering from a malignant abdominal tumour which later proved fatal. This was a considerable set-back to a promising career, but he was retained as the royal physician. When he failed to diagnose typhoid fever as the cause of the Prince Consort's fatal illness, one would have thought his career was at an end. However, Victoria had a deep affection for her physician, and believed that he was more a victim of misfortune than actual incompetence. Whatever his professional short-comings he must be judged kindly and with some admiration for the compassion and kindness he showed to the young poet Keats during his last days in Rome. Here Clark found pleasant apartments for the dying poet and cared for him without expecting or receiving reward. When we remember that there were few at that time who recognised the genius of Keats, least of all the reviewers of the day, we must respect Clark's assessment: "After all, his expenses will be simple, and he is too noble an animal to be allowed to sink without some sacrifice being made to save him. I wish I were rich enough, his living here should cost him nothing . . . I fear there is something operating on his mind . . . I feel very much interested in him."[94] Indeed, there was much troubling the young poet; his mental anguish was if anything greater than his physical suffering – his unfulfilled poetical ambitions and his love for Fanny Brawne.

From London Wilde went to Vienna where he became friendly with the young Semmelweiss who was later to discover the cure for puerperal fever. Wilde was particularly impressed by the maternity system in this city, whereby pregnant ladies could have their infants in absolute secrecy – a facility not without appeal to him. From Vienna he went to Germany, and then onwards to Brussels to meet up with his old friend Charles Lever, who on qualifying had deserted the scalpel for the pen, and was at this time completing his famous novel *Charles O'Malley*.[95] The proofs of this he threw at Wilde, who we are told rocked an enormous four-poster bed with insuppressible laughter as he read of O'Malley's exploits.[96]

Returning to Dublin Wilde began practice at number fifteen Westland Row and he converted an old stable at number eleven Molesworth Street into a dispensary. In 1844 he opened St. Mark's Ophthalmic Hospital and Dispensary for Diseases of the Eye and Ear in Mark Street off Great Brunswick Street (now Pearse Street), and for many years this was the only hospital in the British Isles teaching both aural surgery and ophthalmology. It was the predecessor of what is today the Royal Victoria Eye and Ear Hospital.[97] He was successful in private practice and his reputation was enhanced with the publication of his book on *Aural Surgery*.[98] George Bernard Shaw, however, did not hold his surgical skill in high regard; he recalled many years later that in dealing with his father's squint Wilde "overdid the correction so much that" his father squinted "the other way all the rest of his life."[99]

In the 1840s a young lady, Jane Francesca Elgee, was writing spirited, many would say seditious, prose and poetry for the *Nation*: "You have never felt the pride, the dignity, the majesty of independence. You could never lift up your head to heaven and glory in the name of Irishmen, for all Europe read the brand of 'slave' upon your brow." Her poetry smacked of much the same passion and banality:

> "Hark! the onward heavy thread –
> Hark! the voice rude –
> Tis, the famished cry for bread
> From a wildered multitude."[100]

Wilde was fascinated by all this, and in 1851 they were married; a year later William Charles Kinsbury Wills Wilde was born and in 1854 Oscar Fingal O'Flahertie Wills Wilde was introduced to the world.

Wilde like so many of his contemporaries, was a prodigious worker. Apart from his practice and the running of his hospital he was editor of the *Dublin Journal of Medicine and Chemical Science*.[101] In 1841 he was appointed assistant census commissioner, a post that involved a vast amount of work which was rewarded with a knighthood in 1864 when he was aged forty-nine. Dr Peter Froggatt has put Wilde's mammoth work as census commissioner into perspective: "This was one of the greatest national censuses ever conducted. The results were published in ten foolscap volumes totalling 4,503 pages; two of these volumes containing 710 pages, were written solely by Wilde."[102]

In middle life, Wilde devoted immense energy to cataloguing the Irish Antiquities — a prodigious task which he performed single-handed, and for which the Royal Academy elected him vice-president and presented to him its highest award, the Cunningham gold medal. He also devoted much time to medical biography[103] and he wrote a fascinating book on *The Closing Years of Dean Swifts's Life*.[104]

An unfortunate incident was to blight Wilde's career. Sometime in 1854 William Stokes referred a Miss Mary Josephine Travers to Wilde with an ear complaint. This twenty-nine year-old woman was not beautiful, but she was of ample proportions and Wilde found her attractive. We do not know how intimate the relationship became, and can only assume that being a hot-blooded fellow, Wilde's intentions, whatever his actions, might not have been altogether platonic. After some years the relationship ended in acrimony. She began a campaign of harassment to both Wilde and his wife, and she invited libel action. The bait was eventually taken and the case became a Victorian scandal of sumptuous proportions. In essence the case was not so much one of libel against Lady Wilde, but rather a trial of Sir William for rape. A thrilled public heard with delight declarations such as: "I will only say that 'she went in a maid but out a maid she never departed.' "[105] In the end Speranza was found guilty of libel and fined a farthing, but the costs were substantial. Wisely Wilde had declined to appear as witness (Lady Wilde being the actual defendant), but his colleague Arthur Jacob, also an ophthalmic surgeon of repute, castigated him for failing to do so in the *Dublin Medical Press*: "He owed it to his profession, which must now endure the onus of the disgrace — he owed it to the public, who have confided, and are still expected to confide themselves to his honour — he owed it to Her Majesty's representative who had conferred an unusual mark of distinction on him, to purge himself of the suspicion which at this moment lies heavily on his name."[106] In fairness Jacob's criticism has validity, and it is possible that in a later age Wilde might have had his name erased from the medical register. In any event his career was damaged irreparably and he was a broken man. He retired to his country retreat, Moytura House at Cong in Connemara, where he produced his best known books — *Lough Corrib* and *Lough Mask*.[107] He delegated his professional duties to his natural son Dr Henry Wilson, also an ophthalmologist. He became careless in dress and unkempt in appearance as George Bernard Shaw was to later recall — "Wilde was dressed in snuffy brown and as he had the sort of skin that never looks clean he produced a dramatic effect beside Lady Wilde (in full fig) of being like Frederick the Great beyond soap and water, as his Nietzschean son was beyond good and evil."[108] Three years after the trial the Wilde's lost their beloved daughter Isola, and four years later Wilde's two illegitimate daughters died tragically in a fire, an event that affected him greatly. Any happiness in life was now derived from archaeology, and watching the progress of Oscar and Willy through school and university.

Sir William died on April 19, 1876 after a long and rather obscure illness. Of his last days we have Oscar's account which is really a tribute to his mother:

"Before my father died in 1876, he lay ill in bed for many days. And every morning a woman dressed in black and closely veiled used to come to our house in Merrion Square, and unhindered by my mother, or anyone else used to walk straight up stairs to Sir William's bedroom and sit down at the head of his bed and to sit there all day, without ever speaking a word or once raising her veil. She took no notice of anybody in the room; and nobody paid any attention to her. Not one woman in a thousand would have tolerated her presence, but my mother allowed it because she knew that my father loved the woman and felt that it must be a joy and comfort to have her there by his dying bed. And I am sure that she did right not to grudge that last happiness to a man who was about to die, and I am sure that my father understood her indifference, understood that it was not because she did not love him that she permitted her rival's presence, but because she loved him very much, and died with his heart full of gratitude and affection for her."[109]

There were many tributes after his death, including an elegy by Samuel Ferguson, but perhaps Speranza's verse so full of Victorian poignancy and nostalgia is the most fitting:

> "Read till the warm tears fall my love,
> With thy voice so soft and low,
> And the Saviour's merits will plead above
> For the soul that prayeth below."[110]

There were many other doctors in this "Dublin school," whose lives followed a less hectic course and whose contributions, though more modest, were nonetheless significant. Among these was Arthur Jacob, the ophthalmologist who discovered the neural layer of the retina known as *membrana Jacobi,* and was founder and editor of the *Dublin Medical Press* and one of the founders of the Irish Medical Association.[111] Not all the achievements of the "Dublin school" can be attributed to the physicians of the period. There were many active and enterprising surgeons but surgery was barred from further advancement by the limitations imposed on its practice for want of a means of overcoming pain and infection, and also by blood loss. The first of these barriers was overcome by a Richmond surgeon in 1847 when John MacDonnell (whose son Robert was destined to give the first transfusion of human blood in The Charitable Infirmary eighteen years later[112]) performed surgery under anaesthesia. Eleven days previously ether had been used for the first time in Europe by Liston at University College London. MacDonnell read a report of the operation in the *British and Foreign Medical Review* and decided to operate with either to amputate the arm of a young country girl named Mary Kane, who had tripped and fallen several weeks before while carrying some hawthorn branches.[113] The elbow joint had been penetrated by a thorn and subsequently became infected. Instead of seeing a qualified doctor "she had been advised by one of those persons who tamper with human health and life." When she was sent to the Richmond two weeks later, "she was suffering severe pain in the joint, the outer part of which presented a large ulcer, with spongy flabby granulations, and having an opening from which a profuse discharge took place, and by which a probe could be passed into the joint." In spite of all treatment, "she gradually, during the next four weeks, lost flesh to great emaciation, became decidedly hectic, had several times severe bowel complaint, and at length a slough formed over the sacrum, as she could only lie supine." MacDonnell postponed surgery for one day, so that he could make an apparatus for inhaling the vapour of ether, and having tried this on himself to the stage of senselessness, from which he recovered without ill-effect he proceeded to operate on Friday morning, New Year's Day 1847, in the presence of a large gathering of eminent physicians and surgeons. "There was slight evidence of pain at the moment of finishing the division of the muscles, and again at the time of tying one of the arteries, but the patient declared that she had no unpleasant sensation from the inhalation." MacDonnell regarded ether as one of the major advances in medicine: "I am sanguine respecting the safety, the great utility, and the manageableness of this singular agent . . . I anticipate that we shall be enabled to prolong insensibility with safety, for a considerable time, by skilful alternation of vapour and atmospheric air . . . I regard this discovery as one of the most important of this century. It will rank with vaccination, and other of the greatest benefits that medical science has bestowed on man."

Admirable though the introduction of anaesthesia was, the mortality from surgery remained high because of infection. Joseph Lister, alert to the researches of Louis Pasteur in

Paris, was able to reduce the mortality after amputation from 45.7 per cent to 15 per cent by using carbolic acid to kill the organisms causing infection. "Listerism" was readily adopted on the continent, but it was only accepted slowly in Ireland.[114]

Francis Rynd, a less wellknown figure of the school was the inventor of the hypodermic syringe which allowed doctors for the first time to give morphine by injection rather than by mouth, for the relief of pain.[115] There was also that towering example of the Victorian polymath, the Reverend Dr Samuel Haughton, divine, scientist, and physician. His scientific publications were diverse and at times brilliant, but he is possibly best known for "Haughton's drop," a calculation giving the length of the drop needed to dislocate the cervical spine and so cause instantaneous death in hanging, rather than slow strangulation.[116]

These talented and flamboyant Victorians of the "Dublin school" needed a forum through which to express themselves and present their work. Towards this end William Stokes and Robert William Smith founded the Pathological Society of Dublin in 1838. Corrigan was an active participant from the start and was later its secretary and president. The first meeting was held on December 1, 1838 with Robert Graves in the chair.[117] The physicians and surgeons of the "Dublin school" were, as we have seen, astute observers of the signs and symptoms of disease, but they were not satisfied with merely making a diagnosis. It was their practice to confirm the accuracy or otherwise of their conclusions by careful dissection at post-mortem examination, an event that occurred all too frequently. One of the main aims of the Pathological Society was the study of pathological anatomy, that is the structural changes that occur in the body in response to disease. The balance between the disciplines of clinical medicine and pathology was carefully maintained as Corrigan emphasised to the students of the Society,[118] "But while I would impress upon you the great value of learning pathology, that is, the study of the results of those destructive actions which terminate life, or cause loss or injury of limb, I at the same time feel it to be my duty to impress on you that the study of pathology alone will not make you physicians or surgeons. It is to the combination of pathology with clinical research, that you must look for the acquirement of skill and knowledge that will cause you to be looked up to with confidence in our professional stations." The meetings of the society were organised well so that a variety of disease was presented: "This society," Corrigan said, "possesses a feature which is peculiar to it, and to which, I believe, its success is in a great measure due: I mean the exclusion of mere theoretical disquisitions and disputations . . . Another advantage of this arrangement of the society is, that no valuable time is lost; so that in each week of the session, short as is the time of meeting, a large amount of practical information is collected, and mutually communicated." But there was another function to be served by the society, and this Corrigan held in high regard: "The Irish School of Medicine owes to it (the society), I think I may say, the very high status which it holds at present throughout Europe and America. To it are paid the first visits of distinguished foreigners belonging to our profession, who come amongst us; and thus it has become the means of extending the fame of the Irish school of medicine to every part of the civilised world. I believe I am not wrong when I state, that scarcely a meeting, since the commencement of the society, has been held, that has not been attended by foreigners of eminence from one part or another of the globe. At our last two meetings we have had visitors from classic Italy and majestic Greece." The society served furthermore to bring together different elements within the profession: "Our society opens its meetings to the medical and surgical officers of our army and navy. They are free to come here; and in a city in which there is always so large a garrison, the value of such a society cannot be overrated; for while we receive valuable contributions from them, from their experience in other climes, we, in turn, give in exchange, the information which we have been able, in our respective spheres, to acquire."

Meetings were held regularly in either the anatomy theatre of Trinity College, or the Park Street Private Medical School, and were attended by senior students of the several Dublin medical schools and many doctors. Its proceedings were published, and if we consult Corrigan's bibliography we see that between 1840 and 1867, he published no less than fifty-six case reports most of which were presented to the Dublin Pathological Society and many of which were published in the *Proceedings* of that society. The society proved so popular that other centres soon followed Dublin's example, and by 1840 Cork, London, Liverpool and Philadelphia had similar societies. Legendary names in medicine were conferred with the Honorary Diploma of Membership — Sir Astley Cooper, Sir Benjamin Brodie, Richard Bright, J. Cruveillier, J.L. Schönlein and Karl Rokitansky. When the Royal Academy of Medicine in Ireland (which is still in existence) was founded in 1883, the Pathological Society was incorporated in it as the Section of Pathology.[119]

The life of the Dublin school of medicine was brief, but its light had burned so brightly that it reached across the world. Corrigan was not unaware of the rise of the "school"; he recognised the importance of his own contributions to it, and was proud of the renown the school received internationally. Speaking in a debate in 1869 he urged those present to "look back to the Dublin school of medicine and see what it was when he was a boy — the Dublin school was one in which it was supposed medicine could not be taught. There was a medical school connected with Trinity College attended by about forty students. The Royal College of Surgeons was then struggling into existence. He went to Edinburgh under the impression that medicine could not be taught at home. To what heights had the "Dublin school" risen in a few years? It had risen to an eminence which had no parallel elsewhere in their time. Its name had reached America and every part of Europe."[120] Corrigan moreover saw the school as a commercial as well as academic success:

"The Dublin school of medicine, from having only a class of about 100 students, now had a class of about 1,000, and these were not supported in Dublin at less than £100 per annum each. That was £100,000. If he added about half that number for the young men coming to Dublin to prepare for the Indian Civil Service — for Irishmen were taking the lead in all examinations — he might say that the medical students caused an expenditure of about £150,000 per annum. They had often heard discussions as to the loss of £30,000 a year to

> Dublin if the Lord Lieutenancy of Ireland were abolished,
> yet here the medical students of Dublin spend £150,000
> per annum amongst the hard-working shopkeepers and
> the persons who let lodgings in the city."

He touched often on the influence of the school in his lectures:
"The Irish school of medicine and surgery is, if I am not mis-
taken, exerting a silent but deeply spreading influence upon
society, an influence which is beneficial, and which will I
hope be lasting."[121] He was proud especially of its international influence: "Until lately this country may be said to
have been unknown, or known only to be misrepresented.
Latterly foreigners from all parts of Europe of high mental
acquirements have visited us, and their numbers each year are
increasing; . . . and if the beacon of knowledge is once more
to burn as pre-eminently brightly in my native country, as
tradition says it once did, the honour of re-lighting will
assuredly belong to my own profession." Its success was due,
in Corrigan's opinion to a willingness to examine critically
any doctrine however sacred, and a tolerance that would permit change in scientific thought:

> "To train the mind in such habits of patient observation,
> cool reasoning, and steady deduction, which are the only
> sure foundations for professional skill, I believe no
> school in Europe excels our own. If we turn to some of
> the other schools of Europe, we too often see their pro-
> fessors, ambitious of forming a sect, stimulated by the
> desire of hastily acquiring practice, or grasping at a short-
> lived notoriety, distorting fact to suit their purposes,
> and thus justifying the bitter sarcasm of Cullen, that
> there are in medicine 'more false facts than false theories.'
> Dublin is I trust, free from such imputation, and while
> all that is really valuable is retained all that is idle or
> empty is discarded. There is no blind adherence to what
> is old, nor narrow minded opposition to what is new:
> while we admit all that will bear test of observation,
> while we revere the reasoning of Harvey and the truths
> of Hunter, we are not deluded by the fooleries of
> homeopathy, or the knaveries of animal magnetism."

On yet another occasion he elaborated on the clinical pragmatism that he believed to be the essence of the "Dublin school":

> "There is no such thing as theory in medicine. All theories of medicine are nonsense, just as much as the gone-by theories of phlogiston and anti-phlogiston in chemistry ... In short the true practical physician adapts his practice to his patient, not his patient to his theory. This constitutes the true practice of medicine. It is on its steady adherence to these principles that the high character of the Dublin school of medicine has been raised and which I am sure it will maintain. It is known throughout Europe and America as essentially the 'eclectic school of Europe.' Having no theory or hypothesis to support, it accepts information, and is ready to test alleged improvements, come from where they may. It tests them cautiously and carefully in its hospitals, adopts them if worthy of being adopted, or rejects them if found erroneous."[122]

The "Dublin school" began somewhere around 1830 and lasted scarcely fifty years. Its success was dependent foremost on the extraordinary energies and talents of its main progenators, Graves, Stokes and Corrigan. Others of ability were to follow but they failed to sustain the spirit of the "school." We may well wonder why so vibrant a movement was permitted to decay. The conditions in which subsequent generations practised were not substantially different to those of the mid-nineteenth century; there were the same hospitals, with the addition of some new ones; there were more doctors and nursing improved greatly; a limited amount of money for research became available whereas there had been no provision for research funding in Victorian Ireland; the government participated in health care not always acting in the best interests of the sick, but nonetheless, augmenting greatly the voluntary support on which mid-nineteenth century medicine depended. And yet the "school" disappeared. The *raison d'etre* of the "Dublin school" was its iconoclasm which was fuelled from without rather than within Ireland. The members of the "school" competed with and enjoyed the company of the

European leaders of medicine; their ideals and their standards were pitched well above the mediocrity to which Ireland, through complacency and an insular philosophy is prepared often from unawareness of anything better, to tolerate. Had later generations been prepared to seek and absorb the influence of European and American medicine, the school might have survived, and Irish medicine might have been saved from a period of stagnation and apathy from which it only now shows some feeble signs of emerging. If today's medical profession is to be enriched from a study of the rise and rapid decline of the "Dublin school," it will be by the realisation that its future lies not within the narrow confines of the island that is Ireland, but beyond in the broader intellectualism of international science.

6

Merrion Square

By 1834 Corrigan had moved his home and practice from Bachelor's Walk to number four Merrion Square West.[1] Here he joined the elite of his profession, and the most distinguished members of society.

The Georgian squares of Dublin had few rivals for style in the nineteenth century. When on January 1, 1801, the Act of Union dissolved the Irish parliament in Dublin with Westminster becoming the seat of government for both countries, the aristocracy and nobility departed for London leaving behind a social vacuum that was filled by the clergymen of the established church, the wealthy merchants and the professional classes. Lawyers and doctors were plentiful and both were to dominate the social life of Dublin for a century.[2]

The social change that occurred in Dublin immediately after the Union is described by Maria Edgeworth in her novel *The Absentee*:

"From the removal of both houses of parliament, most of the nobility, and many of the principal families among the Irish commoners, either hurried in high hope to London, or retired disgusted and in despair to their houses in the country. Immediately, in Dublin, commerce rose into the vacated seats of rank; wealth rose into the place of birth. New faces and new equipages appeared. People who had never been heard of before started into notice, pushed themselves forward, not scrupling to elbow their way even at the Castle; and they were presented to my lord-lieutenant and to my lady lieutenant; for their Excellencies might have played their vice-regal parts to empty benches, had they not admitted such persons for the moment to fill their court. Those of former times — of hereditary pretensions and high-bred minds and manners — were scandalized at all this; and they complained with justice, that the whole tone of society was altered; that the decorum, elegance, polish and charm of society was gone."[3]

The Georgian aristocracy left behind them a city that had few rivals for architectural eminence. The Gardiner family on the northside had developed Henrietta and Denmark Street, Gardiner's Mall, Great Charles Street, Gardiner Street and Mountjoy Square, and on the southside architectural harmony was achieved by the Fitzwilliams. The development of Merrion Square began in 1760 and was completed in 1790 together with Upper and Lower Fitzwilliam Street. Fitzwilliam Square and Place were not completed until the 1840s. Standing at the corner where Merrion Square East joins Merrion Square North, the observer's eye is drawn by the gentle undulation of line and shadow on door and window of the Georgian architectural facade towards the Dublin mountains which seem to rise from the end of the street.[4] The houses of these great squares and streets were ideally suited to the professions, with the legal profession favouring the northside squares of Rutland and Mountjoy and the medical profession settling initially in Merrion Square and later in Fitzwilliam Street and Square. Indeed, so popular did Merrion Square become to the medical profession that it was known to irreverent Dubliners as "The Valley of the Shadow of Death."[5]

The houses of Merrion Square provided ample accommodation for medical practice, family life and, of course, entertainment. The staff occupied the basement and coach houses at the rere; the hall floor contained the waiting room, the doctor's consulting room, and a dining-room in reasonable proximity to the basement kitchens. On the second floor the drawing-room ran the width of the house and extended through folding doors to the rere. From the front windows there was the beautiful view of a wooded quadrangular park. Here the *conversaziones*, the after dinner gatherings, and tea-parties were held. The two upper floors contained the bedrooms and nurseries.

Corrigan's neighbours included: William Stokes at number five, Lord Justice Fitzgibbon at number ten, and William

Wilde across the street in the corner house at number one; Sir Philip Crampton's house at number fourteen was a landmark with its flowering pear-tree planted in the year of Waterloo.

The Victorian doctors did not confine themselves to the Georgian squares of the city. They also owned houses in the country, or within a short distance of the city where they passed the summer months. William Stokes had a retreat, Carrig Breac at Howth, and William Wilde went further afield to Moytura House at Cong in Connemara. In 1844 Corrigan leased a plot of ground on Coliemore Road in Dalkey for 999 years from Martin Burke, the owner of the Shelbourne Hotel.[6] Here he built a granite mansion in Tudor style and above the doorway placed a granite bust of himself encircled by a laurel wreath. The house which he named *Inniscorrig* is beautifully situated overlooking the rocky sea shore of Dalkey Sound.[7] He built a small harbour from which he was able to indulge in his favourite pastime of sailing. He designed a fine aquarium where he bred tropical fish and reptiles many of which he presented to the zoo.

In the illustrious ambience of Merrion Square Corrigan's practice flourished. Examination of his fee books from 1858 to 1879 shows that over this period his annual income averaged £4,000, and in 1863 his income reached £6,000.[8] Most of this came from private fees; only about £300 per annum was earned in salary from student fees at the Richmond (a monthly payment of £8 6s 8d) and Maynooth College. Corrigan has recorded meticulously his daily income over these years, showing that most of it was earned in consultation at his rooms in Merrion Square. His fee for travelling to the country was substantial; for example: a visit to Ballinasloe £66; Tipperary £100; Longford £42; Lady Castlerosse, Killarney £105; Limerick £100; Castleshane in Monaghan £105; Sallins £21; Lady Granard in Johnstown Castle £105; the Marquis of Headfort £105.

We learn from the fee books that when Corrigan was in town he worked every day, including Sundays and holidays. On Christmas Day in 1859, £18 in fees were received, and in the same day in 1864 he received £5 for a visit. It would appear that even on family occasions he could not or did not wish to escape from the demands of practice — on the day of his daughter Mary's marriage £1 fee for a visit is recorded; on the anniversary of the death of his daughter Joanna £41 is recorded; on the day of the funeral of his sister Celia £4 is entered. Corrigan's investments grew over the years and in 1862 he had £6,000 stock from which he earned interest. He also had debentures in the King's and Queen's College (£1,000 with an annual interest £20) and the Lying-in Hospital (£200, annual interest £3 13s 10d). Later there are some entries for rental income suggesting that he had invested money in property.

Lombe Atthill, a neighbouring doctor, often visited Corrigan on business, and was thus given the opportunity of observing first-hand "the largest practice in Ireland."[9] Corrigan, he tells us, "was very particular about his fees, and necessarily so for a large number of the patients who thronged his waiting-rooms were members of the lower middle class from the country districts, who not infrequently tried to evade paying the fee."

On one occasion while waiting in the hall for Corrigan to complete a consultation, Atthill engaged a recently appointed manservant in friendly conversation by asking him how he was getting on in his new post only to be told that he was serving his notice, as he went on to explain:

> " 'It was a simple thing,' he said. 'There was a great lot of patients waiting to see the doctor the other day, and amongst them a lady from Cork. Well, the doctor had to go away before he had seen them all; this lady was among those left and was greatly put out, saying she had come all the way just to see him. I said, 'Don't mind; come early tomorrow, and I will take care you see him at once.' Well, she gave me a shilling, and I put her in first the very next day. All went on well till she was leaving the study without giving the fee. So the doctor says, 'My fee, ma'am.' 'Your fee?' says she. 'Did not I give the man in the hall a shillin'?' "

Corrigan's success in practice was due not only to his position in society and in the profession, but also to his personality: "Once, when attending a lady of rank in fever, when he entered her room accompanied by her anxious

husband, he said to the latter, 'She is better!' The visit completed, when they left the patient, the husband asked how he
knew at a glance without examination that the patient was
better. 'I knew it by an infallible symptom — I saw the handle
of a looking-glass peeping from under her pillow.' "[10] On
another occasion we catch the cool draught of a personality
that would brook little nonsense. "One bitter winter's day,"
Francis Cruise recalls, "I met him in consultation in a house
near our square. We saw and examined the patient, who was
in bed upstairs, and then came down to consult. Having been
shown into a comfortless, fireless drawing-room, Corrigan
said to me: 'I won't consult here,' and opened the door into
the back drawing-room where the family were warming themselves over a glorious fire. He said at once: 'Let us exchange
rooms.' The consultation over, we called the family in to hear
our fortunately favourable opinion. 'Now,' said he, smiling,
'Do you think Dr Cruise and I could have done justice to the
case if we had been left perishing in the other room?' All
laughed."

In practice he was careful not to betray the smallest haste
or pressure of time. "No matter how really hurried, he never
let it be seen, and he taught me never to look at my watch in
my consulting room, but to have a clock always at a glance,
but not prominent." Nor it seems did he like to be seen
making too hasty an exit: "Many thought he bore a close
resemblance to O' Connell. He, however, always wore a single
coat, saying that the putting on of an overcoat in the patients'
hall led to unnecessarily protracted enquiries."[11]

Entertainment in the medical houses of Merrion Square
was lavish, and in the social season activity was hectic. At
number four Merrion Square West there were frequent *conversaziones* from 8.30 to 11 pm, garden parties, *déjeuners*,
dances and dinner parties sometimes consisting of as many as
eighteen courses, and then there were the *levées* at Dublin
Castle. During the week Mrs Corrigan and her daughters were
at home for tea from 2 to 6.30 pm to the other hostesses of
the city.[12] The daughters of the doctors of Merrion Square
conformed to an exciting if somewhat daunting social programme. January to March was the season for dances, and the
ambition of medical mammas was to have their daughter pre-

sented at drawing room. "After the implantation of a rather
hairy vice-regal kiss on their left cheeks, the young ladies
would be safely launched on society." Because many regi-
ments were quartered in Dublin, the daughters tended to
marry army officers, often finding their destiny in a far-flung
post of the Empire.[5]

At these gatherings in Merrion Square the aristocracy, and
at times royalty itself, rubbed shoulders with the lawyers, and
the doctors, the clergy and the academics, the writers, the
artists and the officers of the army. The atmosphere on such
occasions was the quintessence of Victorianism: "The Land-
seer pictures, the plethoric side-board, the anti-macassared
armchairs whose knobled headpieces and unaccommodating
arms forbade the impropriety of rest, the red chenille table-
covers, and heavy velvet curtains, all conspired, with dim
melancholy dusk to defeat the light from the globed bat wing
gas-jets in their efforts to dispel a little of the too respectable
gloom."[13]

Among Corrigan's guests we find the most distinguished
members of Victorian society in Dublin. Many a lord lieutenant graced his table. At one function the following are
listed among the guests — The Earl of Meath, Sir E. Grogan,
Sir James Power, Sir James Dombrain, Sir H. Brownrigg,
George Roe, DL, Francis Codd, JP, Mr Corballis, QC, D. Hamil-
ton, the Hon Baron Hughes, the Hon Judge Lynch, Dr
Fleming, Dr Churchill, Mr Coppinger, QC, Mr Morgan O'Con-
nell, Sir Bernard Burke, Col Foster, Dr Stokes, Dr Law, Dr
Steele, Dr Beatty, Dr Evory Kennedy, the Provost of Trinity
College, Dr John Hughes, Dr Ringland, Dr J.S. Hughes, J.
Lentaigne, John F. Waller, LLD, F.W. Brady, QC, Dr Duncan,
Dr J.H. Powell, Dr Tufnell, Dr A. Mitchell, Dr Nelligan, the
Very Rev. B. Woodlock, Rector of the Catholic University,
William Wilde, Dean Myler, Dr Apjohn, Sir James Murray
and Robert Adams. There were eighty-five other guests
besides.[14]

And what of the women in the gathering? "What pretty
women! The tea they had consumed! Indeed, Dublin was the
'tea drinkingest city in Europe.' The ladies dress; low neck to
shoulders, pagoda sleeves, crinoline skirts, hooped end many-
flounced drawn up in four places to show contrasting petti-

coats, heel-less slippers, shawl or mantilla of shot-silk, *crepe de chine* or embroidered silk heavily fringed. These beautiful creatures in their graceful adornments were thrown into high relief by stern gentlemen of seemingly military ferocity dressed in black tailcoats, embroidered waistcoats laden down with heavy alberts, frilled shirts and tight black trousers terminating in black elastic-sided boots."[13] The public gazed, sometimes in wonderment at the gaiety and opulence of the medical eminence, but not always with approval; a paper of the times viewed it all thus: "Many of them care more for social advantage than progress of science. The ambition of this section is not to widen the horizon of knowledge, but to run a house in a fashionable square, and keep a carriage and pair. The patient laborious self-abnegating devotion to the cause of science has little charm beside the musical clink of the sovereign, and the possibility of hooking a knighthood out of the political peculiarities of the country."[15]

In the home of William Stokes at number five Merrion Square we would find among the doctors, artists, writers, actors and actresses who found in their host a warm and sensitive cultural appreciation of their achievements and endeavours. Indeed if we are to take Pentland Mahaffy at his word, Stokes had been a considerable influence on at least one artist, his "very dear friend," George Petrie: "The remarkable researches of George Petrie built on the antiquities and the music of Ireland, would never have seen the light, but for the constant pressure and encouragement of William Stokes, who though he was neither a musician nor an artist, felt the beauty of artistic work with a keenness and tenderness beyond the depth of ordinary man."[16] Petrie, a child of Scottish parents had been educated at Samuel Whyte's Academy in Grafton Street, a remarkable institute where Brindsley Sheridan and Thomas Moore had attended before him. The influence of art was present from an early age; as a child he had seen Sarah Curran, weeping when she saw his father's portrait of Robert Emmet. Instructed in painting and engraving by the Brocas brothers and later at the Dublin Society's drawing school where he became friendly with Francis Danby and James A. O'Connor, he applied his artistic skills to painting the archaeological treasures of Ireland. Few books of Irish scenery and topography of the time were without his engravings, and though his work was said to be deficient in colour and execution, he had a remarkable eye for detail.[17]

By applying scientific and logical principles to archaeology, Petrie dispelled the fantasies of Vallency and Betham. As a member of the Ordnance Topographical Survey of Ireland, with Larcom, O'Donovan, O'Curry and Clarence Mangan, he contributed much to this uncompleted project. In his travels he collected Irish folk music, and his collection the *Ancient Music of Ireland* contains over 2,000 tunes. When Petrie died in 1866, Stokes devoted the remainder of his life to producing a biography of his friend — "Archaeologist, painter, musician, man of letters, as such, and for himself, revered and loved."[18] Indeed the Stokes family was to pay a further tribute to Petrie: Stokes's daughter, Margaret, later edited his *Christian Inscriptions in the Irish Language.*[19]

Stokes also influenced the celebrated and very beautiful actress Helen Faucit. Of Stokes she said, "I seemed to have been fumbling in the dark before I knew well what I wanted, but did not know how to reach it. He revealed to me myself — at least he discovered what I was feeling and wanted to bring forth in my art."[20] She often visited the houses of Merrion Square when playing in Dublin which she did frequently until her marriage in 1851 to Theodore Martin the biographer of the Prince Consort, of whom it was said he "valued his prize less highly after it was captured than before."[21] Perhaps Stokes was taking things a little far when seeing Helen he declared, "Woman the repository of all that is pure, and delicate, and moral in this life." Both had a passion for Shakespeare. She was acclaimed as a Shakesperian actress and had written a book on *Shakespeare's Female Characters* and Stokes was a member of a little Shakespeare Society in Dublin which numbered among its members Mahaffy, Samuel and Lady Ferguson and Professor Dowden.

We can take it that Stokes's nature was such that his feelings for Miss Faucit were platonic, but not so those of two other guests to his home, William Wilde and the artist Frederick Burton. Wilde had not yet met his future wife, Speranza, and his pursuit of Miss Faucit would have been ardent, whereas his rival Burton, who remained a bachelor all his life, was of a more reticent disposition. This pair vied for the favours of the actress from the early forties, when she was appearing in *Antigone* at the Old Theatre Royal.[22] "At every appearance she was greeted with enthusiasm, as she came on stage attired in classical garb embroidered in crimson and gold, the music of Mendelsshon blending with the silvery inflexions of her voice." Her suitors were a contrasting sight, each in a box on either side of the stage. Burton was extremely handsome and charming of manner, whereas Wilde was small, attractive, persistent and full of personality. The actress, however, it seems became involved with neither other than to allow Burton to paint her.

Sir Frederick Burton linked together many famous personalities of the mid-Victorian era with an iridescent thread of delicate watercolour. Like Petrie he had been a pupil of the Brocas brothers. He gained renown as a portrait painter, escaping the demands of a patronising society by retreating to the west of Ireland, or to the forests of Franconia to paint moving studies of peasantry, *The Arran Fisherman's Drowned Child* and *The Widow of Wohlm* being popular examples of this period. *Helelil and Hildebrand*, or *The Meeting on the Turret Stair* as it is also known, was inspired by a translation of an old Danish ballad by Stokes's father Whitley.[23]

The Victorian doctors appreciated the relevance of the artist in society, and patronised the arts. Eccentric Clarence Mangan was well known to the doctors of Merrion Square, as indeed he was to most Dubliners, a fact that is hardly surprising if we heed Wakeman's description of the poet, "Poor Clarence Mangan with his queer poems and jokes, and odd little cloak, and wonderful hat, which exactly resembled the tiles that broomstick-riding witches are usually represented with, his flax-coloured wig, and false teeth, and the inevitable bottle of tar-water, from which he would sip and sip all day, except when asleep, with a plain deal desk for a pillow . . ."[24] He would often cap this bizarre ensemble with a huge pair of dark green spectacles on a face as colourless as parchment, so that in the words of Duffy, "He looked like the spectre of some German romance rather than a living creature." An extraordinary sight he must have been, strolling through Dublin in most settled weather with a very voluminous umbrella under each arm. Stokes was shocked one day when doing his rounds in the Meath hospital to see his friend, unkempt, destitute, and extremely ill.[25] He had Mangan moved to a private room, clothed in flannels, and supplied with whatever comfort was necessary for the remaining days of his life. When he died Stokes asked Frederic Burton to make a drawing of the death mask, which is now in the National Gallery of Ireland. Mangan is said to have died of cholera but his addiction to opium hastened his decline:

> "I exult alone in one wild hour —
> That hour in which the red cup drowns
> The memories it anon renews
> In ghastlier guise, in fiercer power —"[26]

Carlyle who visited Ireland in 1849 has left an interesting pen-picture of Merrion Square society.[27] Stokes and he did not take to each other. "In Merrion Square Dr Stokes *in*: clever, energetic, but squinting, rather fierce, sinister-looking man, — at least some dash of that susceptible in him: to there, nevertheless, to-morrow evening . . ." If first impressions were to augur for the future, then dinner was doomed to ignominious failure:

> "Stokes's dinner was well replenished both with persons and other material, but it proved rather unsuccessful. Foolish Mrs Stokes, a dim Glasgow lady, with her I made the reverse of progress, — owing chiefly to ill luck. She did bore me to excess, but I did not give way to that; had difficulty however in resisting it; and at length once, when dinner was over, I, answering somebody about something chanced to quote Johnson's 'Did I say anything that *you* understood, Sir?' the poor foolish lady took it to herself; bridled, tossed her head with some kind of indignant-polite ineptitude of a reply; and before long flounced out of the room (with her other ladies, not remembered now), and became, I fear, my enemy forever!"

Carlyle's opinion of the other guests, with the exception of Petrie and Burton is even less complimentary, and his kindly host does not appear to have enjoyed the evening at all:

> "These (Petrie and Burton) and a mute or two were the
> dinner; Stokes, who has a son that carves, sitting at the
> side; after dinner there came in many other *mutes* who
> remained such to me. Talk, in spite of my endeavours,
> took on Irish-versus-English character; wherein, as I
> really have no respect for Ireland as it now is and has
> been it was impossible for me to be popular! Good
> humour in general, tho' not without effort always, did
> maintain itself. But Stokes, 'the son of a United-Irishman'
> as I heard, grew more and more gloomy, emphatic,
> contradictory . . ."

At least in Petrie, Carlyle found a kindred spirit and the two
struck up a friendship later to be renewed:

> "Petrie, a Painter of landscapes, notable antiquarian,
> enthusiastic for Brian Boru and all that province of
> affairs; an excellent simple, affectionate loveable soul,
> 'dear old Petrie,' he was our chief figure for me: called
> for *punch* instead of wine, he, and was gradually imitated;
> a thin, wrinkly, half-ridiculous, yet mildly dignified man;
> old bachelor, you could see;* speaks with a panting
> manner, difficult to find the word; shows real knowledge,
> tho' with sad credulity on Irish antiquarian matters;
> not knowledge that I saw on anything else."

Frederic Burton also achieved the dubious compliment of a
special notice in Carlyle's *Diary*, but did not fare as well as
Petrie: "Burton, a young portrait-painter; thin-equiline man,
with long thin locks scattered about, with a look of real
painter-talent, but thin, proud-vain, not a pleasant 'man of
genius.'"

Charles Lever often visited the Stokes and Wildes although
he was not impressed by Merrion Square company, complaining of stupid dinner parties where men of physic and law
talked an uninteresting and unintelligible jargon. Witty and
irrascible his company was irresistible. Of him Trollope said,
"Of all the men I have encountered, he was the sheerest fund

*Petrie was, in fact, father of a large family.

of drollery." Lever had qualified in medicine with difficulty, but he found the practice of medicine not only arduous, but insufficient to afford his gambling debts, and he was forced to turn, very successfully, to literature. When Lord Derby bestowed upon him the Counsellship of Trieste he did so with the trite observation, "Here is £600 a year for doing nothing, and you are just the man to do it."[28]

Like so many Irish writers he chose exile from Ireland for much of his life, but was compelled to return periodically for intellectual refreshment in Dublin. "Though compelled by his duties to live abroad, he felt it an absolute necessity to revisit Ireland periodically, and have the tone of his mind refreshed by nights in Trinity College, or at the table of some old friends, who told him all the newest good things and revived him with the music of the Irish brogue."[29]

In Dublin he feasted not only his body with the best of food and wine, but also his mind in wit and story: "My friend, Dr Beatty, with whom I had a bottle of Carlowitz last evening told me not a bad thing. Christmas Day was celebrated at his house by a plum-pudding of vast circumference; but the doctor missed the whiskey which he had given out to rob it of dyspeptic terrors. That night he taxed his cook with the omission, who naively replied, 'The puddin' and I tossed to see which should have the whiskey, and the puddin' lost."[30]

According to one of his biographers, W.J. Fitzpatrick, Lever owed many of his good stories to Stokes, "A man of gloom to his patients, but a real Rabelais of humour when freed from the restraints of professional pomp and mystery."[31]

The children of Dominic and Joanna Corrigan grew up in the opulent society of Merrion Square. Their eldest son, John, chose the army for a career, joining the Third Dragoons. William selected the legal profession and became a prominent barrister. Mary, the eldest girl, married Richard Martin, the son of a prosperous Catholic business family,[32] and Celia, remained unmarried, a constant companion to her parents.

7

The Great Famine

In The Charitable Infirmary Corrigan had devoted himself almost exclusively to the practice of clinical medicine, and to the development of the "Dublin school." In these pursuits he had been eminently successful; he had an international reputation, a medical school in which he could influence the course of medical education, and a private practice that was to make him wealthy. All of this would have been more than most doctors would ever hope for. Corrigan, however, saw other peaks to scale, and even from his position of eminence some of these were obscured in cloud. He realised that master though he was of clinical medicine, he was unlikely to match the discoveries of his younger years. He appreciated that successful though he would remain in the practice of medicine, most illnesses were little influenced by what he could provide. As for teaching, it no doubt gave him considerable satisfaction, but he knew that far-reaching reforms were necessary in medical education. Perhaps more than all, he felt compelled to influence the overall provision of health care to the wretched inhabitants of a nation whose level of misery and neglect is now difficult to conceive. These sentiments were to lead him inevitably towards politics, and his course was to be punctuated by a series of controversies, any of which might have halted his advancement.

From afar we can see and perhaps understand the opposing forces. The medical establishment had admitted Corrigan to its lower echelons and in return he was expected to conform rigidly to the decrees of its leaders. Medicine, even today, has no room in its hierarchy for outspoken criticism from within its ranks. The system is well-controlled and organised by the colleges and medical associations. A miscreant is dealt with effectively in one of two ways; either, he is excluded entirely from the establishment ranks of power and ignored, usually with the desired effect, or he is taken into the establishment, sometimes elevated, and ultimately made to see that the most effective way to advancement is by adherence to the dictates of the system. The latter course would have been unacceptable to Corrigan and besides, the colleges, the effective source of power and control in the profession, closed their doors on him without ever believing that he would destroy their defences and make them look very foolish for an intransigence that was sectarian rather than doctrinal.

Then there was the government which may have had its own reasons for giving support to the medical maverick. An organised medical profession is a phenomenon that governments do not encourage, and the terrible events of the great famine were about to bring members of the profession closer than they had ever been before. Successive lord lieutenants began to read the pamphlets written by Dr Corrigan of the Richmond Hospital; they came to know him in a professional capacity, and most became his friend. Indeed he was to act as confidant and advisor in the Vice-Regal Lodge on more than a few occasions.[1]

The first major debacle was in 1842. Corrigan, writing from the Richmond with his former colleague Robert Harrison, surgeon to The Charitable Infirmary, and professor of anatomy and surgery in Trinity College,[2] published a pamphlet examining a bill then being drafted for the regulation of medical charities in the country.[3] This bill dealt with the provision of support for dispensaries and fever hospitals, the selection and remuneration of medical officers, and the means of administering the system. The central issue as far as the Royal Colleges were concerned was one of power — who should control the Medical Charities Board? Corrigan and Harrison advocated that the administration of the funds should rest with the Poor Law Commissioners, "The authority which furnishes the supplies and which is answerable to the public for their expenditure, must be permitted to follow the funds, and to examine into and report upon that expenditure." The colleges wanted the lord lieutenant to control the finances. Corrigan and Harrison favoured the recommendations in the bill for a board consisting of seven physicians or surgeons to be nominated by the lord lieutenant, whereas the colleges were adamant that the board should consist of representatives from the Royal Colleges of Physicians and Surgeons, and Apothecaries Hall.

Corrigan and Harrison's pamphlet discussed these and many other relevant issues and this was circulated to the country's dispensary doctors with a questionnaire seeking their views. This was an unique means of assessing opinion in the profession, and the hundred or so replies show that the rural doctors appreciated being able to voice their opinions, which they did with erudition and in many cases eloquence. [4] Corrigan and Harrison published an analysis of this democratic survey in a second pamphlet, [5] but they also included the proposals that had been drafted by the colleges and circulated privately to, among others, the lord lieutenant. This infuriated the colleges, and their ire knew no bounds when it was learned that Corrigan and Harrison had gone to the chief secretary, Lord Eliot, to acquaint him with their contrary views. Dr Maunsell, secretary of the Royal College of Surgeons in Ireland, wrote to Eliot accusing Corrigan (but not Harrison) of attempting to influence him unfairly: "The Committee are informed that the expression of opinion has been pointedly interfered with by an individual, who appears to represent himself as honoured with your Lordship's confidence on this subject."[6] Understandably Lord Eliot did not take kindly to this insult: "Dr Corrigan is not more in my confidence than the other gentlemen of the medical profession with whom I have been in communication on the subject of the Medical Charities Bill; but I believe him to be a man of high honour and respectability, and incapable of doing that which you represent him to have done."[7] He informed Maunsell that he felt it only right that Corrigan should be made aware of the allegations being made against him, and he placed the whole correspondence in Corrigan's hands. Corrigan with Lord Eliot's permission, published the lot, and a few more pertinent letters besides, in the *Dublin Evening Post*. [8]

The college should have withdrawn quietly, but there followed a protracted correspondence in the daily papers, which as one paper commented was not to the credit of the profession:[9] "For the gentlemen of the College of Surgeons, collectively and individually, we entertain the most sincere respect; and for such of them as we are acquainted with — not a few — the warmest friendship. It pains us exceedingly to be obliged to say that the conduct of the Committee in this case was ill-judged."

Corrigan had won this battle, but shortly afterwards the government announced its intention of not proceeding with the bill. He later commented, "I cannot but think that they came to this determination disgusted with the opposition their best efforts for the amelioration of the state of the sick-poor encountered."[10] Corrigan had now alienated the medical establishment, and made some powerful enemies who were to show that they had long memories and knives to match. He had, however, one powerful friend in a high place.

In the autumn of 1845 the Irish peasant was performing the most important task of the year. From his small patch of land he was digging the potato crop planted in the spring. The "lumpers" as the commonest variety was known would provide enough food for him and his family for the next year, and monotonous though his diet might be, it was nutritionally adequate. He could not afford to plant other crops such as corn, and only a few enterprising communities had learned to fish the plentiful waters that permeated the island. In this autumn of 1845 there was concern in the minds of some who had viewed with trepidation the increasing dependence of the populace on the potato for nourishment. From England came news of a devastating potato blight spreading from the Isle of Wight to Kent.[11] As reports of blight in the Irish potato crop began to reach Dublin in 1846, Corrigan published a pamphlet directed towards the authorities and the wealthy minority of Irish society.[12] Aware that he might be "censured by many as an alarmist," he made no apology for anticipating "how helpless on occasions of great panic is the public mind." By analysing the epidemics of the previous century he demonstrated that important though contagion, poor sanitation, poverty, and climate were in propagating epidemics of fever, there was one outstanding feature common to all epidemics — famine. Furthermore, he observed that the commonest cause of famine in Ireland had been the failure of the potato harvest. "The people of Ireland," he said, "are peculiarly liable to become the victims of such a pestilence. The effect of competition among a superabundant unemployed population, had been to reduce their wages to the lowest sum on which life can be supported. Potatoes have hence become their stable food. If this crop be unproductive, the earnings of the labouring classes are then quite insufficient to purchase the necessary quantity of any other food . . . The potato has, I believe been a curse to our country . . . When a bad crop occurs there is no descent for them in the scale of food: the next step is starvation." He deplored the fact that corn was abundant but out of reach of the poor: "They *starve* in the midst of plenty, as literally as if dungeon bars separated them from a granary. When distress has been at its height, and our poor have been dying of starvation in our streets, our corn, has been going to a foreign market. It is, to our own poor, a forbidden fruit." He urged politicians to study Ireland's needs so that future epidemics might be prevented. The remedy he claimed was "to be found, not in medicine, but in employment, not in the lancet, but in *food*, not in raising lazarettos for the reception of the sick, but in establishing manufactories for the employment of the healthy."

If, with the wisdom of hindsight and possessing the scientific knowledge accrued over the past century, we wish to identify a cause for the great famine, and thereby to apportion blame for the resulting catastrophe, we need look no further than Corrigan's pamphlet: it was the dependence of the peasant on the potato which once destroyed left no alternative to starvation. Successive governments failed to appreciate this all too obvious fact, and refused ostrich-like to heed the warnings of previous failures of the potato crop. One report from Erris conveys very clearly the nation's dependence on "Raleigh's gift":

"Previously to the potato blight of last year, the peasantry of Erris appear to have been a contented race, growing abundance of potatoes for their annual consumption, having plenty of wool for clothing, and of butter and milk, the produce of the cattle reared on their mountain farms. Each peasant generally had a small take called 'a sum' consisting of two, three, or more acres of arable land, and from twenty to thirty acres of mountain, at a very low rent, sometimes as low as thirty shillings for the whole. With the exception of the five or six weeks during which he planted his potatoes, his time was spent in comparative idleness. As there was always a supply of potatoes roasting in the ashes on the hearth, there was no need of set hours for meals. They ate when hungry, drank when thirsty, and slept when they wished for repose. As almost their only food was the potato, and they made no other provision for the future, the blight has proved the death warrant of thousands."[13]

The mortality from the epidemic fever was often startling but statistics failed to give any real impression of the terrible suffering that was endured by the survivors. To many, Corrigan declared, death would have been a happy release, and he warned: "The offspring will inherit for generations to come, the weakness of body and apathy of mind, which famine and fever engendered." Corrigan was too astute a judge of human nature to rely solely on a humanitarian appeal to "those who are placed in power, and who possess wealth." Drawing on the statistics from previous epidemics he commented on the surprising fact that fever affected the wealthy in much lesser numbers than the poor, but when it did so the mortality was ten times higher. "It seems, therefore," he wrote, "that while the rich possess constitution and means which enable them to resist the ordinary contagion of fever, the seizure, when it does come is in itself demonstrative of a greater amount of virulence."[14] He was critical of the recent Poor Law Act which allowed for the conversion of workhouses into fever hospitals in times of emergency: "Sickness should not be made a chain to drag a man into a poor house." He ended his pamphlet with a plea: "If there be no famine, there will be no fever — and if active and timely exertion be made to afford sufficient employment and wages to our people, I believe there will be, neither *famine* nor *fever*."

Corrigan seems to have been convinced that there would be a major famine to be followed as always by a number of often fatal illnesses known collectively as "epidemic fevers." His anticipation of these events was not in itself remarkable, but his conviction that their occurrence could be of catastrophic magnitude calls for closer examination.

The potato had been affected previously by blight; no fewer than twenty-four failures of the potato crop were recorded up to 1851.[15] On three occasions prior to 1845 (1739, 1800 and 1816) famine had been followed by devastating epidemics of fever. When Corrigan proclaimed "No famine, no fever," he did not refer, as MacArthur has pointed out in his masterly analysis of the medical aspects of the famine, to the localised everyday outbreaks of infection in the hospitals, and from time to time in the cities, "but to a great tide of pestilence which engulfed the whole country."[16]

The cause of the famine of 1845-50 was a fungus disease of the potato due to *Phytophthora infestans* which appears in the form of black spots on the leaves with, on the under surface, a whitish mould containing the spores.[16] These are carried to other plants by the wind, rain and insects. The fungus thrives in wet damp conditions. The remarkable feature of the 1845 blight was the speed with which it devasted large crops. In the summer of 1846 the potatoes looked remarkably well, and there did seem every reason to anticipate an abundant harvest.[17] Then almost the entire harvest disappeared in a week. Lombe Atthill later described the landscape: "Driving, say, for half a mile or more through smiling meadow or pasture lands, you would suddenly perceive an offensive stench, borne on the wind; then into view would come a field, often of large size, one mass of blackened stalks, a clear indication that the tubers were already rotting."[18]

The extent of the calamity was not appreciated immediately. It was disquieting to have to accept that millions might be reduced almost overnight to starvation, and then there was always the hope that the next crop would, as in the past, alleviate the hunger. The starvation consequent on the failure of the potato crop did not in itself cause the many fevers of the great famine, but when the meagre resistance of the poor was lowered further by malnutrition, the organisms of infectious disease so prevalent in the filthy hovels that housed most of the populace were permitted to spread without hindrance. Even the most rudimentary forms of hygiene, which were practised by the poor in times of epidemic were abandoned through the weakness and apathy associated with starvation. The potato was the sole food of about one-third of the population, and a main article of diet of many more.

The frightful conditions of the poor have been enumerated by Pim:

"A great part of the population were living in a state of extreme poverty. The laws relating to land were such as to discourage any general attempt at improvement. A large proportion of the landlords were embarrassed, and in many instances they had ceased to reside on their property. The extent of land under the management of receivers appointed by the courts had increased to an alarming degree. From the poverty of the people living on potatoes grown in their own gardens, there were in many districts no retail dealers in food. Indian meal, which would have been an excellent substitute for the potato, had been so long systematically excluded, that its use was unknown and its value disregarded. The poor-law contained no principle of expansion capable of meeting such a difficulty. Many of those who should have administered it were far away. The extent of the unions rendered the due administration of relief impracticable; while the poor-law taxation, by diminishing the funds applicable to the payment of labour, increased the amount of pauperism."[19]

The facilities for dealing with the everyday health problems of the nation had been improving, but they could not cope with a disaster, however small, in any part of the country. The close of the eighteenth century had seen the government beginning to accept some responsibility for health care with the provision of the houses of industry, where the helpless poor "reduced to that state by sickness or misfortune" were authorised to beg, or were cared for in the houses.[20] Those not fortunate enough to qualify for a begging licence or for admission were put to honest toil by imprisonment and hard labour. This comprehensive solution of dealing with the poor was not, of course, practical: "Beggars were met on every road and seen at every door; it was a regular trade, and my father had to issue a kind of ticket, which he distributed to those who were supposed to reside inside the bounds of his parish. They were supposed not to be relieved at his house without producing this — a useless role, as it in no way lessened the number of those who daily applied for alms at the hall door."[21]

Charitably-minded people formed societies for the dispensation of relief to these unfortunates, the most prominent and active of which were the mendicity societies, which as MacArthur puts it "aimed at driving the beggar off the streets by both making it difficult for him to ply his trade and at the same time presenting him with a hard alternative means of livelihood."[20] In England the Elizabethan Poor Law system provided for the aged, the young, the permanently infirm and the unemployed, but political distractions in Ireland had taken precedence over social welfare and the Poor Law system was not extended to Ireland until 1838. The country was then divided into 130 unions, each with its workhouse and board of guardians. These workhouses proved unpopular institutes which is hardly surprising to judge from Carlyle's sceptical account of one that he visited in 1849:

"Three or four hundred big hulks of fellows tumbling about with shares, picks and barrows, 'levelling' the end of the workhouse hill; at first glance you would think them all working; look nearer, in each shovel there is some ounce or two of mould, and it is all make-believe; five or six hundred boys and lads, pretending to break stones. Can it be a charity to keep men alive on these terms? In face of all the twaddle of the earth, shoot a man rather than train him (with heavy expense to his neighbours), to be a deceptive human *swine*. Fifty-four wretched mothers sat rocking young offspring in one room: *vogue la galére*."[22]

Government also attempted to cope with the problem of poverty through the creation of employment in public works. For many years parliament voted considerable sums for the construction of harbours and post roads, and canals, the erection of bridewells, gaols and workhouses, the building of churches, and the widening of the Dublin streets. This form of relief was, however, badly administered:

"The relief works, too, when started, were for the most part not only of a useless nature, but very badly managed. There was no proper organisation and little, if, indeed any, supervision. A batch of men would be started, say, to cut down a hill on some out-of-the-way road: they dawdled, worked in fits and starts, and in the cold wet weather got chilled, and died by the score. Then roads were laid out, and never finished; and, in truth, most of these would have been, if finished, absolutely useless."[23]

In the early nineteenth century government began to make efforts to provide for the sick poor. Three different types of institute were founded: dispensaries, of which there were 632 by 1845, where the poor could receive free medical advice and medicine, county infirmaries (thirty-four by 1843) "receptacles for the infirm and diseased" and fever hospitals, of which over a hundred had been erected by 1845. Then in 1815 the Richmond lunatic asylum was opened for the care of the insane, and this was followed by the erection of ten large district asylums each serving several counties. Hand in hand with these official measures private citizens erected, as we have seen, "voluntary hospitals" in Dublin where by 1845 there were no less than thirty, of which twenty-one were specialist institutions, including four lunatic asylums, six maternity and four fever hospitals.

However inadequate these facilities may seem today they did represent a vast improvement in a short space of time and more importantly were indicative of a changing philosophy in parliament, which by the mid-nineteenth century accepted responsibility for the social welfare of the nation. McDowell was of the opinion that "the Irish poor enjoyed better medical services than their fellows in wealthier and healthier countries."[24] Improved though the conditions might be as compared to the previous century, and comparable though they might be to other countries, they were nonetheless inadequate and could not hope to contend with the consequences of a famine. The government realising this passed the Temporary Fever Act in 1846 which empowered the lord lieutenant to appoint commissioners of health to constitute a Central Board of Health.[25] This board was empowered to set up fever hospitals and to provide medical assistance, nursing and comforts wherever there was an "appearance of fever in a formidable shape."[26] Nominations to the board were made by the secretary for the Home Department, Sir James Graham, to the prime minister Sir Robert Peel. Sir Randolph Routh, Dr Dominic Corrigan, Sir Philip Crampton, Professor Robert Kane and Edward Twistleton, Esq., were appointed.[27] Randolph Routh had been a senior commissariat officer in the Waterloo campaign; he was to superintend the distribution of famine relief in Ireland from 1845 to 1848. Corrigan was appointed on the basis of his experience and writings on famine fever; Sir Philip Crampton was a recent president of the Royal College of Surgeons in Ireland, surgeon to the Meath hospital and surgeon-general. He was a distinguished appointee with much experience in governmental administration in health affairs. Professor Robert Kane (shortly to be knighted) was a distinguished chemist who was also a doctor though he never actually practised. He had been professor of chemistry at the Apothecaries Hall, and he held a chair of natural philosophy at the Royal Dublin Society. He had been influential in establishing a Museum of Irish Industry, which subsequently became the Royal College of Science and he had published a book on *The Industrial Resources of Ireland*.[28] He had founded the *Dublin Journal of Medical and Chemical Science* which he edited for some time, and he was a fellow of the Royal College of Physicians.[29] He had sat on previous boards of enquiry, and earlier in the year Peel had made him a member of the Relief Commission for Ireland not so much for his expertise but because as Peel put it, "He is an Irishman, a Roman Catholic, and we have not one on the commission. He has gained some practical knowledge from having served on other commissions . . . he has written on industrial resources of Ireland. But mainly he is a Roman Catholic."[30] His inclusion of the Central Board of Health was not therefore surprising. The last member of the board was Mr Twistleton, the resident Irish Poor Law Commissioner, who like Kane had sat on previous commissions and was familiar with the administrative problems of providing relief in Ireland.[31]

Corrigan was now in a position to put into effect the measures which he had so ably stated in his publications, and yet the board seems to have run into trouble from its earliest moments. To begin with it completely underestimated the risk of an epidemic, and this is surprising in view of Corrigan's conviction that a major famine must lead inevitably to an epidemic. The board noted that the fever admissions of 1840 were very much higher than those of 1846 and concluded that because no serious devastation had followed in 1840, there was no need for alarm. The board's greatest error was in assuming that the next year's potato crop would be normal, as indeed had been the case in previous blights. In fact, the board seemed in agreement that many circumstances favoured a major epidemic, but surprisingly it assured the government that such would not occur. The summer of 1846 passed without, it seemed, any great cause for concern, and the act was allowed to expire on the appointed day, August 31, 1846, a serious error of judgement. As the winter approached the board's optimism proved ill-founded. One and a half million acres of potatoes had been lost in the blight, and reports of unprecedented fever outbreaks were coming in thick and fast from the rural areas. The lord lieutenant rapidly reappointed the Central Board of Health which quickly got down to work. It was to remain in existence until August 1850, during which time it would open 373 temporary fever hospitals and employ 473 additional doctors for fever duty, as well as publishing directives for the management of the epidemic, and dealing with requests from all over the country.[32]

The board had to attempt to make provision for the control of a number of different infectious diseases within one massive epidemic that was sweeping through a debilitated nation. The commonest fevers were typhus and relapsing fever, both of which are spread by the common louse. The organism causing typhus fever belongs to a group known as *Rickettsia*. These cause extensive damage to the blood vessels throughout the body, especially in the skin producing the characteristic spotted rash and in the brain, causing delerium and stupor from which the disease acquires its name (*tuphos* — mist).[33] The *Rickettsia* swallowed by the louse on biting an infected person, multiply and are passed in the insect's faeces on the skin of a fresh victim from where they enter the blood with the scratching associated with louse infestation. Relapsing fever is due to a spirochaete, a larger organism than the *Rickettsia*, which again multiplies in the louse and infection takes place through the skin. The onset of fever is sudden and severe, often accompanied by sickness and vomiting and its course is punctuated by relapses that coincide with the release of spirochaetes into the blood.

Another disease, commonly seen in times of great deprivation, bacillary dysentery also plagued the unfortunate victims of the famine. This disease is caused by bacilli which are transmitted by food, fingers, and flies. They multiply in the intestine and produce ulceration and inflammation of the intestinal wall, with severe bloody diarrhoea, pain and exhausting straining; the illness often progresses to gangrene of the bowel.

Along with these illnesses the endemic diseases — tuberculosis, rheumatic fever, smallpox, and typhoid fever continued their unrelenting attack on the weakened population, and such was the array of infection facing the unfortunate doctors in the front-line that any attempt at an accurate estimate of the prevalance of one form over the other is not possible. To add to the misery two non-infectious diseases arising from a deficiency of essential foods were rife among the famine victims, scurvy and famine dropsy. Lack of vitamin C causes scurvy, a condition in which the gums become spongy, and ulcerated with eventual loss of the teeth; haemorrhages appear on the skin, and in advanced cases there is bleeding into the muscles and under the skin causing severe pain. In famine dropsy the lack of essential nutrients and protein causes swelling of the abdomen and oedema of the legs.

The misery and suffering during the Great Famine was of such a magnitude that many in Britain, and not a few in Ireland, refused to believe the terrible reports being carried in the papers. It was only when a number of visitors respected for their sanguinity began to write of the horrific conditions that the people of Britain realised how great was the catastrophe. One such report came from William Edward Forster:

"The impression made on me by this short tour can never be effaced. Bad as were my expectations, the reality far exceeded them. There is a prevailing idea in England, that the newspaper accounts are exaggerated. Particular cases may or may not be coloured, but no colouring can deepen the blackness of the truth.

When we entered a village, our first question was, how many deaths? 'The hunger is upon us,' was everywhere the cry, and involuntarily we found ourselves regarding this hunger as we should an epidemic; looking upon starvation as a disease. In fact, as we went along, our wonder was not that the people died, but that they lived; and I have no doubt whatever that, in any other country, the mortality would have been far greater; that many lives have been prolonged, perhaps saved, by the long apprenticeship to want in which the Irish peasant has been trained, and by that lovely touching charity which prompts him to share his scanty meal with his starving neighbour. But the springs of this charity must rapidly be dried up."[34]

There were many such accounts; they differed not in detail but in the writers ability to portray his disgust and the extent of the devastation that faced him at every turn . . . From Belmullet in 1847:

"We entered a cabin. Stretched in one dark corner, scarcely visible, from the smoke and rags that covered them were three children huddled together, lying there because they were too weak to rise, pale and ghastly, their little limbs, on removing a portion of the filthy covering, perfectly emaciated, eyes sunk, voice gone, and evidently in the last stage of actual starvation. Crouched over the turf embers was another form, wild and all but naked, scarcely human in appearance. It stirred not, nor noticed us. On some straw, soddened upon the ground, moaning piteously, was a shrivelled old woman, imploring us to give her something — baring her limbs partly, to show how the skin hung loose from the bones, as soon as she attracted our attention. Above her, on something like a ledge, was a young woman, with sunken cheeks, — a mother I have no doubt, — who scarcely raised her eyes in answer to our enquiries, but pressed her hand upon her forehead, with a look of unutterable anguish and despair. Many cases were widows, whose husbands had recently been taken off by the fever, and thus their only pittance, obtained from the public works, was entirely cut off. In many the husbands or sons were prostrate under that horrid disease, — the results of long-continued famine and low-living, — in which first the limbs, and then the body, swell most frightfully and finally burst."[35]

From Erris:

"In one cabin I saw six children lying heads and points on their miserable beds on each side of the turf fire, while the father and mother, wasted and emaciated, sat crouching over the embers. In another cabin, I saw the father lying near the point of death on one side of the fireplace; over the ashes sat a wretched little boy, wholly naked, and on the opposite side of the hut, beneath a ragged quilt, lay the body of an old woman who had taken shelter there and died. As she belonged to nobody, there was nobody to bury her; and there have been many instances of bodies lying five or six days unburied, before any one could be induced by threats or rewards to inter them. I saw many graves made within a few yards of the cabin door. In some places bodies have been interred under the floors on which they died; and in others they have been covered by the ruins of the cabins they occupied . . ."[36]

The burial of the victims of famine fever presented a major problem, and inability of weakened survivors to dispose of their dear ones caused not only intense emotional and spiritual anguish, but was also a major factor in the propagation of disease. Ingenious efforts were made to deal with the problem of burial:

"Skibbereen, 6th of February, 1847 — This place is one mass of famine, disease and death; the poor creatures hitherto trying to exist on one meal per day, are now sinking under fever and bowel complaints – unable to come for their soup, and this not fit for them: rice is what their whole cry is for; but we cannot manage this well, nor can we get the food carried to the houses from dread of infection. I have got a coffin with moveable sides constructed, to convey the bodies to the churchyard, in calico bags prepared, in which the remains are wrapped up. I have just sent this to bring the remains of a poor creature to the grave, who having been turned out of the only shelter she had – a miserable hut – perished the night before last in a quarry, she was found with some flax around her, lying dead! You will perceive, my dear sir, by this fact, how we are placed, and were it not for my strong reliance on Almighty God, I could not bear up against these scenes."[37]

Sometimes desperation overcame even the Catholic superstitions that are so much a part of death and burial: "One day Stephen Regan met a dog dragging a child's head along. He took the head from the dog and buried it and set a tree over it. The family to whom the child belonged were getting relief for the child and for that reason did not report its death."[38]

The numerous reports, both official and casual, make sad and at times sickening reading. Often the horror of the moment distracts the writer from commenting on the efforts, frequently heroic and selfless, being made by both the authorities and voluntary agencies to alleviate suffering. Many absentee landlords on hearing of the famine determined to stay well away from their properties, but there were others who valiantly tried to support their unfortunate tenants:

"Many of these landlords, as well as the clergy, are most assiduously working in all ways in their power. They have imported large quantities of meal and rice, which they sell at prime cost; there being in many districts no dealers to supply these articles; and are making soup at their own houses, and dispensing daily to their famishing neighbours. Many of their ladies too have come nobly forward in the cause, and, at the sacrifice of much comfort, are much engaged in visiting or attending to the poor, employing the women in knitting, spinning, etc. But as the landlord cannot obtain his rents, and the incomes of other classes are diminished, the burden of supporting great numbers of people, fearfully increasing every day, falls heavily upon the few; who are now less able than ever to bear it."[39]

Of the many vivid and at times poignant accounts of conditions during the famine none matches in eloquence and force the appeal written in December 1846 by Mr Cummins, a justice of the peace in Cork, to Lord Wellington urging Britain to come to Ireland's aid;

"Being aware that I should have to witness scenes of frightful hunger, I provided myself with as much bread as five men could carry, and on reaching the spot I was surprised to find the wretched hamlet apparently deserted. I entered some of the hovels to ascertain the cause, and the scenes that presented themselves were such as no tongue or pen can convey the slightest idea of. In the first six famished and ghastly skeletons, to all appearance dead, were huddled in a corner on some filthy straw, their sole covering what seemed a ragged horse-cloth, and their wretched legs hanging about, naked above the knees. I approached in horror, and found by a low moaning they were alive, they were in fever — four children, a woman, and what had once been a man. It is impossible to go through the details, suffice it to say, that in a few minutes I was surrounded by at least 200 of such phantoms, such frightful spectres as no words can describe. By far the greater number were delirious, either from famine or from fever. Their demoniac yells are still ringing in my ears, and their horrible images are fixed upon my brain. My heart sickens at the recital, but I must go on. In another case — decency would forbid what follows, but it must be told — my clothes were nearly torn off in my endeavours to escape from the throng of pestilence around, when my neck-cloth was seized from behind by a grip which compelled me to turn, I found myself grasped by a woman with an infant, just born, in her arms, and the remains of a filthy sack across her loins — the sole covering of herself and babe. The same morning the police opened a house on the adjoining lands, which was observed shut for many days, and two frozen corpses were found lying upon the mud floor, half devoured by the rats.

My Lord, you are an old and justly honoured man. It is yet in your power to add another honour to your age, to fix another star, and that the brightest in your galaxy of glory. You have access to our young and gracious Queen, lay these things before her. She is a woman, she will not allow decency to be outraged. She has at her command the means of at least mitigating the sufferings of the wretched survivors in this tragedy. They will soon be few, indeed, in the district I speak of, if help be longer withheld. Once more, my Lord Duke, in the name of starving thousands, I implore you, break the frigid and flimsy chain of official etiquette, and save the land of your birth — the kindred of that gallant Irish blood which you have so often seen lavished to support the honour of the British name — and let there be inscribed upon your tomb *Servata Hibernia*."[40]

The famine fevers raged in Dublin with no less virulence than in the country. The city hospitals were better equipped to deal with epidemics but were soon overwhelmed by an influx of famine victims, many already ill with fever, from the country. Crowds of fever stricken patients beset the closed gates of the fever hospitals which erected temporary tents and sheds to accommodate as many as possible. In March of 1847 Cork Street Fever Hospital accommodated within the main hospital and in the temporary sheds and tents 14,766 patients of whom about 2,000 died. The pattern was similar in the fever hospitals throughout the capital.[41]

39. Hall and stairway of a Merrion Square house. By courtesy of Dr. P. Horne. *(see p. 173)*

40. "Inniscorrig", Coliemore, Co. Dublin. The country home of Dominic Corrigan. By courtesy of the present owners. Photograph by E. O'Brien. *(see p. 173)*

41. George Petrie (1789-1866). From a drawing by Charles Grey in the Royal College of Surgeons in Ireland. By courtesy of the College of Surgeons. Photograph by J. Hall. (see p. 177)

42. *Helen Faucit (1817-1898). From a drawing of Miss Faucit as Antigone by Frederick Burton. By courtesy of the National Gallery of Ireland.* *(see p. 178)*

43. *William Wilde and William Stokes sharing a bottle of beer. From a photograph taken by Lord Justice Fitzgibbon. By courtesy of the Royal College of Surgeons in Ireland.* (see p. 178)

44. *Frederick William Burton (1816-1900). From a portrait by George Francis Mulvany. By courtesy of the National Gallery of Ireland.*
(see p. 179)

45. *James Clarence Mangan (1803-1849). From a water colour of Mangan's deathmask by Frederick Burton. By courtesy of the National Gallery of Ireland.* *(see p. 179)*

46. *Charles Lever (1806-1872). From an engraving of a portrait by Phiz published in "Our Mess", Volume I, 1843. Photograph by D. Davison.* *(see p. 181)*

47. Robert Kane (1809-1890). From an engraving of a portrait by George Mulvany. By courtesy of the National Library of Ireland. Photograph by D. Davison. *(see p. 193)*

48. A peasent's hovel. By courtesy of The Illustrated London News.

49. Emigrants for America and Canada waiting on the quayside at Cork. By courtesy of the Radio Times Hulton Picture Gallery.

50. The Royal College of Physicians of Ireland, Kildare Street, Dublin. From an engraving in the Irish Builder. *By courtesy of the National Library of Ireland.*   *(see p. 241)*

51. The Great Hall of the College of Physicians. From an engraving in the Irish Builder. *By courtesy of the National Library of Ireland.*
                                                                                         (see p. 241)

52. *Dominic John Corrigan (1802-1880). From a portrait of Stephen Catterson Smith, Snr. in the Royal College of Physicians of Ireland. By courtesy of the College of Physicians. Photograph by D. Davison.*
(see p. 242)

53. Dominic John Corrigan (1802-1880). The statue by John Henry Foley in the Statue Hall of the Royal College of Physicians of Ireland. By courtesy of the College of Physicians. Photograph by D. Davison.
(see p. 242)

54. Henry Marsh (1790-1860). The statue by John Henry Foley in the Statue Hall of the Royal College of Physicians of Ireland. By courtesy of the College of Physicians. Photograph by D. Davison.
(see p. 243)

55. *William Stokes (1804-1878). The statue by John Henry Foley in the Statue Hall of the Royal College of Physicians of Ireland. By courtesy of the College of Physicians. Photograph by D. Davison.*
(see p. 243)

56. Robert Graves (1796-1853). The statue by Albert Bruce-Joy in the Statue Hall of the Royal College of Physicians of Ireland. By courtesy of the College of Physicians. Photograph by D. Davison. *(see p. 243)*

57. *Dominic John Corrigan (1802-1880). From a photo-engraving on porcelain. By courtesy of Dr. P. Horne. Photograph by J. Hall.*

The government did provide large sums of money, but once the fever flames were blazing, there was little that could be done to contain the conflagration, other than alleviate the suffering of the victims, and try to anticipate how best to rehabilitate the nation once the fires burnt themselves out as they must inevitably do. One of the greatest problems in providing food for the rural areas was transport. There were virtually no railways, and what roads existed were often inadequate. Another problem was that the Indian meal provided had to be cooked thoroughly to be digestible and often it was eaten half-boiled, the result being that, "Instead of nourishing the people, (it) actually increased the mortality, inducing, as it did, bowel complaints that soon proved fatal."[42]

If a fisheries policy could have been implemented speedily thousands of lives would have been saved. Indeed grants were made to Claddagh fishermen to enable them to redeem their nets from pawn and to repair their boats,[43] but for the most part ignorance and the customary dependence on the potato, rendered all such efforts futile:

> "Dunfanaghy is a little fishing town, situated on a bay remarkably adapted for a fishing population: the sea is teeming with fish of the finest description, waiting, we might say, to be caught. Many of the inhabitants gain a portion of their living by this means; but so rude is their tackle, and so fragile and liable to be upset are their primitive boats or coracles, made of wickerwork over which sail cloth is stretched, that they can only venture to sea in fine weather; and thus, with food almost in sight, the people starve, because they have no one to teach them to build boats more adapted to this rocky coast, than those in use by their ancestors many centuries ago."[44]

One of the remarkable features of the disaster was the charity and benevolence of groups in Ireland, England and most notably America. The most prominent of these was the Society of Friends to which Ireland owes an incalculable debt. This body of charitably-minded people not only collected nearly £200,000, (of which nearly £140,000 came from America),[45] but also saw to its intelligent disposal through the selfless energies of its members, among whom one of the most energetic was Jonathan Pim.[46]

Estimates of the number who died or emigrated during the famine often conflict, and there were many exaggerated assessments of the magnitude of the catastrophe. In Dr Curran's obituary notice (he died from typhus) the writer estimated that nearly a million persons had died from famine, or its consequences, up to the latter part of 1847. This, according to MacArthur, is certainly an exaggeration, but the estimate, "If made applicable to the whole of the famine, may not be far from the truth."[47] This sober assessment would not seem to be inaccurate, and is supported by examination of the census returns. In the middle of the year 1845, some months before the first appearance of the potato blight, the census returns give the population of Ireland as 8,295,061 and in the middle of 1853, "when things may be said to have been restored to a normal condition, it had, on the same authority, fallen to 6,198,984, this being equivalent to a reduction, within the space of eight years, of 2,096,077 or more than a fourth of the former population."[48] Examined from another point of view, it was calculated that the natural increase between 1841 and 1851 should have resulted in a population of over nine million, whereas the census return for 1851 showed it to be just over six and a half million.[49] We can accept then that more than two million of the population was lost in a decade. The exact number that died will never be known, but a careful examination of the evidence available makes it "reasonably certain that some 800,000 people, almost one-tenth of the entire population at that time, perished between the autumn of 1846 and the spring of 1851,"[50] though some historians have put this figure as high as a million and a half.[51] Emigration accounted for the remainder — just over a million.[52] Of these the majority went to the United States and British North America.[53] Many met a fate as bad, if not worse than that from which they sought escape. The mortality on the ships carrying these unfortunate emigrants was often of horrific proportions and they soon earned the name "coffin ships." Robert Graves has recorded that two emigrant ships "the *Ceylon*, with 257 steerage passengers, had 117 deaths, and 115 in fever on her arrival. The *Loosthank* with 349 steerage passengers, had 117 deaths, and only 20 escaped fever."[54] In nine months nearly 10,000 Irish emigrants to Canada alone had perished from fever.[55] For those who landed and survived life was to prove hard in a hostile environment, where as Woodham Smith has written it was to take the emigrant Irish a long time to adjust:

> "It is a matter of history that the Irish political record has some black spots. Irish emigrants, especially of the famine years, became, with rare exceptions, what their transatlantic environment made them, children of the slums, rebuffed, scorned by respectable citizens and exploited by the less respectable. The Irish were the most unfortunate emigrants and the poorest, they took longest to be accepted, longest to become genuinely assimilated, they waited longest before the opportunities the United States offers were freely available to them.
>
> The story of the Irish in the New World is not a romantic story of liberty and success, but the history of a bitter struggle, as bitter, as painful, though not as long-drawn-out, as the struggle by which the Irish at last won the right to be a nation."[56]

The mortality from fever among doctors had always been high, but during the Great Famine the number of deaths was unprecedented. Stokes with his colleague Cusack compiled a bill of medical mortality showing that whereas mortality among combatant officers had been 10 per cent during the war years, 1811-1814, the mortality among dispensary medical officers for the twenty-five years prior to 1843 had amounted to 24 per cent, one in every two deaths being due to typhus.[57] Exact figures for mortality throughout the Great Famine are not available but many fell victim to the fevers they sought to cure: "In Munster in one year (1847) 48 died, mostly of typhus: seven died similarly in that year in Cavan . . . Of the 473 medical officers appointed by the board of health to special fever duty, one in every thirteen died at his post."[58]

Many of the hospital returns during the famine period are incomplete because of the death or illness of the medical officer. In the Sick Poor Institution in Meath Street, where Corrigan had experienced the major famine of 1826-27, the figures for four months of 1848 "representing probably over 6,000 cases are missing, because of the 'almost contemporaneous' deaths of two members of the medical staff from typhus, and the illness of three others from the same disease."[59]

The Central Board of Health had been established to combat the dreadful forces of hunger, disease, poverty, decay and death. It was doomed to failure from the outset, not so much because it misread the portents, but because the most it could have possibly hoped to achieve was palliation of suffering, and perhaps some shortening of the duration of the famine. The board became the scapegoat for a nation experiencing an appalling catastrophe. The board now had power to appoint medical officers, and one of its duties in this regard was to make recommendations on an appropriate scale of fees. This was to involve Corrigan in a controversy that was to do much damage to his career and personal credibility. The board recommended a fee of five shillings per day in addition to any permanent salary that the doctor might have. This payment was meagre especially in view of the fact that previous health boards had made greater awards and if for no other reason that many doctors were themselves dying from the fever epidemic. Moreover dispensary doctors were not well paid, the average income at the time being only seventy-one pounds per annum.[60]

The profession was astounded by the five shillings a day salary. William Wilde promoted a public meeting of the profession on the occasion of Dr Curran (who later died of typhus fever) refusing appointment to a fever hospital,[61] and 1,160 practitioners signed a memorial to His Excellency George William Frederick, Earl of Clarendon, Lord Lieutenant-General and General Governor of Ireland: "It is right to draw your Excellency's attention to the fact, that statistical returns for upwards of twenty-five years exhibit a fearful mortality from fever among the medical men of this country, and recent events have shown that from the same cause we have to deplore the loss of many of the best and most efficient practitioners who contracted typhus fever in the discharge of their duties among the sick poor. We most strongly, but respectfully protest against the ... five shillings per day ... offered by the Board of Health for the discharge of that onerous responsible and dangerous duty."[62] To which they received the reply that "the lordships of the treasury are of the opinion that the remuneration is as high, as under the circumstances of the case, they should be justified in granting."

The newspapers took sides with the profession, with the exception of *The Evening Post*, which attempted to attribute the profession's indignation to political ends: "We began to think (we could not help it) that there was more in this than met the eye, and we could not resist the conclusion which has finally grown upon us that consideration for the 'hardships and injustice sustained by the profession' formed a very small element in the agitation and that one of the main objects was to make use of the alleged grievance as a means of exciting the opposition of the profession against the government in the approaching general election."[62] This did little to appease the outraged doctors. The government hid behind the Board of Health, and it was not long before Corrigan was singled out to take the brunt of public and professional opprobrium. The *Nation* pointed out that only a year earlier Corrigan had protested against fever hospitals being built in proximity to poor houses, but "he had not, as yet, felt the pulse of an excellency. However, since he has done so new light has burst on him and closed his mouth. In every part of Ireland, for the last six months, fever hospitals have been erected in connection with – generally speaking, on the ground with – the poor houses; and every frightful consequence predicted by Dr Corrigan has occurred ... Put the man in office himself, change his point of view, immerse his head in a cocked-hat ... and (he) becomes a partner in the insulting offer to the members of his own profession, of five shillings a day as state payment, for constant fever practice, in sinks of contagion whose destructive atmosphere no man knows better than he."[62]

The profession had in the opinion of the popular press been treated ignominiously by the government when it submitted its memorial to Lord Clarendon: "Men of European fame, whose opinions dictate to life in the schools of Paris and of Germany, – men who still have preserved for Ireland, the foremost rank in surgical and medical science, — men of all religions, of all politics, stood together, — an Irish profession at last." The *Lancet* was of the opinion that the members of the Board of Health should have resigned rather than be party to the award "or else they must take the universal reprobation of their brethern."[62]

Slowly the medical and lay press began to turn its frustrated acrimony towards Corrigan, not because he was negligent in his duties as a member of the board, but because he had in effect been the most diligent of its members. David La Touche criticising the board's general inefficiency stated that he "seldom found anyone there but Dr Corrigan," and this is born out in the records of attendance at the board's meetings; from March 31 to August 14 1847, Sir Philip Crampton attended 42 meetings, Sir Robert Kane 2, Mr Twistleton 12, and Corrigan 87.[63]

The most vitriolic attack of all was to come from his colleague Robert Graves in the Meath hospital, who in a thirty page letter to the *Dublin Quarterly Journal of Medical Science*[62] launched a personal attack against Corrigan that in a later age would have been answered by a libel writ. Graves and his colleagues were furious that the government in appointing the Board of Health did not ask the Colleges of Physicians and Surgeons who they would wish to nominate. The government had, in fact, appointed a recent president of the College of Surgeons, Sir Philip Crampton, and Sir Robert Kane, a fellow of the College of Physicians, who, though not an actively practising doctor, did have more knowledge of the potato blight than any doctor and was chosen for this reason. Graves hoped that he would soon hear "That my friend Sir Robert Kane has succeeded in the process of self-analysis so as to eliminate and get rid of the MD element from himself, as being the most unprofitable portion of his composition."

Corrigan was not of course a fellow of either college and it is this fact that seems to have irritated Graves more than all else: "As to my friend Dr Corrigan, no one will deny his ability or industry, but many will doubt his wisdom in accepting the amount of responsibility which has necessarily devolved on him; for during Sir Philip Crampton's absence in London and Sir Robert Kane's uniform non-attendance, Dr Corrigan was for many weeks *The Board of Health* and, consequently, neither the College of Surgeons nor the College of Physicians was represented at that board." Had the doctor from the Liberties been rising a little too speedily for Graves' liking? "But Dr Corrigan may be excused from becoming a little giddy when he ventures into the same car with Sir Philip, and, to the amazement of all, suddenly finds himself at an altitude so elevated, that his companion, although a veteran aeronaut, betrays distinct evidence of alarm."

Graves goes on to question Corrigan's ability to attend to the business of the board in view of his many other commitments. As he was the most diligent of its members he must therefore, in Graves' view, accept censure for the board's inadequacies. All of which might be fair enough, but Graves failed to take account of the vast effort Corrigan had put into the board, and that poor though the five shillings a day award might be, the board was achieving a certain amount of success against fearful odds; moreover any success it did have was due to Corrigan's industry: "The country at large owed much to the unceasing energy and immense capacity for work which Corrigan then displayed. After a hard day's work of hospital and private practice it was no unusual thing for him to devote six or eight hours to tedious office work, receiving and answering communications from all parts of Ireland."[64]

In the course of his very long letter Graves expressed fears about the government's real intentions in relation to the profession: "The moment that charity ceased to be the sole guardian of the sick poor — the moment that public boards, government officials, and local committees, took into their hands the superintendence and administration of medical relief — that moment Mammon interfered and spoiled the goodly work. Medical practitioners had now to deal with hard task masters, who, misinterpreting the motives of their former exertions, argued, that the labour so long gratuitously bestowed, could always be commanded at a small price . . . But, in truth, the English government has of late been pursuing systematically a line of conduct tending to depreciate the medical profession in the eyes of the public." These sentiments on state-controlled medicine have since been reiterated by successive generations of doctors. He realised that the profession should not rely on support from the public: "They feel no sympathy . . . and they think that all MDs have a right to die for the benefit of the public . . . ."

Many of the points raised by Graves were valid, but his attack on Corrigan was unkind and excessive. Bearing in mind the difficulties under which Corrigan was labouring to make the board function at all, Graves' criticisms were misdirected, and he should have concentrated on the government. But Graves tended to act impetuously. Stokes, who kept out of the whole debacle, summed up Graves' character thus: "It is to be observed that as his mind was open and unsuspicious he occasionally fell into the error of thinking aloud without considering the nature of his audience, and of letting his wit play more freely, and his sarcasm when defending the right cut more deeply than caution might dictate."[65]

Corrigan chose to remain silent, and resisted the call from the journals and the press for his resignation from the board. To do so would have merely given credence to the accusations levelled against him. He would have done well to let the storm clouds pass but unwisely he chose this time to seek election to honorary fellowship of the King's and Queen's College of Physicians in Ireland. Immediately the *Lancet* spoke out: "But at the present juncture for any professional body to do an action which might and would be construed into an approval by the profession of the Board of Health, and its five-shilling-a-day plan of remuneration for medical services, is nothing less than an act of gross professional treachery and treason."[66] It went on to point out that its stand was not a personal one against Corrigan: "His election to the honorary fellowship of the College of Physicians in Ireland would do that college a credit," but to elect him would be taken as "a sign and seal on the part of the College of Physicians of their approval of a board which has, whatever its intentions degraded the Irish medical profession and, against whose acts the great majority of the college has already protested in signing the representation."

Successful though Corrigan now was he had been denied access to the hierarchy of the profession, namely one of the Royal Colleges through whose offices he might have hoped to influence the course of medicine. The *Lancet* again put his position quite bluntly: "The matter stands simply thus: Dr Corrigan is not a member of any Irish college, but is a graduate of the University of Edinburgh, and though he has been several times, and by several presidents of the College of Physicians (of England) solicited during the last few years to join that body, he has hitherto always indignantly refused."[66] If this is correct, it is difficult to see why Corrigan would have refused the honour. In what appears to be a curious strategy he had "upon the late jubilee at the Royal College of Surgeons . . . used every influence to gain the fellowship of that body without examination, but he was rejected."[66] Presumably he saw this as a means of gaining fellowship of the Irish College of Surgeons, and he may have had ambitions towards securing two very firm feet in the medical establishment — one in each college. Corrigan had always been interested in surgery, and there are certificates for the years of 1833, 1834 and 1837 showing that he attended student lectures in surgery and the clinical lectures in surgery at The Charitable Infirmary, and this when he was a physician to the Hospital.[67] This was a most unusual course for an eminent physician to take. In fact in 1843 he sat for the surgical diploma of the College of Surgeons of England. "On presenting himself before the Board of Examiners he was asked: 'Are you the author of the essay on patency of the aortic valve?' On replying in the affirmative he was presented with the diploma without further question."[68] His surgical colleagues thought highly of him and they elected him president of the prestigious Dublin Medico-Chirurgical Society in 1840. Whatever his intentions may have been with the surgeons, he was in serious difficulties with his colleagues, the physicians. The *Lancet*, in fact, alleged that much canvassing had taken place and that "as the corporation is very small, men are about to be brought from England, and their expenses paid, in order to vote for the job on Monday."[69] If these tactics were employed they were to no avail. Graves and those fellows who had been so incensed by the Maunsell episode and by his role in the Board of Health saw to it that he was black-beaned.

For one of Corrigan's eminence and fame to suffer black-beaning by the Irish College of Physicians was a devastating

ignominy. There may have been some sectarian influences
to the College's action, and indeed, the college's history is
such in this regard that it would not be difficult to sustain
this viewpoint. However, there is little in Corrigan's papers
to suggest that this was so, and he did touch frequently on
this subject believing that there was no place for religious
discrimination in medicine: "The study of our profession is,
from its very nature, essentially calculated to create and
nurture habits of charity and mutual forbearance. Its study
trains the judgement not to censure the errors of others, but
to labour to correct its own. Taught from the earliest periods
of our education, to exercise our own powers of observation
and reasoning, we learn to accord to others that liberty of
thought which we claim for ourselves, and as we hourly meet
doubts and difficulties in the study of those laws which relate
to the material body, we shrink from the presumption of
daring to dogmatise for others upon what relates to an im-
material soul."[70] And when addressing the British Medical
Association in 1867 he had said of the medical profession:
"And among the bonds that unite the three divisions of our
kingdom together there are none stronger than those of our
profession, soaring in its exercise above all sectarian discords.
We know no difference of race, or creed, or colour, for every
man is our neighbour, and when we remember that the
Redeemer, while on earth, chose the healing of the sick as
one of the most impressive evidences of His divine mission,
we must ever hold in respect the exercise of a profession that
devotes its efforts to the same object."[71] No, it seems that
the college's motive in black-beaning Corrigan was more base
than even the warped ideology of sectarianism. In a letter
many years later to Michael Hicks Beach he wrote, "I was
black-beaned from the college being a candidate for the degree
of honorary fellow and a report was then forwarded depre-
cating my good repute . . . This was done in the hope of preventing me from receiving from her Majesty the honour of
'Physician to the Queen'." He goes on to say, "It required
much strength to face this, but I did face it out for about
ten years when the opportunity to end it came."[72]

The government watched all of this in silence. The famine
reached its horrible climax. Corrigan and his colleagues did

what they could in the Hardwicke Fever Hospital, and on the Board of Health Corrigan worked tirelessly to organise and coordinate medical relief.

In 1847 there were signs that the worst of the epidemic might be over, when one of the most dreaded of fevers, cholera, broke out in Ireland in December, 1848.[73] There had been an epidemic of cholera in England earlier that year, and this soon reached Belfast from Scotland. The mention of cholera in the nineteenth century could cause great public anxiety and sometimes panic. The medical profession often bore the brunt of public frustration and hostility. There are many reported instances of attacks on doctors, their houses and hospitals.[74] In the English epidemic of 1832 it was widely rumoured and believed that doctors were using the cholera epidemic to increase the supply of cadavers to the medical schools for dissection. In the same epidemic, Stokes and a surgical colleague diagnosed a mysterious death in Kingstown (now Dun Laoghaire) as cholera, and both only escaped injury by driving dangerously away from the angry mob who feared not alone for themselves, but for the disastrous effect an announcement of cholera would have on the holiday season.[75]

The cholera bacillus (*Vibrio cholerae*) was not discovered until 1884, and in the mid-nineteenth century the mode of spread of cholera (by contaminated water) was not known.[76] The medical profession of the period was however, much preoccupied by the cause of this mysterious disease. There was no shortage of "theories of cholera" which included "the telluric, electric, and izonic theories; the animalcular and fungoid; the zymotic and humoral; and the theories naming ingesta, or putrid effluvia, or a specific poison as in small-pox."[77] The profession was divided into two main camps: the contagionists, among whom in Ireland Graves was the most vocal, maintained that cholera could be passed from a victim to a healthy person, and the non-contagionists, among whom stood Corrigan, who held that the disease was not spread in this way because persons coming into contact with cholera often escaped infection. Although each viewpoint seems irreconcilable the reasoning in both theories was not, in fact, very different. The controversy did, however, have serious implications in the application of measures to control cholera. The anticontagionists wanted to abolish quarantine,[78] and the Central Board of Health influenced by Corrigan adopted this view, and advised that isolation of cholera patients was unnecessary. In August 1848 the Central Board of Health published a set of general instructions and precautions to deal with the threatened epidemic of cholera: "The Central Board of Health are anxious to impress upon all persons, the important differences that exist between cholera and fever, with respect to the mode of propagation of these epidemic diseases. Fever, it is well known, is highly contagious, or easily propagated from one individual to another, while all experience shows that cholera is rarely, if ever, contagious; consequently, the separation of the sick from the healthy — a measure so essential to check the spread of fever — is not required in cholera, and the friends and relatives of persons attacked with cholera may be under no apprehension of catching the disease, and need not be deterred from paying to the sick, in their own dwellings, every needful assistance and attention."[79] Graves opposed this decision vigorously, and many of the local health committees acted on his advice rather than adhere to the official pronouncements.[80] Moreover, the public seem to have recognised that isolation was beneficial. The ill were moved to barns or sheds, and the door was built up with turf to shut off the patient and the nurse from the healthy. Food was passed in through the window, often on a shovel, by relatives or friends who were careful not to handle vessels used by the infected person. The burning of infected houses by neighbours was widespread; sometimes the fear of infection was so great that the walls and roof of the house were broken so as to bury the bodies of the fever-victims, or the house was fired without removing the bodies.[81]

The cholera epidemic was severe and the mortality in the towns was particularly heavy. The official figures give the cholera deaths as 2,502 in 1848, 30,156 in 1849, and 1,768 in 1850, but MacArthur believes that this is an exaggeration of the true mortality from cholera.[82] How much the misguided recommendations of the Central Board of Health contributed to the spread of the disease is difficult to determine. Even though Corrigan was wrong in believing that cholera was not contagious, and despite the board's recommendations emphasising this and discouraging isolation, its advice on the general measures for coping with the disease were sound. The board did not, for example, advise dispensing completely with hospital care, but it warned that if treatment was withheld while awaiting admission to the already overcrowded and exhausted hospitals, the delay might be fatal. The board, moreover gave advice that if heeded might have done more than isolation to limit the spread of the disease: "Do not allow any stagnant water or dung heaps to remain around your dwellings — clean out all sewers without delay; this should be done at once, without waiting for the approach of the disease; it will be unsafe and it will be too late to do it when cholera shall have broken out . . . Be careful that the water used as drink is of good quality."[79]

Cholera was not the only "new" epidemic to afflict the unfortunate nation in the waning months of the Great Famine. Sir William Wilde and Professor Arthur Jacob, the two most eminent oculists of the day, visited the principal workhouses in the country where an infective disease of the eyes known as "purulent or catarrhal ophthalmia" was threatening the sight of many of the inmates. In two years, (1849-50) over 40,000 were afflicted, of whom nearly 800 suffered partial loss of sight, some 300 lost the sight of one eye, and over 100 became completely blind.[83]

The Great Famine finally petered out in 1850, and with the end of the fever acts in 1850 so too did the Board of Health conclude its work. Looking back on its activities it is easy with knowledge and the righteous virtue of hindsight to judge its mistakes too harshly, and to discount the significant role it played in ameliorating the suffering of the famine victims, and in limiting the spread of disease. MacArthur, in his masterly analysis of the medical aspects of the famine is of the opinion that there was only one measure that would have had an immediate and far-reaching effect, namely, the provision of a large number of hospitals to isolate all the sick as cases arose and thus limit infection.[84] However, he asks realistically: "In view of the obstruction offered later to the board by local authorities when the epidemic was actually upon them, what would have been their response, and that of the treasury, to proposals to provide hospital beds to accommodate tens of thousands of fever cases which did not then exist, and which might never exist?" Once the starving millions of the country were in the grip of the louse-borne typhus and relapsing fevers there was little that disinfective measures could do to eradicate these diseases. Stoving of contaminated clothing and bedding in heated ovens and by boiling might have been of benefit but could not have been organised on a scale large enough to have any significant effect. Even today, as MacArthur has emphasised, "Only by wholesale treatment of a population with the new insecticides and this compulsorily enforced by some authority with the power of military law could epidemic typhus and relapsing fever of a like degree be stamped out effectively and with despatch."[84] It was unfortunate that the board did not enjoy the confidence of the medical profession and that it had been so vindictive in its dealings with Corrigan who had devoted more time and effort to famine relief than most of his colleagues. The medical profession as a whole reacted in an emotional and immature manner to the five shillings a day award to dispensary doctors, and it was a serious defect of judgement on Graves' part to castigate Corrigan rather than the government for not obtaining a more equitable sum. MacArthur has pondered how it was that his opponents "fancied that, by some magic which Corrigan did not possess, they in his place could have softened the stony heart of the treasury in London; clearly they had never studied the peculiar quality that distinguishes the nether millstone."[84]

Stokes, aware of the great difficulties with which Corrigan and the board had had to contend, wrote:

> ". . . if many (lives) were lost, perhaps ignorantly, let us think on the number saved. We cannot be suddenly wise. Nations, as well as individuals, must purchase experience, even though the cost be ruinous. And whatever fault we may find with the modes adopted for relief to the sufferers in the famine of 1847, we must applaud the intention, and be grateful for the efforts that were made."[85]

The Great Famine is said to have ended in 1850, but it would be more correct to say it abated. Ireland was never without poverty, and the dependence on the potato was to persist with the result that further famines were inevitable. Before the close of the Victorian era Ireland would have no less than four more famines.[86] Social conditions were to change little in the nineteenth century, and Carlyle found Ireland a depressing place in the aftermath of the famine:

"Flat, flat, waste of moor; patches of wretched oats — then peat bogs, black pools; the roofless cottages not far off at the time. Potatoes — poor cottier digging his little plot of them, three or four little children eagerly 'gatherin' for him: pathetic to look upon."[87]

The workhouses he found to be particularly repellant:

". . . the first I had ever seen, quite shocked me. Huge arrangements for eating, baking, stacks of Indian meal stirabout; 1,000 or 2,000 great hulks of men lying piled up within brick walls in such a country, in such a day! Did a greater violence to the law of nature ever before present itself to sight, if one had an eye to see it?"[88]

William Wilde in a letter to Sir Thomas Larcom expressed the dissatisfaction shared by so many of the profession at the way Britain had handled the famine:

"The present year is now drawing to a close; and all who have witnessed its singular and melancholy scenes must look back upon it with wonder and with dread. Its history will be a darkened page in the annals of our country, recording events whose nature may warrant the incredulity of after times. It will be difficult to believe at a future, and we hope, a happier day, that, within a short distance of the capital of England, the seat of British intelligence, British power, wealth, and plenty, nearly a million of her subjects died of hunger or its consequences; of want, not resulting from their own improvidence, but from the long-threatened, yet not till then complete failure of a crop which was their only support. The record of this great and dreadful fact is engraved in characters so deep and strong that age will not efface them."[89]

Stokes also was sickened and depressed by not only the famine but by the repressive hand of British politics on Ireland's development:

> "Oh! that we could all unite in striving for civil and religious liberty that this fair and lovely land, for which God has done so much and man so little, might put forth its smothered energies which now burst forth only to ruin and destroy."[90]

Wilde's and Stokes's recriminations are directed more at Victorian society than at the British government though it must collectively with society share in the opprobrium. If we are to pass judgement, or to apportion blame for the disaster we must first examine the nineteenth century social and political milieu so that our conclusions are made within the context of the conditions of that society; any assessment made superficially on the basis of contemporary attitudes will serve only to confuse. Britain stands culpable for ignoring the repeated warnings of earlier famines, and Corrigan's prediction of serious fever epidemics. Once the famine had gripped the nation in circumstances so favourable to epidemics of disease, the government probably did as much as might be considered reasonable. It could, it is true have done more, but it might also have done appreciably less. In making our assessment of that terrible decade in Irish history, it is salutory to reflect that so called twentieth century civilisation permits calamities of equal and even greater magnitude to occur in parts of the world no further from affluence and plenty than Ireland is from England.

8

Leader of the Profession

As Ireland emerged from the depression of the Great Famine, Corrigan's fortunes began to change for the better. In 1847 the government demonstrated its regard for his efforts on Her Majesty's behalf by creating him physician-in-ordinary to Queen Victoria in Ireland, an honour never before granted to a Catholic.[1] That the government valued his administrative ability is evident from the fact that in 1850 he was approached unofficially through Sir Philip Crampton by the lord lieutenant, then Lord Clarendon, to become medical commissioner in Ireland.[2] This, he declined because the salary of £1,200 per annum would not compensate him for his private practice which he would have had to relinquish. In a letter to Sir Philip he wrote: "The salary named is too small. It would involve too great a sacrifice of professional income on my part and too serious a loss to my family." He must have thought long and hard about declining a position that would have given him the authority not only to direct the Poor Laws and medical relief in the country, but also "the general direction of the profession."[3] He may have felt that in addition to loss of income he would have been denied the freedom to express himself as an individual.

Corrigan did, however, accept a government appointment on the Lunatic Asylums (Ireland) Commission from 1856-68.[4] Characteristically he was soon at loggerheads with his fellow commissioners on the important matter of medical supervision of asylums. The commissioners wanted the resident physician and manager to be in charge whereas Corrigan sought a practising doctor to visit daily in addition, so that the responsibility did not rest only with one individual, as he believed it "wrong to commit the medical, surgical, and moral treatment of the inmates of a lunatic asylum, female as well as male to the uncontrolled management of any one individual."[5] He realised that the mentally ill were at a great disadvantage:

> "It must be remembered that the inmates of a lunatic asylum present no analogy to the inmates of any other public institution. The inmates of gaols, workhouses, and hospitals are sane, and can bring their complaints before visitors while in those institutions, and will be listened to, or on leaving, can have them investigated; while the poor creatures who are the inmates of a lunatic asylum may be terrified into silence, incapable of stating their wrongs or their complaints, and perhaps well-grounded assertions of past ill-treatment will be considered as the mere delusions of their imagination."

He was aware that abuses to the mentally ill were not uncommon, and to illustrate this he cited a case of an old man who was killed by cold shower treatment with the coroner's verdict of death due to heart disease being returned. An inquiry showed that, "six hundred and eighteen gallons of water, at a temperature of forty-five degrees, not many degrees above freezing, must have been discharged uninterruptedly over the person of Dolley as he stood in the shower bath, of which the construction was such, as to render, during its continuance, respiration more than ordinarily difficult." Corrigan had no difficulty in providing examples of abuse; his concern was not so much for the cases of abuse discovered, "but to reflect on how many may be concealed."

On this issue he was successful, as we learn from Mapother: "In reporting, a majority, (of the Commissioners) all now deceased, denied him the right of giving his opinion that there should be always an extern physician whose daily visits would prevent there being the suspicion that harshness or cruelty was practised by the managers. Dr G. Hardy (later Lord Cranbrook) moved for his written statement and such officers were consequently appointed."[6]

Throughout his life, Corrigan persisted in his efforts to obtain better conditions for "our weak-minded fellow-creatures." In 1872 he again drew attention to the abuses he had experienced as a visiting commissioner: "In – – – Asylum a male patient, in ward number two was found at our visit, strapped down in bed; in addition he was confined in a strait-waistcoat, with the sleeves knotted behind him; as he could only lie on his back, from a contrivance we shall presently describe, his suffering must have been very great. His arms were, moreover, confined with wrist-locks of hard leather, and his legs with leg-locks of similar kind, the strapping was so tight that he could not turn on either side, and any change of position was still more effectually prevented by a cylindrical stuffed bolster of about ten inches thick, which ran round the sides and top and bottom of the bed, in the centre of which the lunatic was retained as in a box, without power to turn or move. On liberating the patient, and raising him, he was very feeble, unable to stand, with pulse scarcely perceptible, and feet dark red and cold. The man had been under confinement in this state for four days and nights . . . When examined as to this case, the manager stated he was aware of the man's being in bed, but not of his having all these instruments of restraint upon him. No record of this case of restraint appears in the morning statement book."[7]

In 1849, two years after the Royal College of Physicians had black-beaned him, Trinity College bestowed on him its highest medical honour, a doctorate of medicine.[8] The College of Physicians appears to have remained resolute in its determination to keep Corrigan out. Then in 1855, eight years after the black-beaning, Corrigan made a move that must have confounded his enemies in the college. Dr Dominic Corrigan, physician-in-ordinary to Queen Victoria in Ireland, humbly sat with the final year students, many of whom he would have lectured, for the college's graduating examination, the Licentiate. In this he was, of course, successful and there was little that could now be done to stop his advancement to full fellowship of the college one year later. Then in 1857 William Stokes proposed him for highest office – the presidency – and he defeated his opponent Sir Henry Marsh who had been four times president by eighteen votes to three.[9] Corrigan had again demonstrated his determination and tenacity of purpose in overcoming apparently insurmountable odds to achieve his objective. He was to occupy the presidency for five successive years, a feat not since equalled. Corrigan's success was not only a personal triumph; the election of a Catholic to the highest office open to a physician was seen then as an outstanding event. "The people of Ireland regarded his career with peculiar interest and his success with gratified pride. This feeling was in no way sectarian, it was rather racial or national. They felt that intellectual triumph was their best and noblest vindication against the contumely which had fallen on them in consequence of the ignorance enforced upon the nation by the Penal Laws."[10]

What sort of an institute was this College of Physicians that Corrigan had so much difficulty in entering and of which he was now president? The college established as the Fraternity of Physicians by Dr John Stearne in 1654, was the second oldest medical corporation in the country.[11] In 1667 Charles II granted a royal charter and the Fraternity of Physicians became the College of Physicians in Dublin, and in 1692 under a new charter it was designated the Kings and Queen's College of Physicians in Ireland.[12]

If Corrigan looked back on the college's two hundred years of history, as he almost certainly did, he cannot have been impressed by the way it had managed its affairs. He may, in fact, have had difficulty escaping the impression that it had survived more in spite of than because of its own endeavours. The college had been established to improve medical standards, but this it did to only a limited extent. It violated the vast legacy of its first president Sir Patrick Dun time and time again, so much so that in 1799, Dr Robert Perceval, the then president, castigated the fellows accusing them of spending £333 14s 11d from Dun's funds to pay the law expenses of both sides in a case in which the college was defendant. He added that it was not expedient that management of Dun's estates should remain in the hands of the college. A committee appointed by the Irish House of Lords to enquire into the administration of the bequest, concluded that it had been grossly misused and that the college having no hospital in which to practice, had neglected the clinical development of medicine. The committee added furthermore that the fund had been misappropriated in providing claret for the president, twice paying for books purchased, in law suits in which the college was both plaintiff and defendant, and in loans to indigent members of the college, which in some instances had not been repaid. The upshot of the House of Lords Committee Report was the establishment of the hospital known today as Sir Patrick Dun's Hospital, an institute for which the benefactor had not, in fact, made stipulation. The college, furthermore, through neglect and indifference managed to lose most of Dun's library, which would today be a priceless legacy.[13]

Dun had left lands in Waterford, which the college never visited until 1811, by which time it appears the estate had shrunk by some 200 acres or so. Dr Hill who visited the estate drew up a strongly worded report:

"For a more ludicrous representation of the complete unacquaintance of the College respecting the real condition of their estates could not be made, then to exhibit them fretting on every frivolous occasion, rushing into law suits, under the guidance of agents as uninformed as themselves, and pertinaciously litigating, and squandering the money about an acre on one side, whilst twenty might easily be stolen from them in another . . . The foregoing circumstances, cannot but excite surprise in the mind of any person who should be told that a learned and honourable corporate body, invested with the sacred character of trustees, should have slumbered for more than a century in profound unacquaintance with the actual state of the trust; should never have possessed any connected series of maps of the estates; nor visited them till the present day."[14]

This comedy of errors had not escaped the satirical pen of Erinensis who wrote thus of the college in 1826:

"The proceedings of medical corporations might be counted by their abuses. Add up these items in their annals and you arrive with arithmetical certainty at the moment of their labours. Their monotonous existence seems to be disturbed only by an occasional transition from indolence to the most mischievous activity. From the number of their avocations they have scrupulously

excluded the interest of science and the ungrateful cultivation of humanity. The greatest efforts of which they
happen to be guilty, from time to time, never transcend
that impassable barrier of exertion — *self*."[15]

The college had in the opinion of Erinensis failed in its charter
granted obligation to improve medical standards:

"By some fatality, however, incident to English legislation when Ireland is the patient to be treated, this
benign prescription of an incorporated College of
Physicians, intended to secure the longevity of the
inhabitants, entirely failed in its object. In spite of
the new college, its charter, and its great powers, the
quacks continued to furnish the old quantity of work
for the coffin-makers by the exercise of their mortal
craft, just as if no such measures had ever been pro-
jected to check this unnecessary expenditure of life."[15]

Corrigan must have reviewed this catalogue of mismanagement
with some dismay but he was not one to dwell for too long
on the past; development was needed to ensure the future.
The college's greatest deficiency, in Corrigan's opinion, was
the lack of a dignified place in which to hold its meetings.
It had over the years made feeble efforts to obtain premises,
but for most of its life its meetings had been held in the home
of the president. In 1818 rooms were made available in Sir
Patrick Dun's Hospital and it was here that the college met
when Corrigan became president.

In 1860 just as Corrigan began his first term as president,
the Kildare Street Club wrote to the college offering their
premises for £6,000, as the Club was preparing to move to a
new building lower down the street. Corrigan made an offer
of £5,000 for the premises, fittings and furniture and this was
accepted. He then asked the fellows to subscribe; he and
Nelligan gave £500, Sir Henry Marsh £200 and William Stokes
£150. A fortuitous event was to provide Corrigan with the
challenging prospect of erecting a purpose-built premises for
the college. A fire swept through the premises of the old
Kildare Street Club claiming three lives, embarrassing a maid
and manservant who had to make good their escape from the

latter's bedroom, and leaving only the billiard rooms and
racquet court of the club standing.[16]

On July 7, 1862 the foundation stone for the new college
was laid and the event was reported at length in the papers:
"The ceremony was performed by His Excellency the Lord
Lieutenant, in the presence of a distinguished assemblage of
nobility and gentry, including a considerable number of ladies
and the leading members of the medical and surgical profession. A platform was erected in the centre of the ground,
and at either side seats were enclosed for visitors who had
received invitations. The several fellows of the college were
present in their robes to receive His Excellency, who was
accompanied by Mr Hatchell, private secretary, Captain Willis
and Captain Moore ADC in waiting. The dais intended for His
Excellency and the fellows of the college was handsomely
carpeted, and His Excellency was conducted to a seat prepared
for him . . . His Excellency then proceeded to lay the first
stone, which was suspended by a windlass, a few feet from
the ground. In the cavity prepared for it was placed a glass
bottle containing some current coins of the realm."[17]

Not only would there be a new building; the college was
to change policy. The president lost no time in settling an
old score:

"The present year will be remarkable in our annals, not
alone as the era of the foundation of our new college,
but for an important improvement in legislation affecting
our body. For this advantage we are indebted to the
Chief Secretary for Ireland, the Right Hon. Sir Robert
Peel whose absence we regret, as we hoped to have the
pleasure of thanking him in person on this occasion.
The act introduced and passed by Sir Robert Peel will
come into operation on the first of September next.
Previously to the passing of this act we could only
elect to the fellowship of our college the graduates of
three universities, practically we were limited to one;
but after the first of next September we shall be no longer
thus trammelled. We shall have power to award without
distinction to all those of our profession whose personal
conduct and professional merits deserve it the fellowship of our college. We shall attain our true position,

recognising perfect freedom in education, and our only question henceforth will be, as it ought to be, what a man knows, not where he learned it. It is only just to the memory of Sir Patrick Dun to observe that no such restriction as that I have noticed, hampering the action of our college, existed in the charter obtained by him. It was imposed by an Act of Parliament of 1800."[17]

Corrigan determined to stay at the helm until the new college building was complete, but at the end of his first term of president, John Nelligan opposed him for the office and the voting was even at fourteen for each. Corrigan had no hesitation in using his casting vote in favour of himself.[18]

The press reported favourably on Corrigan's successive elections to the presidency of the college:

"At the stated annual meeting of the College of Physicians, held on Friday last, the college unanimously elected Dr Corrigan as president of the college for the third time. The compliment thus paid to this eminent physician is, we believe, altogether without precedent. The president must feel that this rare distinction, coming as it does from his professional brethren, is a worthy endorsement of the high esteem in which he is held by the public — an endorsement as elevating to the character of the profession, which allows no spirit of jealousy to prevent heaping honours year after year upon the foremost man in their ranks, as it is complimentary to the distinguished recipient of these honours."[19]

On July 1, 1864 the college met for the last time at Sir Patrick Dun's Hospital and the first meeting in the new hall took place on July 5.[20] The fellows expressed their satisfaction:

"We cannot permit the present occasion of meeting for the first time in our new hall to pass by without expressing the satisfaction we feel at the altered circumstances in which the college is now placed from what it has been so long a period, and the obligation we are under to our president for having initiated the movement which has led to this result, as well as for the deep interest he has taken at all times in carrying out the undertaking."[21]

Corrigan was conscious of the great honour his colleagues had bestowed upon him and he was extremely sensitive in matters of protocol relating to the college. Arriving at the lord mayor's inaugural dinner in the Mansion House in 1864 he found that he was not seated at the high table, whereupon he left immediately. The lord mayor wrote apologising for the fact that due to an unprecedented attendance by the nobility he had had to seat the guests in accordance with the roll of precedence as set down by the Ulster King at Arms. Corrigan replied that no personal feeling had influenced him, but that it had been customary to place the president of the College of Physicians in a high place, and that no profession merited the compliment more than his. The newspapers found this the stuff of good satire and the *Globe* reported the incident with relish:

> "The Irish papers have been full of the grievance of Dr Corrigan, who went to the Dublin lord mayor's dinner and went out again *impransus*, or in plain un-Esculapian saxon — fasting. He is physician to the Queen, or something grand like that. By right of his dignity he should have been placed (at least he thought so) *inter primores*; that is at the table raised upon a dais, where the lord lieutenant with his host and the grand officers of state regaled themselves. But when he approached that end of the Round Room, lo! the seats were all pre-occupied, and the doctor was invited to join the judges and general officers, the members of parliament and the privy counsellors, the captains and sheriffs, the aldermen and country squires and the clergy at a long table on the floor. Many a gentleman of high degree might have deemed this all very good company, but not so the physician to the Queen. He took the affront in high dudgeon and he wheeled about incontinently on his well-booted heel, gave himself a spin of indignation, and trotted off, unimpresssed by the savour odours which might have tempted a weaker appetite to stay."[22]

When Corrigan retired from the presidency of the college in 1864, his friend William Stokes proposed that a committee should be set up to "take into consideration how it may further mark its appreciation of his conduct as president."[23] The first action the committee agreed to was that Mr Catterson Smith should paint a portrait to be hung in the college hall.[24] This was the first time that such an honour had been paid to any fellow of the college, but it was deemed an inadequate demonstration of regard and a subscription was established for a statue to be executed by Mr Foley.[25] On June 3, 1869 the public installation of the statue took place in front of a large gathering. Dr Thomas Beatty spoke of those qualities in Corrigan that had led to this unique honour: "First, because by the force of his strong manly intellect, his early, and continued perserverance and industry, his successful labours as a hospital physician, his large private practice, his reputation as a brilliant lecturer and writer, and honorable conduct as a professional brother, he had achieved for himself a high position among the most eminent physicians of the country." Of the sculpture itself Beatty said: "I cannot conclude without expressing my admiration of the manner in which our countryman Mr Foley, has executed the work with which he was entrusted. The statue of Sir Henry Marsh, which stands beside that of Sir Dominic Corrigan is from the same studio. It has been regarded by all observers as a masterpiece of art; and, as in the case of the bronze statue of Goldsmith at Trinity College, it was thought unlikely, if not impossible, that even Foley himself could create its equal, so his effort to rival that of Sir Henry Marsh was looked to with anxiety and apprehension. But the transcendent genius of the great Irish sculptor enabled him to keep pace even with himself, and as in the case of Goldsmith, he produced at least its equal in the splendid statue of Burke that stands beside it, so we have now before us another striking specimen of his art in the statue of Corrigan, a work of the highest order of merit, and worthy to take its place beside that of Marsh."[26]

William Stokes also paid tribute to his colleague and thanked the subscribers for "so valuable a gift, and so admirable a work of art." Finally the Reverend Professor Samuel Haughton said, "He felt proud that there was at least one institution, the College of Physicians, where apart from politics or religion, they could pay a tribute to genius and distinguished ability."[23]

This honour was one of the most unique in Corrigan's career. His statue now stands in the statue hall of the college with Marsh, Stokes and Graves. He had the very unusual distinction (shared only by Stokes in 1876) of having an honour of this magnitude bestowed on him in life; its significance was not lost on the recipient who had been black-beaned from the college rolls less than two decades earlier. The medical profession had made amends for its short-sighted action in 1847, and now the government placed its seal of approval on an unique career. On Janury 17, 1866 Corrigan received a letter from Lord Wodehouse at the vice-regal lodge informing him of the Queen's intention of raising him to the dignity of a baronet. He replied, "I shall endeavour to prove myself not undeserving of this high mark of Her Majesty's approbation, and it will be equally my duty to continue to retain the kind and favourable opinion of Your Excellency the expression of which has obtained from Her Majesty the distinction conferred upon me."[27] On January 30, 1866 the *London Gazette* announced, "The Queen has also been pleased to direct letters patent to be passed under the Great Seal granting the dignity of a Baronet of the United Kingdom of Great Britain and Ireland, unto Dominic John Corrigan, of Cappagh and Inniscorrig, in the county of Dublin, and of Merrion Square, in the city of Dublin, MD, one of Her Majesty's physicians-in-ordinary in Ireland, and the heirs male of his body lawfully begotten."[28]

The *Daily Express* had the following comment to make: "*Sir Dominic J. Corrigan, M.D., Bart.* We understand that Her Majesty has conferred the dignity of a baronetcy on Dr Corrigan, physician-in-ordinary to the Queen in Ireland. The fact Dr Corrigan has always advocated moderate Liberal opinions, and has recently come forward, with an independence which has won very general respect, to oppose the attempt of the ultramontane prelates to obtain absolute control over the education of the Roman Catholic youth, has not stood in the way of his obtaining an object of ambition to which he is entitled from his high reputation, personal character and social rank. The compliment bestowed upon him may be regarded as a recognition, though a partial one, of the just claims of the medical profession in this country,

which has not hitherto obtained from the state its due proportion of the public honours."[29] Only four doctors had
preceded Corrigan for the distinction of a baronetcy in
Ireland; three were physicians — Thomas Molyneux, Edward
Barry, and Henry Marsh all of whom were fellows and presidents of the Royal College of Physicians, and one was a
surgeon, Philip Crampton, Corrigan's life-long friend.[30] The
honour was in recognition not only for the high position he
held in the profession, but for his services and work in connection with the Central Board of Health, as commissioner
of education during the introduction of national education
and as a member of the senate of Queen's University.[31]
The distinction crowned an extraordinary rise to the pinnacle
of both the medical profession and society. Victorian Dublin
was, of course, unique in its system of honouring the profession, some would say outrageously so; it became known
later as "the city of dreadful knights." Towards the close of
the century no physician or surgeon would accept anything
short of a baronetcy. John Banks refused for many years to
accept an ordinary knighthood and finally settled for the
KCB.[32] It has been argued with some justification that the
merit of these awards can be judged by the fact that neither
Graves, Colles nor Stokes received a title. Colles was in fact
offered a baronetcy but declined to accept. Graves and Stokes
did deserve honour from the Crown, but it is not difficult to
find the reason for their exclusion from the titled ranks.[33]
The apparent injustice of the system is common to all forms
of political reward; the efforts made by an individual for a
popular political or social cause can be assessed readily and
duly acknowledged, whereas the value of a scientific or
artistic endeavour only becomes apparent in time, often
posthumously, and is subject to the vagaries of fashion and
posterity. Neither Stokes nor Graves had much time for
medical politics though both served as officers of the College
of Physicians and the British Medical Association; neither,
however, became involved in general politics. Stokes, in fact,
found medical politics quite distasteful. His caustic comment
on medical politicians when speaking once to the British
Medical Association can hardly have endeared him to his
audience: "The man among us, who by his unselfish labour,

adds one useful fact to the storehouse of medical knowledge, does more to advance its material interests than if he had spent a life in the pursuit of medical politics."[34] Stokes was an idealist and as such he would have made a poor politician. Returning in melancholy mood from an archaeological visit to Lough Mask and Corrib he remarked, "But in truth a little time will level these ancient castles and the high-born and honourable inhabitants, and the feeling which their communion creates, and then 'utility' will have its reign, and 'common sense' laughing at the past and the beautiful will build factories with the remains of history, make money, and die."[35]

Corrigan had a number of interests outside of medicine. He was a keen naturalist, an accomplished yachtsman, and an inveterate traveller. His love of natural history had been cultivated in youth by Cornelius Denvir at Maynooth, and in the lectures he gave in later years he "showed a very considerable knowledge of its various branches."[36] In his aquarium at Inniscorrig he bred a variety of tropical fish, some of which he presented to the Royal Zoological Society of Ireland with which he had been associated for many years.[37]

The zoological gardens were opened to the public in 1830 and in September of the following year the zoo itself was opened. Though London zoo had been founded some years earlier, the public were not admitted for a number of years and the Dublin zoo can therefore claim to be the first amenity of its kind to open to the public in these islands, and one of the first in the world.[38] The main founders of the zoo were Sir Philip Crampton and Dr Whitley Stokes. There is no record that Corrigan was a founder member as has been stated, but he was certainly associated with the society from its earliest days. He was a member of council in 1833 and participated in what has been stated to be the most important meeting of the society held in Hunts Hotel, Dawson Street, on May 15, 1833 in which a new code of laws for the society was debated. Corrigan opposed the appointment of a president on the grounds that "his taste would predominate during his year of office, and the arrangement would most probably have the effect of diverting the energies of the society into some new branch of science, according to the whim of each

246 Conscience and Conflict

person presiding."[39] He could hardly have forseen that he was to become the first president to hold office for five years, from 1859-63.

In 1840 he was joint honorary secretary with Robert Ball, and "it was owing to his energy and that of a few more, that the society did not become extinct in the famine year of 1847."[40] This was not the first time that a doctor had come to the aid of the animals. Some years earlier "when the society was in need and the animals in danger of perishing, the surgeon-general (Sir Philip Crampton) had given an un-limited letter of credit for their preservation and that of the society."[41] The medical profession of the time played a very active role in the government of the zoological gardens; almost half the members of the council of 1861-62 had medical qualifications.[41]

In 1864 Corrigan was the hero of a small drama in the zoo. A soldier, wishing to obtain his discharge from the army, put his hand into a wolf's cage and was quickly seized by the animal. A policeman who had been standing nearby rushed to the cage and "belaboured the wolf's head with his baton, the enraged animal held his grasp — the blood flowed copiously, and the surrounding crowd were terror-stricken and scream-ing." Corrigan who happened to be nearby seized the police-man's baton and forcing the narrow end of the handle between the wolf's jaws with a sudden twist brought the point against the roof of its mouth. "The wolf in agony, let go of the hand and fled to a corner of the cage howling." Corrigan then dressed the hand and sent the man to the Richmond hospital for further treatment, where he was arrested as a deserter. An interesting account of the event appeared in the *Dublin Evening Post* written by a "correspondent" who was none other than Corrigan's daughter Cecilia.[42]

Corrigan took one long holiday each year and during this he did what he enjoyed most — travelling. He was usually accompanied by the entire family, or on occasion his son William would sail to join the party: "Papa, Mamma, Cecilia and I were in Paris, Schaffhausen, the Tyrol, Vienna (where William joined us from his yachting tour of Ireland), Dresden, Berlin, Aix-la-Chapelle and Antwerp, from August 21 to October 6, 1858."[43] These annual holidays rarely lasted less than six weeks and often took longer than two months. Over the years the family visited North Italy, Rome, Naples, the Pyrenees, Spain, Greece, Munich, Edinburgh, London, Hamburg and Wales. In Europe Corrigan took the opportunity to visit the hospitals and medical schools in the capital cities. He also observed illnesses peculiar to other countries and sometimes he wrote about these. In 1834 an article appeared on "plica polonica" an unusual condition common in Poland in which the hair is plaited and matted and allowed to grow to a great length.[44] In 1861 he presented to the College of Physicians the treatment practised for hydrophobia or rabies in the Isle of Salamis.[45]

In 1862 he recorded his travels to Greece with Mary in an interesting book entitled *Ten Days in Athens with Notes by the Way*,[46] but perhaps the most interesting diary of his travels is an unpublished one in which he recounts the family holiday to France and Italy in 1859.[47] In Paris the Corrigan family witnessed the entry of La Grande Armée of Austria with the Emperor at its head. Travelling by boat from Marseilles to Naples he made friends with an Englishman and commented, "It is surprising what a staple fund of abuse these three things furnish to some English travellers — Ireland, Catholicism and O'Connell . . . There are two ways of meeting these attacks — one is by controverting the facts on meeting the arguments but this always leaves you on the defensive, and the defendant always labours under the disadvantage even when he succeeds in only defending his own position of leaving his opponent unscathed. The other is not to trouble yourself with the defence but become in reply the attacker and put your opponent on his defence. This is the shorter and in my mind the better adapted for the epigrammatic style of travelling. And it is sometimes amusing to see how soon the equanimity runs into a little irritability when the attacker is obliged to defend himself." This strategy was often effective though Corrigan admits that he did not always come off best: "But as in despatches of our greatest men I will conceal my own defeats and only say the enemy came on with overwhelming force and I thought fit to retire and effected my retreat in good order." One conversation went thus:

E. You are I fear beginning again to murder in Ireland.
C. I only left London a few days since and while I was
    there news came in of a horrible murder in Sheffield.
    A poor man sitting at the door of a house in the
    public street in the evening was shot dead by some
    of his brother tradesmen . . .

On another occasion his English friend who had been to a
dinner party in Cork remarked on the peculiarity of the
accent and gave Corrigan an imitation of it. Corrigan was not
impressed: "When I was first in London I almost thought I
should be obliged to get an interpreter. I was at Morley's
Hotel and my first interview was with a waiter in the morning who came to my room to know if I 'appened' to have a
'hud boot.' I was very much puzzled to know what he meant
but after a little he enlightened me by telling me it was
'tother one of this' at the same time holding up an odd boot
— to view." The Englishman remarked that such an accent
would only be found among the lower classes, but Corrigan
disagreed: "I was on my way to the House of Commons a
few days since and inquired of a policeman. He told me to
go thro' the 'hopposite harch', and soon afterwards in the
House I heard one leading statesman observing on the impropriety of indulging in hostile expressions towards the 'hem-
peror of the French' to whom another in replying spoke on
the necessity of maintaining the 'hundependence' of the
country." Corrigan relates with some glee that, "This was too
much for my good natured companion and he immediately
had recourse . . . to bet one hundred to one that we two
should sit for six hours in the House of Commons and not
hear an aspirate used where it should not be. As I never bet
and we were then on a steamer in the Mediterranean and the
House of Commons was up I could not take up the bet . . ."
    In this diary he wrote with wonderment tinged with
admiration on the practice of mixed bathing in Italy: "A lady
had just taken to the water and she swam out to fully half a
mile from the shore accompanied by a boat with four sailors
and it rowing alongside her lest she should feel weak in the
current. However she swam well back. She wore a Turkish
jacket and short wide trousers with a girdle round the waist,
her long black hair floating loose on the water." He over-

came his temerity, however, and began to enjoy this daring continental practice: "I was soon after in the water and on one side of me was a group consisting of a lady bathing, a gentleman leaning over a rail on the platform chatting to her, and beside her in the water some of the men in charge of the baths teaching a boy to swim, while on my other side were some ladies engaged in an animated discussion as to the respective swimming merits of two of their male friends who deferred to their judgement."

In Naples he was appalled at the begging: "They have not the slightest idea of doing the least act of civility without begging," but he was most impressed with the bay. Always anxious to return with something for the Dublin zoo he captured some lizards in Pompeii "and brought at a wine shop on the road a bottle to hold them."

In 1860 he visited the spa known as the Medical Station in Arcachon in Bordeaux and was so impressed with the town and the beneficial effects of the climate to health that he made the topic the subject of his presidential address to the Royal College of Physicians.[48] This was later published in a pamphlet and translated into French. His address begins: "Among the aids on which we depend for the restoration of health, or for its preservation, however, theories and medicines may vary from time to time, there is one that we always and most properly hold in high esteem, *change of climate* ... The subject is one claiming more attention every day, as increased facilities of travelling by steam vessel and railway have now placed it within the reach of thousands who could not before have attained this important hygienic agent."

Arcachon unlike so many celebrated European resorts was not subject to the cold piercing wind of the north, and its bay had other advantages besides: "It is a large inland bay, of about twenty miles by ten wide, communicating with the Atlantic in the Bay of Biscay by a narrow channel nearly three miles long, tortuous, and about a mile across. This passage is long and narrow, and so completely is the whole basin surrounded by 'dunes,' or low ranges of sandhills, that no storm that rages over the Atlantic ever raises the waves in the bay ... In addition to the sandhills or dunes, the north-east, and east and south are belted by an almost interminable forest of pines of great size and height." It is these pine trees that most interested Corrigan: "The whole air is perceptibly impregnated with the balsamic odour of turpentines, and we know that the balsams and turpentines in vapour are remedial agents of much power in bronchial affections . . ." The pines possessed not only medicinal properties, they had been used also to prevent the inexorable advance of the sands which in 1721 had completely buried the church of "Notre Dame d'Arcachon." He found the bungalow style of the houses of Arcachon most pleasing: "The watering places of Arcachon now consist of hundreds of such isolated houses, with magnolias, oleanders and orange-trees, giving the whole place the picturesque appearance of clusters of Indian bunga-lows in an American pine clearing." The Victorians were fascinated by the effect of climate on disease, and a re-commendation from one as eminent as Corrigan was sure to boost tourism. Such seems to have been the case and the citizens of Arcachon expressed their gratitude by naming a street *Allée Corrigan* which remains to this day in that now popular seaside resort.[49]

On another occasion he visited the spa town of Aix-les-Bains, where his first night was not pleasant.[50] Forced to stay in a *maison meublée* the baronet found his bed none too comfortable: "The foot of my bed had been allowed to sink to a considerable angle, so that as I attempted to sleep I slid down to the foot, and this gave rise to a very uncomfortable dream of my being at the foot of a tall ladder, up which I was endeavouring to climb with my back to the rungs, and every moment when I dreamed I had achieved some distance I felt myself suddenly sliding, as if down the slope of a fire-escape, until I was jerked suddenly by my arrival at the bottom, which I found, on my awakening, was the foot-board of the bed." However, better accommodation was soon found, and we are given a vivid description of Corrigan's morning trip to the baths. Wrapped in snow white towels he was conveyed in a sedan-chair by two attendants, a journey that gave him some cause for concern: "I felt as if a single false step on the part of my bearers would toss me out on one side or the other like the contents of a hand-barrow, and without the possibility of my helping myself, and I felt this

the more as my conveyance mounted flights of steps."
Divested of his towels, two able-bodied attendants took up
position one standing in front of him and the other behind,
and "directed a tube in full force of hot water upon back,
shoulders, arms, and legs . . . This process being at length
completed I stood up, and was assisted, if necessary, by one
of the attendants to a round iron bar secured in the wall at
each end (but separated from it by a small space), on which I
rested my hands, with my face to the wall, much in the same
position in which I might suppose a garotter to be placed for
his flogging. While this is being done the second attendant
fits on the open end of one of the discharge tubes a rose like
that of a garden watering-pot, lays on a stronger and hotter
force of water, and makes it play over neck to heels — now
hence, now there, now everywhere, until it makes one feel
as if this needle-bath were flaying him, and yet the sensation
is not of pain, but it is of pleasure verging on pain . . ." He
never quite overcame his fear of the sedan trip to the douches
and he preferred to walk "greatly aided by my morning dress
of genuine Irish frieze, obtained as a kind gift from the
Poul-a-Phouca or Ballymore-Eustace Mills. It is of all materials
the best for the out-door morning walk, not lying close to the
skin, and confining in its loose woolly texture so much air as
to make it a very superior non-conductor of heat."

Corrigan was an authority on spas and baths. He wrote on
the subject in the medical journals criticising Irish baths for
a "deficiency of a sufficient supply of vapour" which he considered detrimental to health.[51] The baths then being built in
Dublin and Blarney resembled more the sauna than the
Turkish bath, and those who had invested money in these
were understandably alarmed by Corrigan's opposition. A
lengthy and polemical correspondence followed. Dr Barter,
"the celebrated hydropathic physician," warned Corrigan
and his supporters: "I sincerely trust that if they again venture
before the public, they will endeavour to master their subject
and not lend their names to fill the pages of a respectable
journal with statements based on utter ignorance, and thus
occupy my time, as well as the time of others, in reading,
correcting, and contradicting their puerilities."[52] Finally
the whole correspondence and what purports to be the final

statement (we shall not judge) appeared in a pamphlet by one who signed himself "Photophilus."[53]

Another travel article by Corrigan, appeared in the *Dublin Post* of Saturday, September 4, 1858 as "Jottings from Rien Faire, Paris, August 30, 1858."[54] In this he described the inefficiency and filth of a Parisian passport office: "When I went in, the middle of the room for its whole length was occupied with a crowd of French and foreigners, men and women of all ranks and degrees of cleanliness and odours, without any order." During hours of delay and inefficiency he was passed from one official to another, until finally, "another man jumped down a big black stamp upon what the clerk had previously written; and again at the door going out, where another very dirty man stamped again with another dirty stamp upon what somebody had also written, so that the main part of the business of each in succession appeared to be to obliterate what his predecessor had written." Departing from the passport office his attention was drawn to "a nice modest-looking French girl" who was "obliged to stand for several minutes opposite the desk of a close cropped, big-whiskered, black-looking fellow, who first deliberately gazed her all over, and then going over feature by feature wrote under 'Front,' 'Sourals,' 'Yeux,' 'Nez,' 'Bouche' such descriptions as he thought fit, while his fellows, at either side looked up and grinned now and then. I looked at the process, and for an instant in her face. She looked up at me for a moment, while an almost imperceptible flitting passed across her countenance, which said as plainly as words could speak, 'This should not be so!' I am sure an Irish or English girl would have broken her parasol across his head, and a British jury would have brought in a verdict of 'Served him right.'" The whole business had taken him five hours and he resolved: "We shall never have passports in our country. Were it ever to be attempted, Wat Tyler's hammer would be swung again."

In Boulogne he was tricked into taking a horse drawn car whereas one was supplied *gratis* by the railway company. Of this he says, "You have often heard our car men abused for the heinous crime of taking up a passenger and his luggage, and charging a shilling for a jaunt from Gibbon's Pier to the Kingstown Railway Station." Well, after being charged two francs for a five minute jaunt in Boulogne, Corrigan viewed the matter with humour. " 'Done,' thought I, pointing to my friends in the omnibus carried *gratis*. Driver laughed; I thought I might as well do the same. Kingstown drivers beaten hollow; and as I always make a bad rhyme, which drives away vexation of being outwitted, made this:

> You're better off for what you have;
> I'm not much worse off for what I gave. "

The French diet was a little too rich for Corrigan's taste, and he did not approve of the French penchant for alcohol and tobacco, "The merits of 'cognac,' 'chartruese,' 'kirch-wasser,' and 'elixer of spa,' are discussed by gentlemen *sous les arbres*, who naturally refer to ladies for their opinions, and mixed in these colloquies now and then the puff of a mild cigarette, but not from Irish lips."

Corrigan sailed often from his harbour at *Inniscorrig* and here he held a regatta in August of each year; this was one of the few days he took off from work outside of the annual holiday. He was an active member of the Royal Irish Yacht Club, and on July 16, 1863 in the absence of the vice-commodore through illness he acted as president when the lord lieutenant, the Earl of Carlisle, was entertained by the club.[55] The sailing committee of the day included his son William. His Excellency "entered the dining-room of the club-house, where a most sumptuous and *recherche déjeuner* had been prepared for some 70 specially invited guests ... Some prize strawberries had been supplied for the lord lieutenant's table from the gardens of J.N. Boswell, Esq, of Monkstown, which attracted general notice. Besides the principle *déjeuner*, luncheon was supplied in another apartment to some 200 guests." Speaking to the occasion Corrigan said, "When the mind alone is cultivated the intellect often becomes overpowered, and I ever find that the hand which wields with vigour the oar or the cricket-bat is not the less able to carry away the prize medal. The beautiful Bay of Dublin can be looked on as the 'cloth of gold' where the brotherly and manly sports attached to the yachting world can be and are cultivated to perfection; and with respect to the fair ladies I see around me, I feel sure I can say for them that they would not the less accept a hand because it came rough and hard from holding a tiller or pulling a rope."

And what of family life? The Corrigan household appears to have been a happy and devoted one. Corrigan was an early riser usually arriving in the hospital at 8 a.m. His afternoons were spent in his consulting rooms in Merrion Square; then he would dine with Lady Corrigan and at 7.30 p.m. both parents would meet with the rest of the family in the parlour, after which he might spend until the small hours working in his study. Lady Corrigan remains a background figure about whom little appears in his diaries and letters. As the daughters Mary and Cecilia grew older they accompanied their father to *levées* in Dublin Castle or to meetings of the General Medical Council in London where they would all stay at Morley's Hotel.[56]

The Corrigan's had their share of family suffering. One daughter, Joanna, died at the age of seventeen in 1858 from what we know not. There is a poignant line in Mary's diary[57] which reads, "She was exquisitely lovely and perfect in every way," and eleven years later her father has a note in his fees' book: "Ann. of dear Joanna's death." There is another entry in the fees' book on March 16, 1866: "Letter from Melbourne announcing poor John's death there on 6th Jan."[58] John was the eldest son and heir to the baronetcy. He joined the Seventy-fourth Highlanders as ensign, became lieutenant by purchase, and then joined the Third Regiment of the Dragoon Guards as captain. He wrote interesting despatches for the newspapers on the Kaffir War, in one of which he described the death of Colonel Fordyce to whom he was ADC and who died in his arms in the field.[59] He himself was seriously wounded in the head during this war and received a medal for his services. When his regiment was stationed in Dublin he acted as Brigade-Major at the Curragh Camp. It was while serving in India that he became ill and when on sick furlough in Melbourne he developed an illness of only two days duration which was fatal. His remains were interred in the Roman Catholic cemetery in Melbourne. His father had a memorial erected on his grave and a tablet was placed in the chapel of the Royal Hospital at Kilmainham. John Corrigan's only son John succeeded to the title baronet but died at the age of twenty-three in 1883 and the title became extinct.[60]

The next son William became a highly successful barrister. He was close to his father and both shared a common interest — sailing, often going away together for weekends on their yacht. In July 1873 we find Corrigan jumping to the defence of his son's profession, the law. The occasion is of interest as it illustrates again Corrigan's intense nationalism — what is good enough for Britain is good enough for Ireland. It is not clear why Corrigan was selected to put the case for the Irish Bar, but presumably his son then a practising barrister asked him to do so. "During the course of the inquiry into the loss of the City of Dublin Steam Packet Company's steamer, *Columba* this week, a very important question was raised by Mr Corrigan (i.e. Dr Dominic Corrigan) on behalf of the Irish Bar as to the *locus standi* of Mr Hamill, an English barrister, who conducted the inquiry on behalf of the Board of Trade, instructed by the solicitor of the same body."[61] The question being asked by Corrigan was simply — was a member of the English Bar competent to represent the Board of Trade as a practising barrister in an Irish court of justice? Corrigan put it this way: "Mr Hamill was a member of the English Bar, and the members of the Irish Bar felt naturally aggrieved at an English barrister coming over here and, in fact, taking the part of an Irish barrister. They felt that that was an Irish court of justice. They knew that in the English courts of justice if an Irish barrister presented himself he would not be listened to for one moment unless he was also a member of the English Bar." The appeal was unsuccessful but Corrigan conducted a lengthy correspondence of the subject over many years and was never satisfied with the result.[62]

The eldest daughter Mary who recorded lovingly so many details of her father's career was married by her uncle, the Very Rev Monsignor Woodlock, to Richard Martin in 1863, and the pair went on their honeymoon to Munich accompanied by "Papa."[63] Richard became High Sheriff of the City of Dublin, an appointment for which his father-in-law was prepared to use his influence, and he was later knighted.[64] Mary lived to be the last surviving child; she does not appear to have had any children.

The second daughter Cecilia Mary did not marry. She died on September 2, 1880.

9

Towards Politics

Corrigan was a popular and innovative teacher. His medical lectures were planned carefully, and he never failed to attract a large audience. Many of his lectures were published in the medical journals, but unlike Graves and Stokes he never wrote a textbook of medicine. Gratifying though he may have found the role of teacher, he realised that the extent to which he could influence educational policy was limited, and he was aware from as early as his student days that medical standards were haphazard and in need of urgent reform. One way to influence reform was to become part of the organisation responsible for medical education, and in 1859 he was appointed to the General Medical Council as the representative of the Queen's University. He was to occupy this position for twenty-one years during which he devoted much thought and energy to securing a uniform standard of medical training.

The Medical Act of 1858 establishing the "The General Council of Medical Education and Registration of the United Kingdom," as the council was officially called, was passed after eighteen years of parliamentary wrangling during which time no less than seventeen medical bills floundered.[1] Before 1858 there was a number of separate licensing bodies conferring professional titles as varied in the powers of practice they granted to the recipient, as in the standard of education they demanded (or, as was often the case, did not demand). The council was created to serve the public good in a number of ways; it was to keep and publish the *Medical Register* of qualified practitioners so that "persons requiring medical aid should be enabled to distinguish qualified from unqualified practitioners;" it was to supervise and improve medical education and it was this function that was to most concern Corrigan; it had the power of taking disciplinary action in cases of serious professional misconduct; and finally it was to publish a national pharmacopoeia.

Critical though Corrigan was of the standard of medical education, he was equally concerned about the dismal general education that many students of medicine possessed. He was well-qualified to speak on this subject having been a commissioner of national education in Ireland for many years, and a member of the senate of Queen's University since its inception in 1850. "I wish I could congratulate the profession or the public on the standard of education in the profession improving of late years. I am sorry to say the reverse is the fact, and that, on the contrary, in preliminary and professional education there is, generally speaking a great deterioration." This unsatisfactory state of affairs he attributed to the willingness of the medical schools to lower their standards to secure students: "Step by step each college descended below its neighbour in the sliding scale until it has come to this, that now a candidate rejected at one college has beforehand prepared for his immediately setting out for the next lowest on the scale, that will gladly sell its diploma on easier terms."[2]

As the council set about the task of compiling the *Register* it was horrified to learn that among 1,750 students preparing for the examination of the Society of Apothecaries only 350 had passed a preliminary examination in general education. The profession's standing in society was, in Corrigan's view, seriously threatened by this defect in basic educational requirements, and he wanted legislation to ensure an overall minimal standard for students wishing to take up medicine as a career: "The preliminary education, moreover, of our students in general education, instead of being supervised by any one respectable body is left almost to chance for no less than eighteen bodies have the power of examining in art and science students going to the medical profession, and giving certificates, some in the United Kingdom, some in Canada, some in Tasmania, that such students are sufficiently educated in general acquirements to enter the study of medicine." He pointed out that the Home Guards, the Admiralty and the Law did not trust the examination of "peripatetic and irresponsible bodies scattered over the world. Can we hesitate for a moment in coming to the conclusion that for students entering the study of medicine threre should be one uniform and sufficient preliminary examination and that such examination should be under the control of a central authority in each division of the United Kingdom, defining what is wanted, and what the examination should be...It is evident that, under the present system, young men get into our profession who could not pass an examination for a place of a letter-carrier."

The medical council did indeed act on this important matter but at its own pace, which was, as we shall see, much too sedentary for the Dublin representative who believed that once a defect had been identified there was no point in postponing its correction. It was not until 1874 that the then president, Sir George Paget was able to say, "*Now* a preliminary education is enforced on all. The future influence of this on the social status of our profession can scarcely be over-rated."[1]

If there were problems in acquiring a uniform standard of general education there were even greater ones in achieving uniformity in medical education. Corrigan declared: "We have in the United Kingdom nineteen licensing bodies, conferring no less than thirty separate licences and fifty-three titles. The result is necessarily a downward tendency in competition." He gave the profession a stern caveat: "It appears to me that if your system be not altered, the civil authorities of the country must ignore all our licensing bodies, and like the army and navy authorities, institute an examination for themselves. I should deeply regret to see this, but to this I fear it must come unless we bestir ourselves."[2]

He was not impressed by the *modus operandi* of the council and stated this quite plainly in allegorical fashion: "There is an incident related in one of our popular sea-stories, of the mate of a cutter who imposed upon the simple minds of his crew by showing a great press of sail aloft, and with loud trumpeting on deck, calling on all about him to admire how he carried on to forward the good ship on her way; but all the time he cunningly trailed a sail along under the lee-quarter, so that the good ship could make no way. I believe we have ... such obstructives to deal with seeming to carry on, but secretly taking care that no progress is made; for their object is that we should remain stationary." He was not alone in his opinion of the council's attitude to the urgent business before it. Sir James Paget made the cryptic comment: "We sat for eight days and on six of them decided to do nothing." In a ten year period upwards of twenty medical bills were lost in parliament, and five minor bills became law.[1]

He was especially concerned at the council's dilatory approach in restricting foreign medical graduates. In particular he criticised its intention to admit doctors to its register without examination. His fears were not without justification: "In the amended bill that has been put forward by the council there is one clause that I make no apology for bringing under earnest attention. It is that the General Medical Council shall have a power to admit *without examination* to the registry, and thus make them eligible for all appointments in the United Kingdom, the holders of foreign diplomas equally with our own graduates and licentiates, on satisfactory evidence being laid before it that those degrees or licences have been granted after a sufficient course of study and examination . . . I hope the whole profession will seriously consider this proposed clause, and will unite with me in resisting it, not merely for their own sake, but for the public good. It is notorious that both in Germany and America there are universities that sell their diplomas, just as they sell beer or Indian corn, to all who can afford to pay for them."[3]

Corrigan gave examples of universities that sold diplomas, one being the German University of Erlangen. His allegation was challenged by the university which indignantly declared in the *British Medical Journal* that since 1863 it had abolished for all time the conferring of degrees *in absentia*, and that the "degree of MD, had not been conferred on any foreigner, and consequently, on any Englishman, without his personally attending, and passing an examination by written papers, as well as *viva voce.'*[4] Corrigan in reply pointed out that the university had only itself to blame for not informing the council that it had stopped "selling its diploma without examination, remitting to any purchaser its university degree in return for a bill of exchange, just as an Erlangen brewer would forward a cask of Bavarian beer on order," and he added quite reasonably that there was no reason to suppose that the venerable institute might not at some future date revert to its old ways. As to the assurance given by the university that its graduates must sit a *viva voce* examination, well, this cannot be taken too seriously either: "To any one of honest intelligence the phrase *viva voce* examination could convey that the candidate presented himself at the seat of the university, and was examined there by its authorities. Not at all; for in one of the documents in my hands the applicant, resident within this kingdom, was referred for the *viva voce* examination – to whom do you suppose? To one of their own graduates in the neighbourhood of the applicant, and the applicant was informed that on passing such a *viva voce* examination and payment of £32 he was to have the degrees."[2]

The council maintained that by freely admitting foreign degrees there would be created in the course of time a state of reciprocity between the European countries. Corrigan saw this argument as nothing short of ridiculous and suggested that if that was what the council sought it should abolish all degrees and restrictions so that eventually "as Mr Gladstone (in his celebrated free trade speech at Paris) said of custom-houses, all universities and colleges would be only remembered as things of the past."[2] He advocated instead the French system, "that the holder of a foreign diploma, desirous of being placed on the *Register*, should be entitled on such diploma to present himself for examination to some of our licensing bodies; and on passing its examination and obtaining its diploma, to have his name placed on the *Register*.

He urged the council to reconsistute itself and incorporate in its constitution "a code of regulation, both as to preliminary and professional examination, and that all graduates and holders of licences or degrees from our several corporate bodies should be subject to such examination before being permitted to hold any public appointment, supported wholly or in part by public grant." The General Medical Council did not, in fact, obtain the legislative powers that Corrigan so earnestly advocated until 1886, when the applicants for registration were required to pass examinations in medicine, surgery and midwifery, and it was given the power to ensure that these examinations were of sufficient standard. The council was in addition empowered to register colonial and foreign practitioners on a reciprocal basis provided standards were maintained.[1]

A subject of great controversy and discussion, in the mid-nineteenth century, not only in medicine but in society generally, was the admission of women to medicine. Male Victorian society generally found the notion repugnant, and was supported in this by many women, among them the Queen. Elizabeth Garrett Anderson, by insisting that private tuition was the equivalent of apprenticeship, had obtained the licence of the Society of Apothecaries of London in 1865, but the door was quickly slammed shut when the Apothecaries made attendance at a recognised medical school compulsory. The medical schools in turn did not deem it proper or desirable to admit women. Corrigan, in debating the matter at the Council supported the admission of women to medicine because he saw it as a fundamental right but he found the prospect of women doctors distinctly disagreeable: "In the senate of the Queen's University, the question was discussed, until an opinion was obtained from the law officers of the Crown that we had not the power of granting degrees to women; and on this discussion I was the advocate of women's admission into the profession but I also distinctly stated that, supposing women obtained their medical degrees, no consideration should induce me to meet them in practice. Those two things may seem inconsistent; but, while I advocated the principle that there should be free admission for women in competition for whatever honours or distinctions were open to them, I could not conceal from myself that I could not go into consultation with a woman and discuss with her the particulars of cases that must occur in hundreds every week, without losing totally that respect for her sex which I have no wish to lose: and, if I were asked as regards the members of my own family whether I would advise either one or the other to go into the medical profession, my answer would be that I would rather see them buried."[5]

It was felt at the time that medicine as a career would be morally debasing to women. This view was shared by both Corrigan and Stokes who put it thus: "Is it not very much better that a certain number of women should not make the

profession of medicine and surgery a source of employment
to them, or that the moral condition of the female should,
more or less, be damaged by having to attend to matters which
are in fact antagonistic to the delicacy of women . . . Is the
unsexing of women, which would certainly be threatened by
a large surgical or medical education, a desirable thing?"[6]

Corrigan did not believe that women would be physically
capable of coping with the demands of medicine, but he did
not subscribe to the view that just because women were
admitted to medicine they would wish to enter other fields
of employment: "Are we to assent to such a ridiculous pro-
position as that, if we admit women into the medical profession to study medicine and practise it, therefore, forsooth,
a little girl of thirteen or fourteen may be sent as 'midship-
man' upon a ship of war?" How very strange he would find
today's world.

Another argument put forward in favour of women doctors
was that ill women were often reluctant to permit a male
doctor to examine them. Corrigan regarded himself as better
qualified than most to refute this view: "It has been stated in
one of the works which have issued from the press in favour
of the movement and in most pathetic language, that there
are thousands of women's lives lost in Ireland from their dis-
inclination to employ male doctors; and it is said that in the
nunneries hundreds of women sink annually on that account.
I have a very fair share of opportunity of knowing what the
opinions of the women in convents are. I have asked hundreds
of them whether they would like to have women-doctors,
and the invariable answer has been, 'We would not have one
of them near us.' Now that is the opinion of the most modest
women possible in any community."[5] What one wonders,
would have been the lot of a nun who answered otherwise to
the baronet, accompanied no doubt by Reverend Mother.

At any rate the General Medical Council by a majority of
two-thirds declared after much debate, "that, notwithstanding that there are in the opinion of the council, special
hindrances to the practice of medicine by women which
cannot safely be disregarded, the council is not prepared to
say that women ought to be excluded from the practice of
medicine."[7] In practice this attitude was to be of little help

to women as none of the licensing bodies in the United Kingdom would admit women to an examination which could then be registered. Such were the prejudices against women doctors in London and Edinburgh that they turned to Dublin where "they met in most quarters with an extremely cordial reception, and the Irish College of Physicians and the Queen's University of Ireland both assented to their request and agreed to admit women to examinations and diplomas."[8] Queen's University later vetoed the proposal but the College of Physicians held fast and in 1877 five women were registered as licentiates of the King and Queen's College of Physicians of Ireland. The General Medical Council did not admit women doctors officially until 1878, but like colonial and foreign practitioners, they were to be placed in a separate department of the *Register*.[1]

However frustrating Corrigan found the council's methods of dealing with business, it is evident from his speeches to the council that he enjoyed greatly putting his point of view, even if he did not always succeed in getting his own way. Sir Richard Quain, president of the council from 1891 to 1898, recalled the repartee between Corrigan and the Scottish representative, Alexander Wood: "The humorous and sparkling jokes and witticisms of the Irish baronet were met by the cool, calm, and judicious reasonings of the representative of the Edinburgh College of Physicians, who was generally regarded as coming off victorious in the fight."[1]

At its annual session from May 24 to June 5, in 1876 the General Medical Council debated Lord Carnarvon's Vivisection Bill. Among the speakers was Mr Lister the discoverer of antisepsis which was to so alter the whole practice of surgery. He believed that "the pain inflicted on pheasants in a single day's shooting was greater than that caused by vivisection in the British Islands in a whole year."[9] But credit for "the best speech on the vivisection question" went to Corrigan. At first "he energetically opposed any interference with the bill at all, on the ground that it could not be said to come within the scope of the council's duties." If the council dealt with vivisection, why should it not also deal with game laws, shoeing horses, and ringing pig's noses. When he was unanimously over-ruled on this ploy he entered the fray with enthusiastic oratory. He believed that if further legislation on cruelty to animals was needed, the medical profession should not be selected for "penal enactment" but that the subject should be treated in its relation to society at large. "When medical men were selected and held up to odium, and charged with cruelty in scientific experiments, the best thing to do was to return blow for blow." Corrigan alluded to the treatment of oysters, and the crimping of salmon. "What," he asked, "do people do with regard to foxes' tails? When a fox is taken, his tail is cut off while the animal is alive, in order that it might retain the beauty of the hairs. Foxes' tails so obtained are worn by ladies on their dresses at country balls, and the lady who is able to show the greatest number of foxes' tails on her flounces is the belle of the evening; and yet that lady and her admirers would help to promote a bill in parliament to charge scientific men with cruelty!" And what of ostrich feathers and the dear wren? "I have often been shocked by seeing my pretty pet bird, the golden wren, with its trustful eye, stuffed and appearing as an ornament on a lady's bonnet. These little creatures, which are our friends everywhere — in the hothouse, in the greenhouse, in the garden, and which one could not look at without loving — were trapped, and their skins are taken off while they are still alive, in order that they might retain their beauty." Corrigan told the council he had been to Hurlingham, and that "many of the members of parliament who went to Hurlingham came to the house and attacked the doctors." At Hurlingham where Corrigan had seen "a number of the finest ladies in the land," the practice was to cut off the pigeon's tails which was to them like a rudder of a ship. "When they were let loose having been deprived of their tails, they were obliged to fly straight forward, and there was, therefore, an exceedingly unfair advantage on the side of the sportsman, who was enabled thus to take more deadly aim at the birds." He went on to relate a scene at this venue which he said he could never forget, and because of which nothing would ever induce him to go there again. "A poor little pigeon was shot so that its bowels were hanging out, and while it was flying away in that condition it turned round to where the ladies were sitting, and the poor creature endeavoured to take shelter on the silk dress of a lady. There was a wonderful expression of sympathy; but what was it for? Not for the poor creature with its bowels hanging out, but for the lady's silk dress!"

Corrigan was an active member of the General Medical Council for twenty-one years. He travelled regularly from Dublin to London often taking Mary with him. To judge from his fees books he spent about thirty days a year in London on council business, making about five visits annually.[10] He must have wondered often if he was not wasting his time, and his frustration became manifest on more than one occasion. Addressing the profession at large he commended it for tolerating the constitution of the council for so long. Who, he asked, paid for it: "You do; the whole profession that I see around me. The bodies that send their representatives to the General Medical Council pay not one shilling towards it. By whom are the council elected? Not by you; not one of the whole council is your member. The council are no more representative of the profession than would the members of the House of Commons be representatives of the people if they were elected by the several corporations throughout the kingdom."[2] A decade later little had changed. The Medical Act of 1858 was due once again to come before parliament for amendment, and Corrigan aware of his age, (he was 76) felt he had no option but to place his views before the whole profession in the *British Medical Journal*[11] of 1878: "in the hope that they may form the groundwork for other thinkers." Once again he urged that the medical council should be representative of the whole profession: "The great mass of the profession, which supports the General Medical Council and pays all its expenses, has been, and continues to be, debarred from any participation in its management . . . There are twenty-four members. Of these, there are six Crown nominees named by the Crown. Are they paid by the Crown or by public money from the state? Not a shilling is contributed by Crown or state which appoints them. They are paid out of money extracted from the working men of the profession." Likewise, he pointed out the representatives of the universities, the surgical and medical colleges, and the Apothecaries Hall did not contribute to the expenses of the council. He proposed reducing the council to nine members and a president. He dismissed the Crown representatives as being of no use and added with customary bombast: "I provide for sufficient influence on the part of the government without them." University representation he proposed should be reduced from eight to three, one from England, Ireland and Scotland, and the other medical corporations should be dealt with likewise. This would leave "three seats for the active working members of the profession — one for England, one for Ireland, one for Scotland — elected by the registered practitioners resident for a certain period in the respective part of the United Kingdom for which they would be entitled to vote." Six years after his death the new act of 1886 incorporated many of Corrigan's democratic suggestions. "Henceforth, five practitioners were to be elected to the council by the postal votes of the profession as a whole, and if the council desired, as it did at a later date, this number could be increased."[1]

Corrigan was also involved in the regulation of another branch of medicine — pharmacy. He was mainly responsible for the passing of the Pharmacy Bill of 1875 which sought to institute a "pharmaceutical society, and to regulate the qualifications of pharmaceutical chemists in Ireland, and to establish certain relations between the pharmaceutical societies of Great Britain and Ireland."[12] The Bill was brought in by Hicks Beach and passed after a number of modifications. The new Pharmaceutical Society in recognition of Corrigan's work made him its first president, a post he occupied from 1875-78.[13]

Corrigan's intimacy with government over the years could not fail eventually to attract him towards national politics. He had been a member of the Central Board of Health, he was a Commissioner on Lunatic Asylums, in addition to being a member of the senate of the Queen's University and of the General Medical Council. He had first experienced parliamentary procedure in 1861 when he accompanied Sir William Wilde to London to give evidence on the Dublin Waterworks' Bill then before the House of Lords.[14] He was chosen to do so because of a long letter he had written on the subject to Sir John Gray in which he elaborated on the scientific necessity for an adequate water supply for the city of Dublin.[15] This controversial topic was a cause for concern for many years, and the medical profession, most notably, Sir Philip Crampton (in memory of whose endeavours a strange monument was erected) had attempted often to impress upon the government the importance of the project.

At the end of the eighteenth century the city was supplied with water from the city basin in James Street by "a curious system of metal and wooden pipes," from which issued lateral pipes of lead conveying water to each house where it was stored in tanks operated by a ball and cock.[16] The main supply only operated at certain times and each person was obliged under penalty to keep the storage reservoir in working order. In 1802 iron pipes were laid to replace the wooden pipes that decayed rapidly, and a new tax called the *metal main* was imposed upon the citizens. As the population of the city increased the supply of water from the city basin became inadequate and two additional reservoirs were excavated, one on the Royal Canal at the extremity of Blessington Street, and the other on the Grand Canal at Portobello, at a cost of £30,000 paid from the fund of the metal main. Modern city planners might take note of the efforts made by their predecessors to render the innovations of progress pleasing to the eye as well as being an amenity for the denizens: "These reservoirs are intended, like that of James Street, to be promenades for the citizens in the city, and are laid down with gravel walks and shrubberies."

The purity of the water in this system left much to be desired: "The appalling impurity of the water was caused by the principal use of the harbour (the reservoir on the Royal Canal) — exportation of manure to consumers in the country. This material was dumped on the quay, and transferred to barges, of which there were usually about thirteen, each manned by a crew of three. The quay sloped towards the water, which received the dung and urine of horses, offal and excreta produced by crew members, great quantities of bilge water from the boats, and manure which dropped into the harbour while being shovelled or wheel-barrowed into the vessels."[17] This water passed unfiltered to the houses of the city, and to such institutes as the House of Industry Hospitals where it passed through a grating, the bars of which would prevent the passage of dead cats and rats, into storage tanks.[18] Apart from pollution there was another great disadvantage in the canal system — the pressure of water was insufficient to help in extinguishing fire and Sir Francis Cruise recalled, "I remember well a terrible fire in Westmorland Street, where a houseful of people were burned alive, no water reaching the higher parts of the house."[19]

Corrigan knew that many diseases were caused by the water pollution, and he dispelled the popular belief that filters purified water: "The best filter that ever was constructed will not make impure water pure, or convert unwholesome water." He described experiments done in the House of Industry Hospitals showing that ova and small worms could pass through even a fine sand filter. He stressed the limitations of chemical analysis of water: "Chemistry cannot tell us the difference between the air of a district where to breathe it is death from cholera or yellow-fever, and the invigorating breeze of the most healthful mountain top." He also discussed the dangers of lead poisoning from pipes, and presented three cases that had been under his care. "All these considerations, I think, lead us to the conclusion that we ought not to take our supply from the canal water, which must ever be liable to all the injurious impregnations that are likely to arise from comparatively stagnant water, from the multifarious animal, vegetable and mineral substances carried as articles of traffic, and from the canal itself being the receptacle for the sewage of every boat carrying live lumbar." He pleaded that expense should not be spared as future generations would gladly pay for the benefits to be derived from a clean water supply, but he did not go so far as to suggest the means of achieving this: "I am not competent to offer any suggestions, but I cannot think that with granite mountain ranges within a few miles of our city, it would be difficult to obtain a supply of water that would be wholesome and palatable, and fit for our manufacturing purposes."[15]

Corrigan's first encounters in national politics did not meet with success. He contested unsuccessfully the mayorality of Dublin when James Mackay was elected.[20] In 1868 Sir Benjamen Lee Guiness, member of parliament for the city of Dublin, died and Dominic Corrigan put himself forward as a candidate in the Liberal cause. The medical profession had long regretted its inadequate representation in parliament, and many of his colleagues subscribed towards Corrigan's expenses. It has been said that one of his reasons in seeking a seat was to achieve superannuation for the medical profession.[21] If this is so, there is no evidence that he brought it forward in parliament. He had tried to achieve superannuation for doctors when he was on the Central Board of Health during the famine, because he considered it highly unjust that a doctor should die in the course of his duties and leave behind a destitute family. Mapother tells us that: "Sir Dominic consented to stand for Dublin City and Drs Lyons and McDonnell and I acted as treasurers of a purely professional fund. Over £1,200 was quickly subscribed, although a strong protest was signed by Conservative doctors on the grounds that the destruction of their church was then threatened. It was urged that a single vote could not influence the inevitable disestablishment. But, political convictions have always outweighed professional interest."[22]

The odds against Corrigan were formidable. Arthur Edward Guinness was contesting the seat. He was the eldest son of the well-known and popular Benjamen Lee Guinness who had successfully re-organised the family brewery into a thriving export business which made him the richest man in Ireland. He had been the first lord mayor of Dublin in 1851. He had begun the restoration of St Patrick's Cathedral at a cost of £150,000, and at the time of his death he was engaged in the restoration of Marsh's Library.[23] Apart from the popularity of young Guinness there were other disturbing factors. The measures of the Gladstone government had alarmed the conservative element of the profession and furthermore Corrigan believed that his religion would lose him much of the profession's support. But perhaps his refusal to compromise his liberal opinions was to prove more damaging than all else: "He spoke out in bold and manful terms on the Land Question in especial, and, appealing to first principles, he pointed out that earth, air, and water, coming directly from the natural laboratories of Providence, all mankind were entitled to a just and sufficient share of them for the preservation of life. Bad landlords were an anomaly and an anachronism; they should, he argued, be compelled by law to perform that which good landlords accomplished by their own free will."[24] This line of thought did not appeal to the wealthy landlords, and one member of parliament accused him of preaching communism. Corrigan wrote to the papers asking if this accusation was not unreasonable and he challenged the correspondent to disagree with the principles which led him to take this stance: "As I look over the earth, the dominion of which God gave to Adam for all men, I see in it three great elements which are no man's own — the air, the water and the land . . . They are God's own gifts to man, and man must manage them for mankind . . . Some may say if you deny that every man's land is his own, you advocate communism, or the seizing of lands from the landlords. Indeed I do not. If I advocate justice to the tenant, I do not advocate injustice to the landlord."[25]

The seat was contested with fervour but Corrigan came last in the poll with a little over 200 votes separating him from Guinness and Pim who were returned.[25] Voting at this time was complicated by the practice of freemen votes which could be purchased and Guinness secured 2,000 votes in this way. If the poll had depended on the votes from the wards alone Corrigan would have been elected with Pim. The freeman vote was no longer permitted after 1879.

Characteristically this defeat only served to make Corrigan all the more determined to enter Westminster, and he lost no opportunity in gathering support for the next election. Where better than a church to enlist popular Catholic support? On Sunday, May 23, 1869 a public meeting "most numerously and influentially attended," was held in the old 'John's-lane Chapel,' to decide how best to complete the spectacular new church which the Augustinian Fathers were erecting to replace their old chapel.[26] His Eminence, Cardinal Cullen, Archbishop of Dublin was in the chair. The Lord Mayor, Mr. Edward Fottrell was joined on the platform by prominent members of the clergy, the professions, judiciary and business. The church was packed to capacity. The meeting opened with a resume by Dr Crean of the church's history, which was, to say the least, illustrious:

"The site of the church is the hallowed spot upon which the priory, the hospital, and the Church of St John the Baptist formerly stood, and where our Catholic fore-fathers made an asylum for the sick, the aged, and the dying. This home of charity flourished from the days of the illustrious St Laurence O'Toole until the church, the priory, and the hospital itself was levelled to the earth by the sacriligous hands of the ruthless spoiler. This present chapel, which sprang from the ruins of the old nearly 200 years ago, is the last of the old chapels of Dublin . . . But now, eternal thanks to the wisdom of an all-ruling Providence, it is going to be replaced by a temple of Catholic worship rivalling in architectural splendour and beauty the churches of olden times."

Grandiose ambitions are costly and, over the preceding ten years £18,000 had been collected, but expenditure of £4,000 on the site, and £19,000 on the building left a deficit of £5,000.

Sir Dominic Corrigan then addressed the meeting: "Standing in this old church so many memories crowd back on my mind that I cannot refrain from trespassing on you, I hope for only a few moments . . . Within a few yards of the spot on which I now stand I drew my first breath. I was born on the spot where now rises that grand porch and tower raising its head to heaven, on the summit of which will soon appear aloft the cross, the symbol of our redemption and of Catholic worship." He reminded the packed congregation that his recent failure to achieve a seat in parliament would soon be rectified: "It is not very long since you gathered round me and cheered me in another place and I hope it will not be long before we meet again on the same platform, which, although not so holy as this is at all events useful to our country." With the skill of a consumate politician he thrilled his audience with an account of their struggle against the oppressor, taking care to advocate only tolerance and passive resistance. When he spoke of his intimacy with O'Connell the chapel resounded with applause: "One of the last times I ever saw him was when he sat on the steps of that altar, and when I sat with him, and when Father Matthew preached from the pulpit behind me, and when after the ceremonies he came with me to the Old Castle of St John, beside where I was born, and with me mounted the old round stairs to the top of the Castle of St John." The latest phase in the Catholic struggle, Corrigan said, had been emancipation, an achievement which he believed to be a turning point in Irish history. Was he directing his remarks to the Cardinal and the hierarchy when he intimated that another form of religious intolerance, might again retard Ireland's development? "We never can hope for our country unless men of every creed meets his brother man as his equal, and there can be no equality in the country so long as there is religious unequality. There can be no friendship among men, there can be no nationality unless there is religious equality . . . When we have established equality then we shall look for the regeneration of Ireland."

For a man in pursuit of votes Corrigan's subscription of £10 to the Augustinian fund does seem paltry. From what can be ascertained in a careful search of his papers and the fee book, it would seem that Corrigan was more generous in his endowment of professional bodies than of the Catholic church. There is a record of an earlier business dealing with the Augustinian fathers, in which altruism was not a dominant feature. The site for the new church in Thomas Street included among other properties those once owned by Corrigan's father John. These had passed out of the family's hands, but in 1854 Corrigan and his son William, then a successful barrister, bought the property back in a sheriffs' sale. Apparently a Nicolas Gogarty of Thomas Street was in debt of £500 16s 3d to Dominic Corrigan, who pressed for payment and the sheriffs' sale of Gogarty's property, goods and chattels secured £120. A year later father and son sold the property for £220 to Bishop Daniel O'Connor and Father John Walsh of John Street for the purpose of building the new church, thus earning themselves a hundred pounds' profit.[27]

Sir Arthur Guinness was unseated on petition in 1869. According to Corrigan the circumstances were well known: "A petition was presented against the return (of 1868), and the election for one of our opponents was declared void on the ground of bribery. A new election was ordered in 1869 and you returned me by a large majority!"[28] Corrigan's nearest rival in a sharp contest was Captain King Harmon. On February 21, 1871 Sir Dominic Corrigan made his maiden speech to the House at Westminster.[29] He stated that he had the gratification of being with both parties of the House — the minority party who he thought with, and the majority party who thought with him. In discussing a criticism of the matter under debate as being 'un-English,' he said, "Not long since it was considered very un-English and un-Irish too (laughter) to have an election without big stones or brickbats." He hoped after the last hustings reminiscences of this kind would be deposited in the British Museum — he believed it was a piece of limestone which had been adroitly seized by an honorable member who had not long since come into the House (renewed laughter). "It was not very long since a number or gentlemen had united in a well-known borough to form themselves into a joint-stock company for the purpose of returning certain members. It was not very long since an election would have been considered un-English which had not been characterised by bribery." Did the honourable members sense the cool draft that would in time develop into a gale?

At home the papers waxed enthusiastically about the performance of the new parliamentarian: "The parliamentary *debut* of our distinguished representative, we learn from various sources was a complete success. He was listened to with marked attention, applauded with much heartiness, and keenly appreciated to all present. His delivery was very happy. Calm and deliberate, without labour on affectation, he evolved his arguments with clearness and point, but never sought to erect a superstructure of wearying detail or to enforce his opinions by reiteration, while in his illustration he was delicately humorous and most apposite."[30] Corrigan's style in parliament was deliberate and at times repetitive and according to Mapother modelled on that of the Liberator. He once said to Mapother, "I want to let one idea take root before I try to plant another."[31]

It is difficult to determine how enthusiastic Corrigan's medical colleagues were in supporting him for election. There were to be sure some staunch supporters who gave of time and money to secure his election, but there were also those belonging to the established church who did not wish to see change in their lifetime, and besides there were those who did not espouse his liberal sentiments. He deemed it important that the medical profession be represented in parliament: "The only effective way of attaining the objects desired is by the personal presence of members who are practically acquainted with the subjects before them, capable of furnishing information at the moment required, correcting errors or combating objections as they arise."[32] He was critical of the profession for not seeking greater representation in parliament: "We have always many men among us who would be most useful to the state and to their profession; but they hold back, and too often the excuse is that it would interfere with their practice, which means it would interfere with money-making."

As events turned out Corrigan's medical background was to have little bearing on his parliamentary career. At Westminster he directed his attention to two main issues — non-sectarian university education and the temperance cause, and when Britain appeared to be over-reacting to events in Ireland, he was quick in pleading for his countrymen's rights. He threw himself into his new role with customary vigour. He travelled frequently to London, leaving by the evening packet from Westland Row and often returning after only two days. It was his habit to leave London by the Friday night mail and drive directly from the terminus at Westland Row to the zoological gardens to breakfast with the council on the Saturday morning. Between April and August of 1871 he visited London no less than seven times.[33] Though he remained on the board of the Richmond hospital and continued to do some private practice, he had effectively resigned from medicine when he was elected to parliament. Nonetheless his influence on Irish medicine was considerable and abroad his reputation continued to grow. "Fame has some of the attributes of Time; it withdraws its object from the ordinary level of humanity, and produces an effect of remoteness. Thus it happened that when, in recent years, the name of Corrigan was mentioned in medical society on the continent it was a surprise to most to learn that he still survived, so thoroughly had his name been identified with the great masters of the past whom they were want to revere."[34]

10

Westminster

Corrigan believed that the Irish drinking habit was a cause for grave concern. He had seen the effects of excessive drinking among the poor of the city, and in parliament he turned his attention towards legislative methods for restricting the sale of alcohol. There was before parliament at the time of Corrigan's election a Sunday Trading Bill[1] which sought to forbid the sale of all goods except pastries on Sundays. This bill would have had the effect of prohibiting the sale of alcohol on Sundays, but Corrigan did not favour the religious overtones in it: "He did not believe that by legislation people could be made either moral or religious, or that anything in the New Testament imposed upon society such Sabbath observances as were contained in the Bill."[2] In 1872 speaking to another bill which sought to restrict the sale of alcohol on Sundays to hotels only, he brought to the attention of the house an unique aspect of the Irish drink habit: "The effect of the drinking habits in Ireland under the custom of what was called 'rounds' was peculiarly pernicious; and they led, not only to the ruin of the men themselves, but also to the great waste of their wages which received on the Saturdays, were too often dissipated in whiskey on Sunday."[3] The sadness and the misery caused by whiskey drinking were, Corrigan told the house, difficult to imagine. He quoted from the *Freeman's Journal*: "The police courts presented a frightful appearance this (Monday) morning. A great majority of those in attendance bore the marks of violence, such as black eyes and broken heads. In the northern division there were 140 cases, in the southern 114. A person looking at the crowd without knowing the cause would think a great battle had taken place." An aside from a member that happily such instances did not occur in England touched a sensitive point in the Dubliner who retorted: "I have not quoted as I might have done abundantly from English newspapers for in them I find cases of drunken navvies dashing out the brains of their paramours and murdering their children on Sundays."

The Sunday Closing Bill, as it became known, did not pass parliament and Corrigan then sought to have the act amended, so that it would be unlawful to sell alcohol on Sundays and holy days.[4] The vintners in Dublin and elsewhere in the country were becoming distinctly alarmed at the persistent efforts of Sir Dominic to restrict what they saw as their livelihood. Aware of this Corrigan informed the house that he wished to dispel the notion held by some that his move was "an attempt to interfere with a supposed immemorial right of the trade." He attempted to persuade the publicans at a meeting of the Dublin Licensed Grocers' and Vintners' Association.[5] He listed the support for his bill, not least being the Catholic bishops, some of whom had organised voluntary Sunday temperance with most gratifying results as the Archbishop of Cashel testified: "A drunken man is to be rarely seen amongst us on Sundays. Rioting and blasphemy, the inevitable consequences of excessive drinking, which before the introduction of our law prevailed to a lamentable extent have ceased to desecrate Sunday and to disgrace our towns . . . It has not, to my knowledge led even in a solitary instance to the setting up of unlicensed or shebeen houses."

One of the objections to Corrigan's bill was that unlicensed premises would become an even greater evil than licensed ones, and that Sunday closing would legislate unfairly against the poor who unlike the rich did not have clubs in which to drink. Corrigan answered these arguments by giving the experiences of the bishops with voluntary Sunday closing, and he did not see any reason why the poor should not also have their clubs. The publicans agreed to compromise by opening only "from 2 o'clock p.m. till 6 o'clock p.m.," but Corrigan saw this as an "inducement to the intemperate to come into towns to drink in the licensed house," after which they would repair to the unlicensed ones.[6]

At Westminster he argued strongly that stricter legislation

on drinking was necessary in Ireland than in England: "Beer is the general drink in England; beer taken to excess stupifies; whiskey maddens." He returned again to the difference in the drinking habits of the Irish, a phenomenon that is considered by contemporary psychiatrists to be one of the main causes of the serious problem of alcoholism in Ireland: "In England each man drinks his beer in such quantity as he likes; in Ireland, in country parts especially, they drink in rounds in parties of five or six; each stands his round in turn, treating the party in glasses of whiskey."[4] The support for Corrigan's Bill was considerable. He was able to list among his supporters His Eminence Cardinal Cullen, thirteen archbishops and bishops of the Catholic church, three bishops, sixteen deans and twenty-one archdeacons of the Protestant church, the heads of the Presbyterian bodies and the Wesleyan Methodists. He had, in addition, memorials signed by 1,026 justices of the peace, and representatives of the gaols and asylums. His opponents were for the greater part nameless, but in politics money generally overcomes eminence and honourable idealism, and the purveyors of liquor wielded their fiscal power effectively. Corrigan's bill was defeated by thirty-three votes, and realising that he could not hope to achieve total Sunday closing, he supported the move for limited opening then being advocated for England, and accepted an amendment that was carried giving the authorities the power to close public houses on Sundays should a majority of the citizens so desire.[7]

Though defeated in parliament Corrigan continued to press for restrictive legislation through the Association for Closing Publichouses on Sundays of which he became president. In this role he attempted to change the public's attitude to drinking:[8] "Let each man in Ireland, whether in parliament or in possession of a vote to return a member, think for himself and we can have no doubt the result will be — 'close the public-houses on Sundays.' " He pleaded with the public to look at the interests of the two sides to determine which had the more honourable motive: "It is, I think, impossible for anyone not to admit that on the one side are the advocates of Sunday closing, without a personal object to gain, and that on the other side are those, the majority of whom derive a profit from the sale of whiskey on Sundays." The Association for Closing Publichouses on Sundays had its own newspaper – the *Dublin Temperance Banner*[9] in which it outlined its objectives and published the results of what would today be called opinion polls. Members of the association visited every family in each of the municipal districts of Dublin, Belfast, Londonderry, Cork, Limerick and Waterford leaving a questionnaire which was collected the following day. The result of this unusual poll was that 78,158 heads or representatives of families voted, of whom 69,270 were in favour of Sunday closing.[10] But even these overwhelming statistics were not enough to overcome the opposition of the huge vested interest in the sale of alcohol. The Irish publicans were no longer alone in fighting the Sunday closing movement; their English counterparts were much alarmed at the momentum the movement was gathering in Ireland and they began to exert financial pressure in the most effective areas of parliament, so much so that Benjamin Whitworth, the member for Kilkenny suspected some dishonest dealings: "There was a good deal of money contributed to defray the expenses of opposition; he would like to know how it was spent? He thought a good deal of it was spent in the house itself, some perhaps legitimately, but he was afraid that most of it was not."[11]

As President of the Association for Closing Publichouses on Sundays Corrigan had difficulty at times in preventing his members from pressing for total prohibition of alcohol, and he assured opponents of the movement that once Sunday closing was achieved, "We will then declare this association dissolved."[12] Though he did not achieve success with the Sunday Closing bill in parliament, he remained as President of the Association for Closing Publichouses on Sunday until 1878 when the objective was in sight.[13] An astute politician might have warned Corrigan that to support a temperance movement in Ireland was politically unwise but this would not have been likely to deter him from the course he took at Westminster. He believed genuinely that alcohol was a cause of profound misery in Ireland, and in this he was right. He recognised with remarkable prescience that the Irishman's affinity for alcohol was abnormal, and that his drinking pattern was very different from that of the Englishman. One hundred years later the problem is one of the most serious affecting the progress of the nation.

Corrigan showed himself always ready to take up the cause of his countrymen when Westminster threatened to wield its punitive might in the face of Irish unrest. He believed that the English did not understand the Irish character and that Britain, being quick to over-react to events in Ireland, was more likely to aggravate than quell disturbance. He told the house that he regretted its tendency to deal differently with Ireland than with other parts of the United Kingdom: "He was sorry to see occurrences were occasionally passed over in Scotland and England which would bring down heavy censure on Ireland."[14] His point was well illustrated in the Phoenix Park Riots in 1871 when a crowd gathered to petition for the pardon of prisoners, and the meeting ended in a riot with the police. Corrigan urged parliament to leave well alone and not add fuel to the fire with retaliatory arrests and trials. He said: "The object of the meeting was legal, for surely it would be conceded that the people were entitled to meet to petition for the pardon of prisoners, whether the crime was treason or murder." He assured the house that the number of injuries had been greatly exaggerated, and he warned that an enquiry would not arrive at the truth but only succeed in prolonging the whole business. He dismissed as ridiculous the suggestion that the meeting was particularly offensive because it was held near the vice-regal lodge. The site of the fracas was, he pointed out, the same distance from the lodge as was the Marble Arch from Buckingham Palace. As to the inference that the riots had been designed to interfere with the people's recreation, he asked if the members of parliament were aware of the size of the Phoenix Park: "Kensington Park, Hyde Park, and St James' Park put in line would not equal in measurement half the length of the Phoenix Park." There was no need, he assured the house to seek "a mysterious Fenian plot" just because there had been large numbers of the populace present. In the People's Gardens on a Sunday there might be 5 to 6,000 visitors of all classes, and in the zoological gardens another 6,000. He regretted that there was nowhere in Dublin suitable for a large meeting and he suggested that part of the park should be set aside for such events. Corrigan ended his appeal by asking that the law which was the same for both lands should be administered in the same way in Dublin as in London. "Ireland," he warned, "was content to be the sister of England, but would not be her Cinderella . . . Let bygones be bygones. Let us look to amend the future, and try to forget the bitterness of the past." Parliament listened, but did not heed him. Trials followed, and two years later there was little sign of a satisfactory conclusion. He took the same line in the debates following a Galway election in which there were twenty-four prosecutions for undue influence and intimidation. He pointed out that there was wrong on both sides, and that the truth would never be arrived at. "Leave Galway to itself, and all will be friends again, a consummation devoutly to be wished." Aware that neither party would adopt his suggestion he informed the government that he would not be voting with it.[15]

He also used his influence in parliament in an attempt to secure release of Fenian prisoners, and his views on the subject are of interest if for no other reason than the relevance of the issues to contemporary political events in Ireland: "I think the government view to take would be were the crimes for which the men are now in confinement, crimes against society altogether apart from Fenianism or were the crimes or acts of those men of political origin, committed in the furtherance of a political object? If the latter and I think this may be admitted it appears to me we ought to consider the acts of those men not as moral but as political crimes."[16] The exemption of the political prisoner from criminal culpability was as polemical then as it is today, but Corrigan was quite explicit in his opinion. "In a late election at Waterford a soldier acting under command in charging ran his lance through an unoffending man standing in his own doorway — That act viewed 'per se' was murder but it truly and really was not. The Fenian who blew down the wall of Clerkenville Prison blew it down to liberate his chief — He killed some persons by the explosion but murder was not his motive . . . I would now only put this practical question — would it be just or would it be politic to liberate those men? — I feel quite convinced it would be both."

In parliament Corrigan was gaining a reputation, at least at home, of being bold and courageous in debate. His style was fluent and impressive, his English simple but perfect, and he could marshal facts with great skill. But he had faults; he had an irritating tendency towards repetition in his efforts to clinch the argument, and this may at times have alienated his supporters. His temper was "easily discomposed," and he could interrupt on a point of order not always valid.[17]

Corrigan's greatest efforts at Westminster were on behalf of university education. His interest in education was not confined to medicine. As a commissioner for national education, he had been instrumental in establishing the network of national schools throughout the country, and as a member of the senate of the Queen's University from its foundation in 1859 until his death thirty years later, he supported non-denominational education much to the annoyance of the Catholic hierarchy. The history of university education in Ireland is a complex issue the outcome of which influenced the history of Ireland more than its many wars had done. The Catholic hierarchy were victorious, if indeed that word is applicable, over successive Liberal and Conservative British governments, but Catholic intransigence proved every bit as illogical as had Protestant bigotry in the past, and the establishment of denominational in favour of secular university education was to do much to perpetuate the sectarian divisions that persist in Irish society. Dublin University founded by Queen Elizabeth I is the oldest of Ireland's many universities. The foundation stone of its college, Trinity College, was laid by Thomas Smyth, lord mayor of Dublin on March 15, 1593. It was not in fact the first university in Dublin. In 1320, in the office of Pope John XXII, a university had been established but it only lasted a short time.[18] Trinity College was originally designed for the higher education of Protestants, but for many years after its foundation a number of Catholics were educated there. This was stopped in 1637, when Archbishop Laud was Chancellor and from then until 1793 Catholics and Dissenting Protestants were debarred from taking degrees. The Relief Act of 1793 allowed "Papists . . . to hold or take degrees or any professorships in, or be masters or fellows of any college to be hereafter founded in this kinddom, provided that such college shall be a member of the

University of Dublin." As there was no immediate prospect of a new college, Catholics were permitted to take degrees in Trinity College but were debarred from scholarships and fellowships. This was a serious disability to the small Catholic intelligentsia, and Richard Lalor Sheil, a Catholic graduate of Trinity College, a member of parliament and a notable playwright brought in a bill in 1834 "for the admission of Roman Catholics and other dissenters to scholarships and certain professorships" which was promptly thrown out. Parliamentary agitation, however, continued and in 1845, an act of parliament was passed "to enable Her Majesty to endow New Colleges for the advancement of learning in Ireland." As a result of this bill, grants were provided for the erection of three colleges at Belfast, Cork and Galway, to be known as the Queen's Colleges. Each college was to have a staff of twenty professors in addition to a president, registrar, librarian and bursar and contrary to practice in Trinity and the British universities all appointments were to be made by the Crown rather than the university.[19] A fundamental principle of the new colleges was to be "the absence of all interference, positive or negative, with the conscientious scruples of the students in matters of religion."[20] Only students who completed prescribed courses in one of the colleges could proceed to examinations in a new university established in 1850 to be known as the Queen's University. Medical candidates might be exempted from part of the prescribed course in medicine on presenting certificates of attendance at other recognised medical schools, provided they attended at least one-third of the medical lectures in one of the Queen's colleges.[21]

The Catholic hierarchy had deliberated for a number of years on the impending establishment of the Queen's Colleges and Corrigan had, in fact, presented the bishops with his views in 1845. He did make one interesting, if somewhat impractical, suggestion on the method of selection of university professors: "A man may profess the very highest knowledge of a subject and yet be *a very bad teacher of it*. Among men who will aspire to professor's chairs there will not be probably any great difference as to the amount of information *possessed by each* but there will be the widest difference *as to the manner* and clearness in *conveying* information.

The men wanted for professor's chairs in the colleges are men not possessing profound and eruditic knowledge of their subject, but men capable of conveying the knowledge possessed in a clear form. The examination of the candidates should then be by hearing them lecture *extempore* on a subject chosen on the moment."[22]

The Presbyterians and the Catholics sought representation on the staffing of the Queen's colleges. The government met some of the Presbyterian demands for the Belfast College, but when the bill received royal assent in 1845, the Catholic claims were all but ignored. Only seven of the sixty professors appointed were Catholic.[23]

The Queen's University was to be administered by a senate, the nominated members being the lord chancellor of Ireland (Maziere Brady), the two archbishops of Dublin (Richard Whately and Daniel Murray), the chief justice of the Queen's bench (Frances Blackburne), the master of the rolls (Thomas Berry Cusack), the chief baron of the exchequer (David Richard Pigot), and a number of individuals distinguished either in their particular professions or for their services to the government. These included, the Third Earl of Rosse, the astronomer; Lord Monteagle, an Irish peer and former Whig minister; Thomas Wyse, then British ambassador at Athens; Sir Philip Crampton, the surgeon-general who was also a member of the senate of London University; Richard Griffith, geologist, civil engineer, and chairman of the Board of Works; Thomas Aiskew Larcom, formerly of the Ordnance Survey, then deputy-chairman of the Board of Works; James Gibson, barrister of Belfast, and law advisor to the general assembly of the Presbyterian church; Robert Kane and Dominic Corrigan. Less than one-third of these senators were Catholics, and of these only Kane and Corrigan were to prove regular attenders. The Viceroy, himself was nominated as first chancellor of the university when Prince Albert declined to accept the position.[24]

The Queen's colleges and University ran into trouble from the start. Both Catholic and Protestant objected to the colleges being under the control of the government, but the main objection was that the colleges were undenominational. Victorian idealism did not permit the separation of education from religion.[25] Religion was in fact regarded as "the queen of the sciences"[26] and its exclusion as a subject from the curriculum was unacceptable to Catholics. In 1849 , Paul Cullen was appointed Archbishop of Armagh and he immediately committed himself to the destruction of the 'godless' Queen's College and University. Cullen had been in Rome for nearly thirty years where he had been rector of the Irish College. He was "inflexibly hostile to mixed education."[27] He presided over the Synod of Thurles in 1850, at which it was decreed that no Catholic bishop or priest should hold office of any kind in the Queen's colleges; and the clergy were required to discourage the faithful from attending them. Cullen did not mince his words; in *A Letter to the Catholic Clergy* he wrote:

> "All Catholic parents have been warned of the 'grievous and intrinsic dangers' of the institutions; they have been called upon to save their children from their influence; and the terrible account has been announced to them which they shall have to render to Jesus Christ, for the souls purchased by His Blood, if they betray these little ones, who are so precious in His sight, into grievous dangers, or suffer them to be perverted by a corrupt system of instruction."[28]

Cullen's intransigence and total inflexibility on the issue of mixed education, together with an unsuppressible energy was to influence university education for centuries ahead, in ways not yet fully apparent.

In spite of Catholic opposition the "godless colleges" and the university got down to the business of organising an educational programme. The Queen's colleges were independent corporations with the right to design their own course and examinations, but their educational programme was determined almost entirely by the senate of the Queen's University.[29] The university's headquarters were in Dublin Castle and all examinations were held in St Patrick's Hall in the Castle until 1877, when they were transferred to the Exhibition Building at Earlsfort Terrace. The senate met on average eight times a year and had an effective membership of under nine. These included the three presidents of the colleges in Cork, Galway and Belfast; Maziere Brady vice-chancellor (until his death in 1871), who was lord chancellor of Ireland under three liberal administrations: James Gibson QC, who attended until his death in 1880, and Dominic Corrigan, who remained a senator for thirty years and succeeded Brady as vice-chancellor in 1871. Robert Kane who was president of Queen's College, Cork, believed that the Queen's system had not done too badly against difficult odds. In the first seven years the colleges had enrolled 534 students at Galway, 772 at Belfast, and 798 at Cork of whom 25 per cent were Catholics.[30] Kane commenting on these figures wrote:

"Thus, in the Queen's University, founded in a country paralysed, at the time, by the most fearful visitation of famine and pestilence that had visited this portion of the globe since the middle ages; in a country depopulated to an extent beyond aught on record; where the very classes for the education of whose sons the Queen's colleges were founded, were reduced, in a large proportion, to ruin, and in all, to the verge of destitution, by the financial distresses of the time — the Queen's University and the Queen's colleges, exposed to all those dangers which, with institutions as with man, necessarily beset the path of infancy; subject to all the various kinds of influence which could withold or withdraw pupils from their walls, yet, actually, matriculated more students, and conferred more degrees in the corresponding interval of time from their foundation, than did the University of London and its affiliated colleges, supported by the wealth, the energy, and the influence that belong to the metropolis of the British Empire."[31]

The Catholic clergy with Cullen at its head was not content with the Papal Rescripts of 1847 and 1848, and the dictates of the Synod of Thurles condemning the Queen's colleges. The bishops determined to found a Catholic University modelled on Louvain University. Cullen invited John Henry Newman to become the first rector of the university in 1851. He was, as Dowling,[32] commented peculiarly well-qualified for the post:

"He was a Catholic, a recent convert; he was a scholar; and he had experience of university life that few Englishmen at his age or of his time could boast of, and which no Catholic Irishman could possibly have had. He had come into contact with some of the greatest minds of his day; and that contact was still scarcely broken. His sermons, his lectures, his writings were living proof of his learning, of his depth of thought, of his originality, and of his power of exposition."

The Catholic University was opened at number eighty-six St Stephen's Green in November 1854, and the Catholic School of Medicine was founded in Cecilia Street. As the university had no charter, it could not confer degrees, but the school of medicine was recognised by the Royal College of Surgeons of Ireland and was able to grant degrees.[33] The university was also without endowment and relied for financing from voluntary collections in Irish dioceses and parishes and from Catholic concerns abroad.[34] The college had a sublime setting on St Stephen's Green where the Georgian dignity of numbers eighty-five and eighty-six was augmented by the erection of the beautiful Byzantine University chapel designed by John Hungerford Pollen, which became the centre of religious life in the university. This is not the only memorial that Newman left as testimony to his brief rectorship of the university; of greater durability are his famous lectures on *The Idea of a University*.[35] His intellectual vision was so much more liberal than that of Cullen, we can only marvel that Cullen chose him as rector in the first place, and it can hardly have come as a surprise to their contemporaries when Newman resigned in 1858. Gwynn[36] summarised Cullen's idea of a Catholic university as one that not only should "prevent Catholics from going to Protestant universities, but that the hierarchy should have the most absolute power over its organisation in every detail." Newman could not tolerate Cullen's bigoted outlook. If Cullen's views are to prevail, he wrote to a friend, the university "will simply be priest-ridden. I mean men who do not know literature and science will have the direction of the teaching. I cannot conceive the professors taking part in this. They will simply be scrubs."[35] Cullen soon tired of Newman's liberal views on university education. He wrote in 1858:

"The rector has not been in Ireland at all this year and things cannot go on without someone in charge. Furthermore, Father Newman has organised things in such a costly manner that they cannot be supported from the collections, and while the students are few, he has nominated very many professors who have nothing to do. Moreover there are complaints regarding discipline. Father Newman kept a kind of boarding school for a dozen young men in his own house and some of these went to dances and kept horses for hunting. Father Newman justified this system by saying that there should be more liberty at the university than in the secondary schools, but the people reply that collections are not necessary to educate young men in dancing and hunting. I spoke repeatedly against these matters, but it seems that Father Newman so greatly admired the University of Oxford that he could not bring himself to condemn practices which are in force there."[37]

Dr Bartholomew Woodlock, brother-in-law to Dominic Corrigan, was appointed to succeed Newman as rector of the Catholic University.

The clergy resented bitterly the expenditure of £30,000 annually of public money on the Queens' University, while the Catholic University was "left to struggle unrecognised by the state and unaided by public funds."[38] There followed a decade of vacillation by government at a loss as how best to accommodate the Catholic University within the structure of the Queen's University. There were many proposals, most of which were resisted by the Protestants who condemned endowment of any institute that was not non-sectarian.

In 1865 Corrigan published privately a pamphlet setting down his views on university education.[39] In this he proposed that the Queen's University should become an examining body with its examinations open to all comers, whether educated at the Queen's colleges or not. He maintained that not all subjects needed the full facilities of an university: "History, geography, mathematics, logic and some languages may be learned at home, under private tuition, or at colleges or schools throughout the country; but modern languages and the demonstrative and more practically useful sciences, can only be learned where there is a complete staff of professors with all the appliances." Furthermore, he advocated that the university be non-sectarian not only in relation to the students, but also in the composition of its senate and the appointment of its professors, of whom an equal number should be Protestant and Catholic.

These proposals understandably caused quite a stir. The Catholic church can only have been horrified that so eminent a Catholic would support non-denominational education, but the only record of any statement among Corrigan's papers is a non-committal comment from the president of Maynooth:[40] "I have read it with great interest. It does not go as far as I should wish." Professor Nesbitt from Queen's College in Belfast published a pamphlet in reply to Corrigan's views[41] in which he pointed out that the Queen's colleges were founded "not to give greater facilities for obtaining degrees, but to extend academical education," and that Corrigan's advocacy of equal religious representation on the senate and staff would in fact enhance rather than diminish sectarianism. As far as the Protestants of the North were concerned "they would at once dissociate themselves from an institution smitten with the taint of sectarianism." Nesbitt did not believe it practical to have equal religious representation on the professorial staff, and his argument does have some validity, even if it lacks credibility: "No one dreams that Catholic intellect is less acute than Protestant; but to get an adequate supply of Catholic intellect of the required maturity, it is necessary to have a sufficient seed-plot for its cultivation, and at present it would not be easy to point to such." Sir Robert Peel's views were not dissimilar. He wrote to Corrigan: "I have read it with much attention, I am glad to observe you endorse the views of O'Connell and other eminent men as regards the advantage of mixing together for purposes of secular education young men of different religious persuasions, and that you repudiate the foundation of state establishments of sectarian colleges. Pardon me however if I venture to differ from the opinion you profess of the necessity of distinguishing, under the head of separate religious denominations, the number

THE PHYSIC-ALL BARONET.

"Preserver of my father, now of me,
The medicine of our house!"

58. A caricature of Dominic Corrigan by Spex in Ireland's Eye, *July 11, 1874, p. 174. By courtesy of the National Library of Ireland.*
(see p. 243)

59. *Photograph taken in Dublin Zoo in 1855. The group are positioned around the sledge used by Sir Edward Belcher in an expedition to the North Pole in 1853 in search of Sir John Franklin and his party. Left to right: D. Corrigan, Dr. George W. Hatschell, Jacob Owen, Robert Ball, Sir Francis W. Brady, Dr. George J. Allman, P. Supple, Jnr, Mr. Lowe (Superintendent), Mr. Walsh (Carpenter), J. Supple, Snr. (Keeper), Patrick Rice (Keeper). By courtesy of Dr. T. Murphy. Dublin Zoological Gardens. Photograph by D. Davison.* (see p. 246)

60. *Sign for Allée Corrigan, Arcachon in Bordeaux. Photograph by E. O'Brien.* (see p. 249)

61. *Allée Arcachon, 1981. Photograph by E. O'Brien.* (see p. 249)

62. The Promenade, Arcachon. Photograph by J. Hall from a postcard.

63. The Old Jetty, Arcachon. Photograph by J. Hall from a postcard.
(see p. 249)

64. A mobile bathing cabin in Arcachon. Photograph by D. Davison from a postcard. (see p. 249)

65. The Promenade, Arcachon in 1866. Photograph by D. Davison from a postcard. (see p. 249)

66. *Tombstone on the grave of John Joseph Corrigan (1831-1866) in Melbourne, Australia. The inscription reads: "In memory of Captain John Joseph Corrigan, 3rd Dragoon Guards who departed this life, January 6, 1866 aged 35 years. Eldest son of Sir Dominic J. Corrigan Bart. M.D. Ireland. Requiescat in pace". By courtesy of the Royal College of Physicians of Ireland. Photograph by D. Davison from an old photograph.* (see p. 254)

67. *"The Miss Corrigans 6.10.1861". Mary (standing) and Cecilia Mary Corrigan. Courtesy of the Royal College of Physicians of Ireland. Photograph of D. Davison from an old photograph.* *(see p. 255)*

68. *Cecilia Mary Corrigan. By courtesy of the Royal College of Physicians of Ireland. Photograph by D. Davison from an old photograph.*
(see p. 255)

69. *Dominic Corrigan in later years. By courtesy of the Royal College of Physicians of Ireland. Photograph by D. Davison from an old photograph.*

70. *Augustinian church and monastery, John Street, Dublin. From an engraving in the Dublin Builder. By courtesy of the National Library of Ireland.* (see p. 270)

A XX M.P.

" There came a bark that, blowing forward, bore
Sir Arthur, like a modern gentleman
Of stateliest port ; and all the people cried,
' Arthur is come again ! ' "

PUB. BY C SMYTH.   57. DAME STREET.

71. *A caricature of Sir Arthur Guinness by Spex in* Ireland's Eye: *February 21, 1874, p. 44. By courtesy of the National Library of Ireland.* (see p. 272)

72. *Paul Cardinal Cullen. From an unsigned portrait in the Pro-Cathedral House. By courtesy of the Pro-Cathedral. Photograph by D. Davison.* (see p. 286)

73. *The Most Reverend Dr. Bartholomew Woodlock (1819-1902).*
From the All Hallows Annual, *1899, p. 8. By courtesy of All Hallows*
College, Dublin. Photograph by D. Davison.   *(see p. 287)*

74. William Ewart Gladstone (1809-1898). From a carte-de-visite.
Photograph by D. Davison.   *(see p. 313)*

75. Francis Cruise (1834-1912). From a photograph in the Royal College of Physicians of Ireland. By courtesy of the College of Physicians. Photograph by D. Davison. *(see p. 327)*

76. *Wreath laying in the Corrigan family vault in St. Andrew's Church, Westland Row, Dublin on the centenary of the death of Sir Dominic Corrigan. February 1st, 1980. Professor O. Conor Ward, Vice-President of the Royal College of Physicians of Ireland and Dr. Eoin O'Brien, President of the Section of the History of Medicine of the Royal Academy of Medicine in Ireland.* (see p. 328)

of members of the senate of the University. Neither do I think nor have I ever heard that the present constitution of the senate is considered a grievance by Catholic parents or pupils. I differ also entirely from the inference you draw for the religious persuasion of the several professors in the other Queen's colleges, . . . sectarian ascendency in conformity with local predominant influences has never had anything to do with the appointment of professors; merit and merit only guiding the selectors to the best of our judgement, . . . and truly it would not be just to exclude or to eliminate an eminent man seeking a chair in one of the colleges on the plea that his religious faith, with which his teaching as professor would have nothing to do, was not of the required complexion."[42]

Lord Palmerston was of the same mind as Corrigan on nonsectarian education: "What the Irish Catholics want to accomplish under cover of this reasonable purpose is to substitute their sectarian college entirely for the Queen's colleges, which are founded on the principle of mixed education. This is an aim which we must not allow them to accomplish . . . My opinion on the contrary, is that the aggregate university body of the Queen's colleges should examine for degrees all comers, wheresoever educated." He was prepared to be explicit on the likely outcome of such an arrangement: "What the Catholic priesthood want is that this Catholic college should be the only place of education for the young Irish Catholic, and that it should be, like Maynooth, a place where young men should be brought up to be bigoted in religion, to feel for Protestants theological hatred, and to feel political hatred for England."[43]

An interesting view of the pamphlet is given in a biographical sketch of Corrigan in the *Illustrated London News*. The pamphlet it said, was "distinguished by its containing his own views, not those of any party, and probably the right view, as it has received the abuse of the bigoted and opposite parties of the two sides of Ireland — the Presbyterian on the one hand, and the Ultramontane on the other."[44]

In 1866 the government, anxious to pacify the Catholic bishops without upsetting the Protestants, issued a supplemental charter to the Queen's University, which empowered the university to hold a matriculation examination distinct from that of the Queen's colleges, and to grant degrees to those who had so matriculated even though they had not pursued their studies at the Queen's colleges or matriculated from them. As Corrigan had recommended just such a measure in his pamphlet, it is hardly surprising that he was among the senators of the Queen's University who voted for acceptance of this controversial charter by a slim majority of two. The charter was, however, fiercely resisted and Dr William Mac-Cormac of Belfast initiated proceedings in chancery the effect of which was to render the charter inoperative.[45]

The Catholic hierarchy had so far desisted from entering into open opposition of Corrigan's views on university education, possibly out of consideration for his relationship to the rector of the Catholic University. Another Catholic, James Lowry Whittle published in 1866 a pamphlet, *Freedom of Education: What it Means* in which he appealed to educated Catholics to beware of the bishops demands which would ultimately restrict their independence in education.[46] This was dismissed by Cullen as being "as ignorant as it is presumptuous."[47] When, however, Corrigan in his campaign for election in 1870 reiterated his views on non-sectarian, or as he called it, mixed education, in a speech in the Rotunda,[48] the hierarchy decided the time had come to make its position quite clear to him. The Very Rev John Spratt was chosen to inform the Baronet that if he wished to represent Dublin in parliament he must also represent the Catholic church's view — totally. John Spratt, a respected figure, had been Provincial of the Carmelite Order; he had built Whitefriar Street Church, and founded St Peter's Orphanage, St Joseph's Night Refuge and the Asylum for Catholic Female Blind. He was almost as prominent as Father Matthew in the temperance campaigns and he was active in attempts to revive native industries.[49] He wrote to Corrigan: "I hope the sincere interest I feel in your election for the city as the worthy and gifted representative of the united Liberal party will plead my excuse for respectfully drawing your attention very earnestly to one of the subjects dealt with in your speech at the Rotunda last week. Since then, I have become aware that with reference to the education question the views you are supposed to maintain cause great uneasiness, I will not say dissatisfaction, in high quarters amongst the clergy. To yourself personally there can be but one feeling, that of friendly admiration, but the education question being the only one now left unsettled, upon which as Catholics we have a natural interest, the clergy and Catholics generally feel they have a right to make quite sure that their future representative in parliament shall fully, fairly and unconditionally represent and sustain their views regarding that most important question."[50] In reply Corrigan stated that his views on the subject were well known for many years: "That there should be one great National University for Ireland; that it would have no concern whatever with teaching; that all university degrees, emoluments and honours should be equally open to all candidates without distinction, let them be educated where they may, in college, at school or at home, in short that the whole business of the university should be to ascertain what a man knows and not where he learned it."[51] However upset the church may have been by his views on university education, it must have regarded his pronouncement on primary education as almost heretical: "On primary education my opinion is that there should be the same 'Freedom of Education.' That the state should be equally impartial to all denominations giving equal aid to all, to those who desire to have denominational education and to those who do not." He warned that dissension among the Catholics would be disastrous at the election but added that if his views did not obtain general approval he would withdraw from the contest. "Desirous as I am of the honour of representing Dublin I am more anxious for the success of the Liberal cause and I will not stand in the way to imperil its success."

There followed a number of meetings of which some notes exist indicating that the clergy were playing for time and awaiting the return of Cardinal Cullen from abroad.[52] Then on July 26, 1870 the following demands were delivered verbally to Corrigan whose request for them in writing was declined. He insisted, however, in having them transcribed: "That Sir D. Corrigan should give an unqualified declaration of support for middle class denominational education as understood by the bishops. That he should vote for a grant for a Roman Catholic college . . . That while Sir D. Corrigan was not to be asked to retract his opinions upon mixed education yet in all probability he would be questioned, and it was expected he would be so dexterous in his replies as not to say too much in favour of the question and not to express any opinion repugnant to that of the Roman Catholic bishops."[53] There followed a number of recorded exchanges between Corrigan and members of the clergy, with the latter threatening on one occasion to publish a correspondence with Corrigan which would deny him success if he did not change his stand on mixed education.

Then on August 7, a long letter arrived from Cardinal Cullen in which he made his position very clear:

"I thank you for your address to the electors of Dublin, which you had had the kindness to send, and I trust you will allow me to make some observations on it, as I promised to do. I shall merely refer to that part of it which treats of education, a question in which, in common with all Catholics I take a deep interest, because if Catholic children receive a bad or uncatholic education, they run a great risk of losing religious feeling altogether, whilst if they be trained up in the fear and love of God according to Catholic principles, they will be generally able to preserve their faith, and to perform the works which their religion prescribes . . . I must add that the eyes of the Catholics of Ireland at present are turned to Dublin, and that it is expected that this city will give an example to the whole kingdom by electing a member firmly resolved to uphold the right of Catholic parents to give a Catholic education to their children, and to require that whilst doing so they shall have a full share in all the advantages and endowments which have been enjoyed or are enjoyed by persons of other religious denominations."[54]

The Cardinal accused Corrigan of neglecting the question of intermediate education through the royal and endowed schools most of which were in the hands of Protestants: "There will be no equality in the country unless Catholic intermediate schools be put on the same footing in regard to endowments as Protestant schools of the same class." He argued that Catholics must be given the same opportunity as Protestants in university education:

> "In the next place I must observe that the proclaiming
> of freedom of education would be a delusion and a
> mockery unless Catholics be first placed on a level with
> Protestants, and steps be taken to endow one or more
> Catholic university colleges and subsidiary institutions.
> As things are at present Protestants and non-Catholics
> have possession of vast endowments for educational
> purposes. Trinity College has princely estates, and an
> immense annual income: the Royal schools which are
> ancillary to Trinity College have also large possessions,
> and the Queen's Colleges receive a yearly grant of
> £30,000 from the taxes of this country paid in a great
> part by Catholics — Trinity College and the royal schools
> are openly Protestant, and the teaching of that college
> has dragged thousands of young Catholics into the abyss
> of heresy or apostasy. The Queen's colleges have been
> condemned by the Holy See and the Catholic bishops
> as dangerous to faith and morals, and are well calculated
> to promote indifferentism to all religion. Catholic youth
> cannot therefore frequent such institutions with a safe
> conscience: they are left in that sad condition to which
> confiscation and persecution reduced them, and not
> having a Catholic university or Catholic intermediate
> schools, they are placed in a state of inferiority when
> compared with their Protestant fellow subjects . . . Cer-
> tainly neither freedom nor equality in education can
> exist, as long as one class constituting only a fraction of
> the population is amply endowed, while at the same time
> Catholics, the great mass of the people, are obliged to
> provide from their own resources for the education of
> their children in the higher branches of knowledge."

He then elaborated on the concept of a Catholic university:
"As to a Catholic university, I need only repeat the Fifth
Resolution of the bishops adopted in Maynooth last year,
namely, that since the Protestants of this country have had
a Protestant university for 300 years, and have it still, the
Catholic people of Ireland clearly have a right to a Catholic
university." The Catholic church could not reconcile itself

to the paradox in its argument, that if Catholics who were exposed to other religions lost their faith, the tenets of their beliefs cannot have been sound: "If young Catholics of seventeen or eighteen years of age be compelled to keep company and to attend the same schools with youths of different religion, the great probability is that these Catholics will abandon the practice of confession, of fasting, of mortification and other works which are hard to flesh and blood, especially when they see that their teacher and their companions laugh at or ridicule such practices, and express their contempt of young men who forsooth are foolish enough to be guided by the precepts and doctrines of the ancient church." Cardinal Cullen was not prepared to compromise at all: "With respect to primary education I beg to state that the demands of Catholics comprize Catholic schools, Catholic teachers, Catholic training schools, Catholic books and Catholic inspectors. Less than this will not satisfy the Catholics of Ireland . . . I would have it clearly understood that no public aid should be given to any school established for the purpose of perverting Catholic children, or for any proselytising purposes. Proselytism is productive of such evil results, and is carried on to so great an extent in Ireland, that where there is a question of schools too much care cannot be employed in guarding against it." He made a veiled threat to Corrigan by implying that he had the means of turning Catholic opinion against him: "I shall now conclude by observing that I think a sentence in your letter to Dr Spratt will be turned against you by your opponents. You say that on university education 'my views have been for some years before the public. I entertain the same views now.' Many Catholics will say that they cannot support you because some few years ago you wrote very strongly in favour of mixed education and the Queen's colleges, and you now profess your adherence to what you wrote then." The Cardinal would accept nothing short of a complete retraction of Corrigan's views on education. "The only way I see for getting out of this difficulty is by publishing a distinct condemnation of those colleges and of the principle on which they are founded."[54]

Corrigan replied three days later. He restated his views as given to Dr Spratt but elaborated on a few points: "That there

should be one great National University the constitution of
which should be such as to fairly represent all parties and thus
command the confidence of all. That its degrees honours and
emoluments should be open to all candidates wherever educated in colleges, school, whether boarding or day schools or
at home. That it should have no concern with teaching its
function being solely that of examining. That the charter of
the existing universities *viz*. Trinity College and Queen's University should be repealed so as that there should be but
one University of Ireland. That the state should impartially
distribute among the colleges whatever funds may be allotted
to such colleges giving equal aid to all."[55] Corrigan made one
tempting suggestion to the Cardinal, but this he knew would
not be enough to divert him from a doctrinaire advocacy for
Catholic education. "In my letter to Dr Spratt and in my
address I have gone much further than I went in my pamphlet
of 1865 for while in the latter I ventured only so far as to
propose to establish a National University thinking we were
not strong enough to touch Trinity College, I am now of
opinion that we are strong enough to deal with it." Corrigan
in closing threw down the gauntlet to the Cardinal by informing him that he was going for parliament with or without the
support of the Church: "I hope your Eminence will kindly
excuse me if I have failed to explain myself on all points
satisfactorily but the writ for the coming election has just
been issued this day and the pressure on my time and thought
is very great. I can only in conclusion assure your Eminence
that no effort will be wanting on my part to carry out to the
utmost of my power your Eminences recommendations."
Another letter followed by return of post, and it is of interest
to see that Corrigan's brother-in-law, Dr Woodlock, was now
drawn into the fray. He together with Cannon Farrell and Dr
Spratt called on Corrigan to seek clarification of a few issues.[56]
They wanted to know if Corrigan would advocate continuing
the endowments to Trinity College, and the Protestant royal
and charter schools and other like institutes "instruments of
a now happily bygone Protestant Ascendency" or if he would
advocate redistribution of funds for education on the principle of equal rights for all. Corrigan in reply pointed out that
as far as private endowments were concerned parliament

could not interfere, but he assured the clergy that he would
seek the redistribution of all public endowments for education on the principle of equal rights for all. He also assured
them that he opposed granting public monies to any proselytising institutions.

Cardinal Cullen interpreted Corrigan's agreement on these
points as a capitulation, so much so that he even went along
to vote for Corrigan and for the quaker Jonathan Pim, another
Liberal, as is recorded in one of his letters:

> ". . . Dr Corrigan the Liberal candidate, formerly a great
> advocate of mixed education, denounced the Queen's
> College most vehemently and declared for Catholic edu-
> cation. Pim, the Quaker, went on in the same strain. The
> Tories declared for the Protestant church and mixed edu-
> cation . . . I voted (today) for Pim and Corrigan. I sup-
> pose no cardinal ever voted for a Quaker before. The
> contest is very close and it is impossible to know who
> will win . . . If the Liberals get a large majority, the poor
> (established) Church will soon count her last days . . ."[57]

Corrigan was to make his strongest stand in parliament on
the education issue. He had shown courage in the stance he
took against Cardinal Cullen and the Catholic clergy, and he
was to display the same fortitude and integrity in Westminster.
There was vastly more at stake than mere educational facilities; these were, of course, important and Corrigan had
strong views as to how an illiterate nation should be best
educated so that the students of its universities might take
their place with the graduates of Britain and Europe. But he
saw with remarkable clarity well beyond the educational
demands being made on behalf of the Catholics by the
hierarchy. The great achievement of Catholic emancipation
would in his view be reversed if the religious intolerance of
the pre-emancipation period was now practised by the
Catholics, and he believed that the church's insistence on
educational facilities at all levels solely for Catholics would
guarantee future religious intolerance and sectarian strife.
His stand against the church and his efforts at Westminster
for mixed education must today be viewed with admiration,
but his failure to implement them fully was predictable and

unfortunate for a country that does not yet appreciate the true meaning of religious freedom.

Gladstone in tackling the thorny problem of Irish university education first brought in his Irish church act of 1869 for the disestablishment and disendowment of the Anglican church. All denominations were now legally equal and independent of the state. It should therefore have followed that the state would not establish or endow any denominational institution. A year later Trinity College announced its intention of abolishing all religious tests in the college and university,[58] and the Convocation of Queen's University commented with optimism:

> "In this direction is to be found the true solution of the Irish university education question. There should be no university in this country recognised or supported by the state where persons of all denominations would not stand upon equal footing; and . . . to establish a denominational university or college for any one religious sect would tend to perpetuate those feelings of intolerance and ill-will amongst . . . the different religious persuasions from which Ireland has already suffered so much."[59]

Cullen saw the church's disestablishment as a major triumph for the Catholic cause:

> "In the future, the Protestants will find themselves as the Catholics, without any privileges. Let us hope that this act of justice will have a good effect in Ireland. The poor Protestants are all very irritated. They never did imagine that England would have abandoned their cause."[60]

If Gladstone had entertained hopes that disestablishment would make the Catholic clergy more amenable on the university education question, he was soon disillusioned. "The Royal Assent was scarcely given to the Irish Church Act" the *Express* remarked, "until Cardinal Cullen and his confreres raised a howl of religious discord." The Catholic hierarchy was, if anything, more insistent in its demands for "a complete system of education based upon religion."[61]

In 1871 Corrigan's efforts on behalf of Irish education

were acknowledged when he was appointed vice-chancellor of the Queen's University — to succeed the late Right Honourable Sir Maziere Brady.[62] In this role he no doubt felt that he could speak authoritatively in parliament on Irish educational requirements. Aware that Gladstone was preparing a bill aimed at solving the university problem, Corrigan wrote to the lord lieutenant, Lord Spencer,[63] proposing two plans either of which would provide Ireland with "freedom of education." He began by reviewing the difficulties with the existing universities:

"The *University* of Dublin which many consider identical with *Trinity College* is as to its governing body, as to its fellowships, professorships, scholarships, etc. open to all religious persuasions and it admits to degrees in two ways by attendance on lectures or by examination at stated periods without attendance on college lectures. This would seem at first sight to be a settlement that ought to be satisfactory to all but it is not recognised to be so for the following reasons. Roman Catholics and Presbyterians and members of other persuasions object that although the religious tests have been abolished by law, the provost and senior fellows, the governing body of Trinity College, the junior fellows, the professors and the examiners will for years to come be either all of the Protestant church or be such in so vast a majority that Trinity College in its government, in its teachings and examinations will retain sectarian character — that however free in theory it will be as sectarian as before in its tendencies and its influences."

Corrigan then dealt with the Queen's University:

"The Queen's University in Ireland is not permitted (with the exception to a certain extent of its medical degree) to confer degrees on any except candidates who have been educated at the Queen's colleges and who must have resided for three years at Belfast, Cork or Galway. The objections of many on conscientious grounds to the Queen's colleges are as strong as Trinity College and in some instances even stronger and the compulsion on students to spend three years of their lives in the provincial towns of Belfast, Cork or Galway excluding the metropolis (Dublin) is universally ridiculed."

This was not in his view freedom of education. In contrast, he observed, parents in England could have their children educated where they wished and then they could obtain their degrees from the London University. This he did regard as freedom of education.

Corrigan then proposed two solutions either of which would be acceptable:

"There are two ways of correcting this social and educational injustice, one the bold and comprehensive measure which would establish one university in Ireland — a university whose powers as those of the London University would be purely examining and which would take away from Trinity College the power of conferring degrees leaving it and all other colleges and private tuitions on an equality and which would enable all colleges, schools and private tuition to compete fairly on the common platform of the central university. This plan should put matriculation examination as well as examination for degrees solely and wholly under the direct control of the Central University. All prizes scholarships etc. whether in medals or money should be given by this university alone. The other course would be that too often adopted in dealing with Irish questions   half measure. To leave Trinity College (University of Dublin) untouched, to allow it to carry out its own reforms and to enable the Queen's University in addition to its existing powers to be a university not only for examining students from the Queen's Colleges but a university for the purpose of *ascertaining by means of examination* the persons, who have acquired proficiency in literature, science and other departments of knowledge by the pursuit of such course of education and of rewarding them by academic degrees and certificates of proficiency etc. I would however far prefer the first."

Spencer did not share Corrigan's enthusiasm on the topic and he anticipated much opposition on "a subject which burnt the ministerial fingers so much but a short time ago."[64] Corrigan was none too pleased with this pessimistic assessment of the situation so he took the matter up directly with Gladstone expressing his concern at the lord lieutenant's dilatory handling of the subject.[65]

> "I entertained a strong impression which has now grown into a stronger conviction that a bill should be introduced because of the combined movement of Home Rule and education which is now being proposed in Ireland. There is this palpable standing grievance which I think cannot be defended that while a parent in England may educate his son where he choses and then send him forward for the examination for his degrees to the London University, a parent in Ireland is denied this freedom of education and is now forced by law to send his son to a college in Belfast, Galway or Cork before he can present him for the examination for his degree in the Queen's University. I think it is not wise for the government to leave with our opponents the vantage of this grievance in the approaching contest. Either of the alternatives I have ventured to propose should I think turn the tide. The first I still consider would be the better but it might meet with much opposition. The second would I anticipate be accepted — by the House of Commons as it would only associate the Queen's University in Ireland to the London University in England giving all parents full liberty to educate their children where they chose. This would be full freedom of education in Ireland and would annihilate this monster grievance."

Corrigan wrote to Gladstone again in 1873[66] expressing the view that there might be too much opposition if he attempted to deal with the entire university question, and he suggested that he should try for no more than an extension of the powers of the Queen's University "to enable it to admit students wherever educated, to examination of its degrees." This was in effect, a plea for the enforcement of the supplemental charter of 1866.

Gladstone did, in fact, pay close attention to many of Corrigan's proposals but he did not heed his advice to take the university question cautiously one piece at a time. He produced a set of sweeping proposals guaranteed to alienate every party with an interest in university education and the defeat of his bill led predictably to the fall of his Liberal government. He proposed that there should be a new national and non-sectarian university in Ireland, the University of Dublin, which would teach and examine and to which sectarian and non-sectarian colleges alike might be affiliated, provided they met certain educational requirements. The affiliated colleges were to include Trinity College, the Catholic University, the Queen's colleges of Belfast and Cork (Queen's College, Galway, was to be suppressed) and Magee College, Londonderry. The Queen's colleges were to retain their endowments and the new university was to receive £50,000 a year towards which Trinity College was to contribute £15,000. The Catholic University was not to receive an endowment.[67] The debate on this University Education (Ireland) Bill gave Corrigan the opportunity to express his views on the subject to the house.[68] He explained to the members the anomalous position of the Queen's University which many members might reasonably have supposed was intimately connected with the Queen's colleges. As Vice-Chancellor of the University he could attest that, "The Queen's University knows nothing whatever of the proceedings in the colleges." How ridiculous it was then that, "Catholic students may go from Carlow College, and from St Mary's College Dublin, from St Patrick's College, Thurles, St Kyran's and from private tuition to London University; but they will not be admitted to the Queen's University, sitting in Dublin, unless they spend the whole time of the undergraduate course in one of the Queen's colleges, in Belfast, Cork or Galway." Corrigan then put forward his proposal for a great National University of Ireland, the function of which should be solely to examine candidates regardless of whether they were educated in college, school, or at home. There must not, he insisted, be any religious favouritism in education. "The state should be equally impartial to all denominations, giving equal aid to all — to those who desire to have denominational education, and to those who do not. Those words, sir, explain, I hope sufficiently, the character in which I rise — not as the advocate of mixed education, but as the advocate of a perfect freedom of education, giving equal facilities for education to all." He supported the bill insofar as it set out to establish a National University, but he deplored the fact that certain colleges were to be affiliated to the university, and given rights of representation not shared by others, and that the university was to be a teaching as well as examining body: "If a university were to examine only those students who were educated within its walls, then I might have little objection to its both teaching and examining its own pupils, because there would be no room for partiality; but the case is totally different when there is to be a university established which is not only to teach and examine its own pupils, but the pupils of other universities and colleges."

Corrigan then criticised the proposed constitution of the Council of the University which was to be made up mainly of professors, a bad policy in his opinion, because each would seek to promote his own interest. He objected violently to the proposal that the lord lieutenant should be chancellor to the university: "I consider it an indignity little short of insult to do it, and that, if done, it will destroy the independence of science; and the conviction will be that the only way to university distinction and emoluments under such chancellorship, will be up the back stairs of the Castle." He was also unhappy about the lack of provision for Catholic representation on the proposed council of the university: "There is no security whatever in the Bill for fair representation of the religious persuasions on the council. The members may be all Catholics, or Protestants, or Presbyterians. The probability — nay, almost the certainty — will be, that for many years to come, one-half the members of the council will not be Catholic, and that even that minority will be at length weeded out." Promises from the government on this were not enough, there had to be safeguards in the Bill: "In 1845 on the formation of the Queen's colleges, the Roman Catholic bishops presented a memorial to the government, praying that a fair proportion of the professors and other office-bearers in the new colleges should be members of the Roman

Catholic church." Legislation on the matter was declined by the government and instead reassurance of adequate representation was given, but this had not been enough: "The professors now number sixty in the three Queen's colleges, and how many Catholic professors in the whole of the three colleges, including arts and professional education? — only nine . . . This is called mixed education . . . I often remonstrated against this weeding out of Roman Catholics, but was met by the assurance that it could not be avoided, as the most competent person was always appointed, and the most competent person happened to be — of course, by accident — nearly always a Protestant." Furthermore, Corrigan said, when the Queen's College was founded appointments were made by the lord lieutenant, but this was to have lasted only until the senate was ready to take up the task: "And now, at the end of nearly thirty years after that solemn promise was given, there is seen in Ireland what is not seen in any other — even the most despotic — country in Europe, that professors, sixty in number of arts and sciences are the mere nominees of a viceroy." He was even more critical of the lack of endowment to Catholic education in Ireland:

"But suppose all these defects I have observed upon were removed, there still remains the intolerable injury that will be felt deeply and more deeply everyday — that while Trinity College is left in possession of at least £50,000 a year wrung by oppression and confiscation from the Catholics: . . . Catholic colleges and Catholic schools derive nothing from the state. . . . Is it fair not to give the Catholic laity for their university education a similar grant? Let a similar act of justice be done for them as has been done for the clergy. Let them have a fair start in this new educational competition. If they then fail in the competition for degrees, emoluments, and honour, they will not be able to say they have not had fair play; but if they fail under the proposed bill, which leaves thousands on thousands with Protestant and Presbyterian colleges, and gives nothing to them, they will attribute their failure to injustice; and every rejection of a Catholic candidate that will occur will be a never failing repetition of heart-burning, sectarian discord, and disaffection in Ireland."

Corrigan had made his case strongly at Westminster, and successive governments including Gladstone's were influenced by his proposal for one national university modelled on the University of London. He was convinced that neither Catholic nor Protestants would be well served by a sectarian university and there were many to whom his strictures on this topic caused deep offence, not least of whom were the Catholic bishops. While Cullen would have approved of his efforts for equitable endowments, he viewed his adherence to the principle of non-sectarian education with dismay and was furious that all his efforts to restrain him came to no avail. He was prepared to bring considerable pressure to bear on Corrigan, as Corrigan has recorded: "Indeed two of the clergymen from my own parish St Andrews, one of them the administrator, called on the editor of the *Freeman* to request him, which he refused to do, to insert a requisition calling on me to resign in consequence of not being guided by their views."[69]

Gladstone's university bill succeeded in antagonising all the main interests: "Trinity College, threatened with loss of revenue and its historic status; the Catholic prelates, because their university was to be left unendowed; and both Protestant and Catholic supporters of the Queen's University which the scheme proposed to extinguish..."[67] The bill was defeated in the House of Commons by the votes of the Irish members both Catholic and Protestant and Gladstone's government fell, to be succeeded by the Conservatives led by Benjamin Disraeli. In 1879 he solved, at least temporarily, the university problem by reverting back to the supplemental charter of 1866. His proposals were much along the lines advocated by Corrigan in his pamphlet and later speeches. The Queen's colleges, Trinity and the University of Dublin were left undisturbed, but the Queen's University was replaced by a new university similar to London University. This university to be known as the Royal University, was to be an examining institution only. Except for medicine, students would not be required to reside in or attend lectures at any institute. It was empowered to confer degrees on any student who matriculated in the university and passed the examinations prescribed by its senate. The government of the university was vested in a thirty-six member senate of whom six were to be elected by convocation and the rest to be appointed by the crown. (Corrigan was invited to join the senate in the last year of his life). The government erected university buildings at Earlsfort Terrace, and provided an endowment of £20,000 yearly. The Royal University was established in 1881, and the Queen's University was dissolved the following year.[70] This phase in Ireland's university history lasted twenty-seven years until 1908 when parliament dissolved the Royal University and created two new universities: the National University of Ireland, with constituent colleges at Dublin, Cork and Galway; and Queen's University, Belfast, which replaced the old Queen's College. Attendance at lectures was compulsory in both universities. The governing bodies were to be representative of the hierarchy, Catholic and Protestant, and the president of University College, Dublin was to be a Catholic. There was to be no religious test.[71] The result of this measure was that Trinity College (Dublin University) catered for Protestants (this effect was largely of Catholic making, as Catholics were effectively banned from entering Trinity College), and the National University became, in effect, the Catholic University. This resolution of the complex university question would have given Cullen much satisfaction, but to Corrigan it would have been the denigration of his efforts on behalf of religious tolerance in Ireland. As the twentieth century draws to a close with sectarian discord a constant threat to the country, Cullen's bigoted intransigence may now be seen as a reactionary influence which succeeded in perpetuating the religious divisions of many centuries, not only in the classrooms of the schools, but also in the halls of the universities, where the maturing intellect of an emerging nation should have been permitted unrestrained freedom in the intellectual pursuit of art and science.

11

The Closing Years

When Gladstone dissolved parliament in 1873, Corrigan decided not to seek re-election. He informed his supporters of his decision in a letter to the daily newspapers in which he concluded that he had been loyal to his election promises: "I can truly say that I adhered to every pledge I made; that I was never absent from the House of Commons on any question of importance or of local interest to my fellow-citizens; and that when I occasionally differed from some sections of my constituents on novel questions on which I had not pledged myself, I still gave my best attention to all views put before me — reserving, however, on such question, the privilege of finally acting on my own judgement."[1]

The Catholic prelates gave him one last chance to accept their demands for sectarian university education in exchange for which they would pledge their support in the election. Characteristically he would not compromise his stand on this issue: "A suggestion (was) made to me almost immediately on the arrival here of the news of dissolution, made *of course* without authority that I should not lose an instant in waiting on His Eminence and giving him an assurance that I would not repeat my errors of past parliamentary life but would at once pledge myself to support his views and that a pastoral would then issue calling upon all Catholics to support me, which would ensure my success. I did not give utterance to it but I thought of the lines in a play in which I performed when a boy, 'And has the Douglas sunk so low.'"[2]

The Liberal party after much dissension selected Lord Mayor Brooks to replace Corrigan, and to run with Pim. Brooks was according to Corrigan a "most bigoted orangeman." Corrigan was astonished at the behaviour of the

Catholic priests who did not give their support to a Catholic candidate to replace him:

> "I have to relate what I consider, the lowest humiliation to which our party could be brought . . . There was a meeting of clergymen held in Dr Lyon's house on Saturday last to consider the expediency of starting at least 'one Catholic candidate.' It was determined to adopt this step and Dr Lyons was selected. Canon Farrell and Dr Woodlock, Rector of the Catholic University, went to the cardinal and with his sanction they went as a deputation at once to the Mansion House to ask the lord mayor to associate a Catholic with him but with the slavish assurance (for I can apply no other epithet to it), that if Mr Brooks thought the association of a Catholic with him would in the least imperil *his* (Mr Brooks' return) they would not start the Catholic. Mr Brooks said he would consult his committee and the committee declined the proposed function."[2]

The press was critical of the manner in which Corrigan had been treated: "We must say the Liberals of Dublin have not treated their late representative with generosity. He brought to their case a distinguished name which will always hold a high place in the history of Irish medicine, and we are not aware that his party have any reason to complain of any want of zeal on his part in their service."[3] Even the Conservative *Daily Express* while viewing the disarray in the Liberal camp with no small degree of pleasure, regretted the departure of Sir Dominic: "So much for our opponents, whose camp it will be seen is in a disordered state with a veteran commander put on the retired list as the only way of appeasing a mutinous party, and his post given to a deserter from the other side, who has never before led them in political battle."[4]

The election was a devastating defeat for the Liberals. Of the 103 new Irish members, fifty-nine were Home Rulers, thirty-two Conservatives, and only twelve were Liberals, whereas there had been fifty-seven in the previous parliament. The Home Rulers by declaring for denominational education secured the support of the Catholic clergy who played a dominant role in the election.[5] In Dublin, Arthur Guinness headed the poll for the Conservatives, and Brooks was elected for the Liberals with Pim losing his seat by less than 2,000 votes.[6] There was much criticism of the way the Liberals had mismanaged the election: "Examination of these results can leave no doubt that had the Liberals united, and not divided themselves into two sections, both unitedly, could have carried the election, and prevented one of the seats from lapsing to a Conservative. This fatuity is to be deplored . . . Had 376 more electors from the Liberal side polled for Brooks, and all those 5,214 votes been split with Pim, both Liberals would have been returned and Dublin would retain its former position in Liberal representation, instead of being now practically disfranchised in the present parliament."[7]

Corrigan was disillusioned by the behaviour of the Catholic hierarchy who it seemed would stoop very low indeed to achieve denominational education. He had been wise, especially in view of Pim's subsequent fate, not to contest the election. He would have had no chance of success against, what he later referred to as a "threefold alliance" which he could not "in the interests of justice to himself and others call a holy alliance."[8] He elaborated further in a letter to Sir Bernard Burke:

"The news of dissolution came you know very suddenly on us on Saturday last 24th inst. I had previously some weeks before had an authorised announcement made that it was my intention to stand for the city at the next election which we then supposed would not take place earlier than the coming autumn. I had little time to think but in course of that day and next Sunday reports reached me from several quarters that our clergy would unite with the Home Rulers and publicans to defeat me in revenge for my misdeeds. The publicans in revenge for my Sunday Closing Bill, the Home Rulers for not being as mad as themselves and the clergymen to show that thus everyone would be punished who dared not to go the whole length with them in the education question."[2]

Corrigan now began to enjoy a well-earned retirement. He continued to travel to London for the meetings of the General Medical Council, and to see private patients at Merrion Square, but more of his time was given to sailing and tending to his aquarium at *Inniscorrig*.

He wrote a delightful sketch entitled, "Reminiscences of the Dissecting Room," which appeared anonymously in the *British Medical Journal* of 1879,[9] but the author was quickly identified in the daily newspapers:

> "We violate no journalistic secrecy in saying that the author of the pleasant little sketch is our distinguished countryman, Sir Dominic Corrigan, Bart., We would heartily wish that Sir Dominic would give the public vastly more of his 'recollections' than they as yet possess. His life was cast in a peculiarly interesting period, and he was always an earnest worker in whatever was of public concern. In his own profession, the profession in which he has had many rivals, but no superior, and few equals, he has seen many striking changes in various ways . . . In the politics of half a century he has witnessed many strange vicissitudes, and he was a sharer in many hard struggles which he and his Catholic co-religionists had to fight against a domineering ascendency, and for a religious freedom and equality which even yet have not been wholly achieved."[10]

He continued to lecture in medicine and was glad to pass on the wisdom of his years to his "young friends" as he liked to call the medical students. In 1873 he was honoured by an invitation to deliver the address at the annual distribution of prizes at St Mary's Hospital Medical School in London, and in this he took the opportunity to recollect his struggles and fortunes in the profession.[11]

He was an active member of the O'Connell Monument Committee and was present at the laying of the first stone on August 8, 1864.[12] This committee spent more time discussing and arguing trivia than doing the business for which it had been appointed. By 1876 Corrigan was thoroughly fed up with the men involved in the project. He chaired a particularly stormy meeting in the Mansion House at which were discussed the merits of having O'Connell cloaked or uncloaked (favoured by Corrigan as he only wore a cloak in his decline[13]) hatted or hatless and the wishes of the late Mr Foley in the affair, and at one stage he had to vacate the chair.[14] The Catholic clergy in particular seem to have irritated him and eventually he could stand no more. "Pray let us have done with this correspondence. I have requested long since to be relieved altogether from the trusteeship. Your proposal is that I should continue in the trusteeship. I decline this altogether. Pray don't blame me for appearing curt."[15]

As age crept upon him he began to shed a number of responsibilities. In 1878 he resigned from the Board of Superintendence of the Dublin Hospitals on which he had served since its formation. The event was commented on in the press: "If the Dublin hospitals have grown to be among the few institutions which lift our city to the level of the greatest capitals, we know nothing which has contributed more to their fame than the name and deeds, the zeal, research and all but inspired success of the greatest among Irish physicians. There is no other man living who less courts public applause, or whom the public voice is more entirely united in applauding. When little past the threshold of age it has been his rare fortune to taste the perfect assurance of immortality — to see his statue set up among the monarchs of his profession, and hear his name quoted as part of the world's property in the highest of the schools."[16]

In 1878 his friend William Stokes died. The two had remained friends and collaborating colleagues for over the half century during which the "Dublin school" had thrived. We know from a correspondence in 1868 that there had been a major rift between them possibly because Stokes voted against him in one of his bids for re-election as president of the College of Physicians. Whatever the cause Stokes had made retribution when he supported the erection of the Foley statue to Corrigan in the College of Physicians. Corrigan was able to do a good turn for Stokes in 1868 by supporting his son (later Sir William) for appointment to the staff of the Richmond hospital.[17] But the relationship between the two great physicians must have reached its zenith when in 1876, Corrigan attended a ceremony in the College of Physicians for the inauguration of Stokes's statue, also sculpted by Foley: "It occupies the near righthand corner of the handsome and cheerful quadrangular hall of the college, facing, on the left, the statue of Sir Dominic Corrigan, Bart; diagonally opposite is the statue of Sir Henry March, Bart; while the fourth angle awaits the statue of Dr Graves — whose life was written by Dr Stokes — now rapidly approaching completion. Sir Dominic Corrigan had been president of the college five, Sir Henry Marsh four, Dr Stokes three, and Dr Graves two years."[18]

Corrigan was disappointed by the developments in university education and in 1877 he attempted to resign from the senate of the Queen's University but was persuaded by Lord Leinster, then chancellor, to stay on,[19] and in 1879, he received a letter from Dublin Castle: "I am directed by His Grace the Lord Lieutenant to communicate to you that it is his wish to place your name on the senate of the New University which is about to be incorporated, by Royal Charter under the name of 'The Royal University of Ireland.'"[20]

Corrigan may have sensed that his health was failing and that the end might not be far off. Indeed Francis Cruise his physician tells us that there was "a slight threat of a paralytic seizure" sometime in 1879.[21] On December 11, 1879 he wrote to the administrator at St Andrews Church to ensure that the family vault was in good order: "I find by my papers that I paid in the year 1859 one hundred and fifty pounds for a vault in the church. I hope it has been preserved intact for I have not had heart for years to visit my poor child's resting place."[22] He had enjoyed excellent health all of his life except for attacks of gout that sometimes kept him in bed but more often merely prevented him visiting his patients. As Mapother puts it "age touched him lightly." Up to his fortieth year he was one of the boldest followers of the Ward hounds, "and his daring leap over the lough of the bay is often talked of."[23]

The last fee recorded in the fee book is £4 on December 27, 1879. There follows a note by Mary:

"Father got ill in his study 4 Merrion Square West on 30th December, 1879 at about 1 oc pm — Dined with Lady Corrigan and then family at 7.30 in parlour as

usual but eat nothing . . . Mama and Mary with him.
Cecilia and William came soon after and Richard. Dr
Cruise came. Papa lay on the sofa. He went up to bed
at 9 oc that evening leaning on Cecilia and me. We sat
up all night. He got worse next morning. Dr Banks came
too with Dr Cruise. William, Richard, Cecilia, Mama and
I never left him for one moment without one of us with
him day and night from 30th December 79 to February
1st 80 when our idolised father died. He knew us all; to
the last he was so gentle, loving, we adored him if possible more than ever — It is a desolate world without
him. Rev Ms Donnelly said he never heard anyone say
the Act of Faith so fervently. Richard was most devoted
to try to do and get anything for Papa and always came
3 or 4 times a day. William his beloved son was deeply
devoted — how they loved each other. Two splendid,
noble characters."[24]

According to Dr Cruise his illness was a stroke of the left
side. During the last illness his physician frequently slept in
an adjoining room "in readiness for any emergency."[21] The
newspapers carried daily bulletins on his progress.

"Surrounded," Cruise tells us, "by his devoted loving wife,
son and daughters and nursed to perfection by experts,"
Corrigan lingered on for some weeks. "With characteristic
simplicity and courage he made his preparation for death,
received the last rites of Holy Church, and patient and calm
awaited his hour. He spoke of it to me with perfect resignation the day before he died. The end came most peacefully
and happily" on Sunday morning, February 1, 1880 in his
seventy-ninth year.

The *cortége* was one of the largest the city had ever witnessed. Following the chief mourners were the carriages of
the president and fellows of the College of Physicians, and a
carriage conveying the college mace, draped in crepe, borne
by the beadle. After leaving the house at Merrion Square the
procession made a *detour* through Kildare Street, past the
College of Physicians, opposite to which it halted for a few
seconds and then proceeded round by St Stephen's Green
and Merrion Square to St Andrew's Church in Westland Row,
where on February 5 the remains were interred in the family

vault beneath the building.[25] The services were conducted by his brother-in-law the Most Rev Dr Woodlock, Bishop of Ardagh.[21]

The obituaries and tributes were many. Let us choose just one: "By the death of Sir Dominic Corrigan, the medical profession loses one of its most conspicuous members, the University of Edinburgh one of its most illustrious graduates, and the Irish race one of its finest specimens. Though a perfect Irishman, Sir Dominic was as much at home in London, as in Dublin, and though a Catholic in religion, he had too much humour and too much humanity in his constitution to be a bigot."[26]

Mapother in his biographical essay in the *Irish Monthly* in 1880 wrote: "Some public memorial or what would exemplify his career more fully, an endowment in favour of struggles in the profession he loved so well, is certain at no distant day to be established."[23] Nearly a century was to pass before the medical profession gave further recognition to one of its most illustrious predecessors. In The Charitable Infirmary the hospital library was named after him in 1969, and in 1970, thanks to the exertions of Dr Harry Counihan, the headquarters of An Comhairle na nOispidéal were named *Corrigan House*. However, the greatest tribute that the profession and the citizens of his native city can pay to Dominic Corrigan is the naming of the new hospital at Beaumont — *The Corrigan Hospital*. This modern institute will incorporate The Charitable Infirmary and St Laurence's Hospital (formerly the Richmond, Whitworth and Hardwicke hospitals) — the two institutes that Corrigan served so loyally.

Appendices

APPENDIX A

FAMILY TREE[1]

NOTES ON FAMILY TREE

1. This family tree, which is not complete, illustrates by the clerical following following of many members of the family, the dominant catholic influence.
2. It has been suggested but not confirmed, that John was related to Michael Corrigan, the third Archbishop of New York (b. 1839) whose father Thomas originated from Kells in 1828. *(Memorial of the Most Reverend Michael Augustine Corrigan, D.D. Third Archbishop of New York.* Compiled and published by authority. The Cathedral Library Association, New York, 1902 in National Library of Ireland).
3. A cousin of the O'Connor Don, head of the most important sept of one of Ireland's most illustrious Catholic families, the members of which are descended from Conchobhar, King of Connacht (d. 971) and the last two High Kings of Ireland were of this line, viz., Turlough O'Connor (1088-1156) and Roderick O'Connor (1116-1198). (Maclysaght, E. *Irish Families. Their Names, Arms and Origins.* Dublin. Hodges Figgis, 1957. pp. 88-90).
4. Emigrated to USA and married there.
5. Emigrated to New Orleans; died of Yellow Fever 2 weeks after arrival.
6. Became a Carmelite Nun.
7. Became a distinguished member of the Loreto Order at Niagra.
8. Both became nuns in the Sacred Heart Order.
9. Francis Sylvester Mahony alias "Father Prout", ecclesiastic and man of letters. Best remembered as author of "The Reliques", and a poem immortalising the Shandon Bells at the foot of which he is buried. (Kent, C., *The works of Father Prout,* London. George Routledge and Sons, 1881).
10. A remarkable philanthropist whose charitable works included the establishment of the Children's Hospital, Temple Street, Dublin. (Russell. Rev. S.J., "Mrs. Ellen Woodlock. An admirable Irishwoman of the last century". *The Irish Monthly.* 1908. 36. 171-6).
11. A man with rebel sympathies who was involved in the Rising of 1798.
12. Dominic Corrigan and Joanna Woodlock probably met in Thomas Street where both families lived; they married in 1829.
13. Became President of All Hallow's College, Second Rector of the Catholic University in succession to Cardinal John Newman, and Bishop of Ardagh and Clonmacnoise (O'Mahony, T.J., "The Right Rev. D. Woodlock," *The All Hallows Annual,* 1902. pp. 7-19).
14. Became a member of the Society of Jesus.
15. Captain of the 3rd Dragoon Guards. Died on sick furlough in Melbourne.

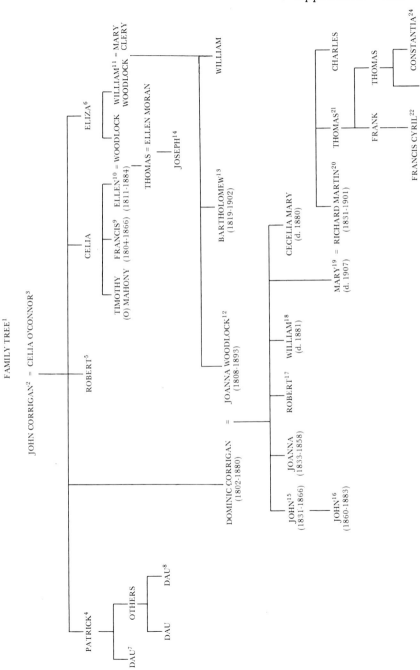

FAMILY TREE[1]

JOHN CORRIGAN[2] = CELIA O'CONNOR[3]

PATRICK[4]   ROBERT[5]   CELIA   ELIZA[6]

DAU[7]   DAU   OTHERS   DAU[8]

TIMOTHY (O) MAHONY   FRANCIS[9] (1804-1866)   ELLEN[10] = WOODLOCK (1811-1884)   WILLIAM[11] = MARY WOODLOCK   CLERY

THOMAS = ELLEN MORAN

JOSEPH[14]

WILLIAM

DOMINIC CORRIGAN (1802-1880)   =   JOANNA WOODLOCK[12] (1808-1893)

BARTHOLOMEW[13] (1819-1902)

JOHN[15] (1831-1866)   JOANNA (1833-1858)   ROBERT[17]   WILLIAM[18] (d. 1881)   CECELIA MARY   MARY[19] = RICHARD MARTIN[20] (d. 1880)   (d. 1907)   (1831-1901)

JOHN[16] (1860-1883)

CHARLES   THOMAS[21]

FRANK   THOMAS

FRANCIS CYRIL[22]   MARY[23] (1892-1975)   CONSTANTIA[24]

16. Succeeded to Baronetcy at age of maturity; died aged 25 years in Silesia.
17. Died in infancy.
18. Became a successful barrister.
19. Mary and Richard died without issue. She bequeathed her country home at Cappagh to the Irish Sisters of Charity for "an Hospital for the Public Benefit", and thus continued the charitable cause begun by her great aunt Ellen Woodlock, when a convalescent home for the Children of the Children's Hospital, Temple Street was established there, and this later became St. Mary's Orthopaedic Hospital.
20. Proprietor of the large timber merchants, Richard Martin & Co., he was High Sheriff of the City of Dublin, Justice of the Peace and Deputy Lieutenant for Dublin, Deputy Chairman of the Royal Bank of Ireland, Director of the British and Irish Steam Packet Company (one of its ships was named *The Lady Mary* after his wife) and a member of the Privy Council. ("Obituary. The Right Hon. Sir Richard Martin. Bart. P.C., D.L.," *The Irish Builder.* Oct. 24. 1901. p. 914).
21. Thomas and Charles Martin were the founders of the firm of T. & C. Martin formerly of the North Wall and later Westmoreland Street, Dublin.
22. Donated Corrigan papers, letters and memorabilia to RCPI in 1944.
23. Mother Mary Martin; foundress of the Medical Missionaries of Mary.
24. Sister Constantia Martin, member of the Dominican Order, Sion Hill, Blackrock.

Corrigan Coat of Arms

In 1880 Dominic John Corrigan on application to Sir John Bernard Burke, Ulster King of Arms and Principal Herald of All Ireland, was assigned the Armorial Ensigns of his family to be borne by him, his descendants, and the descendants of his father, as follows: *Or, a Chevron between two Trefoils slipped Vert in Chief and a lizard in base proper. For Crest, A Sword in pale point downwards, in front thereof two Battle Axes in saltire, all proper. And for Motto, CONSILIO ET IMPETU.*

(Corrigan Archive, RCPI)

APPENDIX B

CHRONOLOGY

1800		— Irish Parliament abolished by Act of Union.
1802		— December, 1st. Born Thomas Street, Dublin.
1810		— Royal College of Surgeons Hall opened on Stephen's Green.
c.1812	Age 10—	Commenced schooling at the Lay College, Maynooth.
1815		— Battle of Waterloo.
1815		— Laennec discovers mediate auscultation.
c.1818		— Commenced Medical Studies, with Dr. O'Kelly at Maynooth.
1820		— Enrolled at Peter Street School and School of Physic, Trinity.
1820		— George IV becomes King.
1823		— Thomas Wakley founds the *Lancet*.
1825	Age 23—	Graduated M.D. Edinburgh.
1825		— Commenced practice at 11 Upper Ormond Quay.
c.1825		— Appointed Medical Assistant to St. Catherine's Parish.
1825		— Dublin first lighted by gas.
1826		— Appointed Physician to the Sick-Poor Institute of Meath Street.
1827		— Robert Adams describes heart-block.
1829		— Published — "Inquiry into the causes of bruit de soufflet and fremissement".
1829		— Published — "On the epidemic fever of Ireland".
1829		— Married Joanna Woodlock.
1829		— Emancipation Bill receives Royal Assent.
1830		— Attended lectures at Dublin Lying-in-Hospital (Rotunda).
1830	Age 29—	Appointed Physician to the Charitable Infirmary, Jervis Street
1830		— Published "Reports on the diseases and weather of Dublin."
1831		— Appointed Consulting Physician to Maynooth College.
1832		— Moved to 13 Bachelors Walk.
1832		— British Medical Association founded.
c.1832		— Lectureship in Peter Street Medical School.
1832		— Published, "On Permanent patency of the mouth of the aorta, on inadequacy of the aortic valves".
1832		— Anatomy Act passed.
1833		— Daughter Joanna born.
1833-46		— Lectureship in Practice of Medicine, the Dublin School of Anatomy, Surgery and Medicine, Digges Street.
1833-37		— Attended Lectures in Surgery at the Charitable Infirmary.
1834		— Moved to No. 4, Merrion Square West (now No. 92).
1837		— Accession of Queen Victoria to throne.
1837-40		— Appointed Temporary Physician to Cork Street Fever Hospital
1837		— Colles states law of maternal immunity in syphilis.
1837		— Appointed Lecturer to Apothecaries Hall.
1938		— Founder member of Dublin Pathological Society.
1838		— Published — "On Cirrhosis of the Lung".
1838		— Published — "On Aortitis as one of the causes of angina pectoris."
1839		— Appointed Physician-in-Ordinary to His Excellency The Lord Lieutenant.
1840	Age 38—	Appointed Physician to House of Industry Hospital.

1841		— Corrigan and Stokes unsuccessful applicants for King's Professorship of the Practice of Medicine at Trinity.
1841		— Clinical Lectures on Fever in the *London Gazette*.
1842		— Pamphlets on Bill for Medical Charities (with Harrison).
1843		— Diploma of MRCS (Eng.).
1843-54		— Appointed Lecturer to Richmond Hospital School.
1844		— Commenced building of Inniscorrig.
1845		— Francis Rynd introduces the hypodermic syringe.
1845		— Queen's College founded.
1845-50		— The Great Famine.
1846		— Appointed to Central Board of Health for Ireland.
1846		— Stokes describes heart block.
1846		— Paper on "Corrigan's Button".
1846		— Morton introduces ether anaesthesia.
1847	Age 45 —	Board of Health controversy.
1847		— Semmelweis discovers cause of puerperal fever.
1847		— Black-beaned for Honorary Fellowship of King's and Queen's College of Physicians.
1847		— MacDonnell performs first operation under anesthesia in Ireland in The Richmond Hospital.
1848		— Proclamation of a 2nd Republic in France.
1849		— M.D. *Honorus Causa*, University of Dublin.
1850		— Death of daughter Joanna aged 17.
1850		— Appointed to first Senate of Queens.
1854-6		— Crimean War.
1855		— Successfully sat for Licentiate of College of Physicians.
1855		— Catholic University Medical School opened in Cecilia Street.
1856	Age 54 —	Elected Fellow of College of Physicians.
1856		— Presidential Address to Dublin Pathological Society.
1859		— Appointed Commissioner of National Education.
1859-63	Age 57 —	Elected President of King's and Queen's College of Physicians.
1859		— Elected President of Royal Zoological Gardens.
1860		— Advocated Vartry Water Supply
1860		— Turkish Bath Correspondence.
1861-5		— American Civil War.
1962	Age 60 —	Published "Ten Days in Athens".
1862		— Lunatic Asylum Correspondence.
1862		— Florence Nightingale establishes school of nursing at St. Thomas's.
1864		— Royal College of Physicians holds first meeting in new hall.
1865		— Robert MacDonnell performs the first blood transfusion in Ireland in The Charitable Infirmary.
1866		— Created Baronet of the Empire during Ministry of Lord Russell.
1866		— Death of eldest son in Australia.
1866		— Published "Cholera Map of Ireland".
1866		— Resigned from Maynooth College.
1866		— Resigned from House of Industry Hospitals.
1866		— Succeeded at House of Industry Hospitals by his friend Dr. Lyons.
1866		— Elected Consulting Physician and Member of Board of the House of Industry Hospitals.
1867		— Lister introduces antisepsis in surgery.
1867		— Address to BMA on Medical Education.

1870		—	Elected M.P. for City of Dublin.
1871	Age 69 —	Elected Vice-Chancellor of the Queen's University.
1874		—	Elected Corresponding Member of *Academie de Medicine de Paris*. (Only other Irishman — Richard Carmichael.)
1875		—	President of the Pharmaceutical Society of Ireland.
1875		—	Observations on Aix Les Bains.
1878		—	Suffered slight paralytic stroke.
1878		—	Paper on General Medical Council constitution.
1879		—	Published "Reminiscences of the Dissecting Room".
1880	Age 78 —	Died, February, 1st, at 4 Merrion Square West.
		—	Interred February, 5th, in family vault, St. Andrew's Church, Westland Row.

APPENDIX C

CORRIGAN BIBLIOGRAPHY

This bibliography was first published in 1980. (Mills, R. and O'Brien, E., "Corrigan Bibliography", *Journal of the Irish Colleges of Physicians and Surgeons*, 1980: *10*: pp. 50-54). A number of papers by Corrigan have since been discovered and are included in this revised bibliography.

ORIGINAL PAPERS

1. MD Thesis. On Scrofula. Edinburgh. 1825.
2. Aneurism of the aorta; singular pulsation of the arteries, necessity of the employment of the stethoscope. *Lancet* 1828: *1*: 586-590.
3. Inquiry into the causes of bruit de soufflêt and fremissement. Part 1. *Ibid* 1829: *2*: 1-5.
4. Inquiry into the causes of bruit de soufflêt and fremissement. Part 2. *Ibid* 1829: *2*: 33-35.
5. On the epidemic fever of Ireland. Unsigned review. *Ibid* 1829: *2*: 614.
6. On the epidemic fever of Ireland. Part 2. *Ibid* 1829: *2*: 600-605.
7. On the motions and sounds of the heart. *Dublin Med Trans* 1830: *1*: 151-203.
8. Reports on the diseases and weather of Dublin. Part 1. *Edin Med and Surg J* 1830: *34*: 91-100.
9. Reports on the diseases and weather of Dublin. Part 2. *Ibid* 1831: *36*: 24-35.
10. On Spinal irritation; a lecture. *Lancet* 1831: *2*: 163-169.
11. On permanent patency of the mouth of the aorta, or inadequacy of the aortic valves. *Edin Med and Sur J* 1832: *37*: 225-245.
12. On the treatment of recent catarrh. *Dublin J of Med Sci* 1832: *1*: 7-15.
13. A new mode of making an early diagnosis of aneurism of the abdominal aorta. *Ibid* 1833: *2*: 375-383.
14. Pemphigus *Cyclopaedia of Practical Medicine* 1834: *3*: 266-271.
15. Plica Polonica. *Ibid* 1833: *3*: 401-403.
16. Rupia. *Ibid* 1834: *3*: 633.
17. Note on bruit de soufflêt, *Dub J Med Sci* 1836: *8*: 202-205.
18. Observations on bruit de cuir neuf, or leather creak as a diagnostic sign in abdominal disease. *Ibid* 1836: *9*: 392-401.
19. Traite Clinique des Maladies du Coeur précéde de Recherches Nouvelles sur l'Anatomie et la Physiologie de cet organs — Par J. Bouillaud. tom. ii. 1836: *Ibid* 1836: *9*: 486-504.
20. On the mechanism of bruit de soufflêt. Part 1. *Ibid* 1836: *10*: 173-197.
21. On the mechanism of bruit de soufflêt. Part 1. *Ibid* 1839: *14*: 305-319.
22. On aortitis as one of the causes of angina pectoris, with observations on its nature and treatment. *Ibid* 1838: *12*: 243-254.
23. On cirrhosis of the lung. *Ibid* 1838: *13*: 266-286.
24. Observations on the exhibition of remedies in the form of vapour in pulmonary disease; with descriptions of a diffuser for the administration of iodine, chlorine etc. *Ibid* 1839: *15*: 94-105.
25. Observations on the treatment of acute rheumatism by opium. *Ibid* 1840: *16*: 256-277.
26. Practical observations on the diagnosis and treatment of some functional derangements of the heart. *Ibid* 1841: *19*: 1-15.

27. Manner of using the stethoscope. Clinical Lecture. *Lon Med Gaz* 1841: *27*: 905-911.
28. Clinical Lectures. Lecture III. Fever No. 1. *Ibid* 1841: *28*: 11-13.
29. Clinical Lectures. Lecture IV. Fever No. 2. *Ibid* 1841: *28*: 89-92.
30. Clinical Lectures. Lecture V. Fever No. 3. *Ibid* 1841: *28*: 171-174.
31. Clinical Lectures. Lecture VI. Fever No. 4. *Ibid* 1841: *28*: 251-253.
32. Clinical Lectures. Lecture VII. Fever No. 5. *Ibid* 1841: *28*: 298-301.
33. Clinical Lectures. Lecture VIII. Fever No. 6. *Ibid* 1841: *28*: 490-494.
34. Clinical Lectures. Introductory Lecture. *Ibid*: 1841: *i.n.s.* 823-826.
35. Doctor Corrigan's adjusting bed for invalids. *Dublin Hosp Gaz* 1845: *1*: 6-8.
36. Paralysis (from arsenic) Lumbago and Sciatica — Cure by "firing" — Mode of application — Superiority of it over blisters and actual cautery. *Ibid* 1846: *2*: 209-211.
37. On famine and fever as cause and effect in Ireland; with observations on hospital location and the dispensation in outdoor relief of food and medicine. Dublin, Fannin & Co. 33 pp. 8º, 1846.
38. Lectures on the nature and treatment of fever, Dublin, Fannin & Co. 33 pp. 8º, 1853.
39. Clinical observation on the treatment of dropsy connected with "Bright's Disease of the kidney" by iodine of potassium; etc. *Dublin Hosp Gaz* 1855: *1*: 369-373.
40. Clinical lecture on remittent jaundice; etc. *Ibid* 1856: *3*: 17-19.
41. Clinical lecture on pneumonia; etc. *Ibid* 1856: *3*: 177-179.
42. Clinical lecture on — Ovarian Tumour; etc. *Ibid* 1856; *2*: 353-355.
43. Clinical lecture on — Glandular Tumours of Pelvis; etc. *Ibid* 1857: *4*: 356-358.
44. Clinical lecture on — Cirrhosis of the lung; etc. *Ibid* 1857: *4*: 369-371.
45. On the mechanism of muscular murmur in the heart. *Ibid* 1857: *4*: 49-50.
46. Clinical lecture on — Permanent patency, of several years duration, etc. *Ibid* 1858; *5*: 1-3.
47. Clinical lecture on — Aneurism of the abdominal aorta, etc. *Ibid* 1858: *5*: 33-36.
48. Clinical lecture on — Endocarditis, etc. *Ibid* 1858: *5*: 49-52.
49. Clinical Lecture on — Bleeding Vascular Tumours of Rectum, etc. *Ibid* 1858: *5*: 97-100.
50. Clinical lecture on — Diphtheria; etc. *Ibid* 1859: *6*: 49-50.
51. Clinical lecture on — Aneurism of Arch of Aorta; etc. *Ibid* 1860: *7*: 81-83.
52. Introductory Lecture. (Summer Session 1866). The Medical Press and Circular Office. Dublin. pp. 16. 8º. 1866.
53. The Cholera Map of Ireland, with Observations. Browne & Nolan, Dublin. 18 pp; 1 map: 8º. 1866.

CASE REPORTS

54. Plastic bronchitis; etc. *Dublin J med Sci* 1840: *17*: 495-496.
55. Organic stricture of the pylorus. *Ibid* 1840: *17*: 507-508.
56. Formation of external abscess in empyema. *Ibid* 1840: *18*: 143-145.
57. Peculiar syphilitic eruption. *Ibid* 1840: *18*: 145-146.
58. Scarletina, etc. *Proc Path Soc Dublin* 1841 Nov; *27*: 108-109.
59. Bright's disease of the kidney. *Ibid* 1841 Nov; *27*: 109-110.
60. Permanent patency of the aortic valves. *Ibid* 1841 Dec; *18*: 122.
61. Duct of the gall bladder communicating with the stomach, etc. *Ibid* 1841 Dec; *18*: 122-123.
62. Chronic laryngitis, etc. *Ibid* 1842 Mar; *19*: 167-169.

63. Dilatation of the arch of the aorta, etc. *Dublin J med Sci* 1842: *21*: 139.
64. Bright's idsease of the kidney. *Ibid* 1842: *21*: 142-143.
65. Aneurism of the Heart. *Ibid* 1842: *21*: 143.
66. Pneumonia. *Ibid* 1842: *21*: 143.'
67. Phthisis, emphysema. *Ibid* 1842; *21*; 297.
68. Lymph on the base of the brain. *Ibid* 1842: *21*: 308.
69. Apoplexy. *Ibid* 1842; *21*: 309.
70. Large branch of the pulmonary artery opening into tubercular cavity. *Ibid* 1842: *21*: 319.
71. Caries of the petrous portion of the temporal bone; etc. *Ibid* 1843: *22*: 392.
72. Pneumonia supervening on scarlatina; etc. *Ibid* 1843: *22*: 393.
73. Dilatation of the air cells. *Ibid* 1843: *22*: 404.
74. Variola after vaccination; etc. *Ibid* 1844: *24*: 288.
75. Contraction of the parietes of the thorax succeeding to pleuritis. *Dublin Quart J med Sci* 1846: *1*: 222.
76. Ulceration of small intestine. *Ibid* 1846: *1*: 231.
77. Cancerous degeneration of liver. *Ibid* 1846: *1*: 247.
78. Strangulation of the intestines by bands of firm cellular structure crossing the peritoneal sac in several directions. *Ibid* 1846: *1*: 248.
79. Pericarditis with pleuritis. *Ibid* 1846: *1*: 495.
80. Endocarditis in progress of cure. *Ibid* 1846: *1*: 495.
81. Endocarditis. *Ibid* 1846: *1*: 496.
82. Anaemia. *Ibid* 1846: *1*: 506.
83. Purulent effusion under the arachnoid supervening on fever. *Ibid* 1846: *1*: 510.
84. Ovarian tumours containing hydatids etc. *Ibid* 1846: *1*: 519.
85. Pneumonia in the lung of a child. *Ibid* 1846: *2*: 523.
86. Endocarditis; etc. *Ibid* 1847: *4*: 235.
87. Perforation of lung and pulmonary pleura. *Ibid* 1848: *6*: 452.
88. Valvular disease of the heart; etc. *Ibid* 1850: *10*: 500.
89. Pericarditis. *Proc Path Soc Dublin*. 1850 Dec; *7*: 230.
90. Pneumonic abscess. *Dublin Quart J Med Sci* 1851: *11*: 196.
91. Foreign substance passed from the intestines. *Ibid* 1854: *17*: 228.
92. Cases of discharge of ligamentous substance from intestines; etc. *Dublin Hosp Gaz* 1854: *1*: 38.
93. Tubercular peritonitis. *Ibid* 1854: *1*: 74.
94. Cases of slow copper poisoning, with observations. *Ibid* 1854: *1*: 229.
95. Some observations on chloroform. *Ibid* 1854: *1*: 308.
96. Case of compound poisoning by Atropia and Opium; Stimulation by Firing, etc. *Ibid* 1854: *1*: 325.
97. Bright's disease of the kidney, etc. *Ibid* 1854: *1*: 346.
98. Enlarged and hardened liver with remittent jaundice. *Ibid* 1856: *2*: 359.
99. Endocarditis. *Proc Path Soc Dublin* 1857 Dec; *5*: 256.
100. Endocarditis. *Ibid* 1858 Jan; *16*: 276.
101. Calcareous deposits in the aorta. *Ibid* 1858 Feb; *13*: 299.
102. Disease of the aorta. *Dublin Hosp Gaz* 1858: *5*: 134.
103. Clinical observations on pica or dirt eating in children. *Ibid* 1859: *6*: 225.
104. Disease of the aortic valves; etc. *Proc Path Soc Dublin* 1860 ns: *1*: 141.
105. On treatment of hydrophobia in Salamis. *Dublin Quart J med Sci* 1862: *33*: 193.
106. Calcareous deposit surrounding the origin of aorta. *Ibid* 1864: *38*: 197.
107. Small-pox pustules in trachea. *Ibid* 1865: *40*: 421.
108. Pneumothorax. *Ibid* 1865: *40*: 436.

109. On Endocarditis. *Ibid* 1865: *40*: 473.
110. Biliary calculi. *Proc Path Soc Dublin* 1867 ns: *3*: 174.
111. On the treatment of incontinence of urine in childhood and youth by collodian. *Am J Obstet Dis Woman & Child* 1871: *3*: 361.
112. Curious Case of Somnambulism. *Chambers Journal*, 1879: *822*: 619-20.
(A number of the case reports were published in both the *Dublin Quarterly Journal of Medical Science and The Proceedings of the Pathological Society of Dublin.*)

MEDICAL EDUCATION AND REFORM

113. Address delivered at the Opening Meeting of the Dublin Medico-Chirurgical Society. Session of 1837-8. Hodges and Smith. Dublin. 8º. pp. 16, 1838.
114. With Robert Harrison. Observations on the Draft of a Bill for the Regulation and Support of Medical Charities in Ireland. Graisberrig and Gill. Dublin. 8º. pp. 19. 1842.
115. With Robert Harrison. Supplement of Observations on the Draft of a Bill for the Regulation and Support of Medical Charities in Ireland. Graisberrig and Gill. Dublin. 8º. pp. 43. 1842.
116. With E. Kennedy. Medical report of the north Dublin union. *Dublin J Med Sci.* 1842: *21*: 508-16.
117. Valedictory Presidential Address to the Pathological Society. *Dublin Hosp Gaz* 1857: *4*: 139-141.
118. Introductory Clinical Lecture. Winter Session. 1858-59. *Ibid* 1858: *5*: 337-341.
119. Introductory Clinical Lecture. Winter Session. 1858-59. J.M. O'Toole. Dublin. 8º. pp. 20. 1858.
120. Letter to Lunatic Asylums (Ireland) Commission. *Dublin Hosp Gaz* 1859: *6*: 88.
121. Lunatic Asylums (Ireland) Commission. Copy of the communication of Dr Corrigan assigning his reasons for dissenting from a report of the commissioners on Lunatic Asylums in Ireland. Printed by The House of Commons. 28 Feb. 1859.
122. Letter on the Turkish bath. *Dublin Hosp Gaz* 1860: *7*: 17.
123. Letter on Dublin Water Works Commission. *Irish Times* Aug 25th 1860.
124. Visiting Physician to Lunatic Asylum. *Brit med J* 1861: *2*: 613-614.
125. On medical Superintendence of Asylums. *Dublin Quart J med Sci* 1862: *33*: 261.
126. Introductory Lecture. Winter Session. 1863-4. Browne and Nolan. Dublin. 8º. pp. 14. 1863.
127. University Education in Ireland. Private printing of 500 copies. 1865.
128. Address in medicine at Annual Meeting of British Medical Association at Dublin, August 7th 1867. *Brit med J* 1867: *2*: 103-107 and *Edin med J* 1867: *13*: 274-284.
129. On Insurance Certificates. *Brit med J* 1868: *1*: 400-401.
130. On Death Registration and "Medical Certificate of Death" *Dublin Quart J med Sci* 1871: *51*: 341-346.
131. Letter from Dominic Corrigan to the corporation of Dublin upon the subject of the Richmond District Lunatic Asylum. Dublin: J. Dollard, 1872.
132. Address at the Distribution of Prizes in St Mary's Hospital Medical School. Morton & Co. London. 8º. pp. 12. 1873.
133. On Insurance Certificates and on Death Registration and "Medical Certificate of Death". Browne and Nolan. Dublin. 8º. pp. 20. 1874.

134. Remarks on the admission of women to the medical profession. *Brit med J* 1875: 2: 13, 14, 20.
135. The Constitution of the General Medical Council – a communication to members of the British Medical Association. *Ibid* 1878: 2: 674-675.
136. Reminiscences of the Dissecting Room. *Ibid* 1879: 1: 59-60.
(Many of these addresses were published also in the daily newspapers.)

POLITICAL SPEECHES AND PUBLICATIONS

(Abbreviations in Hansard: Amendt – Amendment; Res – Resolution; Comm – Committee; Re-comm – Re-Committal; Consid – Consideration; cl – clause; add cl – Additional Clause; 1R, 2R, 3R – Speech delivered on the First, Second, or Third Reading).

137. Speech urging completion of Church of Sts Augustine and John. *Freeman's Journal* 1869 May 24th.
138. *Hansard's Parliamentary Debates* 1871; Vol. *204*:
    1. Elections (Parliamentary & Municipal), Leave, 552.
    2. Ecclesiastical Titles Act Repeat, 2R, 806.
    3. Burial, 2R, 1148.
    4. Ireland – Distribution of Duplicate Works – British Museum, 757.
    5. Ireland – Westmeath & C. Unlawful combinations; Motion for a committee, 1212.
    6. India – Civil Engineering, Res., 1343.
139. *Ibid* 1871; Vol *205*:
    1. Sunday Trading, 2R, 1736.
140. *Ibid* 1871; Vol *206*:
    1. Permissive Prohibitory Liquor, 2R, 1945.
    2. Army Regulations, Comm. cl, 3, 1560.
    3. Army Regulations, Comm. cl, 3, 1576.
141. *Ibid* 1871; Vol *207*:
    1. University Tests (Dublin), Leave, 1164.
142. *Ibid* 1871; Vol *208*:
    1. Local Government Board, Comm. 357.
    2. Parliament – Business of the House, 569.
    3. Foreign Decorations – Convention of Geneva, motion for an Address, 1490.
    4. Ireland – Riots in Phoenix Park, Res 1800.
143. *Ibid* 1872; Vol *209*:
    1. Education of Blind and Deaf Mute Children, 2R, 1505.
    2. Adulteration of Food and Drugs, 2R, 1508.
144. Speech of Sir Dominic Corrigan, Bart MP on "Closing Public Houses in Ireland on Sundays". At a General Meeting of the Dublin Licensed Grocers and Vintners' Association. Published on behalf of the Irish Association for Closing Public Houses on Sundays. March, 1872.
145. *Hansard's Parliamentary Debates* 1872; Vol *210*:
    1. Monastic and Conventional Institutes, Leave, 1712.
    2. Ireland – Civil Service Salaries, Res 2031.
    3. Parliamentary and Municipal Elections; Comm Schedule 1. 1949.
    4. Parliamentary and Municipal Elections; Comm Schedule 1. 1950.
    5. Parliamentary and Municipal Elections; Comm Schedule 1. 1962.
    6. Parliamentary and Municipal Elections; Comm Schedule 1, 1967.

146. *Ibid* 1872; Vol *211*:
    1. Unlawful Assemblies (Ireland), Act Repeal. 2R. 167.
    2. Unlawful Assemblies (Ireland), Act Repeal, 2R. 169.
    3. Ireland — Clare, Lord Lieutenant of, Res 434.
    4. Parliamentary and Municipal Elections, Comm Schedule 1. 884.
147. *Ibid* 1872; Vol *212*:
    1. Sale of Liquors on Sunday (Ireland), 2r, 258.
    2. Sale of Liquors on Sunday (Ireland, 2r, 608.
    3. Sale of Liquors on Sunday (Ireland), 2R, 611.
    4. Railways (Ireland), 2R, 1339.
    5. Ireland — Galway Election Petition, Res 1853.
    6. Intoxicating Liquor (Licensing), Comm cl 1954.
148. *Ibid* 872; Vol *213*:
    1. Intoxicating Liquor (Licensing), cl 24, Amendt 321.
    2. Intoxicating Liquor (Licensing), cl 26, 338.
    3. Intoxicating Liquor (Licensing), add cl Amendt 484.
    4. Intoxicating Liquor (Licensing), add cl Amendt 492.
    5. Intoxicating Liquor (Licensing) add cl Amendt 494.
    6. Intoxicating Liquor (Licensing), Consid cl 674.
    7. Intoxicating Liquor (Licensing), cl 76 Amendt 679.
    8. Ireland — Galway Election Petition, Res 826.
149. *Ibid* 1873; Vol. *214*:
    1. University Education* (Ireland), 2R, 1659.
    2. University Education* (Ireland), 2R, 1751.
       (*Speech is reprinted from a Pamphlet).
150. *Ibid* 1873; Vol *216*:
    1. Ireland — Civil Servants, Res 1862.
151. *Ibid* 1873; Vol *217*:
    1. Sale of Liquors on Sunday, 2R, 96.
    2. Sale of Liquors on Sunday, 2R, 120.
    3. Lunatic Asylum Boards (Ireland), 145.
    4. Navy Assistant Surgeon, 145.
    5. Weights and Measures (Metric System), 2R, 462.
    6. Turkey — Courts of Justice, 900.
    7. Rating Liability (Ireland), 2R, 962.
    8. Endowed Schools Act (1869). Amendt Comm add cl 952.
    9. Customs Outport clerks. Res Report 1242.
    10. Elementary Education Act (1870) Amendt Re-comm cl 3, 773.
    11. Supply — Metropolitan Police of Dublin. 1141.

TRAVEL

152. *Ten Days in Athens, with Notes by the Way*. Longman, London. 8⁰. pp. 277. Illustrated, 1862.
153. Introductory Presidential Address to Association of the King and Queen's College of Physicians. *Dublin Hosp Gaz* 1860: 7: 337-341.
154. Introductory Address. Winter Session. 1860-61. J.M. O'Toole & Son. Dublin. 8⁰. pp. 20. 1 Map, 1861.
155. Observations on Aix-les-Bains. *Dublin J med Sci* 1875: *60*: 485-493.
156. Jottings from *Rien Faire. Dublin Post*. Sep 4 1858.

BIOGRAPHY

1. Obituary. *Brit med J* 1880: *1*: 219.
2. Obituary. *Ibid* 1880: *1*: 227.
3. Obituary. *Ibid* 1880: *1*: 226.
4. Obituary. *Ibid* 1880: *1*: 285.
5. Obituary. *Dublin J med Sci* 1880: *69*: 268-272.
6. Obituary. *Ibid* 1880: *69*: 330-331.
7. Obituary. *Freeman's Journal* 1880: Feb 2nd.
8. Obituary. *Lancet* 1880: *1*: 268.
9. Obituary. *Medical Press and Circular. London* 1880 ns: *29:* 96.
10. Obituary. *Medical Times and Gazette* 1880: *1*: 164-166.
11. Petit, L.M. Obituary. *Revue Scientifique* (Paris) 1880: 2s: *18*: 831.
12. Mapother, E.D. Sir Dominic Corrigan. *The Irish Monthly*, 1880: *8*: 160-171.
13. Moore, N. *Dictionary of National Biography* 1886, p. 252.
14. Cameron, C.A. *History of the Royal College of Surgeons in Ireland*. Dublin: Fannin & Co. 1886, pp. 564-9.
15. Dawes, S.L. Little biographies and the eponymic diseases. (Sir Dominic Corrigan). *Albany Medical Annals* 1908: *29*: 363-365.
16. Cruise, F.R. Catholic Men of Science. Sir Dominic Corrigan (1802-1880) London. Catholic Truth Society. 1912. pp. 20. In *Twelve Catholic Men of Science* ed Sir Bertram Windle, London. 1912.
17. Garrison, F.H. In *An Introduction to the History of Medicine*. W.B. Saunders Company, Philadelphia & London. 1913. p. 352.
18. Riesman, D. The Great Irish Clinicians of the Nineteenth Century. *Johns Hopk Hosp Bull* 1913: *270*: 251-257.
19. Williamson, R.T. Sir Dominic Corrigan. *Ann med Hist* 1925: 7: 354-361.
20. Duffy Hancock, J. The Irish School of Medicine. *Ann med Hist* 1930: *2:* 196-207.
21. Hunter, R.H. Irish Masters of Medicine. No. 3. Sir Dominic Corrigan. *Ulster med J* 1933: *2*: 61.
22. Unsigned essay. Sir Dominic Corrigan. *New Engl J Med* 1936: *214*: 129-310.
23. *Medical Classics*. Williams-Wilkins, Co. Baltimore, USA. 1937: *1*: 672-727.
24. Dixon, E., Sir Dominic Corrigan, Part I. *Dublin Historical Record* 1946: *8*: 28-38.
25. Dixon, E., Sir Dominic Corrigan, Part II. *Ibid* 1946: *8*: 67-76.
26. Neuburger, M. The Famous Irish Triad – Graves, Stokes, Corrigan. *Irish J med Sci* 1948: 6th Series p. 35.
27. Fleetwood, J. *History of Medicine in Ireland*. Browne and Nolan, Dublin. 1951. pp. 193-196.
28. Willius, F.A. and Keys, T.E. Sir Dominic John Corrigan, 1802-1880. *Cardiac Classics*. Henry Schuman Inc, Dover Publications, Inv N York, 1961. Vol 2: pp. 419-423.
29. Widdess, J.D.H., In *A History of the Royal College of Physicians of Ireland*. E & S. Livingstone Ltd. Edinburgh & London. 1963. pp. 184-205.
30. O'Brien, E.T. Dublin Masters of Clinical Expression. III. Sir Dominic Corrigan (1802-1880). *J Irish Colls Phys and Surg* 1974: *4*: 67-69.
31. Lyons, J.B. In *Brief Lives of Irish Doctors*. Blackwater, Dublin 1978. p. 79.
32. O'Brien, E. Sir Dominic Corrigan (1802-1880), Radio Eireann "Miscellany" Broadcast 29.1.'80.
33. O'Brien, E. Ed. Corrigan Centenary Issue. *J Ir Colls Phys & Surg*. 1980: *10*: 1-57.
34. O'Brien, E. Sir Dominic Corrigan (1802-1880). *Ibid*. 11-19.

35. O'Dwyer, W.F. Corrigan and the Charitable Infirmary. *Ibid.* 21-3.
36. Holland, P.D.J. Corrigan and the House of Industry Hospitals. *Ibid.* 24-6.
37. Mills, R. and O'Brien, E. Corrigan Bibliography. *Ibid.* 50-4.
38. Mills, R. and O'Brien, E. Memorabilia and Letters of Dominic Corrigan. Catalogue of an exhibition. *Ibid.* 55-7.
39. O'Brien, E. The Lancet maketh the man? Sir Dominic John Corrigan (1802-1880), *Lancet*: 2: 1356-7.
40. O'Brien, E. Dominic Corrigan and the Great Famine. *The American Irish Historical Society Recorder*, 1981: *41*: 117-9.
41. O'Brien, E. Sir Dominic John Corrigan (1802-1880). The man behind the eponym. *New Engl J Med.* 1981: *304*: 365-6.

REVIEWS AND CRITICISM
(Selected opinions on Corrigan's Publications)

1. On the epidemic fever in Ireland. Unsigned review. *Lancet* 1829: 2: 614.
2. On the motions and sounds of the heart. Unsigned review. *Ibid* 1829: 964-971.
3. Corrigan's opinions on non-synchronism of pulse and impulse. *Ibid* 1830: *1*: 91.
4. Hope, J. Strictures on an Essay by Dr Corrigan on "The Motions and Actions of the Heart". *Lond med Gaz* 1830: *6*: 680-687.
5. Anonymous. On the motions and sounds of the heart by D.J. Corrigan. *Med. Chir. Rev.* 1830: *13*: 122-3.
6. Hope, J. A Treatise on the Diseases of the Heart and Great Vessels. London. 1839. Kidd. pp. 71, 80, 100, 379, 443, 446, 458, 572.
7. Anonymous. A Treatise on the Diseases of the Heart and Great Vessels, comprising a new View of the Physiology of the Heart's Action, to which physical signs are explained. By J. Hope, MD, & C. Kidd, London, 1832, pp. 612. *Dublin J med Sci* 1832: *1*: 58-62.
8. Graves, R. Clinical Lectures. Lecture IX. *London Med and Surg. Gaz* 1833: *3*: 74-80.
9. On Famine and Fever as Cause and Effect in Ireland. A Review. *Dublin Quart J Med Sci* 1846: *1*: 486-490.
10. McCormack, J. Cases Illustrating The Success of "Firing". A New Form of Counter-Irritation. *Lancet* 1846: 2: 612.
11. Wakely, T. (?) Editorial on Central Health Board. *Ibid* 1847: 2: 469.
12. Lectures on the Nature and Treatment of Fever. A Review. *Dublin Quart J med Sci* 1853: *15*: 409-414.
13. Edited by Photophilus — W. Handsil Griffiths. The New Irish Bath versus The Old Turkish or Pure Air versus Vapour. Being an Answer to the Errors and Mis-statements of Drs Madden and Corrigan. William M'Gee. Dublin, 8º. 56 pages. 1860.
14. Ten Days in Athens. A Review. *Edin med J.* 1862: 8: 166-169.
15. Small-pox, review of lecture on. *Brit med J* 1865: *1*: 157-158.
16. Graves, R. A Letter to the Editor of the Dublin Quarterly Journal of Medical Science, relative the Proceedings of the Central Board of Health of Ireland. *Dublin Quart J med Sci* 1847: *4*: 513-544.
17. Nesbitt, M.A. Remarks on Dr Corrigan's letter on University Education in Ireland. William M'Gee. Dublin. 8º. 24 pages, 1866.
18. The University of Erlangen and Sir Dominic Corrigan. *Brit med J* 1867: 2: 54-55.

19. Wilks, S. Notes on the History of Valvular Disease of the Heart. *Guy's Hosp Rep* 1871: *16*: 209-216.
20. Clarke, A., Hadley, W., Chaplin, A. Fibroid Diseases of the Lungs including Fibroid Phthisis. Charles Griffen & Co. Ltd. London. p. 10, 1894.
21. Albutt, C. Diseases of the Arteries including Angina Pectoris. London. 1915. Vol. *2*. p. 427.
22. Ferguson, W.F. Corrigan's investigations on the cardiovascular system; an historical sketch. *Canada Lancet*. (Toronto). 1817: *50*: 205-210.
23. Riesman, D. The Rise and Early History of Clinical Teaching. *Ann. med Hist* 1919: *2*: 136-147.
24. Riesman, D. The Dublin School and its influence upon Medicine in America. *Ann med Hist* 1922: *4*: 86-98.
25. Rolleston, H. Sir Dominic Corrigan, Bart., MD. *Irish J med Sci* 1932: 6th Series. 261-266.
26. Bramwell, E. Corrigan's Original Description of Aortic Regurgitation; A reference to some matters of historical interest. *Edin med J* 1933: *40*: 13-19.
27. Dock, G.L. I. Dominic John Corrigan; His place in the development of our knowledge of cardiac disease. II. The water hammer pulse. *Ann med His* 1934: *6*: 381-395.
28. Willis, F.A. and Keys, T.E. The Influence of the Irish School of Physicians. *Proc Mayo Clin* 1941: *16*: 637-640.
29. Widdess,J.D.H. Corrigan's Button. *Irish J med Sci* 1967. 6th Series. 137-140.
30. Mulcahy, R. Sir Dominic Corrigan. *Ibid* 1961: *430*: 454-463.
31. Mulcahy, R. The Early Descriptions of Aortic Incompetence. *Brit Heart J* 1962; *24*: 633-636.
32. Horgan, J.M. Corrigan on Cardiac Disease. *J Ir Coll Phys Surg* 1980: *10*: 27-31.
33. O'Brien, E. Corrigan's Disease. *Ibid*, 1980: *10*: 32-7.
34. Counihan, H.E. Corrigan on Pulmonary Disease. *Ibid*, 1980: *10*: 38-40.
35. Fielding,J.F. Corrigan on Abdominal Disease. *Ibid*, 1980: *10*: 41-3.
36. Doyle, J.S. Corrigan on Fever. *Ibid*, 1980: *10*: 44-5.
37. O'Brien, W. Fever of the Great Famine. *Ibid*, 1980: *10*: 46-9.
38. Connolly, D. and Mann, R. Dominic J. Corrigan (1802-1880) and his description of the pericardial knock. *Mayo Clin Proc* 1980: *55*: 771-3.

APPENDIX D

STUDENT CURRICULUM OF DOMINIC J. CORRIGAN

(Compiled from the admission cards and certificates of attendance in the Corrigan papers. RCPI)

Course of Instruction	Institute	Teachers
FIRST YEAR. 1820-1821		
Matriculation	The University of Dublin (29.11.1820)	
Chemistry	The Laboratory, Trinity College Dublin (TCD).	Francis Barker M.D. Professor of Chemistry.
Dissecting Course	Theatre of Anatomy, Peter Street.	Mr. J. Kirby and Michael Daniell. Lecturers in Anatomy, surgery, etc.
Anatomy, Physiology and Surgery	Theatre of Anatomy, Peter Street.	Mr. Kirby A.B.T.C.D. & Member of the Royal College of Surgeons, and M. Daniell.
SECOND YEAR. 1821-1822		
Anatomy, Physiology & Diseases of the Eye	Anatomical Theatre, TCD.	Arthur Jacob.
Lectures on the Practice of Medicine	Trinity College Dublin	Martin Tuomy, M.D. Professor of the Practice of Medicine
Dissecting Course	Theatre of Anatomy, Peter Street.	M. Daniell.
Anatomy, Physiology and Surgery	Theatre of Anatomy, Peter Street.	Mr. Kirby and M. Daniell.
THIRD YEAR. 1822-1823		
Anatomy, Physiology and Surgery	The University of Dublin	James Macartney Professor of Anatomy & Surgery.
FOURTH YEAR. 1823-1824		
Pathology	The University of Dublin	James Macartney
Medicine	The Medical School in Ireland (*Schola Medicina in Hibernia*)	John G. Boyton, M.D. Regius Professor of the Institute of Medicine.
Materia Medica and Pharmacy	Apothecaries Hall	M. Donovan.
FIFTH YEAR. 1824-1825		
Bibliothecae Academia	Edinburgh University (12.10.1824)	
Clinical Lectures	School of Physic in Ireland	John Crampton M.D. Prof. of Materia Medica
Materia Medica	School of Physic in Ireland	John Crampton.
Anatomy, Physiology and Surgery	The University of Dublin	James Macartney
Anatomical Demonstrations & Dissections	The University of Dublin	James Macartney.
Morbid Anatomy & Pathology	The University of Dublin	James Macartney.
Lectures on the Institutes of Medicine	School of Physic in Ireland	J. Boyton.
Admission Receipt for £6.16.6.	Sir Patrick Dun's Hospital	James Digges la Touche, Treasurer.
Clinical Lectures	Sir Patrick Dun's Hospital	J. Boyton.
Lectures on Botany	University of Edinburgh	Robert Graham, M.D.

APPENDIX E

MEMBERS OF THE LECTURER'S CLUB FOR 1837-38.

(Compiled from the minute book of the Lecturer's Club of which Corrigan was secretary)

Name	Title	School	Home address
Dr. Apjohn	Prof. Chemistry	R.C.S.I.	28 Lower Baggot St.
Mr. Porter	Prof. Surgery	R.C.S.I.	18 Kildare Street
Dr. Evanson	Prof. Pract. of Med.	R.C.S.I.	36 Dawson Street
Dr. Williams	Prof. Mat. Medica	R.C.S.I.	47 Baggot St. Lr.
Dr. Maunsell	Prof. Midwifery	R.C.S.I.	13 Molesworth St.
Dr. Geoghegan	Prof. Jurisprudence	R.C.S.I.	52 York Street
Dr. Jacob	Prof. Anatomy	R.C.S.I.	83 Ely Place
Dr. Harrison	Prof. Anatomy	R.C.S.I.	1 Hume Street
Dr. Benson	Prof. Pract. of Med.	R.C.S.I.	34 York Street
Dr. Wilmot	Prof. Surgery	R.C.S.I.	120 Stephen's Green W.
Dr. Hunt	Prof. Mat. Medica	Apothecaries Hall	14 Upper Merrion St.
Dr. Kane	Prof. Chemistry	Apothecaries Hall	23 Lr. Gloucester St.
Dr. J.C. Ferguson	Prof. Pract. of Med.	Apothecaries Hall	16 Nth Frederick St.
Dr. M.O.B. Adams	Lect. Midwifery	Apothecaries Hall	27 Nth Gt. Georges St.
Dr. Litton	Prof. Botany	Apothecaries Hall	10 Lr. Cloucester St.
Mr. Alcock	Prof. Anatomy	Apothecaries Hall	17 Sth. Frederick St.
Dr. Stokes	Lect. Pract. Med.	Park Street School	50 York Street
Dr. G. Stokes	Lect. Med. Jurisprud.	Park Street School	16 Harcourt Street
Dr. Beatty	Lect. Midwifery	Park Street School	16 Molesworth St.
Dr. Houston	Lect. Surgery	Park Street School	31 York Street
Sur. Cusack	Lect. Surgery	Park Street School	3 Kildare Street
Dr. Green	Lect. Pract. Med.	Richmond School	14 Harcourt Street
Sur. Nunn	Lect. Jurisprudence	Richmond School	6 Dawson Street
Sur. Cullen	Lect. Mat. Medica.	Richmond School	Jervis Street
Dr. Churchill	Lect. Midwifery	Richmond School	104 Stephen's Green S.

Name	Title	School	Home address
Mr. Power	Lect. Anatomy	Richmond School	24 Great Ship Street
Mr. Adams	Lect. Surgery	Richmond School	16 Sth. Denmark St.
Mr. Flood	Lect. Anatomy	Richmond School	19 Blessington Street
Sur. Baker	Lect. Jurisprudence	Peter Street School	22 Amiens Street
Dr. Mitchell	Lect. Mat. Medica.	Peter Street School	51 Bishops Street
Dr. Bellingham	Lect. Mat. Medica.	Peter Street School	63 Eccles Street
Sur. White	Lect. Surgery	Peter Street School	42 Dawson Street
Sur. Hanlon	Lect. Mat. Medica.	Peter Street School	
Dr. Brennan	Lect. Anatomy	Peter Street School	3 Dawson Street
Dr. Nolan	Lect. Practice Med.	Peter Street School	7 Hume Street
Dr. Power	Lect. Midwifery	Peter Street School	56 Dominick Street
Dr. Brady	Lect. Jurisprudence	Peter Street School	2 Great Charles St.
Sur. Hayden	Lect. Anatomy	Peter Street School	28 Peter Street
Dr. Ireland	Lect. Midwifery	Peter Street School	121 Stephen's Green W.
Dr. Aldridge	Lect. Botany	Digges Street School	4 Duke Street
Dr. O'Reilly	Lect. Jurisprudence	Digges Street School	25 Dominick Street
Mr. Hargrave	Lect. Anatomy	Digges Street School	37 York Street
Mr. Carmichael	Lect. Surgery	Digges Street School	39 Dominick Street
Mr. Colles	Lect. Chemistry	Digges Street School	Aungier Street
Dr. Corrigan	Lect. Practice Medicine	Digges Street School	4 Merrion Square W.
Sur. Irvine	Lect. Anatomy	Marlborough St. School	10 Hardwicke Place
Dr. Denham	Lect. Anatomy	Marlborough St. School	67 Marlborough St.
Dr. Graves	Prof. Inst. of Medicine	School of Physic	9 Harcourt Street
Dr. Crampton	Prof. Mat. Medica.	School of Physic	39 Kildare Street
Dr. Montgomery	Prof. Midwifery	School of Physic	18 Molesworth Street

Notes and References

Full details of works quoted in the text are given when first referred to in each chapter; where the work is referred to again in the same chapter it is indicated in an abbreviated form.

The familiar abbreviations for degrees, diplomas and licenses have been used, and the following abbreviations are also used:

RCSI — Royal College of Surgeons in Ireland
RCPI — Royal College of Physicians of Ireland
TCD — Trinity College Dublin
DNB — *The Compact Edition of the Dictionary of National Biography*, Oxford University Press, 1975.
NLI — National Library of Ireland, Kildare Street, Dublin.

Items in the *Corrigan Archive* in the Royal College of Physicians have been classified as *Letters* (most are numbered), *Diaries* (all are numbered and where the pages have numbers the page reference is given), *Certificates,* (not yet classified), *Pamphlets,* (not yet classified), and *Papers* (a miscellaneous collection of items not already classified). There are a number of Corrigan's published writings among the *Papers,* and these are included in the Corrigan Bibliography, Appendix C.

Chapter 1

1. Dixon, E., "Sir Dominic Corrigan, Part I", *Dublin Historical Record*, 1946: *8*: pp. 28-38. In an indenture between Joseph Catheril and John Corrigan concerning the lease of a house in the Parish of St Catherine, Dublin, dated 3rd February, 1795, John Corrigan is described as a "colliermaker." (RCPI. Corrigan Letters).

2. Kohl, J.G., quoted in *The Great Famine in Ireland and a retrospect of the fifty years 1845-95*, by W.P. O'Brien, London: Downey & Co., 1896: pp. 37-8.
3. Before the dissolution of the monasteries Dublin had a number of hospitals, the oldest being that of St John the Baptist. The Steyne Hospital was founded on the south bank of the Liffey in 1220; the hospital of St Stephen for lepers was on the site occupied by Mercer's Hospital, and Alleyn's Hospital in Kevin Street, was endowed in 1504 by John Alleyn, Dean of St Patrick's for the sick poor. At the dissolution these hospitals were closed, and Dublin was without a hospital until 1718 when The Charitable Infirmary was founded. For a full history of these early hospitals see Evans, E., "History of Dublin Hospitals and Infirmaries from 1188 till the present time", *The Irish Builder*, 1896: *38*: pp. 167, 180, 192, 204, 218, 224, 237, 245, 257.
4. Cruise, F.R., *Catholic Men of Science. Sir Dominic Corrigan (1802-1880)*, London: Catholic Truth Society, 1912: pp. 20. Reprinted in *Twelve Catholic Men of Science*, Ed., Sir Bertram Windle, London, 1912. See also Appendix A.
5. Dixon, E., "Sir Dominic Corrigan, Part II", *Dublin Historical Record*, 1946: *8*: pp. 67-76.
6. Dowling, P.J., *A History of Irish Education*, Cork: Mercier Press, 1971: p. 71.
7. Lecky, W., quoted by Dowling, *ibid*: p. 71.
8. *ibid*: p. 86.
9. Durcan, T.J., *History of Irish Education from 1800*, Wales: Dragon Books, 1972: p. 134.
10. Corrigan Diaries, RCPI. No. 6.
11. Newman, J., *Maynooth and Georgian Ireland*, Galway: Kenny's Bookshops and Art Galleries, 1979: p. 10. For a full history of Maynooth College see Dr Healy's *Centenary History*, 1895. Unfortunately this contains little on the Lay College, and, surprisingly and regrettably, Newman's History has neither references nor a bibliography limiting greatly its use for scholarship. Much of what Newman quotes about the Lay College may be found in: Brady, J., "The Lay College, Maynooth", *Irish Ecclesiastical Record*, 1943: *51*: pp. 385-8.
12. Newman, *Maynooth*, p. 43.
13. *ibid*: p. 166.
14. *ibid*: p. 168.
15. *ibid*: p. 117.
16. *ibid*: p. 167. Details on fellow students at the Lay College may also be found in: Mapother, E.D., "Sir Dominic Corrigan", *Irish Monthly*, 1880: *8*: pp. 160-171, and Corrigan Diaries, RCPI. No. 6. Among others who attended the Lay College (in some instances only for a short period) were: Christopher Boylan, John Richard Corballis, Robert Ffrench Whitehead, John Sweetman, James Blake, Arthur Plunkett, Valentine Dillon.
17. Eighth Report of the Commissioners of the Irish Education Inquiry, June 1827. Quoted in Brady's "The Lay College".
18. Corrigan Diaries, RCPI. No. 6.
19. *ibid*.
20. Widdess, J.D.H., *A History of the Royal College of Physicians of Ireland, 1654-1963*, Edinburgh: E and S. Livingstone, 1963: p. 185.
21. Cruise, *Sir Dominic Corrigan*.
22. Corrigan Letters, RCPI. Nos. 58-60.

CHAPTER 2

1. Kirkpatrick, T.P.C., *History of the Medical Teaching in Trinity College Dublin and of the School of Physic in Ireland*, Dublin: Hanna and Neale, 1912: pp. 56-57, p. 71.
2. *ibid*: p. 66.
3. Widdess, J.D.H., *A History of the Royal College of Physicians of Ireland, 1654-1963*, Edinburgh and London: E & S. Livingstone, 1963: pp. 33-37. The College of Physicians was granted its second charter in 1692, giving it power to penalise unqualified persons practising medicine in Dublin, and it also had powers to supervise the practice of apothecaries, druggists and chemists.
4. Evans, E., "History of Dublin Hospitals and Infirmaries, from 1188 till the present time. 18. Sir Patrick Dun's Hospital, 1788", *Irish Builder*, 1897: *39*: pp. 97, 107, 121, 130, 142, 152.
5. Widdess, J.D.H., *The Royal College of Surgeons in Ireland and its Medical School 1784-1984*, 3rd Ed., Dublin: RCSI, 1984: pp. 62-3.
6. Cameron, C.A., *History of the Royal College of Surgeons in Ireland and of the Irish Schools of Medicine*, Dublin: Fannin & Co, 1886: pp. 513-543.
7. *ibid*: p. 516.
8. Corrigan Certificates, RCPI. For details see Appendix D.
9. Anon., "Reminiscences of the Dissecting Room", *British Medical Journal*, 1879: *I*: pp. 59-60. This paper was written when Corrigan was aged 79; he was immediately identified as the author.
10. Corrigan Certificates, RCPI.
11. Kirkpatrick, *TCD*, pp. 211-13.
12. Corrigan Letters, RCPI.
13. Erinensis. "Sketches of the Medical Profession in Ireland. No. 18. Reduction of the Present Term of Medical Graduation in the University of Dublin considered". *Lancet*, June 16, 1827: pp. 335-339.
14. Cameron, *RCSI*, p. 110. "The Irish medical graduates of Edinburgh increased from one in 1726 to twelve in the year 1750, twenty-two in 1775 and fifty in 1800. The graduates in the last quarter of the eighteenth century numbered 800, of whom 237 were Irish, 217 English, 179 Scottish, and 167 colonists and foreigners".
15. Duncan, A., quoted by Erinensis. *Lancet*, June 16, 1827: pp. 335-339.
16. Makey, W.H., "George Drummond's New Edinburgh", *Edinburgh's Infirmary*, Edinburgh: Lammerburn Press, 1979: pp. 19-22.
17. Graves, R., *A System of Clinical Medicine*, Dublin: 1843: p. 4.
18. Erinensis was an Irish doctor, Dr Peter Hennis Greene, who for many years contributed satirical articles on Irish medicine to the *Lancet*, then under the editorship of the outspoken Thomas Wakley. For a biographical essay and a selection of his writings see: Fallon, M., *The Sketches of Erinensis. Selections of Irish Medical Satire 1824-1836*, London: Skilton & Shaw, 1978.
19. Kirkpatrick, *TCD*, pp. 224-231.
20. Stokes, W., *William Stokes. His Life and Work (1804-1878)*, London: Fisher Unwin, 1898: p. 21.
21. *ibid*: pp. 27-29.
22. Erinensis quoted in Widdess, *RCSI*, pp. 53-4.
23. Widdess, *RCSI*, p. 56.
24. Erinensis, "Sketches of the Surgical Profession in Ireland. No. IV. Mr Kirby", *Lancet*, 1824: *3-4*: pp. 209-218. Reprinted in Fallon, *Erinensis*, pp. 43-53.
25. This engraving showing Macartney seated with a book in his hand, and the head of his dog in his lap is in the RCPI. Written in pen on the margin is

"Presented to Dr Corrigan by Dr Macartney".
26. Kirkpatrick, *TCD*, pp. 216-225.
27. *ibid*: pp. 258-265. Macartney died while writing a paper for a meeting of RCPI. The last words he wrote were:

>All forms that perish other forms supply,
>(By turns we catch the vital breath and die),
>Like bubbles on the sea of matter borne,
>They rise, they break, and to that sea return

28. Blake Bailey, J., *The Diary of A Resurrectionist, 1811-1812. To which are added an account of the Resurrection Men in London and a Short History of the Passing of the Anatomy Act*, London: Swan Sonnenschein & Co., 1896: Extracts from pp. 141-168. This diary was written between 1811 and 1812 by an English resurrection-man named Joseph Naples, who had formerly been a cemetery keeper. The diary was given to Sir Thomas Longmore, who later presented it to the Royal College of Surgeons of England and in 1896, the then librarian of the College, James Blake Bailey published the diary with a history of the practice in London. The book, apart from a comprehensive account of the body-snatching era, also contains an extensive bibliography on the subject to which may be added: Fleetwood, J.F., "The Irish Resurrectionists", *Irish Journal of Medical Science*, 1959: 6th Series: pp. 309-321. Dudley Edwards, O., *Burke and Hare*, Edinburgh: Polygon Books.
29. Kirkpatrick, *TCD*, p. 246.
30. Blake Bailey, *Diary*, p. 88.
31. *ibid*: pp. 50-52.
32. Fleetwood. *Irish Resurrectionists*, pp. 309-321.
33. The derivation of the name is obscure. In the reign of Henry VIII, before the Reformation, the Knights Templar were in possession of the site. Included in their property was an acre, or field, called the Bayl-Yard, presumably under control of the Knights bailiff, whence by corruption may have come the name. Another suggestion is that the toughs or bullies met to settle their quarrels. (Widdess, *RCPI*. p. 184). It is reported to contain the tomb of Murchadh, son of Brian and others slain at the Battle of Clontarf. In the eighteenth and nineteenth centuries it was famous as a dwelling ground, and was used for interments up to 1832 when in the great cholera visitation 500 burials took place within ten days, and 3,200 in six months; it was then closed as a burial place by the Governors from fear of the spread of the pestilence. (Dixon, E., "Sir Dominic Corrigan. Part II", *Dublin Historical Record*, 1946: 8: pp. 67-76).
34. The "Cabbage Garden" formerly known as the Carmelites Garden and situated in the centre of the city at the end of Cathedral Lane off Kevin Street. The burials in the cemetery adjoining St Patrick's had become so numerous that the Viceroy and Council restrained its use by order in 1666, and "three stangs of ground in St Kevin's Parish" were obtained as a burial ground. The name comes, it is said, from Cromwell's troops having grown English cabbage there for their own use. (Dixon, *ibid*).
35. Blake Bailey, *Diary*, p. 31.
36. *ibid*: pp. 37-38.
37. *ibid*: p. 38.
38. Dudley Edwards, *Burke and Hare*.
39. Widdess, *RCSI*, p. 80.
40. Widdess, *RCPI*, pp. 136-137.
41. Riesman, D., "The Dublin School and its influence upon Medicine in America", *Annals of Medical History*, 1922: 4: pp. 86-96.

42. Anon., "The Late Dr Alison", *Edinburgh Medical Journal*, 1859: 5: pp. 469-486. Newbigging, P., "Account of the Illness and Death of Dr William Pulteney Alison, Emeritus Professor of the Practice of Physic in the University of Edinburgh", *ibid*, 1859: 5: pp. 597-50. Haliday Douglas, A., "Harveian Discourse. On the Life and Character of Dr Alison". *ibid*, 1866: 11: pp. 1063-1076.
43. Stokes, *William Stokes*, pp. 31-33.
44. Laënnec, R.T.H., *A Treatise on the Diseases of the Chest and on Mediate Auscultation*, trans. by J. Forbes, New York: S. Wood & Sons, 1830: p. 339. Reprinted with biographical essay and portrait in: Major, R.H., *Classic Descriptions of Disease with Biographical Sketches of the Authors*, Illinois: Charles C. Thomas, 3rd Ed., 1978: pp. 68-71.
45. Stokes, W., *A Treatise on the use of the Stethoscope*, Edinburgh, 1825.
46. Widdess, *RCPI*, pp. 185-186.
47. Two essay papers in Latin written in Corrigan's hand for his final examination are in the Corrigan Papers, RCPI. Paper 1, "The history of a 26 year old girl with abdominal pain" is presented by Robert Graham, Professor of Botany. The student is asked to write on the name of the disease, the reason for the symptoms, prognosis advice and method of treatment. Corrigan's essay on this paper runs to about 1,000 words. Paper 2, "The history of a 62 year old man with inflammation of the intestines" is presented in considerable detail by William P. Alison, Professor of Theoretical Medicine. The student is required to discuss the name of the disease, diagnosis, prognosis, reason for the symptoms, method of treatment and formulae of medicaments. Corrigan's essay runs to about 900 words. Corrigan's Thesis (1,600 words) in Edinburgh University Library is entitled *Dissertatio Inauguralis quadam de SCROFULA complectens. Auctore Dominico Johanne Corrigan.*
48. Corrigan Papers, RCPI. See the printed list of graduates (in Latin) from Edinburgh University in 1825, together with the subject of each dissertation; also the regulations for submission of theses. Other Irish graduates of note from Edinburgh University include George Cleghorn, Robert Perceval, Daniel Cunnigham, Henry Croly and Henry McCormac. See also front endpaper.
49. MacDonnell, J., "Amputation of the arm, performed at the Richmond Hospital, without pain", Dublin Medical Press, 1847: 17: pp. 3-4. It is of interest that John MacDonnell's son Robert was to be the first in Ireland to perform a human blood transfusion in The Charitable Infirmary, Jervis Street on April 20, 1865. (MacDonnell, R., "Remarks on the operation of transfusion and the apparatus for its performance", *Dublin Quarterly Journal of Medical Science*, 1870: 50: p. 257). John MacDonnell's father James was the "father of Belfast medicine", and co-founder of the Belfast Dispensary and Fever Hospital. (Froggatt, P., "Dr James MacDonnell, MD [1763-1845]", *Journal of the Glens of Antrim Historical Society*, 1981: 9: pp. 17-31).
50. Pinkerton, J.H.M., "John Creery Ferguson. Friend of William Stokes and Pioneer of Auscultation of the Fetal Heart in the British Isles", *British Journal of Obstetrics and Gynaecology*, 1980: 87: pp. 257-260.

Chapter 3

1. Atthill, L., The Late, *Recollections of an Irish Doctor*, London: Religious Tract Society, 1911: pp. 195-6.
2. Ormond Quay, on the North bank of the Liffey, is named after James Butler, 1st Duke of Ormond. The house from which Corrigan practised has been demolished.

3. Mapother, E.D., "Sir Dominic Corrigan", *Irish Monthly*, 1880: *8*: pp. 160-171.
4. Warburton, J., Whitelaw, J., and Walsh, R., *History of the City of Dublin*, 2 vols., London, 1818: Vol 2: p.7.
5. *ibid*: Vol 1: p. v. For full details of the census see Vol 2: pp. iii-x.
6. Whitelaw, Rev J., *An Essay on the population of Ireland, 1805*, quoted in *Dublin under the Georges*, by C. Maxwell, Dublin: Gill & MacMillan, 1979: p. 118.
7. The area of the city in which Corrigan practised housed over one-third of the total population of Dublin, 59,788, according to the census of 1821 (Corrigan, D., "On the epidemic fever of Ireland", *Lancet*, 1829-30: *2*: pp. 569-75.)
8. Whitelaw, *Essay on Population*, in Maxwell, *Dublin under the Georges*, pp. 116-117.
9. Stokes, Whitley, quoted in Maxwell, *Dublin under the Georges*, p. 121.
10. Mapother, "Corrigan", p. 161.
11. *ibid*: p. 163.
12. Corrigan, D., *On famine and fever as cause and effect in Ireland; with observations on hospital location and the dispensation in outdoor relief of food and medicine*, Dublin: Fannin & Co, 1846: pp. 33. Corrigan Pamphlets, RCPI.).
13. Corrigan Diaries, RCPI. No. 6.
14. Corrigan Papers, RCPI, Application for Cork Street Fever Hospital.
15. Mapother, "Corrigan", p. 161.
16. Stokes, W., *William Stokes. His Life and Work (1804-1878)*, London: T. Fisher Unwin, 1898: pp. 44-46.
17. Ferguson, J.C., "Auscultation, the only unequivocal sign of pregnancy", *Dublin Medical Transactions*, 1830: *1*: p. 64. For a short biography of Ferguson see: Pinkerton, J.H.M., "John Creery Ferguson. Friend of William Stokes and Pioneer of Auscultation of the Fetal Heart in the British Isles", *British Journal of Obstetrics and Gynaecology*, 1980: *84*: pp. 257-260.
18. Corrigan, D., "Aneurism of the aorta; singular pulsation of the arteries; necessity of the employment of the stethoscope", *Lancet*, 1828: *1*: pp. 586-590.
19. Wakley was a polemical editor and enthusiastic reformer. Under his editorship the *Lancet* became the most outspoken medical journal of all time. Its only rival in propagating reform was the *Dublin Medical Press* founded by Arthur Jacob and Henry Maunsell in 1839 and published as the *Medical Press* in London until 1961. For a biographical essay on Wakley see DNB: p. 2170.
20. For an example of Wakley's support of Corrigan see: Anon., "On the epidemic fever of Ireland", *Lancet*, 1829: 2: p. 614.
21. Corrigan, D., "On the motions and sounds of the heart", *Dublin Medical Transactions*, 1830: *1*: pp. 151-203.
22. Hope, J., *A Treatise on the Diseases of the Heart*, London: Churchill, 1839.
23. Hope, J., "Strictures on an Essay by Dr Corrigan on 'The Motions and Actions of the Heart'", *London Medical Gazette*, 1830: *6*: pp. 680-687.
24. Anon., "On the Motions and Sounds of the Heart By D.J. Corrigan, M.D.", *Medico-Chirurgical Review*, 1830: *13*: pp. 122-133.
25. Anon., "On the Motions and Sounds of the Heart By D.J. Corrigan, M.D.", *Lancet*, 1829-30: *2*: pp. 964-971.
26. Corrigan, D., "On the epidemic fever of Ireland, Part I", *ibid*, 1829: 2: pp. 569-575.

27. Corrigan, D., "On the epidemic fever of Ireland, Part II", *ibid*, 1829: *2*: pp. 600-605.
28. See reference note No. 20.
29. Obituary, *British Medical Journal*, 1880: *1*: p. 219.
30. Corrigan Diaries, RCPI. No. 6.
31. Obituary, *British Medical Journal*, 1880: *1*: p. 219.
32. Obituary, *Freemans Journal*, Feb 2nd, 1880.
33. Corrigan, D., *Address at the Distribution of Prizes in St Mary's Hospital Medical School*, London: Morton & Co, 1873: p. 12. (Corrigan Pamphlets, RCPI.).
34. Anon, *Lives of British Physicians*, London: John Murray, 1830. This is a series of biographical essays on British doctors from Linacre to Gooch, that was published anonymously in 1830. The author was K. MacMichael who had also anonymously written the popular *Gold Headed Cane*, in 1827.
35. Corrigan, *Address to St Mary's*.
36. Book for collection of poetry (Diary No. 8. RCPI.) inscribed to Joanna Woodlock from her "truly affectionate brother William Woodlock", Jan 1829. This was probably a wedding present. The poem is handwritten, and though initialled by Corrigan, it does not appear to be in his hand.
37. Corrigan Diaries, RCPI. No. 6. See also Appendix A.

Chapter 4

1. See Appendix C for complete listing of publications.
2. Cruise, F.R., *Catholic Man of Science. Sir Dominic Corrigan (1802-1880)*, London: Catholic Truth Society, 1912: p. 20. Reprinted in *Twelve Catholic Men of Science*, Ed. Sir Bertram Windle, London, 1912.
3. Gwynn, D., *The Struggle for Catholic Emancipation (1750-1829)*, London: Longmans, Green & Co., 1928: pp. xxi-xxii.
4. Burke, E., quoted in Gwynn, *ibid*: p. 1.
5. *ibid*: p. 183.
6. *ibid*: p. 216.
7. "Proceedings of Committee", Minute Book, 12th Jan., 1831, The Charitable Infirmary, Jervis Street.
8. *ibid*: 13th Jan., 1831.
9. "Proceedings of Governors at Large", Minute Book, 18th Feb., 1831. The Charitable Infirmary, Jervis Street. A total of 77 Governors at large attended the meeting.
10. Charter and Supplemental Charter of the Charitable Infirmary in Jervis Street, Dublin: Cahill & Co., 1941: p. 12.
11. *ibid*: p. 22.
12. Corrigan Diaries, RCPI. No. 6. pp. 35-36.
13. Corrigan to Dr O'Kelly. Corrigan Letters, RCPI, No. 115.
14. Widdess, J.D.H., "The Charitable Infirmary, Jervis Street", in *The Charitable Infirmary, Jervis Street, Dublin 1718-1968*, ed. J.D.H. Widdess, Dublin: Hely Thom, 1968: pp. 3-15, See also: Edwards, E., "History of Dublin Hospitals and Infirmaries from 1188 till the Present Time. X. The Charitable Infirmary (Jervis Street), 1723". *Irish Builder*, 1897: *39*: pp. 6-8.
15. This building remained in use until 1886 when it was replaced by the hospital that stands today. The hospital is due yet another move. The Charitable Infirmary will merge with St Laurence's Hospital in the new hospital now being built at Beaumont and due to open in 1985.

16. In the "General Rules, Bye-Laws and Regulations for the Charitable Infirmary in Jervis Street", for 1831, the staff is listed: Physicians: Dominick (sic) Corrigan, Percival Hunt. Surgeons: James Duggan, William Wallace, John Kirby, R.P. O'Reilly, Andrew Ellis, I.P. Lynch, H.M. Stapleton with one surgical position apparently unfilled. There were at this time eight surgeons and only two physicians.
17. *General Rules, Bye-Laws and Regulations for The Charitable Infirmary in Jervis Street*, Dublin: R.M. Whyte, 1821: p. 4.
18. Corrigan, D., "On Permanent Patency of the mouth of the Aorta, or Inadequacy of the Aortic Valves", *Edinburgh Medical and Surgical Journal*, 1832: *37*: pp. 225-245.
19. Corrigan, D., "On the treatment of recent catarrh", *Dublin Journal of Medical Science*, 1832: *1*: pp. 7-15.
20. Rolleston, H., "Sir Dominic Corrigan, Bart., M.D.", *Irish Journal of Medical Science*, 1937, 6th Series, pp. 261-266.
21. Hope, J., *A Treatise on the Diseases of the Heart and Great Vessels*, London: Kidd, 1839: pp. 71, 80, 100, 379, 443, 446, 458, 572.
22. O'Brien, E., "Corrigan's Disease", *Journal of the Irish Colleges of Physicians and Surgeons*, 1980: *10*: pp. 32-37.
23. It is interesting to note that Hodgkin's description might have been lost to posterity were it not resurrected from the literature by Samuel Wilks in 1878, who also brought to the attention of the profession Hodgkin's description of the malignant blood disorder now known as "Hodgkin's Disease." Wilks, S., "Notes on the History of Valvular Disease of the Heart", *Guy's Hospital Reports*, 1871: *16*: pp. 209-216.
24. Graves, R., "Clinical Lectures Delivered by Dr Graves, Lecture IX", *London Medical and Surgical Journal*, 1833: *3*: pp. 74-81.
25. Graves, R., *Clinical Lectures Delivered During the Sessions of 1834-5 and 1836-7*, Philadelphia: A. Waldie, 1838: p. 315.
26. Stokes, W., quoted by Dock, G., in "Dominic John Corrigan; His place in the development of our knowledge of cardiac disease. II. The Water-Hammer Pulse., *Annals of Medical History*, 1934: *6*: pp. 381-395.
27. Corrigan, D., *Address at the Distribution of Prizes in St. Mary's Hospital Medical School*. London: Morton & Co. 1873. (Corrigan Pamphlets, RCPI)
28. Dock, "Corrigan", p. 389.
29. Anon., "Maladie de Corrigan", *La Lancette Francaise. Gazette des Hopitaux*, 1839. No. 117: p. 1.
30. A water-hammer is made by sealing water in a vacuum in a glass tube which when shaken gives a peculiar knocking sound. A toy based on this principle was popular in the Victorian era, and because the sensation produced by the toy, and the pulse of Corrigan's disease were similar, the term 'water-hammer pulse' was coined.
31. Corrigan, D., "On Cirrhosis of the Lung", *Dublin Journal of Medical Science*, 1838: *13*: pp. 266-286.
32. Corrigan, D., "Practical observations on the diagnosis and treatment of some functional derangements of the heart", *ibid*: 1841: *19*: pp. 1-15.
33. Adams, R., "Cases of diseases of the heart, accompanied with pathological observations", *Dublin Hospital Reports*, 1827: *4*: pp. 353-453.
34. Corrigan Diaries, RCPI. No. 6.
35. Cameron, C., *History of the Royal College of Surgeons in Ireland and of the Irish Schools of Medicine*, Dublin: Fannin & Co, 1886: pp. 513-543.
36. Lecturer's Club Book, (Diary No. 12. RCPI). See Appendix E.
37. Printed letter from Corrigan to solicit support for his appointment to Cork

Street Fever Hospital, 1837. (Corrigan Letters, RCPI. No. 11.).

38. "Proceedings of Committee", Minute Book, 7 June 1831. The Charitable Infirmary, Jervis Street.

39. George Stapleton to Corrigan, 26.10.1837, (Corrigan Letters, RCPI. No. 4.).

40. Evans, E., "History of Dublin Hospitals and Infirmaries from 1188 till the Present Time. No. XXV. Fever Hospital and House of Recovery, Cork Street", *Irish Builder*, 1897: *39*, pp. 171-3, 181-3, 191-3, 201-3.

41. The Minute Books of Cork Street Fever Hospital (now closed) are carefully preserved in Cherry Orchard Fever Hospital, Dublin.

42. Evans, "Dublin Hospitals", p. 171.

43. *ibid*: p. 182.

44. Corrigan Diaries, RCPI. No. 6. pp. 35-6.

45. John Crampton had taught Corrigan as a student and just before his graduation in 1825 he wrote thus to a friend with the following directions — "He lives in Kildare Street. You might have often heard me mention his name in the course of last winter. Tell him I feel obliged to him for the kindness and attention I have always experienced from him, and that I would receive it as an additional mark of his favour if he would allow me to dedicate my thesis to him." In Widdess, J.D.H., *The Richmond, Whitworth and Hardwicke Hospitals, St Laurence's, Dublin 1772-1972*, Dublin: 1972: pp. 77-8.

46. O'Brien, E., "Dublin Masters of Clinical Expression. I. John Cheyne (1777-1836), *Journal of the Irish Colleges of Physicians and Surgeons*, 1974: *3*: pp. 91-93. O'Brien, E., "Dublin Masters of Clinical Expression. III." Robert Adams (1791-1875), *ibid*: 1974: *3*: pp. 127-129.

47. Morpeth to James Power, M.P., 18.6.1840, Corrigan Letters, RCPI. No. 18.

48. John O'Connell to Corrigan, 22.6.1840, Corrigan Letters, RCPI. No.20.

49. Fever patients were isolated in the Hardwicke, non-infectious general medical illnesses were treated in the Whitworth, and the Richmond was a surgical hospital.

50. Warburton, J., Whitelaw, J., and Walsh, R., *History of the City of Dublin*, 2 vols., London, 1818: Vol. 1. pp. 230, 618-623.

51. Widdess, *Richmond*, pp. 12-20.

52. *ibid*: p. 19.

53. Collins, J., *Life in Old Dublin*, Dublin, 1913. pp. 77-79.

54. Evans, E., "History of Dublin Hospitals and Infirmaries from 1188 till the Present Time. XXIV. House of Industry Hospitals", *Irish Builder*, 1897: *39*: pp. 159-162.

55. The hospital was renamed "St Laurence's Hospital", after St Laurence O'Toole by an act of the Dail in 1943.

56. Widdess, *Richmond*, pp. 101-104.

57. MacDonnell, J., "Amputation of the Arm, performed at the Richmond Hospital, without pain", *Dublin Medical Press*, 1847: *17*: pp. 8-9.

58. Lister, J., *Collected Papers*, 2 vols., Oxford: Clarendon Press, 1909.

59. Widdess, *Richmond*, pp. 126-127.

60. *ibid*: pp. 62-63.

61. Corrigan, D., "Clinical Lectures. Introductory Lecture", *London Medical Gazette*, 1841: n.s 823-826.

62. Corrigan, D., "Clinical Lectures. Lecture V. No. 3", *ibid*: 1841: *28*: pp. 171-174.

63. Obituary, *Dublin Journal of Medical Science*, 1880: *69*: pp. 268-272.

64. See Appendix C for complete list.

65. Mapother, E.D., "Sir Dominic Corrigan", *Irish Monthly*, 1880: *8*: pp. 160-171.

66. Corrigan, D., *Introductory Lecture. Winter Session. 1863-4*, Dublin: Browne & Nolan, 1863: p. 14. (Corrigan pamphlets, RCPI.).

67. Corrigan, D., "Introductory Clinical Lecture. Winter Session. 1858-59", *Dublin Hospital Gazette*, 1858: 5: pp. 337-341. Also *Irish Times* report, Corrigan Diaries, RCPI. No. 6: pp. 1-2.

68. Widdess, *Richmond*, p. 79.

69. *ibid*: p. 82.

70. Corrigan, D., "Paralysis (from arsenic), Lumbago and Sciatica – Cure by 'firing' – mode of application – superiority of it over blisters and actual cautery", *Dublin Hospital Gazette*, 1846: 2: pp. 209-211.

71. Widdess, J.D.H., "Corrigan's Button", *Irish Journal of Medical Science*, 1967: 6th Series: pp. 137-140.

72. "Dr Corrigan's New Stethoscope, possessing many splendid and peculiar advantages. Manufactured by G. Oldham & Co. 107, Grafton Street, Dublin. Advertisement in *The Dublin Hospital Gazette*. April 2, 1860.

73. Corrigan, D., "Observations on the exhibition of remedies in the form of vapour in pulmonary disease; with description of a diffuser for the administration of iodine, chlorine, etc", *Dublin Journal of Medical Science*, 1839: 15: pp. 94-105.

74. "Doctor Corrigan's adjusting bed for invalids", *Dublin Hospital Gazette*, 1845: 1: pp. 6-8.

75. Corrigan Diaries, RCPI. No. 6.

76. Garrison, F.H., *An Introduction to the History of Medicine*, Philadelphia: W.B. Saunders, 4th Ed: 1929: p. 420.

77. Widdess, *RCPI.*, pp. 209-210.

78. Corrigan's application for Kings Professorship, Corrigan Papers, RCPI.

Chapter 5

1. O'Brien, E., "The Georgian Era, 1714-1835", in *Portraits of Irish Medicine*, Ed., O'Brien, E., Crookshank, A., with Wolstenholme, G., Dublin: Ward River Press, 1983: pp. 75-113.

2. Belcher, T.W., "Notes on the Mediaeval Leper Hospitals of Ireland", *Dublin Quarterly Journal of Medical Science*, 1868: 46: pp. 36-45. Evans, E., "Dublin Hospitals and Infirmaries from 1188 till the Present Time. 1. The Hospital of St John The Baptist", *Irish Builder*, 1896: 38: pp. 167-170; 180-182; 192-3; 204-5.

3. For details on these institutes consult the excellent series by Evans on Dublin Hospitals in the *Irish Builder* from 1896 to 1898: Vols 38-40: See also Casey, N., "Hospital Architecture in Dublin", in *Portraits of Irish Medicine*, pp. 215-260. Widdess, J.D.H., Ed., *The Charitable Infirmary, Jervis Street. Dublin 1718-1968*, Dublin: Hely Thom, 1968. Kirkpatrick, T.P.C., *The History of Doctor Steevens' Hospital, Dublin 1720-1920*, Dublin: University Press, 1924. Kirkpatrick, T.P.C., "Mercer's Hospital. Its Foundation and Early Days", *Irish Journal of Medical Science*, 1935: 6th Series: pp. 1-15. Smith, C.P.C., "Historic Irish Hospitals: The Royal Hospital for Incurables", *The Irish Hospital*, October 1962: p. 11. Browne, O.D., *The Rotunda Hospital 1745-1945*, Edinburgh: E & S. Livingstone, 1947. Kirkpatrick, T.P.C., and Jellett, H., *The Book of The Rotunda Hospital*, London: Adlard & Son, 1913. Ormsby, L.H., *Medical History of the Meath Hospital and County Dublin Infirmary*, Dublin: Fannin & Co, 1888. Craig, M.J., Ed., *The Legacy of Swift (A Bi-Centenary Record of St Patrick's Hospital, Dublin)*,

Dublin: The Three Candles, 1948.

4. Four of these Georgian hospitals continue to function in the original build-
    ings — Steevens', the Rotunda, St Patrick's and Sir Patrick Dun's. Mercer's
    Hospital closed recently, as will the Charitable Infirmary in the near future.

5. Robins, J., *The Lost Children. A Study of Charity Children in Ireland, 1700-
    1900*, Dublin: Institute of Dublin Administration, 1980: pp. 10-55.

6. Evans, E., "Dublin Hospitals and Infirmaries from 1188 till the Present
    Time. No. 24. House of Industry Hospitals", *Irish Builder*, 1897: *39*, pp.
    159-162.

7. Kirkpatrick, *Steevens'*, p. 19-23.

8. For an account of Mosse's life see Kirkpatrick and Jellet, *Book of the
    Rotunda*, pp. 1-47.

9. Swift, J., "Verses on the Death of Dr Swift (1731)", *Poems*, Ed., H. Williams,
    3 vols, 2nd Ed., Oxford, 1958.

10. Underwood, E.A., *Boerhaave's Men At Leyden and After*, Edinburgh: Uni-
    versity Press, 1977.

11. Kirkpatrick, T.P.C., *History of The Medical Teaching in Trinity College
    Dublin and of The School of Physic in Ireland*, Dublin: Hanna & Neale,
    1912: p. 174.

12. Doolin, W., "Dublin Surgery 100 Years Ago", *Irish Journal of Medical
    Science*, 1949: 6th Series: pp. 97-111.

13. Widdess, J.D.H., *The Royal College of Surgeons in Ireland and Its Medical
    School 1781-1984*, Dublin: RCSI, 1984: pp. 2-3.

14. *ibid*: p. 5-8. Lyons, J.B., *Brief Lives of Irish Doctors*, Dublin: Blackwater,
    1978: pp. 47-49. (For bibliography see p. 171.)

15. Widdess, *RCSI*, p. 8.

16. O'Brien, E., *A Portrait*, pp. 92-95.

17. Cameron, C.A., *History of the Royal College of Surgeons in Ireland and of
    the Irish Schools of Medicine*, Dublin: Fannin & Co., 1886: p. 354.

An interesting insight to Crampton's personality is provided by a correspondence in the form of two poems, one from Maria Edgeworth to Crampton and the other from Crampton to Maria Edgeworth. These are published
by courtesy of the National Library of Ireland.

To Philip Crampton, Esq.,
Surgeon General etc. etc.

With a Fountain Pen
By Maria Edgeworth. 1821.

> *"Go ever flowing ever ready pen,*
> *To him endowed of heav'n, so bless'd of men,*
> *Endow'd with all that genius can inspire,*
> *Of healing science, and inventive fire,*
> *— Bless'd for the use benificently kind*
> *He makes of these the noblest gifts of mind,*
> *Who in the brightness of life's prosp'rous hour,*
> *Delights with wit and humour's happiest pow'r*
> *— OR in disease and sorrow's suffering state*
> *Can soothe alike the lowly and the great,*
> *Of rich and poor, the first the last resource*
> *Whose soul in peril prompt display's its force*
> *Whose rapid glance intuitive can seize*

All that can parry danger, promise ease,
Whose skill, whose voice revives the parting breath
Recalls the victim from despair and death
Or when no human skill has power to save,
Sustains the feeble, animates the brave,
And with true sympathy's consoling art
Can pour the balm that heals the mourner's heart
And with that magic genius, feeling knows
Medicine the soul and body to repose."

The Answer

Caudet non Suis pennis.

Immortal pen! What destiney is thine
To pass from Edgeworth's to a hand like mine,
To feel no more the pow'r that bade thee move,
Through ev'ry mode of wisdom, wit and love,
That taught thee first to wreathe for headless youth
The flowers of fiction with the fruits of truth
And like the eastern sage* who healed by stealth
Combine with pastime, subtile means of health.

Tho' doom'd no more to mend or charm the age,
Oh! deign at least our sorrows to assuage,
Be still the faithful friend of human kind
And serve the body as you've serv'd the mind.

*See the story of the Greek King and his physician, Doubars Arabian Nights.

(M.S. 3241 National Library of Ireland)

18. Erinensis in *The Sketches of Erinensis*, Ed. M. Fallon, London: Skilton & Shaw, 1979: p. 63.
19. Ormsby, *Meath*, pp. 183-190.
20. Meenan, F.O.C., "The Victorian Doctors of Dublin; A Social and Political Portrait", *Irish Journal of Medical Science*, 1968: 6th Series: pp. 133-320.
21. Widdess, J.D.H., *A History of the Royal College of Physicians of Ireland. 1654-1963*, Edinburgh: E & S. Livingstone, 1963: p. 73.
22. Cheyne, J., *Essays on Partial Derangement of the Mind in Supposed Connection with Religion. With a Portrait and Autobiographical Sketch of the Author*, Dublin: W. Curry, Jun & Co, 1843.
23. Stokes, W., *The Diseases of the Heart and Aorta*, Dublin: Hodges and Smith, 1854: pp. 320-27.
24. Cheyne, J., "A Case of apoplexy in which the fleshy part of the heart was converted into fat", *Dublin Hospital Reports*, 1818: 2: pp. 216-23.
25. McDonnell, R., *Selections from the Works of Abraham Colles*, London: New Sydenham Society. For a full biography of Colles see: Fallon, M., *Abraham Colles. 1773-1843. Surgeon of Ireland*, London: William Heinemann, 1972.
26. Colles, A., *Practical observations on the venereal disease and on the use of mercury*, London: Sherwood, Gilbert and Piper, 1837: p. 304.

27. Kirkpatrick, *Steevens'*, pp. 150-153; 167-170.
28. Stokes, W., "Observations on the case of the late Abraham Colles, M.D., formerly Professor of Surgery in the Royal College of Surgeons in Ireland", *Dublin Quarterly Journal of Medical Science*, 1846: *1*: pp. 303-322.
29. Cameron, *RCSI*, p. 388.
30. Doolin, *100 Years Ago*, p. 102.
31. Lyons, *Brief Lives*, p. 19.
32. Anon., "The Dublin Hospitals", *Lancet*, 1826: *6*: pp. 179-180.
33. Graves, R.J., "Clinical Lectures delivered during the Sessions of 1834-5 and 1836-7", Philadelphia: A. Waldie, 1838: p. 33.
34. Davis, A., and Appel, T., *Bloodletting Instruments in the National Museum of History and Technology*, Washington: Smithsonian Institution Press, 1979: p. 1. There is an excellent well researched essay on the history of bloodletting, and cupping, (pages 1-62).
35. *ibid*: p. 5.
36. Drury, M., *The Return of the Plague. British Society and the Cholera 1831-2*, London: Gill and MacMillan, 1979: p. 124.
37. Graves, *Lectures*, p. 53.
38. Davis and Appel, *Bloodletting*, p. 35.
39. *ibid*: p. 36.
40. Graves, *Lectures*, p. 63.
41. Dearlove J., Verguei, A.P., Birkin, N., and Latham, P., An Anachronistic treatment for asthma," *British Medical Journal*, 1981: *283*: pp. 1684-5. Two Russian girls living in London had wet cupping performed by their mothers in an unsuccessful attempt to relieve their asthma.
42. Davis and Appel, p. 24.
43. Erinensis, "Baron Larrey's visit to Dublin," *Lancet*, 1826: 7: pp. 828-9.
44. Quain, R., *A Dictionary of Medicine*, London: Longmans, Green & Co., 1895: p. 413.
45. Widdess, J.D.H., "Corrigan's Button", *Irish Journal of Medical Science*, 1967: 6th Series: pp. 137-140.
46. Fleming, J.B., *Personal Communication*. John Fleming who was professor of midwifery at the University of Dublin from 1952 to 1974 remembers the 'Button' being used for the treatment of sciatica in Sir Patrick Dun's Hospital around 1928 by Dr Drury. He recalls that it left a line of red marks along the course of the sciatic nerve.
47. Graves, *Lectures*, p. 290.
48. Stokes, W., *A Treatise on the Diagnosis and Treatment of Diseases of the Chest*, London, Dublin: Hodges & Smith, 1837. In this work Stokes states the practice of the day in treating chest illness; his own modifications of therapeutic remedies are directed towards protecting the ill patient from the vigorous use of bloodletting, cupping, blistering, etc. though in common with Graves and Corrigan he never completely abandons these procedures.
49. Drury, *Plague*, p. 121.
50. Erinensis, "Sketches of the surgical profession in Ireland", *Lancet*, 1827: 7: pp. 791-4. For his views on a "national school of medicine and surgery" in Dublin see *Lancet*, 1827: pp. 523-7.
51. Graves, *Lectures*, p. 10.
52. The doctors whose names Graves stated have been "spread abroad" included Dease, Blake, Colles, Carmichael, Cusack, Crampton, Marsh, Kirby, Jacob, Houston, Adams, M'Dowell, Apjohn, Harrison, Kane, Montgomery and E. Kennedy, in addition to Stokes and Corrigan.
53. Graves, *Lectures*, p. 11.

54. A full biography on Robert Graves is long overdue. The following biographical essays have been consulted of which the best is: Stokes, W., "The life and labours of Graves", in *Studies in Physiology and Medicine by the late Robert James Graves*, Ed., W. Stokes, London: Churchill & Sons, 1863: ix-lxxxiii. Duncan, J.F., "The life and labours of Robert James Graves", *Dublin Journal of Medical Science*, 1878: *65*: 1-12. Wilde, W., "Biographical memoir of Robert Graves, M.D.", London, 1868. Major, R.H., *Classic Descriptions of Disease*, Illinois, Charles C. Thomas, 3rd Ed., 1978: pp. 279-281. Ormsby, *Meath*, pp. 122-129. Widdess, *RCPI*, pp. 157-166. Lyons, *Brief Lives*, pp. 63-68. O'Brien, E., Dublin Masters of Clinical Expression. V. Robert Graves (1796-1853), *Journal of the Irish Colleges of Physicians and Surgeons*, 1975: 4: pp. 161-163.
55. Graves quoted in Stokes. *Life of Graves*, pp. xxx-xxxi.
56. Graves, *Lectures*, pp. 233-4.
57. Stokes, W., *William Stokes. His Life and Work (1804-1878)*, London: T. Fisher Unwin, 1898: p. 129.
58. Osler, W. quoted in Cushing, H. *The Life of Sir William Osler*, 2 vols. Oxford, Clarendon Press, 1925; p. 322.
59. Graves, R.J., *Clinical Lectures on the practice of Medicine*, Dublin: Fannin & Co., 1848. (First published as *A system of clinical medicine* in 1843.) This book should be distinguished from the *Clinical Lectures delivered during the sessions of 1834-5 and 1836-7*, published in Philadelphia in 1838, from which references to the *Lectures* in this chapter are taken.
60. Hale-White, W., *Great Doctors of the nineteenth century*, London: Arnold, 1935: p. 126.
61. Graves, *Lectures*, p. 110.
62. *ibid*: p. 289.
63. *ibid*: p. 94.
64. *ibid*: p. 291.
65. Corrigan, D., "Practical observations on the diagnosis and treatment of some functional derangements of the heart", *Dublin Journal of Medical Science*, 1841: *19*: pp. 1-15.
66. Brief biography of Jean Bouilland in Major R.H. *Classic Descriptions of Disease*. 3rd. Ed. Illinois. Charles C. Thomas, 1978; pp. 220-3.
67. Corrigan, D., "Observations on the treatment of acute rheumatism by opium", *Dublin Journal of Medical Science*, 1840: *16*: pp. 256-277.
68. Corrigan, D., "Clinical Lectures. Lecture VIII. Fever No. 6", *London Medical Gazette*, 1841: *27*: pp. 905-911.
69. Graves, *Lectures*, p. 89.
70. Widdess, *RCPI*, pp. 162-3.
71. Graves, *Lectures*, p. 192.
72. Graves, *Lectures*, p. 134. Reprinted in *Medical Classics*, 1940: *5*: pp. 33-36 and in Major's *Classic Descriptions*, pp. 280-1. This paper, one of the classics in the literature of medicine, was first published in 1835 — "Palpitations of the heart with enlargement of the thyroid gland". *London Medical and Surgical Journal* (Renshaw), 1835: *7*: pp. 516-17.
73. Stokes, W., *Graves*.
74. Widdess, *RCPI*, pp. 169-70.
75. Stokes, *Diseases of the Chest*.
76. Stokes, W., "Observations on some cases of permanently slow pulse". *Dublin Quarterly Journal of Medical Science*, 1846: *2*: pp. 73-85.
77. Adams, R., Cases of diseases of the heart, accompanied with pathological observations, *Dublin Hospital Reports*, 1827: *4*: pp. 353-453.

78. O'Brien, E., "Dublin Masters of Clinical Expression. III. Robert Adams, (1791-1875),"*Journal of the Irish Colleges of Physicians and Surgeons*, 1974;*3*: pp. 91-93. Cameron, *RCSI*, pp. 395-6.
79. Stokes, W., For details see reference notes 23 and 48.
80. Stokes, *Stokes*, p. 165. For an essay on Stokes's role as a teacher see O'Brien, E., "William Stokes, 1804-78: the development of a doctor", *British Medical Journal*, 1978: *2*: pp. 749-50.
81. Corrigan, D., "Clinical Lectures. Introductory Lecture", *London Medical Gazette*, 1841: *1*: pp. 823-826.
82. Corrigan's classic lectures on clinical medicine were published in a series of papers in the *London Medical Gazette* in 1841. They were revised and re-published in *Lectures on the nature and treatment of fever*, Dublin: Fannin & Co, 1853: p. 33. (Corrigan Pamphlets, RCPI).
83. Corrigan, D., "Clinical Lecture. Introductory Lecture", *London Medical Gazette*, 1841: *1*: pp. 823-826.
84. Acland, H., Memoir of William Stokes in *A Treatise on the Diagnosis and Treatment of Diseases of the Chest*, by W. Stokes, published by The New Sydenham Society, London in 1882.
85. Corrigan, D., *Address delivered at the opening meeting of the Dublin Medico-Chirurgical Society. Session of 1837-8,* Dublin: Hodges & Smith, 1838: p. 16. (Corrigan Pamphlets, RCPI).
86. Corrigan, *ibid.*
87. O'Brien, "Stokes, the development of a doctor".
88. Corrigan, D., "Third Scientific Meeting of 138th session of Royal Dublin Society", *Irish Times*, Jan. 1867 (Corrigan Papers, RCPI).
89. Wilson, T.G. *Victorian Doctor, being the life of Sir William Wilde*, London, Methuen & Co., 1942, p. 122. Thomas George Wilson (1901-1969) was President of RCSI from 1958-60, and with Dr Harry O'Flanagan, the then registrar, was responsible for acquiring the land adjoining the old buildings on York Street where the new College building now stands. He was a keen amateur artist and illustrated his biography of William Wilde with sketches of places and personalities of the period.
90. *ibid*: pp. 214-5.
91. *ibid*: p. 13.
92. de Vere White, T., *The Parents of Oscar Wilde. Sir William and Lady Wilde*, London: Hodder & Stoughton, 1967: p. 38.
93. Wilde, W.R.W., *The Narrative of a Voyage to Madeira, Teneriffe and Along the Shores of the Mediterranean, etc.*, Dublin, 1839.
94. Hale-White, W., *Keats as Doctor and Patient*, London: Oxford University Press, 1938.
95. Lever, C., Charles O'Malley, *The Irish Dragoon*, 2 vols, London: Chapman & Hall, 1857. For a biography of this interesting Dublin doctor-novelist see Fitzpatrick, W.J., *The Life of Charles Lever*, 2 vols, London: Chapman & Hall, 1879.
96. Wilson, *Victorian Doctor*, p. 115.
97. Somerville-Large, L.B., "Dublin's Eye Hospitals", *Irish Journal of Medical Science*, 1944, 6th Series, pp. 445-547.
98. Wilde, W.R.W., *Practical observations on aural surgery and the nature and treatment of diseases of the ear.* London, J. Churchill, 1853. "This work did more to place British otology on a sound scientific basis than anything previously published", see note in Morton, L.T., *A Medical Bibliography*, 4th Ed., Hampshire, Gower, 1983: p. 455.
99. de Vere White, *Parents*, p. 73.

100. *ibid.*, p. 88.
101. Kirkpatrick, T.P.C., "The Dublin Medical Journals", *Irish Journal of Medical Science*, 1932, 6th Series, pp. 243-260.
102. Froggatt, P., "Sir William Wilde and the 1831 Census of Ireland", *Medical History*, 1965: *9*: pp. 302-27.
103. Lyons, J.B. "Sir William Wilde, 1815-1876", *Journal of the Irish Colleges of Physicians and Surgeons*, 1976: *5*: pp. 147-152.
104. Wilde, W.R.W., *The Closing Years of Dean Swift's Life with Remarks on Stella*, 2nd Ed., Dublin, Hodges and Smith, 1849.
105. de Vere White, *Parents*, p. 190.
106. Wilson, *Victorian Doctor*, p. 273.
107. For a list of Wilde's writings see the list on authorship in Wilson, *Victorian Doctor*, p. 337 and also Lyons's essay on Wilde in the *Journal of the Irish Colleges of Physicians and Surgeons*. Some of his works are being reprinted, eg. *Irish Popular Superstitions*, Shannon, Irish University Press, 1972.
108. Wilson, *Victorian Doctor*, p. 306.
109. *ibid*: pp. 315-6.
110. de Vere White, *Parents*, p. 234.
111. Lyons, *Brief Lives*, pp. 61-2.
112. Widdess, J.D.H., "Robert M'Donnell – a pioneer of blood transfusion; with a survey of transfusion in Ireland, 1832-1922", *Irish Journal of Medical Science*, 1952, 6th Series, pp. 11-20.
113. MacDonnell, J., "Amputation of the arm, performed at the Richmond Hospital, without pain", *Dublin Medical Press*, 1847: *17*: pp. 3-4.
114. Widdess, J.D.H., "The Richmond, Whitworth and Hardwicke Hospitals, St Laurence's, Dublin, 1772-1972", Dublin, 1972, pp. 125-131.
115. Widdess, J.D.H., "An historic surgical instrument", *Journal of the Royal College of Surgeons in Ireland*, 1964: *4*: p. 13.
116. Lyons, *Brief Lives*, pp. 110-111.
117. Widdess, *RCPI*, pp. 172-3.
118. Corrigan, D., "Valedictory Presidential Address to the Pathological Society", *Dublin Hospital Gazette*, 1857: *4*: pp. 139-141.
119. Kirkpatrick, T.P.C., "The Royal Academy of Medicine in Ireland", *Medical Press and Circular*, 1937, *195*, No. 5130. For a contemporary review of the activities of the Academy see the "Centenary Issue" of the *Irish Journal of Medical Science*, 1983: *152*: p. 70.
120. Statistical Society Debate, Corrigan Diaries, RCPI, No. 6, pp. 35-6.
121. Corrigan, D., *Address delivered at the Opening Meeting of the Dublin Medico-Chirurgical Society Session of 1837-8*, Dublin: Hodges & Smith, 1838: p. 16. (Corrigan Pamphlets, RCPI).
122. Corrigan, D., *Introductory Lecture. Winter Session, 1863-4*, Dublin: Browne & Nolan, 1863: p. 14. (Corrigan Pamphlets, RCPI).

Chapter 6

1. No. 4 Merrion Square West is now No. 92 Merrion Square and together with the adjoining house No. 91 forms the Irish Continental Bank.
2. Meenan, F.O.C., "The Georgian Squares of Dublin and their doctors", *Irish Journal of Medical Science,* 1966, 6th Series, pp. 149-154.
3. Edgeworth, M., *The Absentee* quoted in *Dublin under the Georges, 1714-1830* by Constantia Maxwell, Dublin: Gill & MacMillan, 1979, p. 97.
4. Merrion Square together with Fitzwilliam Street and Fitzwilliam Place

formed one of the longest uninterrupted Georgian complexes until the state Electricity Board (E.S.B.) was permitted to demolish one block and replace it with a tasteless structure that demonstrates the inferiority of contemporary architects.

5. Meenan, F.O.C., "The Victorian Doctors of Dublin. A Social and Political Portrait", *Irish Journal of Medical Science*, 1968, 6th Series, pp. 311-320.
6. Dixon, E., "Sir Dominic Corrigan. Part I", *Dublin Historical Record*, 1946: *8*: pp. 28-38.
7. Malone, J.B., *Evening Herald*, 26.9.1974. Completed in 1845; later additions have spoilt the original integrity of the house. After Corrigan's time it became the home of Charles Wisdom Healy J.P., whose name is enshrined in Joyce's *Ulysses* as the one time employer of Leopold Bloom.
8. The *Fees Book* (Diary 9, RCPI) is a remarkable document that not only gives meticulous details of Corrigan's income from 1858 to 1879 but also indicates the dates of political meetings, G.M.C. meetings in London, holidays and social and family events.
9. Atthill, L., The Late, *Recollections of an Irish Doctor*, London: Religious Tract Society, 1911, pp. 196-197.
10. Cruise, F.R., *Catholic Man of Science. Sir Dominic Corrigan (1802-1880)*, London: Catholic Truth Society, 1912, p. 20. Reprinted in *Twelve Catholic Men of Science*, ed. Sir Bertram Windle, London, 1912.
11. Mapother, E.D., "Sir Dominic Corrigan", *Irish Monthly*, 1880: *8*: pp. 160-171.
12. Corrigan Diaries (No. 6. RCPI).
13. Little, G.A., "The Past is Prologue", *What's Past is Prologue*, Ed. Doolin, W. and Fitzgerald, O., Dublin, 1952, pp. 90-97.
14. Corrigan Diaries (No. 6, p. 17, RCPI).
15. Meenan, *Victorian Doctors*.
16. Mahaffy, J.P., *Macmillan's Magazine*, 1878, p. 301.
17. George Petrie (1790-1866). For a biographical essay on this remarkable Victorian figure see Strickland, W.G., *A Dictionary of Irish Painters*, Shannon: Irish University Press, 1969, pp. 236-242.
18. Stokes, W., *Life and Labours in Art and Archaeology of George Petrie*, Dublin, 1868.
19. Stokes, M. McNair, *Christian Inscriptions in the Irish Language, chiefly collected and drawn by G. Petrie*, London, 1871-8. For biographical details on Margaret Stokes see D.N.P. p. 2461.
20. Faucit, H., quoted in Stokes, W., *William Stokes. His Life and Work (1804-1878)*, London: T. Fisher Unwin, 1898, p. 83. For biographical details on Helen Faucit see D.N.B. p. 2411.
21. Wilson, T.G., *Victorian Doctor Being the Life of Sir William Wilde*, London: Methuen & Co., 1942, p. 145.
22. *ibid*: p. 144.
23. Frederick Burton (1816-1900). For a biographical essay and list of paintings see Strickland's *Dictionary of Irish Painters*, pp. 130-141. Burton painted portraits of many prominent members of the medical profession in Victorian Ireland, a number of which are reproduced in *A Portrait of Irish Medicine*, Ed. O'Brien, E. and Crookshank, A. with Wolstenholme, G., Dublin: Ward River Press, 1983.
24. James Clarence Mangan, D.N.B. 1309.
25. Stokes, *Stokes Life and Work*, pp. 78 and 248.
26. Mangan, C., "Shapes and Signs", in *Selected Poems of James Clarence Mangan*, Ed. M. Smith, Dublin: Gallery Books, p. 96.
27. Carlyle, T., *Reminiscences of My Irish Journey in 1849*, London: Sampson

Low, 1882, pp. 41-51.
28. Fitzpatrick, W.J., *The Life of Charles Lever*, London: Chapman & Hall, 1879, 2 vols, Vol 2, p. 275.
29. Mahaffy, P., quoted in Fitzpatrick's *Life of Lever*, Vol 2, p. 285.
30. *ibid*: p. 287.
31. *ibid*: p. 296.
32. The Martins were a well-known family of timber merchants — T & C. Martin. The British and Irish Steam Packet Company was owned by the Martins and Mary was later honoured by having one of the company's steamers named *The Lady Martin*. (Dixon, E., "Sir Dominic Corrigan. Part I", *Dublin Historical Record*, 1946: 8: pp. 67-76). See also Appendix A.

Chapter 7

1. Mapother, E., "Sir Dominic Corrigan", *Irish Monthly*, 1880: 8: pp. 160-171.
2. For details on Harrison see the *History of the Royal College of Surgeons in Ireland and of the Irish Schools of Medicine*, by Cameron, C., Dublin: Fannin & Co, 1886, pp. 399-400.
3. Corrigan, D. and Harrison, R., *Observations on the draft of a bill for the regulation and support of medical charities in Ireland*, Dublin: Graisberrig and Gill, 1842, p. 19. (Corrigan Pamphlets, RCPI).
4. Corrigan Letters, RCPI, Nos. 191-284.
5. Corrigan, D. and Harrison, R., *Supplement of observations on the draft of a bill for the regulation and support of medical charities in Ireland,* Dublin: Graisberrig and Gill, 1842, p. 43. (Corrigan Pamphlets, RCPI).
6. Eliot to Corrigan. Corrigan Letters, RCPI, No. 55.
Maunsell to Eliot. Corrigan Letters, RCPI, No. 55.
Eliot to Maunsell, *ibid*: RCPI.
7. Lord Eliot came to Ireland as Chief Secretary, believing in equality of treatment for Catholic and Protestant as a basis for government. (Vale, M., "Origins of the Catholic University of Ireland, 1845-1854. I. Sir Robert Peel's government and higher education for Irish Catholics, 1841-45", *Irish Ecclesiastical Record*, 1954: 132: pp. 1-16).
8. Corrigan Letters, RCPI, No. 55.
9. Corrigan Letters, RCPI, No. 56.
10. Corrigan to Lord Clancarthy (?), Corrigan Letters, RCPI, No. 57.
11. Woodham-Smith, C., *The Great Hunger*, London: Hamish Hamilton, 1962, p. 39.
12. Corrigan, D., *On famine and fever as cause and effect in Ireland; with observations on hospital location and the dispensation in outdoor relief of food and medicine*, Dublin: Fannin & Co, 1846, p. 33. (Corrigan Pamphlets RCPI).
13. Pim, J., *Transactions of the Central Relief Committee of the Society of Friends during the Famine in Ireland in 1846 and 1847*, Dublin: Hodges & Smith, 1852, pp. 202-203. This lengthy report of the Society of Friends' transactions during the famine is a valuable source of contemporaneous material which forms one of the earliest histories of the famine. Jonathan Pim's name is not printed on the work but it is accepted that he was the author.
14. Corrigan, D., *Famine and Fever*. Corrigan was incorrect in attributing a greater virulence to the fever when it affected the rich; their resistance to it was less as Graves pointed out — "In the epidemics of 1816, 1817, 1818, and 1819, it was found by accurate computation, that the rate of mortality

was much higher among the rich than among the poor. This was a startling fact, and a thousand different explanations of it were given at the time; but I am inclined to think that the true explanation was, that the poor did not get so much medicine, and that in them the *vis medicatrix* had more fair play . . . If you look to Dr Cheyne and Dr Barker's Synopsis of the plan of treatment employed by the physicians of those days, you will be prepared, from a mere inspection of it, to admit, that it was at least as hard to escape the physician as the disease". (Graves, R.J., *Clinical Lectures delivered during the sessions of 1834-5 and 1836-7*, Philadelphia: A. Waldie, p. 255).

15. Woodham-Smith, *Hunger*, p. 38.
16. MacArthur, W.P., "Medical History of the Famine", in *The Great Famine*, ed. Dudley Edwards, R. and Williams, T.D., Dublin: Browne & Nolan, 1956, pp. 264-265.
17. Pim, *Transactions*, p. 30.
18. Atthill, L., The Late, *Recollections of an Irish Doctor*, London: The Religious Tract Society, 1911, p. 130.
19. Pim, *Transactions*, p. 23.
20. McDowell, R.B., "Ireland on the eve of the Famine", in Edwards and Williams, *Famine*, pp. 31-6.
21. Atthill, *Recollections*, p. 41.
22. Carlyle, T., *Reminiscences of my Irish Journey in 1849*, London: Sampson Low, 1882, p. 202.
23. Atthill, *Recollections*, pp. 129-130.
24. McDowell in Edwards and Williams, *Famine*, p. 33.
25. Temporary Fever Act. Central Board of Health established by Act 9 VIC c6. See Woodham-Smith, *Hunger*, pp. 196-198.
26. *ibid*: p. 71.
27. MacArthur in Edwards and Williams, *Famine*, pp. 290-1.
28. Kane, R., *The Industrial Resources of Ireland*, 2nd Ed, Dublin: Hodges and Smith, 1845. Facsimile reprint Irish University Press, 1971.
29. O'Raghallaigh, D., *Sir Robert Kane, First President of Queen's College, Cork. A Pioneer in Science, Industry and Commerce*, Cork University Press, 1942. For details of his medical career see Widdess, J.D.H., *A History of the Royal College of Physicians of Ireland, 1654-1963*, Edinburgh, E & S. Livingstone, 1963, pp. 208-209.
30. Woodham-Smith, *Hunger*, p. 57.
31. Twistleton was poor law commissioner for many years and endeavoured to do much for famine relief. However on March 12th 1848 he resigned. "He thinks", Clarendon told Lord John Russell "that the destitution here is to horrible and the indifference of the House of Commons to it so manifest, that he is an unfit agent of a policy which must be one of extermination . . . which no man of honour and humanity can endure". *ibid*: p. 380. It was said of Twistleton that he served on more commissions than any other man of his time. *ibid*: p. 469.
32. *ibid*: p. 198.
33. MacArthur in Edwards and Williams, *Famine*, pp. 262-9.
34. Pim, *Transactions*, p. 155.
35. *ibid*: p. 163.
36. *ibid*: p. 201.
37. *ibid*: p. 188.
38. McHugh, R., "The Famine in Irish Oral Tradition", in Edwards and Williams, *Famine*, p. 421.
39. Pim, *Transactions*, p. 151.

40. O'Brien, W.P., *The Great Famine in Ireland and a retrospect of the fifty years 1845-95*, London: Downey & Co., 1896, pp. 78-9.
41. Evans, E., "History of Dublin Hospitals and Infirmaries, from 1188 till the Present Time. No. XXV. Fever Hospital, and House of Recovery, Cork Street", *Irish Builder*, 1897: *39*: p. 181.
42. Atthill, *Recollections*, p. 129.
43. Pim, *Transactions*, p. 78.
44. *ibid*: p. 148.
45. *ibid*: p. 50.
46. Jonathan Pim was Secretary of the Central Relief Committee of the Society of Friends throughout the Famine period. He later became a Liberal member of parliament with Corrigan.
47. MacArthur in Edwards and Williams, *Famine*, p. 312.
48. O'Brien, *Famine*, p. 252.
49. MacArthur in Edwards and Williams, *Famine*, p. 255.
50. Cousens, S.H., "The Regional Variation in Mortality during the Great Irish Famine", *Proceedings of the Royal Irish Academy*, 1963: *63*: pp. 127-149.
51. Woodham-Smith, *Hunger*, p. 411.
52. MacArthur in Edwards and Williams, *Famine*, p. 255.
53. MacDonagh, O., "Irish Emigration to the United States of America and the British Colonies during the Famine", in Edwards and Williams, *Famine*, p. 388.
54. Graves, R.J., quoted in "The Life and Labours of Graves", by Stokes, W. in *Studies in Physiology and Medicine by the late Robert James Graves*. Ed. W. Stokes, London: J. Churchill, 1863, p. lvii.
55. MacArthur in Edwards and Williams, *Famine*, p. 312.
56. Woodham-Smith, *Hunger*, p. 269.
57. Cusack, J.W. and Stokes, W., "On the mortality of medical practitioners from fever in Ireland", *Dublin Quarterly Journal of Medical Science*, 1847: *4*: pp. 134-145. Stokes has stated that in 1847, 7 per cent of all Irish practitioners died. "Life and Labours of Graves", p. lxii.
58. MacArthur in Edwards and Williams, *Famine*, p. 281.
59. *ibid*: pp. 310-11.
60. McDowell in Edwards and Williams, *Famine*, p. 32.
61. Wilde, W., *Dublin Quarterly Journal of Medical Science*, May 1847.
62. Graves, R., "A Letter to the editor of the Dublin Quarterly Journal of Medical Science, relative to the proceedings of the Central Board of Health of Ireland", *Dublin Quarterly Journal of Medical Science*, 1847: *4*: pp. 513-544.
63. These figures for attendance are given in Graves' letter, and are an indication of the work the Board had to contend with; the Board must have met on almost every weekday of the year!
64. "In Memoriam. Sir Dominic John Corrigan", *Dublin Journal of Medical Science*, 1882: *69*: pp. 268-272.
65. Stokes in "Life and Labour of Graves", p. xvi.
66. Editorial on Central Health Board, *Lancet*, 1847: *2*: p. 469.
67. Certificates in the Corrigan Papers in RCPI show that between 1832 and 1837, Corrigan attended annually a course in the Practice of Surgery and a six month course of Clinical Lectures in Surgery, at the Charitable Infirmary. The certificates for these courses are signed by surgeons Adams, Ellis, Duggan and Brady. It was not unusual for Victorian doctors to train as both surgeon and physician. Thomas Edward Beatty attained the unique distinction of becoming president successively of both the Royal College

of Surgeons and of the Royal College of Physicians. Other Dublin men who began as surgeons and later turned to medicine were George Greene, Samuel Gordon and Francis Cruise (Widdess, RCPI, p. 209).

68. Cruise, F.R., *Catholic Men of Science. Sir Dominic Corrigan (1802-1880)*, London: Catholic Truth Society, 1912, pp. 20. Reprinted in *Twelve Catholic Men of Science*, ed. Windle, B., London, 1912.

69. Editorial on Central Health Board, *Lancet*, 1847: 2: p. 469.

70. Corrigan Diaries, RCPI.

71. Corrigan D., "Address in medicine at the annual meeting of the British Medical Association at Dublin, August 7th, 1867", *British Medical Journal*, 1867: 2: pp. 103-7.

72. Corrigan Diaries, RCPI, No. 2, p. 24.

73. MacArthur in Edwards and Williams, *Famine*, pp. 306-7.

74. Durey, M., *The Return of the Plague. British Society and the Cholera, 1831-2*, Dublin: Gill and MacMillan, 1979, pp. 162-3.

75. Stokes, W., *William Stokes. His Life and Work (1804-1878)*, London: Fisher Unwin, 1898, pp. 49-50.

76. Pelling, M., *Cholera, Fever and English Medicine, 1825-1865*, Oxford University Press, 1978, pp. 3-4.

77. *ibid.*, p. 148.

78. Durey, *Cholera*, pp. 108-109.

79. Corrigan Diaries, RCPI, No. 6. Corrigan defended his viewpoint as late as 1866 when he published *The Cholera Map of Ireland with observations*, Dublin: Browne & Nolan, 18pp., 1866.

80. Stokes, in *Life and Labour of Graves*, pp. li-lviii.

81. McHugh in Edwards and Williams, *Famine*, pp. 416-8.

82. McArthur, *ibid*: pp. 306-7.

83. O'Brien, *Famine*, pp. 230-6.

84. McArthur in Edwards and Williams, *Famine*, pp. 312-314.

85. Stokes, W., quoted by McArthur, *ibid*: p. 315.

86. O'Brien, *Famine*, p. vii. Famines occurred in 1880, 1886, 1891, and 1895.

87. Carlyle, *Reminiscences*, p. 216.

88. *ibid*: pp. 83-4.

89. *Larcom Correspondence* in National Library of Ireland, Dublin.

90. Stokes, *Stokes Life and Work*, p. 101.

Chapter 8

1. Announcement in the *London Gazette*, Nov 26, 1847. "St James Palace, Nov 23, 1847. The Queen has been pleased to appoint Dominic John Corrigan M.D. to be Physician in Ordinary to Her Majesty in Ireland."

2. Crampton to Corrigan. Corrigan Letters, RCPI, No. 33.

3. Corrigan to Crampton. Corrigan Letters, RCPI, Nos. 32, 34.

4. Corrigan, D., "Letter to Lunatic Asylum (Ireland) Commission", *Dublin Hospital Gazette*, 1859: 6: p. 88.

5. *Communication of Dr Corrigan dissenting from Report of Commissioners*, printed by the House of Commons, 28 Feb, 1859. Corrigan, D., "Visiting Physician to Lunatic Asylum", *British Medical Journal*, 1861: 2: pp. 613-614. Corrigan, D., "On medical superintendence of asylums", *Dublin Quarterly Journal of Medical Science*, 1862: 33: p. 261. For a history of the insane and asylums in Ireland see Finnane, M., *Insanity and the Insane in Post-Famine Ireland*, London: Croom Helm, 1981.

6. Mapother, E.D., "Sir Dominic Corrigan", *Irish Monthly*, 1880: *8*: p. 160-171.
7. Corrigan to Dublin Corporation. Corrigan Letters, RCPI, No. 137. Also published — *Letter from Dominic Corrigan to The Corporation of Dublin upon the subject of The Richmond Lunatic Asylum*, Dublin: Joseph Dollard, 1872. (Corrigan Pamphlets, RCPI).
8. Corrigan Diaries, RCPI, No. 6, p. TVW.
9. Widdess, J.D.H., *A History of the Royal College of Physicians of Ireland, 1654-1963*, Edinburgh: E & S. Livingstone, 1963, p. 191.
10. "Death of Sir D. Corrigan", *Freeman's Journal*, 1880, Feb 2nd.
11. Widdess, J.D.H., *A History of the Royal College of Physicians of Ireland. 1654-1963*, Edinburgh: E & S. Livingstone, 1963: p. 1.
12. To perpetuate the glorious memory of the sovereign who had triumphed over the Jacobites, the College was renamed the King and Queen's College of Physicians in Ireland, a cumbersome title that in the 19th century prompted one wag on seeing the letters FKQCPI after the name of a fellow to remark — "What are you at all — some kind of a barrister?" It was not until 1890 that the reference to William and Mary was dropped and the College became simply the Royal College of Physicians in Ireland. (Widdess, *RCPI*, p. viii).
13. *ibid*: pp. 77-8.
14. *ibid*: p. 146.
15. Erinensis, "Sketches of the Medical Profession in Ireland, No. 12. The King and Queen's College of Physicians in Ireland", *Lancet*, 1826, Aug. 10, pp. 651-655.
16. Widdess, *RCPI*, pp. 196-7.
17. Corrigan Diaries, RCPI, No. 6, p. 15; No. 4, p. 15.
18. Widdess, *RCPI*, p. 201.
19. Corrigan Diaries, RCPI, No. 6, p. 2.
20. Widdess, *RCPI*, p. 201. The Convocation Hall in the rear of the College was built 10 years later on the site of the Kildare Street Club's racquet court, and Dominic Corrigan commissioned a stained-glass window by Mr Barff of Dublin. On the viewer's left in the upper part are Corrigan's armorial bearings, beside which are those of his wife's family, Woodlock. Below is the inscription: Ex-dono. D.J. Corrigan, Praesidis, MDCCCLXIV.
21. *ibid*: p. 201.
22. *ibid*: p. 203.
23. Corrigan Diaries, RCPI, No. 6, pp. 33-4.
24. There are two Catterson-Smith portraits of Corrigan in RCPI differing greatly in quality. That commissioned by the fellows in appreciation of Corrigan's services during his five year presidency is by Stephen Catterson-Smith, Snr (1806-1872), and was painted in 1865. It is an inferior work compared with the second portrait, one of the finest examples of portraiture by this very accomplished artist (see front of dustjacket), which was bequeathed by Corrigan's daughter Lady Martin, to RCPI in 1907. (Strickland, W.G., *A Dictionary of Irish Artists*, Shannon: Irish University Press, 1969, pp. 363-376.) For a discussion on art in Irish medicine, see Crookshank, A., "Portraits of Irish Medicine", in *A Portrait of Irish Medicine*, ed. O'Brien, E., Crookshank, A. and Wolstenholme, G., Dublin: Ward River Press, 1983, pp. 1-52.
25. John Henry Foley (1818-1874) was Ireland's outstanding nineteenth century sculptor. See Strickland's *Dictionary*, pp. 357-365, and Crookshank, *A Portrait of Irish Medicine*: pp. 1-52.
26. Henry Marsh (1790-1860). It is difficult now to determine the merits and achievements of Marsh that prompted the subscription of £800 from his

colleagues for the erection of the Foley statue in his memory. He has left nothing worthwhile in the medical literature, and his four year term as president of RCPI is not marked by any notable achievement. For biographical details see Cameron, C.A., *History of the Royal College of Surgeons in Ireland and of the Irish School of Medicine*, Dublin: Fannin & Co, 1886, p. 485-9.

27. Corrigan Letters, RCPI, No. 81.
28. Corrigan Diaries, RCPI, No. 6, p. 24. *Inniscorrig* was Corrigan's seaside home at Coliemore near Dalkey; he also owned land at Cappagh in north County Dublin where he built a house for his daughter Mary and her husband Richard Martin. After her husband's death, Lady Mary bequeathed the house and lands to the Irish Sisters of Charity, for use as "an Hospital for the Public Benefit, and a convalescent hospital for The Children's Hospital, Temple Street was established, and this later became St. Mary's Orthopaedic Hospital.
29. *Daily Express*, May 1866.
30. Cameron, *RCSI*, p. 567.
31. Cruise, F.R., *Catholic Men of Science. Sir Dominic Corrigan (1802-1880)*, London: Catholic Truth Society, 1912, p. 20. Also in *Twelve Catholic Men of Science*, ed. Windle, B., London, 1912.
32. Meenan, F.O.C., "The Victorian Doctors of Dublin. A Social and Political Portrait", *Irish Journal of Medical Science*, 1968: *1*: pp. 311-20.
33. William Stokes received many honours, including *pour la merite*, and his son William whose achievements cannot compare with those of his father did receive a knighthood.
34. Stokes, W., *William Stokes. His Life and Works, 1804-1878*, London: Fisher Unwin, 1898, p. 198.
35. *ibid*: pp. 59-60.
36. Cruise, *Corrigan*.
37. In 1854 a corrugated iron house was constructed for "aquatic animals"; this was later used as a Tea Room and demolished in 1906. There is mention of Corrigan donating a turtle and *sapphirins gurnard*. In 1869 a new Aquarium was opened, and is the present reptile house. Corrigan's last donation to the Zoo was in 1878 when he presented a series of illustrations on natural history. (These details have been researched from the minutes of the Royal Zoological Society by Dr T. Murphy.)
38. Murphy, T., *Some of my best friends are animals*, New York & London: Paddington Press, 1979, p. 18.
39. *In Memoriam. Sir Dominic John Corrigan: Dublin Journal of Medical Science*, 1880: *69*: pp. 268-72.
40. Cunningham, D.J., *Origin and early history of the Royal Zoological Society of Ireland*, Dublin, 1901, pp. 16-19.
41. Minutes of Royal Zoological Society.
     The strong medical representation on the Council is apparent from the unusual photograph taken in the Zoo in 1855 and illustrated on p. 290. The following biographical details of the subjects of this photograph were kindly supplied to me by Dr. T. Murphy:
     George W. Hatschell, M.D. Surgeon to the Lord Lieutenant's Household, Dublin Castle, and to the Constabulary Depot, Phoenix Park, Dublin. Jacob Owen. b. 29 July 1778, d. 26 Oct. 1870. Architect. Had 17 children. One of his sons was James Owen, B.A. 1844, died 1891. Robert Ball, LL.D. b. 1 April 1802, d. 30 March 1857. Residence — 3 Granby Row, Dublin. Secretary, Royal Zoological Society of Ireland, 1837-1857. Appointed

Director of the Museum in T.C.D., 1844. Appointed Secretary to the Queen's University in Ireland 1851. Hon. LL.D conferred by Trinity College, Dublin. 1850. Francis William Brady, Q.C. b. 22 July 1824, d. 26 Aug. 1909. Residence — 22 Lower Leeson Street, Succeeded his father, Sir Maziere Brady, Bt. on 13 April 1871. (Sir Maziere Brady, Lord Chancellor of Ireland, was born 1796, died 1871, he was created a baronet in 1869). Francis Brady married 1st (7/11/47) Emily Elizabeth, youngest daughter of late Samuel Kyle, Bishop of Cork, and 2nd (17/11/92) Geraldine, daughter of George Hatschell, M.D. George J. Allman, M.D., F.R.S., M.R.I.A. b. 1812, d. 24 Nov. 1898. Residence — Belfield, Goose Green Avenue, Drumcondra. Professor of Botany, Trinity College, Dublin, 1844-1855. Professor of Natural History, Edinburgh, 1855-1870.

It is not known how the sledge which forms the centerpiece of the study came to be in the Zoo, but there are some details in the archives. Sir John Franklin and his party disappeared while attempting, in an expedition begun in 1845, to make the passage from Lancaster Sound to Bering Strait. Sir Edward Belcher (1799-1877) was appointed in 1852 to command a British Expedition to search for Franklin. Belcher and his small fleet spent two winters in the Artic but in 1854, he ordered his ships to be abandoned and returned with his officers and crew in ships sent out to make communication with his expedition. Belcher was made an admiral in 1872. In 1960 two notes left by his expedition were found in cairns 600 miles south of the North Pole.

42. Corrigan Diaries, RCPI, No. 6, p. 3.
43. Corrigan Diaries, RCPI, No. 6, p. XYZ.
44. Corrigan, D., "Plica Polonica", *Cyclopaedia of Practical Medicine*, 1834: 3: pp. 401-3.
45. Corrigan, D., "On treatment of hydrophobia in Salamis", *Dublin Quarterly Journal of Medical Science*, 1862: 33: p. 193.
46. Corrigan, D., *Ten Days in Athens with notes by the way*, London: Longman, illus., 1862, pp. 277.
47. Corrigan Diaries, RCPI, No. 10.
48. Corrigan, D., "Introductory Presidential Address to the Association of the King and Queen's College of Physicians", *Dublin Hospital Gazette*, 1860: 7: pp. 337-341. Also published as *Introductory Address. Winter Session, 1860-61*, Dublin: J.M. O'Toole & Son, p. 20, 1 map, 1861. This pamphlet was also translated into French and published in Bordeaux. (Corrigan Pamphlets, RCPI).
49. I visited Arcachon in 1981 and found *Allée Corrigan* to be a pleasant residential road which clearly displays the name of the Irishman in whose honour it is named. Many of the features described by Corrigan in his paper can still be appreciated though the town has expanded considerably and is now a thriving sea-side resort. The French pay liberal homage to science and medicine throughout France and in Arcachon there is another street named to commemorate Alexander Fleming, the discoverer of penicillen.
50. Corrigan, D., Observations on Aix-les-Bains, *Dublin Journal of Medical Science*, 1875: 60: pp. 485-93.
51. Corrigan, D. with Dr Madden. Letter on the Turkish Bath, *Dublin Hospital Gazette*, 1860: 7: pp. 17-25.
52. Barter, R. "Reply to Drs Corrigan and Madden", Refused publication by *Dublin Hospital Gazette*; published in *Cork Daily Herald*, Jan 22, 1860.
53. *Photophilus*, Handsil Griffiths, W., *The New Irish bath versus the old Turkish*

or *pure air versus vapour. Being an answer to the errors and mis-statements of Drs Madden and Corrigan*, Dublin: William M'Gee, 1860, p. 56. (Corrigan Pamphlets, RCPI).

54. Corrigan Diaries, RCPI, No. 6.
55. *ibid*: No. 6, p. 17.
56. *ibid*: No. 6, p. 9.
57. *ibid*: No. 6, p. XYZ.
58. *ibid*: No. 9, 16.3.1866 and 19.3.1869.
59. *ibid*: No. 6, pp. 40 and 69.
60. *ibid*: No. 8, p. 3. See also Appendix A. The tablet in the chapel of the Royal Hospital in Kilmainham measures 42" wide by 36" high with two military figures in relief 9" deep. The inscription reads: "In memory of John Joseph Corrigan (Captain), 3rd Dragoon Guards, who died at Melbourne 6th January 1866, aged 35 years. Eldest son of Sir Dominic Corrigan Bart. This tablet is erected by his brother officers as a mark of their respect and esteem". This information was kindly supplied by Mr. G. Gleeson of the Board of Works.
61. Corrigan Papers, RCPI. Leader in *The Irish Law Times and Solicitor's Journal*, 1873: 7: p. 349.
62. Corrigan Letters, RCPI, Nos. 167-179.
63. Corrigan Diaries, RCPI. No. 6.
64. *ibid*: No. 6, pp. 54-6. See also "Obituary. The Right Hon. Sir Richard Martin, Bart., P.C., D.L. *The Irish Builder*. Oct. 24, 1901, p. 914.

Chapter 9

1. Pyke-Lees, W., *Centenary of the General Medical Council, 1858-1958*, London: W. Clowes & Son, 1958, p. 29.
2. Corrigan, D., "Address in medicine at the annual meeting of the British Medical Association in Dublin, August 7th, 1867", *British Medical Journal*, 1867: 2: pp. 103-7.
3. Report of G.M.C. debate, *British Medical Journal*, 1867: 1: pp. 708-18.
4. Corrigan, D., Memorandum to the University of Erlangan, *ibid*: 1867: 2: pp. 54-5.
5. Corrigan, D., Remarks on the admission of women to the medical profession, *British Medical Journal*, 1875: 2: pp. 13-21.
6. Stokes, W., *ibid*: p. 21.
7. "The Profession of Medicine for Women", *Pall Mall Gazette*, 1875. Corrigan Diaries, RCPI, No. 6, p. 61.
8. Widdess, J.D.H., *A History of the Royal College of Physicians of Ireland, 1654-1963, Edinburgh: E & S Livingstone, 1963, pp. 210-212*. In 1877 five women were registered as licentiates of RCPI, one of whom was Miss Edith Pechey. She had earlier applied for admission to the Queen's University, and the senate agreed by 6 votes to 4 to grant her request, the vice-chancellor, Sir Dominic Corrigan, being one of those who voted in her favour. All that she then needed to do was attend courses at the Queen's University but when she applied to the Belfast College to do so, the council refused to admit her thereby nullifying the decision of the university senate. (Moody, T.W. and Beckett, J.C., *Queen's, Belfast, 1845-1949, The History of a University*, London: Faber and Faber, 2 vols, 1959, Vol. 1, p. 232).
9. Corrigan Diaries, RCPI, No. 2, p. 22.
10. Corrigan Diaries, RCPI, No. 9.
11. Corrigan, D., "The constitution of the General Medical Council — a com-

munication to members of the British Medical Association", *British Medical Journal*, 1878: 2: pp. 674-5.

12. Corrigan Letters, RCPI, Nos. 138-151.
13. Corrigan Diaries, RCPI, No. 4, p. 12. The Pharmaceutical Society of Ireland was incorporated by the Pharmacy Act (Ireland) of 1875 (38 & 39 Vic. cap 57). A president (Dominic Corrigan) and vice-president (Aquilla Smith) and a council of 21 were named by government to carry out the provisions of the act.
14. Corrigan Diaries, RCPI, No. 6, p. 9.
15. Corrigan, D., "Letter on Dublin Water Works Commission", *Irish Times*, Aug. 25, 1860. John Gray, doctor, journalist and parliamentarian was knighted on the occasion of turning the Vartry water into the new course in June 1863. His statue by Thomas Farrell is in O'Connell Street (D.N.B., p. 829).
16. Warburton, J., Whitelaw, J. and Walsh, R., *History of the City of Dublin*, London: Cadell and Davies, 2 vols, 1818, Vol. 2, pp. 1069-75.
17. Widdess, J.D.H., *The Richmond, Whitworth and Hardwicke Hospitals. St Laurence's Dublin, 1772-1972*, Dublin, 1972, p. 79.
18. Despite repeated requests the Richmond Hospital did not receive a grant for Vartry water until 1875 whereas the zoo received a Vartry supply in 1870.
19. Cruise, F.R., *Catholic Man of Science. Sir Dominic Corrigan (1802-1880)*, London: Catholic Truth Society, 1912, p. 20. Also in *Twelve Catholic Men of Science*, ed. B. Windle, London, 1912. Cruise goes on to comment that since the Vartry System was introduced "we have no visitation of cholera, and typhoid fever and zymotic disease in general has greatly diminished. To Corrigan's influence assisted by that of Sir John Gray, Dublin is largely indebted for this huge measure of reform".
20. James W. Mackey was elected Lord Mayor of Dublin in 1866, and was knighted in 1873. *The Lord Mayor's Handbook*, Dublin Municipal Annual, Dublin: Parkside Press, 1944 (N.L.I.).
21. Meenan, F.O.C., "The Victorian Doctors of Dublin. A Social and Political Portrait", *Irish Journal of Medical Science*, 1968: 1: pp. 311-20.
22. Mapother, E.D., "Sir Dominic Corrigan", *Irish Monthly*, 1880: 8: pp. 160-71.
23. D.N.B., p. 856.
24. "Death of Sir D. Corrigan", *Freeman's Journal*, 1880, Feb 2.
25. Corrigan Diaries, RCPI, No. 6, p. 30.
26. Corrigan, D., Speech urging completion of the Church of Ss Augustine and John, *Freeman's Journal*, 1869, May 24.
27. Dixon, E., "Sir Dominic Corrigan, Part I", *Dublin Historical Record*, 1946: 8: pp. 28-38.
28. Corrigan Diaries, RCPI, No. 6, p. 53. Also *City of Dublin Election, Nov. 18th 1868*. Browne & Nolan, 1868, (N.L.I.).

1868		1870	
Guinness	5,587 (Freeman vote − 2,134)	Corrigan	4,494
Pim	5,586 (Freeman vote − 306)	Harmon	3,417
Plunkett	5,452 (Freeman vote − 2,123)		
Corrigan	5,381 (Freeman vote − 285)		

29. *Hansard*, 1871: *204*: p. 552.
30. Corrigan Diaries, RCPI, No. 6, p. 37.
31. Mapother, "Corrigan".
32. Corrigan, D., *Address at the distribution of prizes in St Mary's Hospital Medical School*, London: Morton & Co., 1873, p. 12. (Corrigan Pamphlets, RCPI).

33. Corrigan Diaries, RCPI, No. 9.
34. "Death of Sir D. Corrigan", *Freeman's Journal*, Feb 2, 1880.

Chapter 10

1. "Sunday Trading", *Hansard's Parliamentary Debates*, 1871: *205*: p. 1736.
2. Corrigan Papers, RCPI.
3. "Sales of Liquors on Sunday (Ireland)", *Hansard*, 1872: *212*: p. 258.
4. "Intoxicating Liquor (Licensing)", *Hansard*, 1872: *213*: p. 492.
5. Corrigan, D. *Closing Public Houses in Ireland on Sundays*. Published on behalf of the Irish Association for Closing Public Houses on Sundays, March 1872. (Corrigan Diaries, RCPI, No. 6, p. 43).
6. Corrigan Diaries, RCPI, No. 1, p. 2.
7. "Intoxicating Liquor (Licensing)", *Hansard*, 1872: *213*: p. 494. See also Corrigan Letters, RCPI, No. 190.
8. Corrigan Diaries, RCPI, No. 6, p. 62.
9. *ibid*: No. 1, p. 47.
10. *ibid*: No. 6, p. 62.
11. *ibid*: No. 6, p. 62.
12. *ibid*: No. 2, p. 33.
13. In 1878 the Sunday Closing (Ireland) Act, 41 and 42 Vict., Cap 72 was passed to prohibit the sale of intoxicating liquors on Sundays in Ireland. It extended the restricted sale of alcohol on Sundays to the whole of Sundays outside of the cities of Dublin, Cork, Limerick, Waterford and Belfast where the hours of sale of alcohol were further restricted to between 2 p.m. and 7 p.m. (Reed, A., *The Liquor Licensing Laws of Ireland and Innkeeper's Guide*, Dublin: Alex Thom, 1881, pp. 184-6). This act was extended in 1890 when further efforts were made for the total prohibition of the sale of alcohol on Sundays. (Sargent, W.A., *The Liquor Licensing Laws of Ireland from 1660 to 1890*, Dublin: W. McGee, 1890, p.x).
14. "Ireland – Riots in Phoenix Park", 1871: *208*: p. 1800.
15. "Galway Election Judgement", *Hansard*, 1872: *213*: p. 826. Also "Corrigan Letters, RCPI, Nos. 165 and 166.
16. Corrigan Letters, RCPI, Nos. 36-39.
17. "Death of Sir D. Corrigan", *Freeman's Journal*, 1880, Feb 2.
18. Dowling, P.J., *A History of Irish Education*, Cork: Mercier Press, 1971, p. 160.
19. *ibid*: pp. 164-5.
20. Vale, M.D., "Origins of the Catholic University of Ireland, 1845-1854", *Irish Ecclesiastical Record*, 1954: *82*: p. 12.
21. Moody, T.W. and Beckett, J.C., *Queen's, Belfast, 1854-1949, The History of a University*, London: Faber and Faber, 2 vols, 1959, Vol. 1, p. 75.
22. Corrigan Papers, RCPI.
23. Dowling, *Education*, p. 167.
24. Moody and Beckett, *Queen's*, p. 76.
25. Dowling, *Education*, p. 166.
26. MacSuibhne, P., *Paul Cullen and his Contemporaries*, Naas: Leinster Leader, 5 vols, 1962, Vol. 2, p. 384.
27. Moody and Beckett, *Queen's*, Vol. 1, p. 77.
28. Cullen, Rev P., *A Letter to the Catholic Clergy of the Archdiocese of Armagh*, Dublin: J. Duffy, 1850, p. 18.
29. Moody and Beckett, *Queen's*, Vol. 1, pp. 225-6.

30. *ibid*: p. 277.
31. Kane, R., *The Queen's University in Ireland and the Colleges; their Progress and present State. An address delivered at the distribution of prizes*, Dublin: Hodges and Smith, 1856, pp. 16-17.
32. Dowling, *Education*, p. 168.
33. Meenan, F.O.C., "The Catholic University School of Medicine, 1860-1880." *Studies, 66*, pp. 135-144. The Royal College of Surgeons in Ireland was the first licensing body to give recognition to the new school, and practically all the Cecilia Street students took the letters testimonial of the College.
34. MacSuibhne, *Cullen*, Vol. 5, p. 329.
35. Newman, J.H., *The Idea of a University*, London: Longmans, Green & Co., 1907.
36. Gwynn, D., *A Hundred Years of Catholic Emancipation (1829-1929)*, London: Longmans, Green & Co., 1929, p. 167.
37. MacSuibhne, *Cullen*, Vol. 2, p. 263.
38. Moody and Beckett, *Queen's*, Vol. 1, p. 277.
39. Corrigan, D., *University Education in Ireland*, privately published, 1865 (Corrigan Pamphlets, RCPI).
40. Corrigan Letters, RCPI, No. 67.
41. Nesbitt, M.A., *Remarks on Dr Corrigan's letter on University Education in Ireland*, Dublin: W. M'Gee, 1866, p. 24.
42. Corrigan Letters, RCPI, Nos. 63 and 64.
43. Corrigan Diaries, RCPI, No. 2, p. 6.
44. *ibid*: No. 6, p. 25.
45. Moody and Beckett, *Queen's*, Vol. 1, p. 281.
46. Whittle, J.L., *Freedom of Education; what it means*, Dublin, 1866, p. 5.
47. Cullen, P., quoted in Norman, E.R., *The Catholic Church and Ireland in the Age of Rebellion, 1859-1873*, London: Longmans, 1965, p. 221.
48. Corrigan, RCPI.
49. "Biogram. No. 49. Spratt. Rev. John". *Irish Monthly*, 1887: *15*. pp. 706-7.
50. Corrigan Letters, RCPI, No. 116.
51. *ibid*: No. 117.
52. *ibid*: No. 118.
53. *ibid*: Nos. 118-120.
54. *ibid*: No. 121.
55. *ibid*: No. 122.
56. *ibid*: No. 125.
57. MacSuibhne, *Cullen*, Vol. 4, p. 243.
58. In 1873, two years after Oxford and Cambridge, Trinity abolished religious tests under the Fawcett Act, thereby throwing open scholarships, fellowships, and college appointments, except in the Faculty of Divinity, to all irrespective of creed. Dowling, *Education*, p. 170.
59. Moody and Beckett, *Queen's*, Vol. 1, p. 283.
60. Cullen, P., quoted in Norman, *Age of Rebellion*, p. 382.
61. *ibid*: p. 436.
62. Maziere Brade (1796-1871) was the first vice-chancellor of the Queen's University in 1850, at which time he was Solicitor General for Ireland, and Lord Chancellor of Ireland. He had twice won the vice-chancellor's prize for English verse at Trinity. He was created Baronet in 1869 (DNB, p. 207).
63. Corrigan Letters, RCPI, No. 80(i).
64. *ibid*: No. 80 (ii).
65. *ibid*: No. 80 (iii).
66. *ibid*: No. 80 (iv). Gladstone in his reply to Corrigan wrote "My dear Sir

Corrigan, Any suggestion coming from you with respect to an Irish University Bill deserves my best attention . . .".

67. Moody and Beckett, *Queen's*, Vol. 1, p. 285.
68. "University Education (Ireland)", *Hansard*, 1873: *214*: p. 1659.
69. Corrigan Diaries, RCSI, No. 1, p. 16.
70. Dowling, *Education*, pp. 171-172. Beckett and Moody, *Queen's*, Vol. 1, pp. 186-7.
71. Dowling, *Education*, p. 174.

Chapter 11

1. Corrigan Diaries, RCPI, No. 6, p. 53.
2. *ibid*: No. 1, pp. 16 and 25.
3. *ibid*: No. 1, p. 19.
4. *ibid*: No. 1, p. 19.
5. Norman, E.R., *The Catholic Church and Ireland in the Age of Rebellion, 1859-1873*, London: Longmans, 1965, pp. 455-6.
6. Corrigan Diaries, RCPI, No. 6, p. 53.
7. *ibid*: p. 53.
8. Corrigan Diaries, RCPI, No. 1, p. 47.
9. Corrigan, D., "Reminiscences of the Dissecting Room", *British Medical Journal*, 1879: *1*: pp. 59-60.
10. Corrigan Diaries, RCPI, No. 5, p. 2.
11. Corrigan, D., *Address at the Distribution of Prizes in St Mary's Hospital Medical School*, London: Morton & Co., 1873, p. 12.
12. Corrigan Diaries, RCPI, No. 9.
13. Atthill, L., *Recollections of an Irish Doctor*, London: The Religious Tract Society, 1911, p. 115.
14. Corrigan Diaries, RCPI, No. 2, p. 4.
15. Corrigan Letters, RCPI.
16. Corrigan Diaries, RCPI, No. 4, p. 8.
17. *ibid*: No. 3, p. 22.
18. *ibid*: No. 2, p. 14.
19. Corrigan Letters, RCPI, No. 80 (xvi).
20. *ibid*: No. 80 (xx).
21. Cruise, F.R., *Catholic Men of Science. Sir Dominic Corrigan (1802-1880)*, London: Catholic Truth Society, 1912, p. 20. Also in *Twelve Catholic Men of Science*, ed. Windle, B., London, 1912.
22. Corrigan Diaries, RCPI, No. 5, pp. 3-5.
23. Mapother, E.D., "Sir Dominic Corrigan", *Irish Monthly*, 1880: *8*: pp. 160-171.
24. Corrigan Diaries, No. 9.
25. Obituary, *British Medical Journal*, 1880: *1*: p. 219.
26. Obituary, *Lancet*, 1880: *1*: pp. 268-9.

Index

10, Downing Street,
Whitehall.

Oct 24. 73

My dear Sir D. Corrigan

Any suggestion coming from you with respect to an Irish University Bill desires my best attention; and, as about ten days hence we are to visit Lord Spencer at Althorp, I hope to have a full opportunity of considering